BUSINESS REPLY MAIL

FIRST CLASS MAIL PERMIT NO. 25363 SAN FRANCISCO, CA

Postage will be paid by addressee

PO Box 191826
San Francisco CA 94119-9866

GET WIRED!

GET WIRED!

AND STAY WIRED
BY READING NET SURF,
EXCLUSIVELY
IN WIRED.

If you want to keep up with the Digital Revolution, and the dozens of new sites that are appearing on the Net monthly, you need *Wired* and its Net Surf column – *Wired*'s guide to the best of the Net.

From its online presence (gopher, WWW, Info-rama@wired.com, WELL, and AOL) to its focus on convergence and the communications revolution, *Wired* is one of the most Net-savvy publications in America today.

That's because *Wired* is the only place where the Digital Revolution is covered by and for the people who are making it happen – you.

Since its launch in January 1993, *Wired* has become required reading for the digerati from Silicon Valley to Madison Avenue, from Hollywood to Wall Street, from Pennsylvania Avenue to Main Street.

But *Wired* may be hard to find on newsstands (we're printing almost 250,000 copies and still can't satisfy demand).

So if you want to get *Wired* regularly and reliably, subscribe now – and save up to 40 percent. If for any reason you don't like *Wired*, you can cancel at any time, and get your full subscription price back – that's how sure we are that you will like *Wired*.

If you want to connect to the soul of the Digital Revolution, our advice to you is simple.

--- PLEASE FOLD ALONG THIS LINE AND TAPE CLOSED. (NO STAPLES) ---

I want to get Wired – reliably and regularly. Begin my subscription immediately, if not sooner, saving me up to 40% off the newsstand price. If for any reason, I don't like Wired, I can cancel at any time, and get my full subscription back. I would like (check one below):

Individual subscription		Can/Mex	Other
1 Year (12 issues)	☐ $39.95 (33% off single copy of $59.40)	☐ US $64	☐ $79
2 Years (24 issues)	☐ $71 (40% off single copy of $118.80)	☐ US $119	☐ $149
Corporate/Institutional subscription*		Can/Mex	Other
1 Year (12 issues)	☐ $80	☐ US $103	☐ $110
2 Years (24 issues)	☐ $143	☐ US $191	☐ $210

Foreign subscriptions payable by credit card, postal money order in US dollars or check drawn on US bank only.
* We have a separate rate for corporate/institutional subscribers because pass-along readership is higher. We felt it would be unfair for individual readers to, in effect, subsidize corporate/institutional purchasers.

Name _____

Job title _____

Company _____

Street _____

CityStateZipCountry _____

Phone _____ This is your ☐ home ☐ office ☐ both

E-mail address _____
Very important! This is by far the most efficient way to communicate with you about your subscription and periodic special offers, and to poll your opinion on *WIRED* subjects.

Payment method	☐ Check enclosed	☐ Bill me (for corporate/institutional rates only)	
	☐ American Express	☐ Mastercard	☐ Visa

Account number _____ Expiration date _____ Signature _____

Please Note: The "Bill Me" box above is only for corporations and institutions needing an invoice – which will be for the higher corporate/institutional rates. There is no "Bill Me" option for individuals.

WIRED rents its subscriber list only to mailers that we feel are relevant to our readers' interests. To remove your name from the rental list, please check this box ☐.

AGL

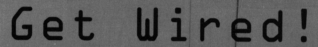

Get Wired!

"Wired looks like Vanity Fair should, reads like Esquire used to and talks as if it's on intimate terms with the power behind the greatest technological advance since the Industrial Revolution."

David Morgan, Reuters

WIRED
Subscribe!

1 Year subscription (12 issues): $39.95
That's 33% off the newsstand price.
Call: 1-800-SO WIRED
Email: subscriptions@wired.com

NEIL SELKIRK

Voyage Into Cyberspace Aboard the Online Service That Has It All...

You've read the book. Now keep up-to-date online.

Every month hundreds of new games come online. How can you possibly keep up? It's easy. The Net Games online directory is updated round the clock. Call YPN for the latest offerings on the Net.

YPN is a service for data.comm.phobes

To watch your favorite show on TV you don't have to know about circuits and tubes. To have fun in Cyberspace you shouldn't have to know about "transmission-control protocols." YPN support makes it simple to navigate the Net—you'll get real help from real people.

Busy? No carrier? Host unavailable?

If you've been out in Cyberspace, you know the frustration of not connecting. YPN can handle the traffic! Call now for your local access number and make an easy connection.

Join us!

The Net is a new medium and a new world. Be a part of it. As a member of YPN you'll get 15 hours of time FREE, plus one of the lowest subscription costs anywhere in Cyberspace!

**Call 1-800-NET-1133 for Local Access Numbers!
15 Hours Free Online Time!
Call Today!**

Praise for net guide™

"Thanks to Wolff and friends, the cyberswamp may just have become a little less murky."—*Entertainment Weekly*

"*Net Guide* is the computer world's online *TV Guide*."—*Good Morning America*

"*Net Guide* will keep you from wandering around aimlessly on the Internet, and is full of good ideas for where to pull over."—*Forbes FYI*

"*Net Guide* is the liveliest, most readable online guide yet."—*USA Today*

"What you need to connect."—*Worth Magazine*

"*Net Guide* is the *TV Guide* to Cyberspace!"—Louis Rossetto, publisher/editor, *Wired*

"One of the more complete, well-organized guides to online topics. From photography to the Church of Elvis, you'll find it here."—*PC Magazine*

"The best attempt yet at categorizing and organizing all the great stuff you can find out there. It's the book people keep stealing off my desk."—Joshua Quittner, *New York Newsday*

"It's changed my online life. Get this book!"—Mike Madson, "Computer Bits," Business Radio Network

"My favorite for finding the cool stuff."—*The Louisville Courier-Journal*

"*Net Guide* focuses on the most important aspect of online information—its content. You name it, it's there—from erotica to religion to politics."—Lawrence J. Magid, *San Jose Mercury News*

"Not only did all the existing Net books ignore Cyberspace's entertaining aspects, but they were process-oriented, not content-oriented. Why hadn't someone made a *TV Guide* for the Net? Wolff recognized an opportunity for a new book, and his group wrote *Net Guide*."—Mark Frauenfelder, *Wired*

"Couch potatoes have *TV Guide*. Now Net surfers have *Net Guide*."—*Orange County Register*

"*Net Guide* is one of the best efforts to provide a hot-spot guide to going online."—*Knoxville News-Sentinel*

"An excellent guide for Internet adventurers. *Net Guide* is well-written and no subject remains undiscovered. *Net Guide* is indispensable for targeted explorations into Cyberspace."—*Het Parool*, the Netherlands

"Assolutamente indispensabile!"—*L'Espresso*, Italy

net chat ™

Your Guide to the Debates, Parties, and
Pick-up Places on the Electronic Highway

A Michael Wolff Book

Kelly Maloni, Nathaniel Wice,
and Ben Greenman

For free updates call 1-800-NET-1133

RANDOM HOUSE
ELECTRONIC PUBLISHING

MICHAEL
WOLFF
& COMPANY, INC.
DIGITAL
PUBLISHING

New York

The Net Books series is a co-publishing venture of Michael Wolff & Company, Inc., 1633 Broadway, 27th Floor, New York, NY 10019, and Random House Electronic Publishing, a division of Random House, Inc., 201 East 50th Street, New York, NY 10022.

Net Chat™ has been wholly created and produced by Michael Wolff & Company, Inc. Net Guide, Net Games, Net Chat, and NetHead are trademarks of Michael Wolff & Company, Inc. All design and production has been done by means of desktop-publishing technology. The text is set in the typefaces Garamond, customized Futura, Zapf Dingbats, Franklin Gothic, and Pike.

Published simultaneously in the U.S. by Random House, NY, and Michael Wolff & Company, Inc., and in Canada by Random House of Canada, Ltd.

0 9 8 7 6 5 4 3 2 1

ISBN 0-679-75814-3

All of the photographs and illustrations in this book have been obtained from online sources, and have been included to demonstrate the variety of work that is available on the Net. The caption with each photograph or illustration identifies its online source.

The book jacket has been designed by Peter Rutten. Copyright © 1994 by Michael Wolff & Company, Inc.

Manufactured in the United States of America

New York Toronto London Sydney Auckland

A Michael Wolff Book

Michael Wolff
President and Editor in Chief

Peter Rutten
Creative Director

Kelly Maloni
Managing Editor

Senior Editors: Nathaniel Wice, Ben Greenman

Research: David Heller, Maria Sturani

Editorial Assistants: Stephanie Engel, Robert Kenney, Ali Lemer, Kendra Wilhelm

Contributing Writers: Caleb Crain, Joel Furr, Jeff Hearn, Kristin Miller, Katie Moore, Jeff Yang, Chris Weller

Photo and Production Editor: Jeff Hearn

Technical Editor: David Wood

Copy Editor: Matt Weingarden

Chief Technology Officer: Stan Norton

Marketing Manager: Bill Folsom

Special thanks:
Random House Electronic Publishing—Kenzi Sugihara, Tracy Smith, Steve Guty, Dennis Eulau, Mark Dazzo, Alison Biggert, Jean Davis Taft, Robin McCorry, and Niki DiSilvestro

Alison Anthoine at Kay Collyer & Boose

Peter Ginsberg at Curtis Brown Ltd.

And, of course, Aggy Aed

The editors of *Net Chat* can be reached at Michael Wolff & Company, Inc., 1633 Broadway, 27th Floor, New York, NY 10019, or by voice call at 212-841-1572, fax at 212-841-1539, or email at editors@ypn.com.

Net Books!

netguide ™

netgames ™

netchat ™

Coming soon

netmoney ™

nettech ™

netsports ™

nettrek ™

Contents

Contents

Part 6. Identity

Part 7. Support

Appendices

FAQ

1. What is chat?

It's what most people do in Cyberspace. With their PC and their modem they connect to a universe of millions of other people who want to get advice, exchange information, express their opinions, vent their rage, find a date, or make love (verbally). Just imagine if you could reach out to everyone who's watching Roseanne or Dave—well, you can on the Net. When the Juice got loose, uncountable numbers of people came online to marvel and gawk with each other. Chat can be real-time—you type a line and then someone else types a line. Chat can be in message form—you put a post on a newsgroup or forum, and shortly thereafter (and for weeks later) people respond to you. Chat can be public or private—using a private room on AOL or CompuServe or an **/msg** command on IRC, or you can communicate one-on-one with email. Chat can be as banal as real life—"Hi!" "Hi to you!"—or as fascinating and powerful, with online friends and lovers (and enemies!) as true as the ones in your RL (real-life) neighborhood.

2. Can I really meet someone online?

Why not? Rush did. If you share a common interest (the Civil War, a 12-step program, Japan, Anime comics, Nirvana, the Democratic Party, bondage and discipline), you'll have little problem starting a Net discussion. That might lead to flirting or flaming (the Net version of a barroom brawl) or a one-night stand. It can lead to painful rejection or to falling in love. It can even sometimes lead to getting together in real life—at a Bennigan's or at a Grateful Dead concert. For Rush Limbaugh it led to marriage.

3. Sounds a bit like a personal ad or like talk radio!

Well, yes and no. There are personal ads on the Net appealing to just about any romantic or sexual interest you might have. And the opinions on the Net tend to be even more vituperative and passionate than anything you've heard from Rush or Howard. The difference is that the Net isn't just for loudmouths or people who can't get a date. It's people expressing all kinds of needs, idiosyncracies, dreams, neuroses. In short, there is no one reason why people go online. People go online for the same reasons they read a newspaper, or take a class, or hang out in a bar, or even watch television—for information, for entertainment, for human contact. The line between real life and virtual life gets finer and finer.

4. What are people talking about?

Whatever interests them! That's the key to understanding the Net. It's not what interests the largest number of people, which is the way most of the media works; it's what interests merely enough people to get the conversation going.

5. Where online does all this take place?

Virtually every online venue has places for chat, both real-time areas and message forums. On CompuServe it's the CB Simulator, the message boards, the real-time chat conferences within forums, and one-on-one invitations; on AOL it's the People Connection, the message boards, the forum rooms, and one-on-one instant messages; on Prodigy it's the Live Chat and Bulletin Boards; on GEnie, it's Bulletin Boards, real-time conferences, and Chat Line channels. On the Internet it's IRC (Internet Relay Chat) and Usenet, mailing lists and MUDs. On BBSs it's echoes and conferences. Of these, the gold standards for live chat are AOL's People Connection and the Internet's IRC.

6. If you can't see and hear people, how do you know they are who they say they are?

There's the rub! You don't. If you're a man online trying to start up a conversation with a woman (or someone who seems to be a woman) but getting only a brush-off, try changing your screen name to, say, Jenny and see what happens.

7. Can I really be anybody I want to be? I've heard that there's a certain etiquette. Are there rules I have to know?

While gender-surfing is common on the Net, some Netizens feel that it runs against "Netiquette"—that is, the mostly unwritten code of ritual and propriety that is more or less accepted on the Net. (One person's role-playing is another's shattering disappointment.) In general, Netiquette is meant to keep the Net open and free for everyone. It is also meant to limit the "noise" that is natural in this worldwide blab school. See the Netiquette sidebar for some basic tenets. In essence, these are conventions that mirror the manners and limits we take for granted in real life. And as you might expect, on the Net you'll meet self-appointed enforcers of Netiquette who will mirror many of the annoying people you know in real life.

8. What if the others don't live up to the Netiquette? Can I shut someone up?

Maybe, but why not just tune the pest out? Network News (nn) and some of the other programs for reading newsgroups include a "kill" feature for filtering out authors or subjects. On The WELL, you can set up a "bozolist" of users whom you never want to hear from again. AOL and most IRC clients include some kind of **/ignore** command. CompuServe's CB has a squelch feature. Some people worry that these kinds of filters harm community spirit—if such arguments give you a headache, just add them to your kill file.

NETIQUETTE

Here are some suggestions:

1. It's not nice to spam (automated universal post) everyone else's conversations about Asian American identity, the new Schwarzenegger movie, and the dramatic uses of memory in Proust with your direct-marketing scheme for water filters.

2. DON'T POST IN ALL CAPITALS. IT'S THE CYBERSPACE EQUIVALENT OF SHOUTING AT THE TOP OF YOUR LUNGS.

3. Warn people before revealing the surprise ending to the new John Grisham novel. Do this by saying "Spoiler" first. ("Spoiler warning: The butler did it" is not acceptable.)

4. Don't post private messages to public forums. Do you really think 3,000 people want to to read "Jaimee, will I see you at Bennigan's on Tuesday?"

5. If you want to be taken seriously, dØn't uze wEErd karakterz Or speLLingz phØr kØØl sLaNg.

6. Learn to ignore people. You don't need to respond every time an interloper posts a "get a life" message on your favorite newsgroup, alt.tiddly-winks.obsessed. Be careful who you flame, how you flame, and where you flame—in fact, try not to flame.

7. Read the FAQ and some

→

9. Before you go any further, just exactly what is the Net? Does it include AOL? CompuServe? The Internet? BBBs too?

Definately. Everything. The whole ball of wax. The Net is the electronic medium spawned by the millions of computers linked (that is, networked) together throughout the world. Known also as Cyberspace, the Information Highway, or the Infobahn, the Net encompasses the Internet, a global, noncommercial system with as many as 30 million computers communicating through it; the commercial online services like CompuServe, America Online, Prodigy, Delphi, and GEnie; the thousands of local and regional bulletin-board services (BBSs); the networks of discussion groups, like FidoNet, that are carried over BBSs; and the discussion groups known as Usenet that traverse the Internet. More and more, the Internet unites all of the diverse locations that make up the Net.

10. I'm game. What do I need to get started?

Computer hardware and software, and a few tricks to find your way around.

recent messages before posting. For some reason the rec.music.rem people get mad at the 10,000th person to ask if Michael Stipe has AIDS. If you're looking for a specific piece of information that's not in the FAQ, like the title of a book or the life-time batting average of a Hall of Famer, request that replies come to you through email rather than to the larger group. After collecting answers, post a follow-up summary for everyone.

8. Don't take it personally if no one picks up on your contribution to a discussion. If you're determined to take part in the conversation, hang back and see what other people are interested in and start contributing to the active threads.

9. If you're in too much of a hurry to make your meaning clear, consider punctuating sarcasm and other nonliteral intentions with a smiley. You can say just about anything you want if you follow it with a winking ;-), smiling :-), or disappointed :-(. There are dozens of variants, including surprise :-o and a Bronx cheer :-p (with drool it's :-p~). A growing minority :-(on cutesy symbols.

10. Try to recognize humor. The people on alt.destroy.the.earth are only joking—well, most of them are, anyway.

11. Can you help me a little with the hardware and software I'll need?

You'll need a personal computer (any flavor). If you've bought one fairly recently, it's likely that it came with everything you need. But let's assume you have only a PC. In that case you'll also need to get a modem, which will allow your computer to communicate over the phone.

So-called 14.4 modems, which transfer data at speeds up to 14,400 bits per second (bps), have become the latest standard. You should be able to get one for less than $150. (Within a year, however, 14,400 bps will feel like a crawl next to faster speeds of 28,800 bps and higher.)

Next, you need a communications program to control the modem. This software will probably come free with your modem, your PC, or—if you're going to sign up somewhere—your online service. Otherwise, you can buy it off the shelf for under $25.

Sometimes you'll want "client software" to make Internet chatting more fun (explained on the sidebar on page 13). Finally, you'll want a telephone line (or two if you plan on tying up the line a couple of hours per night).

ONLINE SERVICES

America Online
- 1-800-827-3338 (voice)
- Monthly fee: $9.95, first month free
- Free monthly hours: 5
- Hourly fees: $3.50
- Email: joinaol@aol.com

CompuServe
- 1-800-848-8199 (voice)
- Monthly fees: $8.95, first month free (standard); $2.50 (alternative)
- Free monthly hours: unlimited basic (standard); none (alternative)
- Hourly fees: $6.- (standard) or $6.30 (alternative) for 300 bps; $8.- (standard) or $12.80 (alternative) for 1200/2400 bps; and $16.- (standard) or $22.80 (alternative) for 9600 bps
- Email: 70006.101@compuserve.com

Delphi
- 1-800-695-4005 (voice)
- Monthly fees: $10,- (10/4 plan); $20,- (20/20 plan)
- Free monthly hours: 4 (10/4 plan); 20 (20/20 plan)
- Hourly fees: $4 (10/4 plan); $1.80 (20/20 plan)
- Setup: $19.- (20/20 plan)
- Full internet access: additional $3.00/mo.
- Email: info@delphi.com

GEnie
- 1-800-638-9636 (voice)
- Monthly fee: $8.95
- Free monthly hours: 4
- Hourly fees: $3.- (off-prime) or $9.50 (prime time) for 2400 bps; $9.- (off-prime) or $15.50

→

12. I'm ready. What kind of access should I get? A commercial service?

No, not necessarily. You have a number of options, varying in price, flexibility, and bandwidth (the amount and speed of data that can travel through a network):

Email Gateway

This is the most basic access you can get. It lets you send and receive messages to and from anywhere on the Net. Email gateways are often available via work, school, or any of the other services listed here.

BBSs

BBSs range from mom-and-pop hobbyist computer bulletin boards (often run from a basement) to large professional services. What the small ones lack in size they often make up for in affordability and homeyness. In fact, many users prefer these scenic roads over the Info Highway. Many of the large BBSs (DSC-BBS, PC-Ohio, and Exec-PC come to mind) are as rich and diverse as the commercial services.

BBSs are easy to get started with, and if you find one with Internet access or an email gateway, you get the best of local color and global reach. Chat is really big on most BBSs—so big that this book contains lots of conversations available only in the BBS world.

You'll find BBSs for your area code in the back of this book. You can

(prime time) for 9600 bps
* Email: feedback@genie.geis.com

Prodigy
* 1-800-PRODIGY
* Value Plan I: $14.95/month includes unlimited core services; 2 hours in plus services, which consist of the bulletin boards, EAASY Sabre, Dow Jones Co. News, and stock quotes; and 30 email messages; additional email cost 25¢ each; additional 'plus' hours cost $3.60 each.
* Alternate Plan I: $7.95/month includes 2 hours of core or plus services; additional hours (core or plus) are $3.60/hour; email costs 25¢ per message sent.
* Alternate Plan II: $19.95/month includes 8 hours of core services; plus services cost an additional $3.60/hour; email costs 25¢ per message sent.
* Alternate Plan BB: $29.95/month includes 25 hours core and plus services; additional hours are $3.60/hour; email costs 25¢ per message sent.

also locate local BBSs through the Usenet discussion groups alt.bbs.lists and comp.bbs.misc, the BBS forums of the commercial services, and regional and national BBS lists kept in the file libraries of many BBSs.

Once you've found a local BBS, contact the sysop to inquire about the echoes (or conferences) you want. These are the BBS world's equivalent to the Internet's newsgroups. With echoes, you're talking not only to the people on your particular BBS but also to everyone on a BBS that carries the echo (in other words, a universe of millions). Even if the discussion of your choice is not on their board yet, many sysops are glad to add an echo that a paying customer has requested.

Many, if not most, local BBSs now offer Internet email, as well as live chat, file libraries, and some quirky database, program, or directory unique to their little corner of Cyberspace.

Commercial Services

Priciest but often easiest. The big ones are America Online, CompuServe, and Prodigy. Also popular are GEnie and Delphi. Commercial services are cyber city-states. The large ones have more "residents" (members) than most U.S. cities—enough users, in other words, to support lively discussions among

---

SENDING EMAIL

I'm on a commercial service. How do I send Internet email?
Each of the major commercial services offers Internet email, with slight variations in form.

From CompuServe
Enter the CompuServe mail area by choosing the **go** command from the menu and typing **mail** (if you don't have CompuServe's Information Manager software, type **go mail**). If you want to send a message to someone on another comercial service, your email will be routed through the Internet, so you must address it with the prefix **internet:**. Mail to John Doe at America Online, for instance, would be addressed **internet:jdoe @aol.com**; to John Doe at YPN, it would be addressed **internet:jdoe@ypn.com.**

To CompuServe
Use the addressee's CompuServe I.D. number. If John Doe's I.D. is 12345,678, you'll address mail to **12345.678@ compuserve.com**. Make sure you replace the comma in the CompuServe I.D. with a period.

From America Online
Use AOL's Internet mail gateway (keyword: **internet**). Then address and send mail as you normally would on any other Internet site, using the **jdoe@ service.com** address style.

To America Online
Address email to **jdoe@aol. com.**

→

their membership. They generally require their own special software, which you can buy at any local computer store or by calling the numbers listed in this book. (Hint: Look for the frequent starter-kit giveaways.)

AOL, CompuServe, and Delphi all provide access to many if not all of Usenet's more than 10,000 newsgroups, and through email you can subscribe to any of the mailing-list discussions.

Delphi provides access to the Internet's IRC channels.

Internet Providers

There is a growing number of full-service Internet providers (which means they offer email, IRC, FTP, telnet, gopher, WWW, and Usenet access), including Your Personal Network (YPN), run by the editors of this book. In practical terms, the Internet enables you to vacation in the 8,000-member LambdaMOO mansion based in Xerox's PARC Lab; drop in on a live bondage scene with doms and subs from Tokyo, Melbourne, and Peoria; or take sides in the latest Jamie-Paul spat on the global *Mad About You* newsgroup.

A dial-up SLIP (serial line Internet protocol) or PPP (point to point protocol) account is the most fun you can have through a modem. It is a special service offered by some Internet providers that gets you significantly faster access and the ability to use

From GEnie
Use the keyword: **mail** and address email to **jdoe@ser vice.com@inet#**. GEnie's use of two @ symbols is an exception to Internet addressing convention.

To GEnie
Address email to **jdoe@genie. geis.com.**

From Delphi
Use the command **go mail**, then, at the prompt, type **mail** again. Address mail to **inter net"jdoe@service.com"** (make sure to include the quotation marks).

To Delphi
Address email to **jdoe@del phi.com.**

From Prodigy
To send email from Prodigy, first download Prodigy's Mail Manager by using the command **jump: mail manager**. Address mail to **jdoe@ser vice.com**. Mail Manager is currently available for DOS and Windows only, with a Mac version due soon.

To Prodigy
Address email using the addressee's user I.D. For John Doe (user I.D.: ABCD12A), for example, you would address it **abcd12a@prodigy.com.**

point-and-click programs for Windows, Macintosh, and other platforms.

Direct Network Connection

Look, Ma Bell: no phone lines! The direct network connection is the fast track of college students, computer scientists, and a growing number of employees of high-tech businesses. It puts the user right on the Net, bypassing the phone connections, and has the advantage of tremendous speed and large amounts of bandwidth.

13. Great, I've got an account. How do I chat?

Email

With email, you can talk to anyone on a commercial service, Internet site, or BBS with Internet access (and to people connected with email gateways, SLIP, and direct network connections).

IP SOFTWARE

Most "serial" dial-up connections to the Internet treat your fancy desktop computer as a dumb terminal that requires a lot of typed-out commands. An IP connection, whether through a direct hookup like Ethernet or a dial-up over phone lines, turns your computer into a node on the Net instead of a one-step-removed terminal connection. With an IP link, you can run slick point-and-click programs—often many at once.

Macintosh users will need MacTCP and, depending on the kind of IP service you're getting, either Interslip or the more advanced MacPPP. Windows users will need the latest version of WinSock. (The latest versions of programs that run over WinSock can be found at ftp.cica.indiana.edu.) Two all-in-one packages of Internet software that you might want to consider for Windows are Chameleon and WinQVT.

Your best best for these programs is to get your online service to give you these programs preconfigured, as the IP address can be mind-boggling to set up.

Email addresses have a universal syntax called an Internet address. An Internet address is broken down into four parts: the user's name (e.g., Kelly), the @ symbol, the computer and/or company name, and what kind of Internet address it is: *net* for network, *com* for a commercial enterprise—as with Your Personal Network (ypn.com) and America Online (aol.com)—*edu* for educational institutions, *gov* for government sites, *mil* for military facilities, and *org* for nonprofit and other private organizations. The dictatorial cyber-maven who drives the Net books to completion and herself and the staff to an early grave would therefore be kelly@ypn.com. But she doesn't answer her email.

IRC

The Internet version of live chat is called IRC, which stands for Internet relay chat. The chat is real-time, which means that if you type something, the people you're chatting with—in Sweden, Sarajevo, or the Sudan—see your words appear immediately on their screens. People from around the world gather in "channels" that are usually focused on a specific theme or subject. When a channel is "hot," there may be as many as 50 chatters. Sometimes, though, it's just you and a friendly stranger. For an example, let's try #hottub, a well-established channel where people pretend that they are in a hot tub together:

A. If your Internet site offers IRC (sometimes such a site is called an IRC client), follow the site's access instructions. This may be as simple as typing **irc** at the main-menu prompt.

B. Once you're there, you can go to a particular channel. For example, to go to the channel

---

INTERNET FUNCTIONS

FTP
FTP (file transfer protocol) is a program that allows you to copy a file from another Internet-connected computer to your own. Hundreds of computers on the Internet allow "anonymous FTP": In other words, you don't need a password to access them. The range of material available is extraordinary—from books to free software to pictures to thousands of games!

Gopher
A gopher is a program that turns Internet addresses into menu options. Gophers can perform many Internet functions, including telnetting and downloading files. Gopher addresses throughout this book are useful for finding collections of information and collections of telnet links to game sites.

Gophers also come in handy for circumventing restrictions on MUD access from some large sites like schools—it's harder to trace a gopher path (the steps the gopher takes to reach the MUD). Gopher menus, however, are likely to be swallowed up by the very latest in Net navigation pleasure: the World Wide Web, a.k.a. WWW or the Web.

The Web
The World Wide Web is a hot new hypertext-based information structure on the Internet. Many believe the Web will become the standard navigational tool on the Net. The Web is like a house where every room has doors to
→

#hottub all you have to do is type **/channel #hottub** and **<return>**. (Whatever you type on IRC appears on the other users' screens as dialogue, so if you don't want to converse but want to give an IRC command, you have to first type a back slash.)

C. If you want to see a list of available channels with the number of people participating and a short description of what the channels are about, type **/list** and press **<return>**.

D. If you would like to create your own channel, follow the same steps you would to join an existing channel, but substitute the new channel name you want. If there isn't already a channel named #redheads on IRC, for example, you would type **/channel #redheads** to create it.

E. To quit IRC, type **/quit** and **<return>**.

CompuServe Live Chat

On CompuServe, chat takes place in the CB Simulator, which you can reach by using the go command from the menu and typing **cb** (or, if you don't have CompuServe's Information Manager software, type **go cb**). You can choose one of 108 channels to join. To join a channel, type **/cha <channel**

every other room—or, more accurately, like the interconnections in the human brain. Highlighted words in a document link to other documents that reside on the same machine or on a computer anywhere in the world. You only have to click on the word—the Web does the rest.

Your dial-up Internet provider undoubtedly offers programs to access the Web. Lynx and WWW are pretty much the standard offerings. Usually you choose them by typing **lynx** and **www** and then **<return>**. What you'll get is a "page" with some of the text highlighted. These are the links. Choose a link, hit the **<return>** key, and you're off.

If you know exactly where you want to go and don't want to meander through the information, you can type a Web page's address, known as a URL (uniform resource locator), many of which you'll find in this book.

With the emergence of new and sophisticated so-called Web browsers (with a graphical point-and-click interface) like Mosaic, MacWeb, and Cello, the Web is starting to look the way it was envisioned—pictures, colored icons, and appetizing text layouts. Unless you have a direct connection to the Internet, you'll need a SLIP for these browsers. If you can't get direct access or a SLIP, do not despair: Dial-up versions of these browsers are expected soon.

number> and **<return>**, or, if you have a graphical interface, just click on the channel. Each of the forums also has a real-time conference area, sometimes broken into specific rooms. Check the forum notice for scheduled chat.

AOL Live Chat

AOL's chat area is The People Connection, which can be reached by using the keyword chat. The first screen you'll see is called The Lobby Window. The left side of the window contains four icons: People, Rooms, Center Stage, and PC Studio. People provides information about the people in whatever room you enter. Rooms gives a list of the rooms where conversation is currently taking place. Center Stage takes you to an online "auditorium," where AOL presents online guests. PC Studio offers a schedule of Center Stage activities and an overall guide to the conversation and topics in each of the rooms. There's a 23-person limit in each room. But as soon as one room is filled, another version of the room is created. And don't limit yourself to the rooms AOL provides. Create your own and invite friends.

IRC

ircII (UNIX, Mac, and Windows)
Standard IRC client. It's a chore to learn the "slash" commands, but that doesn't seem to stop many people from spending all their free time in this program. Mac and Windows versions require an IP connection.

WinSock IRC (Windows)
IRC for Windows. Requires an IP connection.

Homer IRC Client (Mac)
Homer turns IRC into a three-ring circus, transforming arcane IRC command-line "slash" commands into friendly buttons and windows. Dinging sound effects mark channel comings and goings; clanging cuckoo clocks measure the time. With Apple's Speech Manager (available from ftp.apple.com) installed, Homer can even speak the incoming text of individual users in distinct, synthesized voices. If that's not enough, HomerPaint sets up a real-time communal drawing board. Best of all, Homer can run over regular dial-up lines to any Internet provider with regular telnet; the TCP version (which runs over SLIP and PPP connections) includes DCC file transfer, which allows you to trade files with other discussants within an IRC channel. Shareware: $25. Latest version by anonymous FTP from zaphod.ee.pitt.edu/pub. System 7 recommended, at least 4 megs total RAM.

GEnie Live Chat

GEnie's chat area is ChatLines. You can reach it by typing *keyword:* **chat**. ChatLines is part of the LiveWire area and is divided into channels that you enter by typing **/cha <channel number>** and **<return>**. Information on all the channels is available in Channel 1, the Welcome Lounge. To leave, type **/quit**.

Delphi Live Chat

Delphi's chat area is centered in the Main Conference Area (type **go gr conference**). Its subject areas are called groups. To see a list of available groups when you enter the area, type **who** after the conference prompt. When you've selected a group you want to join, type **join <group name>** or **join <group number>** to enter the group. You can create your own conference group by typing **join <name not currently on the menu>**.

Prodigy Live Chat

Prodigy's relatively new chat area is available to Windows and Mac users. *Jump:* **chat**. It's very similar in set-up to AOL's People Connection: Prodigy members can choose from a set of conversation rooms (25-person limit in each room) or create private rooms. Prodigy also features a huge auditorium for guest speakers.

IRC COMMANDS

Basic IRC programs use commands that begin with a / character. Everybody calls these "slash commands." You can always get a complete list of commands by typing **/help** but here are some of the basic ones:

/nick Net_Head
Set your nickname to Net_Head. (No more than nine characters allowed.)

/list
List all the channels. It's a big list. You can limit it to channels with five or more people by typing **/list -min 5**.

/who #hottub
List the users in the #hottub channel.

/join #hottub
Dive into the #hottub channel.

/msg Bubbles Yo, whassup?
Send a private message ("Yo, whassup?") to the user with the nickname Bubbles.

/query Bubbles
Send all subsequent messages to Bubbles (saves typing **/msg Bubbles** for every message).

/part #hottub
Leave the #hottub channel. A common variant is **/leave #hottub**.

/quit Catch you alligators later
Send the message "Catch you

→

Newsgroups

The most widely read bulletin boards are a group of some 10,000-plus "newsgroups" on the Internet, collectively known as Usenet. Usenet newsgroups travel the Internet, collecting thousands of messages a day from whoever wants to "post" to them. More than anything, the newsgroups are the collective, if sometimes Babel-like, voice of the Net—everything is discussed here. And we mean everything.

While delivered over the Internet, the Usenet collection of newsgroups are not technically part of the Internet. In order to read a newsgroup, you need to go where it is stored. Smaller BBSs that have news feeds sometimes store only a couple dozen newsgroups, while most Internet providers offer thousands. Few offer the full range of English and foreign-language newsgroups, because the full aggregate takes up so much disk storage. When space is being saved on the English-language newsgroups, the alt.* hierarchy is usually the first place where cuts are made. If there's a group missing that you really want, ask your Internet provider to add the newsgroup back to the subscription list.

The messages in a newsgroup, called "posts," are listed and numbered chronologically—in other words, in the order in which they were

alligators later" to all the channels you're in, and exit IRC. Command works the same without a message.

/whois Bubbles
Display some details about the identity and whereabouts of Bubbles in IRC. If Bubbles isn't logged in or is using a different nickname, you'll get "Bubbles: No Such Nickname." Try **/whowas Bubbles**, which will tell who last used the nickname.

/away I'm watching The Simpsons!
Mark yourself as "away" from IRC. Anyone who sends you a private message or does a whois on you will see the message "I'm watching The Simpsons!" When you return, **/away** with no message turns the feature off.

/me uncorks a bottle of champagne.
Sends the message "Net_Head uncorks a bottle of champagne."

/ignore Bubbles all
Ignore all messages from Bubbles. Can also be set by Internet address: **/ignore mwolff@well.com** ignores all messages from mwolff; **/ignore *@well.com** all ignores all messages from anyone at The WELL. To turn this feature off, replace "all" with "none": **/ignore Bubbles none**.

/kick #hottub Bubbles
Kick Bubbles out of the #hottub channel. Only works if you have channel-operator status.

posted. Usenet is not distributed from one central location, which means that a posted message does not appear everywhere instantly. The speed of distribution partly depends on how often providers pick up and post Usenet messages. For a message to appear in every corner of the Net, you'll generally have to wait overnight. If you use the newsgroups a lot, you'll start to notice patterns where messages from some machines take five minutes to appear and others take a day.

You can scan a list of messages before deciding to read a particular message. If someone posts a message that prompts responses, the original and all follow-up messages are called a thread. The subject line of subsequent posts in the thread refers to the subject of the original. For example, if you were to post a message with the subject "my most embarrassing date" in alt.romance.chat, all responses would have the subject line "RE: my most embarrassing date." In practice, however, topics in a thread tend to wander off in many directions.

To read the newsgroups you use a program called a reader, a standard offering on most online services. There are several types of readers—some let you follow message threads; others organize messages chronologically. You can also use a reader to customize the newsgroup menu to include only the newsgroups you're interested in.

INSTANT CHAT

You don't always need a place for chat; sometimes you can just shout to someone across Cyberspace.

AOL
Under the Members pull-down menu, choose Send Instant Message. To ignore messages, turn off Instant Message Notice in the Member Preferences under the Members pull-down menu.

Prodigy
Get to the Instant Message Center by clicking the Instant Message button on the Chat Board opening screen. To turn off messages from other people, click the setup options button in the Instant Message Center.

Internet
Talk bubbles@ypn.com sends a message to the user with that Internet address. Talk variants include ntalk, ytalk, hey, yo, and phone.

CompuServe
When logged on, you'll find Invite and Talks under the Conferences pull-down menu. To turn off these types of messages from other users, select the Ignore Invitations or Ignore Talks options under the same Conferences pull-down menu.

Mailing Lists

Mailing lists are like newsgroups, except that they are distributed over the Internet email system. The fact that messages show up in your mailbox tends to make the discussion group more intimate, as does the proactive act of subscribing. Mailing list are often more focused, and they're less vulnerable to irreverent contributors.

To subscribe to a mailing list, send an email to the mailing list's subscription address. Often you will need to include very specific information, which you will find in this book. To unsubscribe, send another message to that same address. If the mailing list has a "listserv" address, you can usually request archives of the list from the same subscription address. Send the command **index <list name>** in the message body.

Echoes or Conferences

Local BBSs often carry what are known as echoes or conferences, which are part of messaging networks among BBSs. You'll find several of these networks mentioned throughout the book: FidoNet, RelayNet (RIME), ThrobNet, AdultNet, AdultLinks (formerly KinkNet), AfterDark, ILink, Smartnet, Intelec, and North America Net. There are hundreds of BBS net-

NEWSREADERS

Newswatcher (Mac) Fancy newsreader. Whole newsgroups can be saved locally in a single file, by article, or by thread. Multiple binaries can be automatically decoded—making it possible to grab all of alt.binaries.pictures.supermodels with a couple of clicks. Requires an IP connection.

Nuntius (Mac) Comparable to Newswatcher, except it can multi-task. Some people prefer the way Nuntius grabs the full text of threads; others hate waiting to read the first message. Nuntius also stores newsgroup subjects on your computer—this chews up disk space but accelerates searches through old messages. Requires an IP connection.

Trumpet (Windows) The most popular Windows newsreader. Thread by subject, date, or author. Like Newswatcher, batch binary extraction. WinNV is also widely used. Available by anonymous FTP from ftp.utas.edu.au in /pc/trumpet/win trump. Requires an IP connection.

Tin (UNIX) Intuitive UNIX newsreader that works especially well for scanning newsgroups. You can maintain a subscription list, decode binaries, and search the full text of individual newsgroups. With its help files and easy-to-use menus, this is our favorite UNIX newsreader.

nn (UNIX) and rn (UNIX) Complex newsreaders (Network News and Read News) favored by UNIX-heads.

trn (UNIX) Maps subjects within newsgroups.

works in Cyberspace, new ones are added daily, and no BBS carries them all—most don't even carry all the conferences on a single network.

Check with local BBSs in your area code to see whether they have the network you want. If they do, but they don't carry the conference you're looking for, ask for it. Most sysops will gladly add a conference for a paying customer.

14. Any suggestions for dipping my toes in the water?

Why not just pick a random entry from the book? Go to MTV's live, mostly teen chat on AOL (page 204); scare yourself and others with tales of overgrown sewer crocodiles in alt.folklore.urban (page 114); or practice your pick-up lines (and typing) in #romance (pages 41-42). Don't get stuck where you started, though; there are tons to check out before picking favorites.

15. I'm starting to get hot for this. But I think I would prefer to be anonymous. Can I?

Yup.

On the Internet you can use an anonymous remailer to forward mail and newsgroup postings.

MAIL READERS

Eudora (Mac and Windows) If the host for your email supports the POP protocol, you're in luck. Eudora makes email even easier than it already was. The commercial upgrade to the free version includes message-filtering for automatically sorting incoming mail, but drops the fun dialog messages (if you start typing without an open window, Eudora beeps, "Unfortunately, no one is listening to keystrokes at the moment. You may as well stop typing." The Windows version requires an IP connection; the Mac version does not.

Pine (UNIX) Menu-driven with a full-screen editor and spell-check. Support of the MIME "metamail" format means that you can "attach" binary files within a letter.

Elm (UNIX, DOS, Windows, OS/2) Programmable "user agent" reader that can also sort, forward, and auto-reply. It does not include its own editor.

Mail (Unix) As the name suggests, a no-frills mail program.

An anonymous remailer works like a mail drop for Internet mail and newsgroup postings. Instead of sending mail directly somewhere, you send it to the remailer with instructions for passing it along under a new identity. The anon.penet.fi Anonymous Server is one of the most widely used. You can get full instructions by sending email to help@anon.penet.fi, but here's a basic overview of the simplest way it can work.

First you have to register. One way is to just email ping@anon.penet.fi. If you've never used the remailer before, you'll be assigned an "anon id." An example might be an124071. This I.D. will stay the same for all future messages you forward from your email address through the remailer—so even though the messages will be anonymous, they'll always be from the *same* anonymous user. Next you have to set a password. Email password@anon.penet.fi with a password as the first and only line of the message body. The password can be any string of upper- or lower-case characters, numbers, and spaces. Let's say you pick the password "suzy".

You can also set a nickname for yourself by sending a message to nick@anon.penet.fi with your desired nickname as the subject.

Now let's say you want to send an anonymous message to the editors of *Net Chat*. Instead of emailing directly to editors@ypn.com, you would address the message to anon@anon.penet.fi, with any subject you like. The first line of the message body, which would not be included in the final message, would read: "X-Anon-To: editors@ypn.com"; and the second line, which also would not be forwarded, would read: "X-Anon-Password: suzy". (If you wanted to post to the alt.sex newsgroup, you would address the first line of the message "X-Anon-To: alt.sex@anon.penet.fi".) The anon.penet.fi machine then automatically forwards your message without your email address.

The remailer also works in reverse, making it possible to carry on anonymous email relationships. Replies to your anonymous messages (or other mail sent to the an124071@anon.penet.fi example) are forwarded to your regular account. The delay caused by all this remailing (to Finland and back!) is usually less than two hours and sometimes as brief as a few minutes.

Anonymity can be even easier to maintain on the commercial services, where you can hide behind an impersonal I.D. number or temporary handle. This isn't always so great—some Internet mailing lists with policies against anonymous subscribers actually prohibit AOL users because they are in effect anonymous.

You should know, though, that some experienced Netizens frown on anonymous messaging because it contradicts the Net principle of openness and because it can be used maliciously.

16. What about those MUDs, MUSHes, and what have you? I thought those were games! Can I chat there, too?

Chat is really what they're best at. There are more than 500 MUDs in Cyberspace. Some of them draw hundreds of people a night; others attract small, intimate groups of regulars. Most are public, with newbies constantly filling the closets, churches, and town halls—the places where newcomers are usually welcomed. Others stay semiprivate—known only through word of mouth.

How do I join a MUD community?

Let's take a walk through a generic MUD. You're probably going to have to connect to the MUD using an Internet function called *telnet*, which lets you log into computers over the Internet instead of over phone lines. Find the telnet command in your Internet service (usually this means just typing **telnet** or finding it in a menu of Internet functions) and add the MUD's address. If the MUD is up, the opening screen will appear. Since on a MUD you're never who you are in real life, the next thing to do is get a character. In many cases, you just type **connect <a character name of your choice> <a password of your choice>**, but in others you have to choose a race, like elf or orc, and a gender (try the one you've had less experience with).

Sometimes you first have to register your character by email while exploring the MUD as a guest in the interim. The commands for getting the essential information (what you absolutely must know to play) are almost always listed on the opening screen. Also, a newbie or public channel on a MUD is often a great source of information and an easy way to meet people.

When you enter a MUD, a description of your surroundings—often a poetic one—will immediately scroll onto your screen. It will sing of the land you have set foot on, tell you of mysterious objects in the area, show you the exits, and announce the other characters going about their business in the same area as you are. Or are they? Don't be surprised if you're eaten alive by a monster or beheaded by a fellow player. Such is MUD life—and death.

If you're still in one piece, let's wander around a bit. There are many ways to move in a MUD (from riding a flying carpet to attaching yourself to another player to teleporting), but the most common—and simplest—way is by typing the name of an exit or by typing a direction: **n** (north), **s** (south), **e** (east), **w** (west), **ne** (northeast), **se** (southeast), **nw** (northwest), **sw** (southwest), **u** (up), **d** (down).

As you travel a MUD, you may find objects along your way. You can trade or sell them, give them to someone else, wear them or wield them in battle, discard them, or—if they appear to be alive—lock them up or kill them, whatever you fancy. There are many action commands—including some for text sex—and it is recommended that you use the help facility on your particular MUD to learn about them.

On some MUDs, you'll start out with a small inventory of items you can add to or discard from as you go along. On combat MUDs, you will also need need to monitor your experience and skill levels.

The amount of power you have to change the MUD—i.e., build in it—depends on the server (MOOs and MUSHes offer the most freedom to build) and the administrator. Building commands are usually preceded by an @ to remind you that when you're building, you're changing the world.

MUD COMMANDS

- **emote <action>** *or* **pose <action>** *or* **<action>** Allows you to describe what your character is doing (varies with server).
- **help** Often gives a directory of help information. You would then type **help <a choice from the directory>** to get topical help.
- **home** Returns the character to his or her home location.
- **look** *or* **l** Displays the description of an area.
- **look <object>** *or* **l <object>** *or* **read <object>** Displays the description of an object or character.
- **news** *or* **faq** *or* **info** Often supplements the help command with more site information (varies with server).
- **page <player>=message** *or* **tell <player>=message** Sends a message that only the specified character can hear (varies with server).
- **quit** *or* **QUIT** *or* **@quit** Disconnects you from the game (varies with server).
- **say <message>** *or* **"<message>** Sends a message to everyone in the local area (e.g., the room) you're in (varies with server).
- **whisper <player>=<message>** Sends a message that only the specified local character can hear.
- **who** *or* **WHO** *or* **@who** Displays a list of all the players currently connected to the MUD (varies with server).

17. Sometimes I just like to listen. Does anybody mind?

You'll be called a lurker, sometimes with affectionate understanding, other times with disdain and spite. On IRC and other forms of live chat, it's not easy to listen in undetected, but in the message-based discussions, you can read without anyone knowing about it. If you're shy, rest assured that you're in good company. It's been estimated that there are more than 100 lurkers on Usenet for every person who contributes to the discussion. When you finally do find something that you can't stand to see left unsaid, you'll—in Net parlance—de-lurk.

18. Sounds interesting. But I really wish I could see the people I'm talking to.

You're a little ahead of your time if you're after live videoconferencing, but there's a growing number of IRC users who leave pictures of themselves for public view by way of the IRC home page (http://urth.acsu.buffalo.edu/irc/WWW/ircdocs.html). Also, if you're on AOL, cruise the PC Gallery (*keyword:* **gallery**), where hundreds of members have uploaded pictures of themselves.

Even though most computer connections still aren't fast enough for video calls (or digitized voice for that matter), there are people developing tools for live sound and video conversations over the Net. If you can borrow access to a high-speed direct connection to the Internet, you have to check out Maven, a program that enables live voice conversations over the Internet (you'll jump the first time you hear someone's live voice coming out of the computer's speaker), and CU-SeeMe, a new program that sets up live videoconferencing over the Internet. Regular dial-up connections are simply too slow to play with these new toys, but if you have an IP connection (see the IP sidebar) you can get a glimpse of the future by downloading the CU-SeeMe software from anonymous FTP at gated.cornell.edu/pub/video. The audio won't work, but you'll be able to see live, extremely jerky black-and-white pictures of people sitting in front of their computer keyboards. Makes you think about the #netsex of the future.

19. I can't wait to make a Net friend—but how do I use this book?

If you know what you want to chat about, turn to the Index, where every subject and place in the book is listed alphabetically. Of course, there's no need to know what you want to talk about; you can browse *Net Chat* and check out sites and conversations as you go along.

The book is divided into seven parts:

- Sex
- Fans
- Fringe
- Net Op-Ed
- Coffeehouse
- Identity
- Support

Each part is broken down by subject: Music, Movies, Pop Fiction, and Sports are some of the topics you'll find under Fans. In most instances, we've gone a step farther. Music, for example, is divided into sections such as Rock, Pop, and Hippie Funk.

All entries in *Net Chat* have a name, description, and address.

The site name appears first in boldface. If the entry is a mailing list, "(ml)" immediately follows; if a newsgroup, "(ng)"; if a BBS echo, "(echo)"; and if a BBS, "(bbs)." The description of the site follows.

After the description, complete address information is provided. A red check mark identifies the name of the network. When you see an arrow, this means "go to…" followed by all the steps you have to take, such as typing a command, searching for a file, subscribing to a mailing list, or typing a Web site's address (called a URL). (Additional check marks indicate the other networks through which the site is accessible; triple dots indicate another address on the same network; and more arrows mean more steps.)

An address is context-sensitive—it follows the logic of the particular network. So, if the entry includes a Web site, the address following the

---

CYBER-COLLOQUIALISM

Chat shorthand
AFK = Away From Keyboard
BAK = Back At Keyboard
BRB = Be Right Back
BTW = By The Way
CUL = "C U" (See You) Later
GMTA = Great Minds Think Alike
HHOK = Ha Ha Only Kidding
HHOS = Ha Ha Only Serious
IMHO = In My Humble Opinion
IMNSHO = In My Not-So-Humble Opinion
IMAO = In My Arrogant Opinion
LOL = Laughing Out Loud
NRN = No Response Necessary (used when emailing to avoid superfluous messages of thanks and acknowledgment)
ROTFL = Rolling On The Floor, Laughing
ROTFLOLPIMP = Rolling On The Floor, Laughing Out Loud, Peeing In My Pants
Re = "Hi again" (used when someone—either the sender or someone else—returns to the group

after a short absence; also seen as "Rehi" or "Re-hi")
TANSTAAFL = There Ain't No Such Thing As A Free Lunch
TTFN = Ta-Ta For Now!
TTYL = Talk To You Later
WB = Welcome Back
WTG = Way To Go!

Smileys or Emoticons
:-) = smile
:-D = smile/laughing/big grin
:-* = kiss
;-) = wink
:-/ = wry face
:-X = my lips are sealed
:-P = sticking out tongue
{} = a hug
:-(= frown
:'-(= crying
O:-) = angel
}:-> = devil

Note for the newbie: Don't use more than one smiley per paragraph.

---

arrow would be a URL that you would type on the command line of your Web browser. If it is a mailing list, the address would be an email address followed by instructions on the exact form of the email message. An entry that included an FTP, telnet, or gopher address would provide a log-in sequence and a directory path or menu path when necessary (see the sidebars on pages 11-12).

> **BOOK TERMINOLOGY**
>
> Terms that identify specific site information in a *Net Chat* entry:
> • **Daily, Hourly, Weekly, Live**: Necessary for keeping up with a discussion. All real-time chat is classified as Live.
> • **Archives:** The address of an archive of a mailing list or newsgroup.
> • **FAQ:** The address where the FAQ can be found.
> • **Register:** The registration address for MUD characters.

In a commercial-service address, the arrow is followed by the service's transfer word (e.g., keyword, go word, or jump word), which will take you to the site. More arrows lead you along a path to the specific area on the site. IRC addresses indicate what you must type to get to the channel you want once you've connected to the IRC program.

The name of a newsgroup entry or BBS echo is also its address, so there is no address information other than the network for these types of sites. (You'll locate the newsgroup or echo at your access provider or BBS—see the Usenet explanation on pages 15-16.)

The notation for BBS addresses differs slightly from that for the other sites. The address for a BBS is its modem number (or numbers) followed by, where applicable, a log-in sequence. BBS discussion networks that carry echoes, like RecoverNet, are listed in *Net Chat* with the notice "check local bulletin boards" and the phone number and name of at least one BBS that carries the network.

20. All right. I'm ready to join. But I don't want to make a fool of myself.

You won't. The Net's huge growth has as much to do with the human passion for hanging out and meeting new people as it does with any business need or technological advance—and the Net is still young enough that just about everyone is happy to see more people joining the party. Post your first message and see it grow into a long thread; wander into your first live conversation and see if people don't chat you up, take you on a tour, or—depending on the moon and the mood—make a pass at you.

21. What if I want to do more than just chat?

Try *Net Guide* and *Net Games*! You should find them in your bookstore right beside *Net Chat*. Look for *Net Money*, *Net Sports*, *Net Trek*, and *Net Tech*—they're coming soon!

Part 1
Cybersex

Pickup scenes

Many people are reaching out to one another on the Net by posting personal ads.

Cyberspace is the perfect place to create a new identity. Even if you have some insane compulsion to be completely honest, the electronic meet market is diverse enough to accommodate almost anyone—from bisexual married women (**alt.personals.bi**) to fat single men (**alt.sex.wanted**), they all have their own personals message boards. So if you're looking for a "tigerish SBF to make my winter nights hotter than July" or casting about for a "twentysomething B&D fiend," try these bulletin boards and newsgroups. And even skeptics who believe that the most important factor in love is location—geography, not G-spot—will be placated by the wealth of Net resources. There are Usenet newsgroups devoted to singles scenes in L.A. or Chicago, as well as the AOL **Neighborhood Singles Groups,** which target communities as small as Saginaw and Austin.

On the Net
Across the board

alt.personals (ng) A nationwide listing board for personals ads, this newsgroup keeps hope alive for

Dinner date—downloaded from CompuServe's Archive Photo Forum.

that SWM in Ohio seeking a black Dolly Parton, or that Illinois couple angling for a threesome. Some Net users post business classified ads in this newsgroup—a woman trying to unload a microwave, a fiction writer looking for an established agent—but the vast majority are standard personals. ✓**USENET** DAILY

alt.personals.ads (ng) GBM desires another. SWM desires SWF for companionship, conversation, and a quickie on the staircase of his apartment building. Vast and sprawling—more than 100 messages each day—alt.personals.ads offers a place for singles of all shapes and sizes to cast a line. And while there are no statistics that indicate how successfully the group pairs people off, with this many options, it's hard to imagine striking out entirely. ✓**USENET** HOURLY

alt.sex.wanted (ng) Demands, demands, demands. That's all you're going to get on alt.sex.

wanted, a nationwide newsgroup that offers a forum for sexual requests. As in most of the sex groups, the users are predominately male, and they seem uniformly interested in having assorted acts performed upon them. ✓**USENET** *FAQ:* ✓**INTERNET**→*ftp* rtfm.mit.edu→ anonymous→ <your email address>→/pub/usenet-by-group/alt. sex.wanted→alt.sex. wanted_FAQ DAILY

AOL Neighborhood Singles Groups America Online has targeted a set of neighborhood newsgroups, hundreds of them, to specific cities—Austin to Boston, Saginaw to Syracuse, and even a handful of Canadian sites. Emphasizing proximity, these groups return to a pre-Net notion of community; there's both comfort and terror in knowing that your chat

> "While there are no statistics that indicate how successfully the group alt.personals.ads pairs people off, with this many options, it's hard to imagine striking out entirely."

partner lives only miles away. For those interested in an actual romance, there's nothing on the Net that comes close. ✓**AMERICA ON-LINE**→*keyword* newsgroups→Search All Newsgroups→*Search by keyword:* singles WEEKLY

AOL Romance Connection A classifieds database that occupies part of AOL's People Connection, the Romance Connection sorts personals by age, region and interest. Conversation is lively, with a healthy understanding of the mix of lust and loneliness that drives most personals services. The Romance Connection also includes a message folder that includes follow-ups from online romance successes. Through this feedback feature, the service claims responsibility for dozens of marriages—but remember, so did David Koresh. ✓**AMERICA ONLINE**→*keyword* romance DAILY

Local Personal Newsgroups (ng) *Sleepless in Seattle* notwithstanding, most people still need to meet to fall in love. For that reason, posting sites for personals are a tricky business. You'll want to jump at anything that excites you, but if the geographic distance thwarts your heart, you'll go away with an even deeper hurt. So turn to your local personals group: While Lone Star lonely hearts like to talk about "fun" and "friendship" (houston.personals); West Coast types go in for faux profundity, like discussion of Camus over Zima at the Viper Room (la.personals). The Bay Area Singles newsgroup offers the lovelorn and horny in the San Francisco/Oakland region an opportunity to meet and mate under the shadow of the Golden Gate. Heavy on gay listings and resolutely upscale, ba.singles also includes occasional discussion of the trials of Califor-

> ## "They keep trying here…night after night after night."

nia dating. Think of these newsgroups as ride boards for your heart—you know where you want to go, but you're not sure if anyone wants to share the trip. Search for local newsgroups by city and region. ✓**USENET** WEEKLY

Odyssey Online For online matchmaking, Odyssey may well be the preeminent service. Couples who've met on this national adult BBS have appeared on *Donahue* and *Good Morning America,* and the BBS has grown immensely since. On your first visit, you'll fill out a personal questionnaire that other members can read to "check you out." In the evenings, the live-talk channels (go chat) like Jaccuzi and Hot Adult are filled with flirtations. View the "Who's Online" list to find out where members are on the BBS and where they're calling from—in case you want to meet someone offline. The message conferences like "Erotic," "Climax," and "Oral" are great places to get noticed and do some erotic reading. Like many adult BBSs, Odyssey features a Match-Maker database, which, based on your answers to personal questions, matches you up with other BBSers. But Odyssey's games (go games) are probably responsible for more matches than the Match-Maker database. The board also provides direct links to a few gay BBSs—connect straight from Odyssey. For local access numbers, voice-call 1-800-947-0936. ☎→*dial* 818-358-6968 →DAILY/LIVE

Singles (echo) While many of the postings on this group are stan-

dard personals fare—"After 16 years of monogamy I quite unexpectedly find myself single again"—not all of the desires are sexual. In fact, if you're feeling especially lonely but you want to scratch the itch by sharing tips on building packet radios or listening to anecdotes about childhood, this echo may be your best bet: There are plenty of well-intentioned singles who won't read your interest in them as an opportunity to wave their desires in your general direction. ✓**THROBNET** DAILY

Singles The two largest rooms in this conference are, of course, the personals postings sites: Men Seeking Women and Women Seeking Men. But in addition to these romance lines, the Singles conference contains an immense amount of discussion that dissects and defines the single life in nineties America. When should sex be introduced? How should you read personal ads? Should you date friends? What is the best way to deal with loneliness? The advice comes in fast and furious, and if you're sensitive about being told what to do, you might want to stay away from this conference. But single WELL visitors with an irresistible attraction to topics such as "Processing Break-ups Healthily (this time)," "Unrequited/Unresolved: My Heart Is Tied Up in the Past," and "Valentine's Day: Boon or Bête Noire?" are encouraged to spend their time browsing, reading, agreeing, and objecting. You might as well try it—you never know who you might meet. ✓**WELL**→*g* sin DAILY

Singles BB This is not just a loud bar filled with guys in power ties and women in push-up bras. One post proclaiming "A REAL MAN" available immediately to "needy ladies" got a three-word response:

"real big ego." Vulnerability gets you many more responses, some phone numbers, and possibly a few friends to laugh about the trials of love. Carol and Al developed a friendship and flirtation by talking about the beach. Janice got sympathy, and offers from a slew of nice guys when she wondered online why men never call "the morning after." The board also has a section of Prodigy "success stories." One raves about the love he found, while another tells about the letter she received from her online beau's all-too-real fiancée. You wonder whether John and his Prodigy date did miss each other in O'Henry fashion—at different Bonanzas in different malls—or if his heart will be broken. But they keep trying here... night after night after night. ✓**PRODIGY**→*jump* singles bb→Choose a Topic DAILY

With a twist

alt.personals.bi (ng) Gene, a fiftyish divorcee in the St. Louis area, wants to expand his horizons by tending to the homosexual fantasies that have been with him since his teens. Susan, a self-professed "hardcore Brooklyn dyke," is looking for a submissive woman to serve her. And Andy in Seattle is sending out a call for any gay filmmakers interested in collaborating in art and life. This newsgroup, which adds dozens of new messages every day, provides a nationwide network of personal postings for bisexual men and women. While some of the other personals sites tend toward the smarmy, alt.personals.bi maintains a fairly high level of dignity and civility, and while most of the postings are from bisexual men and women seeking or responding to search parties, some of the messages are from curious heterosexuals touring in the land of the poly-

morphous. If you're unsure which way to swing, you'll probably want to let your pendulum pass through this newsgroup. ✓**USENET** DAILY

alt.personals.poly (ng) A catchall for personal ads: couples looking for bi women to complete threesomes, gay men looking for partners, married businesswomen itching to be scratched at a conference. The clientele is nationwide and diverse, and consequently difficult to classify, but it seems to comprise roughly the same population as the alt.personals group. All in all, this is a smaller and less crowded version of the larger personals newsgroups. ✓**USENET** WEEKLY

Bisexual (echo) Very similar in content and tone to alt.personals.bi, this group collects classified postings from bisexual men and women across the nation. If you are looking for a good time ("I need a lesbian to introduce me to new horizons"), or looking to give someone else one ("Domfem seeks willing slave"), After Dark's Bisexual conference—with moderately heavy traffic and postings from people nationwide—is a good place to start. ✓**AFTERDARK** DAILY

Heart to Heart Gays and lesbians interested in making new friends or meeting someone special can place a personal ad in the Heart to Heart message board. Subdivided by location and fetish, the boards are very active. Some members are looking for sex and others for a little romance. Do diapers make you hot? Post your ad in the Special Interests folder. But you don't have to be a fetishist to enjoy browsing this board. One member posted an ad about the difficulties of

meeting men who enjoyed romance. He was so inundated with responses that he started his own newsletter. ✓**AMERICA ONLINE** →*keyword* glcf→Heart to Heart DAILY

Romance & relationships

It is surely no coincidence that there is a newsgroup—de.talk.romance—on which

matters of the heart are discussed entirely in German. With all respect to Puccini, the desperation that the Italians portray when a loved one can't be had cannot begin to match the lethality and inevitability of a doomed Teutonic romance. It's a state of mind—so wonderfully expressed in German as "zum Tode betrürt" (in mortal sorrow)—that requires the beautiful lovers Tristan and Isolde to *both* die violently and despairingly. For those with a more pragmatic, Anglo-Saxon disposition regarding romantic matters, though, there are plenty of sites on the Net to talk about dating, sex, marriage, eternal commitment, adultery, and a broken heart. This is the 20th century, after all—on **Couples-L** we casually question the decision to leave the first wife for the second, and on **Relationships** we announce a new love just weeks after parting with a previous prince. The Net could have saved young Werther's live.

Cupid—downloaded from America Online's Mac Graphics Forum.

On the Net

Relationships

Couples Why would you tie your

life to the life of another, especially given the myriad things that can (and do) go wrong? If you are involved in a relationship, are considering getting involved, were recently involved, or remain dead-set against any involvement—that should cover just about everyone—this is the conference for you.

Theoretical history

What is a "successful" relationship? How do you juggle money, sex, and kids? Can a relationship recover from adultery? What's the difference between theoretical and actual honesty? The participants—either safely ensconced in relationships or battle-scarred veterans—dispense their wisdom with clear heads and generous senses of humor, and the conference will serve as a salve for almost any emotional wound. ✓**WELL**→g love DAILY

Couples-L (ml) In love? Falling out of love? Something he/she does driving you crazy? Should you forgive a fidelity slip? Bob, a 70-year-old with "an unresponsive

wife," looks for ways to spice up their relationship. Jenny, a college student, seeks advice on maintaining a long-distance relationship. Steve, a baby boomer, asks whether others are second-guessing their second marriages. Couples-L is about trying to make relationships work. It is emphatically not a sex-talk list. A recent "bored" poster demanded details of sexual practice—"the sicker the better"—and was unanimously shouted down and asked to remove himself to alt.sex.talk.

Long-term commitments

People talk about sex here in the context of long-term commitments, not one-night stands (in Cyberspace and real space). The introduc-

> "On the 21st of July, Chantal asked how to stop loving someone who no longer loved her. On August 8 Chantal sent a breezy 'thanks.' She 'found love somewhere else.' WOW, this really must work!"

tory message asks that all treat each other as they would like to be treated by their partners—and the list is polite and warm. All is not pretty in love, but here you can gain comfort and strength. ✓ **INTERNET**→ *email* listserv@cornell. edu ✍ *Type in message body:* subscribe couples-l <your full name> DAILY

Relationships On the 21st of July, Chantal asked how to stop loving someone who no longer loved her. On the 24th she told how hard it was to see him on the street. On the 28th she placed a personal ad on the board looking for men interested in "serious commitment." On August 7, Barbara told Chantal not to demean herself by pursuing the ex. On August 8, Chantal sent a breezy "thanks." She "found love somewhere else." *WOW*, this must actually work! The posters seem to be really listening to relationship problems and are committed (buzzword) to helping people work out the tough problems that bothered even Adam and Eve. People will listen to you here whether you are a teenager worrying about a first love, a twentysomething guy wanting to know how to tell his roommate he loves her, or a divorcing woman wondering where love went and why. If you are a married man considering consummating his online fling, however, don't look for the go-ahead. Never screw up something real for a cyberdream. ✓ **PRODIGY**→*jump* lifestyles bb→ Choose a Topic→Relationships HOURLY

soc.couples (ng) Soap operas aren't this interesting. Steve's wife is cheating on him with Tom, who's talking to Steve via email. Updates are daily and it seems like everyone on the newsgroup is offering Steve advice. Michele wants

> "A query about how to do a tasteful rabbit-themed wedding brought suggestions from others who had done cow-themed weddings."

a lover who desires sex as often as she does, and a debate erupts between the some-things-are-more-important-than-sex crowd and the you-shouldn't-have-to-repress-your-needs people. Duane wishes that years ago he had gone to his junior prom (his math teacher did try to find him a date—"but that was just adding insult"), and although the prom thing's been covered many times before, new stories quickly filter in. Young men are always here seeking the woman's point of view, and everybody's talking about birth control, dating, and sex. ✓ **USENET** DAILY

Romance

alt.romance/alt.romance. chat (ng) These two groups attract mostly adults; the very notion of "romance" seems to deter high-octane Netpunks. The result is a genteel coffeehouse atmosphere, sedate and responsible, in which matters of the heart are treated with an evenness so admirable it often verges on the uninteresting. Tempted to cheat on your spouse? Well, consider the pros and cons. Worried about your boyfriend's persistent depression and lack of interest? Just talk to him, preferably with empathy

swelling your heart. While postings drift occasionally into the frankly erotic, the romance groups try to stay true to their name— lots of candlelight, flowers, and mature caresses. ✓ **USENET** *FAQ:* ✓ **INTERNET**→*ftp* rtfm.mit.edu→ anonymous→<your email address> →/pub/usenet-by-group/news. answers/romance-faq→part* DAILY

de.talk.romance (ng) Virtually identical to the alt.romance newsgroups except that it's conducted entirely in German. Pursued by a vision of deep kissing on the Reeperbahn? Interested in flexing your Berlitz? *Wilkommen.* All Werthers, young or otherwise, should apply. ✓ **USENET**

The wedding

alt.wedding (ng) While soon-to-be brides form the majority, a steady minority of married men and women —"Married two years, but not over it yet!"—exhaustively cover every facet of a wedding. Weddings are about detail — and trying to offend the least number of people. Whom do you invite? What do you do with uninvited children? How can you include the sister-in-law (SIL, in this newsgroup's parlance) in the ceremony? Many sign onto the newsgroup in the early stages of an engagement, use the forum to vent frustrations, and pick up wedding tips (a query about how to do a tasteful rabbit-themed wedding brought suggestions from others who had done cow-themed and penguin-themed weddings). Countdowns are always in progress, leading up to the signing-off-from-the-Net-for-a-while post just before the big day—"The wedding is Friday night, and today is my last day of work. I'll be back…and might post wedding details then!" ✓ **USENET** DAILY

Kiss and tell

Whatever you tell your closest friends, you're secretly

insecure about sex. Sure you are. Maybe you don't know how to give your partner exactly what he or she wants, or you're out of touch with your own body. Whatever the problem, this is the place to let it all hang out. There's room for everyone. While there's virtually no simulated sex in this section, there's something much better: oddly compelling confessions from men and women about the intimate details of their private lives. **Alt.sex** is consistently one of the most popular newsgroups on the Net and the **Sex-L** mailing list among the most uninhibited.

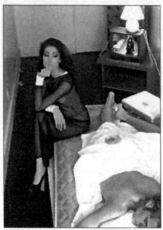

Downloaded from New York Online's kgb Conference.

On the Net

Across the board

alt.sex (ng) Libido is an equal-opportunity employer, and the alt.sex newsgroup attracts a wide variety of users—younger Net-Heads looking for a quick thrill, married couples eager (and often embarrassingly overeager) to share their secrets of conjugal bliss, as well as large numbers of singles, swingles, voyeurs, perverts, and pornographers. Topics range from religion (is AIDS a form of divine retribution?) to erotic tips (maximize the pleasures of fellatio with ice cubes) to public-opinion polls (pubic shaving: yea or nay?), and most of the participants display an endearing mix of prurience and curiosity. ✓USENET *FAQ:* ✓INTER-NET→*ftp* rtfm.mit.edu→anonymous→<your email address>→/pub/usenet-by-hierarchy/news/answers/alt-sex/faq→part* HOURLY

alt.sex.wizards (ng) This is an odd little sex-chat newsgroup that handles issues similar to those discussed on alt.sex. But alt.sex.wizards is significantly more equitable in its gender distribution, with an almost equal number of women, and as a result the topics (are bicycle seats erotic? Is it fair to have sex with the au pair?) have a refreshing quirkiness to them. ✓USENET *FAQ:* ✓INTERNET→*ftp* rtfm.mit.edu→anonymous→<your email address>→/pub/usenet-by-hierarchy/alt/answers/alt-sex/wizards-faq→part* DAILY

Pillow (echo) The pillow talk in question is largely practical advice. What's the proper reaction to a partner's flatulence, especially during oral sex? What drugs jack up your libido and what drugs bring it down? If you don't know the answers to these and other burning questions, tune in to Pillow, where dozens of armchair experts pitch in to solve your most intimate problems. ✓**AFTERDARK** DAILY

Sex-L (ml) Sure, everyone knows about dental dams and French ticklers, but has anyone ever had a nose bridge? Don't answer yet. First make sure you know what a nose bridge is. The Sex-L mailing list is one of the most explicit sites on the Net, whether subscribers are announcing secret desires ("I have a fantasy of sucking the breasts of a lactating young mother. If you are one, what would you think of a request from a friend, not necessarily a lover, who would ask you to let

> "We were making love, I was trying to keep sweat from dropping off my face onto hers, when a small, sensual drip ran to the tip of my nose and onto the tip of hers. It was as if we had a 'nose bridge.'"

him taste your milk? Would you find that an entirely sexual suggestion if he asked you?") or asking for practical advice ("If it wasn't so 'ergonomically' uncomfortable, I could lick her for hours. But it hurts my neck. What's wrong?").

Macho-bewildered stupidity

While many of the postings maintain this compelling texture, a fair number slide into ordinary macho-bewildered stupidity. In the end, sex remains the most fascinating of all human behaviors, and the subscribers to this mailing list chow down at the buffet of eros and libido. So sign up and enjoy. Any other questions? Oh, yeah—the nose bridge. Drum roll, please, as a man from the great state of Indiana explains it all to you: "That reminds me of one of the funniest times. We were making love, I was trying to keep sweat from dropping off my face onto hers, when a small, sensual drip ran to the tip of my nose and onto the tip of hers. It was as if we had a 'nose bridge.'" ✓**INTERNET**→*email* listserv@ tamvm1.tamu.edu ✍ *Type in message body:* subscribe sex-l <your full name> DAILY

Sexual Issues Notwithstanding the Prodigy police, Sexual Issues on the Lifestyle Bulletin Board can get a little racy. A new form of skilled storytelling has arisen in topic threads like "quickies," "accidental nudity," and "sex in public" (on the hood of a car, around the corner from the police station, with the neighbor in the pool). You can also try out your new pickup line here. Women are much more successful in getting responses, but one wonders how many "bored bisexual housewives" there really are home alone. ✓**PRODIGY**→*jump* lifestyles bb→ Choose a Topic→Sexual Issues HOURLY

Sexuality An encyclopedic resource in matters sexual, the WELL's sex conference collects opinions and advice on the sights, sounds, smells, and physical sensations of sex. What's a particularly romantic place to spend a couple of days? How do you know if you've been date-raped? Can you have sex with underwear on? Between practical tips and speculative fantasies (what will sexual habits be like after an AIDS cure?), the conference offers participants opportunities to talk about hundreds and hundreds of additional topics—condom sizes, phone sex, the controversial wet spot. There are almost 80 entries on polyfidelity (that's the paradoxical practice of remaining loyal to more than one person at the same time), and a whopping 42 missives on armpit sex. Comprehensive, intimate, and impressive. ✓**WELL**→ *g* sex DAILY

All about women

Women (echo) Women as sex objects. Women as sex subjects. Women who love the wrong men. Women who love the right men. This group, in short, is about women, and the gauge is so wide that it easily accommodates both Pam, a twentysomething artist struggling with a marriage proposal from a boyfriend she loves deeply but can't imagine committing to, and Lucille, a fortysomething professional about to become a first-time mother. This group tends toward questions of sex and love, though not exclusively, and there are always plenty of men on hand to ensure that even the most substantive discussions are derailed by crass "Hey, baby" talk. ✓**THROBNET** WEEKLY

Virginity or not?

alt.sex.first-time (ng) Some

members preach the virtues of virginity or waiting ("As someone who 'lost it' a number of years after age 18, I believe there is more to life than just banging away at the first opportunity"). Others are waging war to keep the group safe for sex talk ("In my august opinion, anyone who is a virgin after the age of 18, male or female, is a weak-kneed lunatic. Just too scared to live"). The group is fairly new, and promises to satisfy the insatiable curiosity Netters have about other Netters' sex lives. ✓**USENET** WEEKLY

CYBERNOTES

"I am a virgin (at age 20, no less), but by choice. I had a few opportunities to have sex, but turned them down. I was either not in the mood, or didn't have any feelings for the guy. Also, there are too many sexually transmitted diseases out there. I have to keep telling myself this, because I worry that I am still a virgin. Sometimes, I despair that I'm never going to have sex--and by the time I do, I'll be married! Not that that's the end of the world, but I *would* like to have *some* experience by the time I meet the person with whom I am going to share my life."

—from **alt.sex.first-time**

Erotica & porn

Some people like to have sex. Others like to write about it. And others like to write about

it and then post their efforts on bulletin boards and newsgroups. "I stepped into the room and she stepped out of her skirt. I couldn't believe the beautiful body that stood before me..." While there are many Net sites devoted to home-baked erotica and pornography, from the **alt.sex.stories** newsgroup to AdultLinks' **Giffygirls** message board, confessionals aren't the only form of erotica represented online. Drop in on **alt.sex. magazines**, which functions as the *Utne Reader* of smut, collecting excerpts from and reflections on publications such as *Swank*, *Leg Show*, *Red Muff*, and *Barely Legal*.

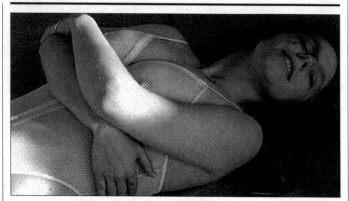

On the Net

alt.sex.magazines (ng) There's a scene in a Woody Allen movie in which Woody is trying to buy a porn mag. Embarrassed, he sandwiches it between a pair of reputable magazines, only to have the cashier hold it aloft and bellow for a price check. That was the seventies. Now, in the nineties, porn mags seem sort of retro, trapped forever in the world of print. But as this newsgroup proves, plenty of publications are still flourishing despite the onrush of high-tech erotica. And not just *Playboy* and *Penthouse*; in addition to these old standbys and their less reputable

cousins (*Hustler*, *Swank*), there are dozens and dozens of less familiar offerings—*Leg Show*, *Honeybuns*, *Lips*, *Red Muff*, and *Barely Legal*, just to name a few. Though the discussion of these periodicals is dominated by netboy libido, there's a decent amount of gay and lesbian traffic, and even an interesting discussion over whether horny straight women should horn in on gay men's magazines. So before you go to the newsstand, do your research here. ✓ **USENET** DAILY

alt.sex.movies (ng) The suicide of 23-year-old porn star Savannah (who had dated MTV jester Pauley Shore and Slash from the band Guns 'N Roses) several months ago elicited a kind of Kurt Cobain reaction here—both sensational and mournful. Other examples of the sharing-caring atmosphere include quick, helpful answers to questions such as "Has Heather Locklear ever done any nude scenes?" and "Where can I find videos of lactating women?" (*Battle of the Ultra Milkmaids* was

one suggestion.) Then there are the Lolita posts that have launched a thousand Oprahs. Check out "The Young-Girl Watcher's Movies & Ratings," which gives four stars to the young Drew Barrymore's *Firestarter*— "Grips the heart of the girl-watcher through exceptionally arousing and memorable scenes." ✓ **USENET** DAILY

alt.sex.services (ng) Curious about the current status of that massage parlor you used to visit on

> **"The suicide of 23-year-old porn star Savannah elicited a kind of Kurt Cobain reaction here— both sensational and mournful."**

the outskirts of Minneapolis? Or about the gay strip club near the Tenderloin that gave new meaning to the term pole-dancing? Aficionados of such establishments flock to alt.sex.services, where they chat about the past, present, and future of the sexual service industry. ✓**USENET** WEEKLY

alt.sex.stories (ng) These mostly anonymous postings aren't very different from the *Penthouse* Forum—there are plenty of camp-counselor stories and sensuous usherettes. Every once in a while, however, an erotic fiction will distinguish itself with such stunningly bad taste that it instantly acquires the feeling of a classic. ✓**USENET** HOURLY

alt.sex.stories.d (ng) It's a common dilemma: You're in the mood to spin an erotic tale, to compose a seductive narrative that will engorge the necessary areas. But you also can't to wait check out the thrilling conclusion of "I Was a Horny Teenage Slut," and you want to find out if anyone has ever had sex with a bona fide giantess. Alt.sex.stories.d serves all your needs, offering a wide variety of sex stories from Net users across America, as well as a steady stream of commentary about the nature of alt.sex groups. ✓**USENET** *FAQ:* ✓**INTERNET**→*ftp* rtfm.mit.edu→anonymous→<your email address>→/pub/usenet-by-group/alt.sex. stories.d→ADMIN:_rec.arts.erotica_introduction DAILY

alt.sex.strip-clubs (ng) This newsgroup provides nationwide recommendations for strip clubs and other sex establishments. Curious about the quality of the waitresses/prostitutes in The Brass Rail in Omaha? Worried that the massage parlor you used to frequent in San Francisco may have taken a

> **"Every once in a while, however, an erotic fiction will distinguish itself with such stunningly bad taste that it instantly acquires the feeling of a classic."**

turn for the worse? Pay a visit to this group; it's a *Michelin Guide* for the groin. ✓**USENET** DAILY

Blue (echo) This is less a discussion group than an ongoing answer to the question "What's your favorite porn flick?" While it sometimes verges on marketplace talk—the commercial aspect of the group cannot be ignored—there's a good deal of good chat about adult films, ranging from the extremely informal ("A buddy and his wife told me about a good adult flick, with a good story and some great looking women, called *House of Strange Desires*") to more professional reviews. ✓**AFTERDARK** WEEKLY

Giffygirls (echo) "Hiya. I'm a middle-aged businessman who lives in Ottawa. I work for a local accounting firm, or maybe a big chemical company with a regional office nearby. Anyway, I have been married for the last 22 years to the same wonderful woman, and Anne and I have two beautiful daughters and a nice split-level house that overlooks a small pond. Here's why I am boring you with this story of domestic bliss. On a

whim, Anne and I recently went to a local motel and took some pictures. We enjoyed ourselves very much, and I have since put the pictures online, and listed them on this Giffygirls group. It seems to be not only a service for posting and downloading, but also a place for discussing the relative merits of popular GIFs. Anne and I feel like budding exhibitionists now, and we're planning on spending lots of time on this group, alerting people to our pictures and trying to find pictures of other couples." ✓**ADULTLINKS** DAILY

Review (echo) While Siskel and Ebert squander their talents on Harrison Ford, Julia Roberts, and Arnold Schwarzenegger, hundreds of Adult Link subscribers are devoting their attention to the other film industry, and this group serves as a meeting place for any and all critical discussion of pornographic films. Whether you're transfixed by Trixie Tyler's *Gang Bang* films, saddened by the death of porn star Savannah, or working yourself into a lather over Hyapatia Lee's highly acclaimed *Girls Doin' Girls 3*, you can add your two cents to the community of male pornography aficionados. ✓**ADULTLINKS** DAILY

Stories (echo) This group is filled to the brim with long fictions, usually with erotic themes, and one representative summary tells enough of the story: "My story is a medieval/fantasy tale of a 17-year-old orphan lad who becomes ensnared in a diabolical plot in the royal family's summer castle to steal some mystical jewels from the prime minister." If this kind of thing appeals to you, there's no shortage of material. If it doesn't, there's no shortage of aggravation. ✓**THROBNET** WEEKLY

Scoring

This is where it happens. It's as close as it's gonna get.

This is cybersex. X-rated. Go back if you're easily offended. And go back if the words get stuck in your throat. Just what exactly is cybersex? It's a lot like phone sex, except it's written (remember, people can save what you write!). It's shared fantasy, interactive porn, a narrative experience. Sometimes it's funny. Sometimes it's hot. Sometimes its the culmination of an email romance, and sometimes just a one-session stand. Sometimes its written by Mickey Spillane, sometimes by Anne Rice, and on the rarest occasions by Philip Roth. Who's having it? Your fair share of teenage boys, but your thirty-something, forty-something, and, incredible enough, fifty-somethings too. Most people you'll meet are men, but there are definitely women cruising the Net! Given their opportunities, they're far more experienced than the men. Of course there's the age-old (in cybertime) question, just how do you know who's who? And does it really matter?

On the Net

Across the board

Adult (echo) A general forum for

Downloaded from the DSC bulletin board.

---

libidinal expression, this group teaches the same lesson that singles bars taught to previous generations: When you're on the make, anything goes. Sometimes, your sexual goals are best served by an obviously insincere compliment ("You are the most fascinating and provocative woman I have ever met"); other times, it's more appropriate to resort to naked self-promotion, whether aggressive ("Does the thought of a honey in full-tilt rut scare you?") or humorous ("I'm going to change my name to Friday…everybody wants Friday to come"). The group enjoys extremely heavy traffic: in peak hours, it's not unusual to have a new message posted every minute. ✓**ADULTLINKS** HOURLY

Adult Sexuality Hello and welcome to GEnie's Adult Sexuality conference. Today our topic is sexual fantasies, and we'd like a volunteer to start us off. Yes, Cuddles? "One of MY fantasies is to do anal, vaginal, and oral all at once (yes, it would require more than one partner <g>) I keep thinking the ulti-

mate experience would be to be COMPLETELY filled…." Okay. Good. Go with that.

Speaking of completely filled, does anyone remember the best way to have anal sex? No, David, not "flip it and rip it." Patti? "I have tried it in a Chinese sling chair, and that seems to work even better than the face-down spread eagle." Yes, yes. The sling chair. Ohh, yes. Your answer brings back memories…but I see we have a hand raised in the back of the room. "Is computer sex a form of adultery?"

Resident seminarian

That's a fascinating question, and perhaps one best answered by our resident seminarian. William? "Sir, the biblical prohibition against adultery is commonly defined as a mental one; that is, that marriage is a state of shared trust and experience, not necessarily only sexual or procreative experience. Consequently, mental infidelity is a serious and actionable form of infidelity." Hmmm. Everyone got that?

Okay. We're almost out of time

> ## "It's time for our Truth Is Stranger Than Fiction presentations. Elaine? 'I once had a lover who insisted that he couldn't have an orgasm until he listened to the Who's "Squeeze Box."'"

for today, so that means it's time for our Truth Is Stranger Than Fiction presentations. Bob, why don't you start? "My penis is so large I have to put my hand at the base when I have sex so that I don't injure my partner." Okay. And we'll end with Elaine. "I once had a lover who insisted that he couldn't have an orgasm until he listened to the Who's 'Squeeze Box.'" ✓**GENIE**→*keyword* family→ Family and Personal Growth Bulletin Board→Adult Sexuality DAILY

Hottub (echo) The aptly named Hottub is filled with the kind of flirting that might float across the deck at a seventies ski lodge. "Many years ago my wife and I met a bisexual nymphomaniac. My wife really got an education from her." "Does anyone want a man who loves to satisfy? I will do my duty to any willing beauty." The Hottub regulars are in their late thirties and early forties, and seem to be complacent suburbanites more interested in spicing up their stable existence than shaking the tree to any great degree. Hottub is one of the tamest of the Adult Link groups; the men are more likely to sign off "Waiting with open arms" than to poke into anatomical specifics. ✓**ADULTLINKS** DAILY

Human Sexuality Forums Bedroom role-playing at 8 p.m. on Friday. Voyeurism as fantasy and reality at 3 p.m. on Saturday. Leather'n'lace techniques at 9 p.m. on Saturday. Hot-tub party at midnight on Wednesday. Every week the forums—there are two (adult and open)—offer more than 70 live, scheduled conferences. The weekly schedule, with new topics each week, is posted under notices in both the forums. But the fun here isn't always scheduled. Spend a few minutes in

the Adult Forum, especially with a female name, and you'll be invited to a private discussion—guaranteed! "Hi Jenny, what's up?" will pop onto your screen.

From that rather inauspicious beginning, you'll end up in either a coy flirting session or a hard-core masturbatory typing scene—with little in between. And many members don't limit their action. If you're a fast typist and quick witted, you can be engaged in two or more conversations at once. The bulletin boards in the Open Forum, with topics like Singles Club, Gay Alliance, and More Than Skin Deep, offer additional discussion and places to meet people. Jacob, for instance, opens up about his shyness in the Singles Club, and Deborah offers to help him plan a party.

Weight

Sonya and Rich, who've been talking for over a year in the Forum since they met in a "What is cybersex?" discussion, talk about Sonya's weight and her self-confidence in the More Than Skin Deep section. And several people join a thread about doing it with a best friend. The Forum moderators, Howard and Martha, have invested a lot of time ensuring that members feel comfortable in the forums—often placing rigid restrictions on who has access to the support-oriented real-time conferences and bulletin

boards in the Adult Forum.

To join the restricted conferences like those for infantilists or gay young adults, you must specifically request access when you send your general request for access to the Adult Forum (18 and over only). With more than 60,000 members, the Human Sexuality Forums are always crowded with people trying to make a connection. Warning: Conferences in the Adult Forum are incredibly difficult to get access to. That's by design, to protect the privacy of the community. ✓**COMPUSERVE**→*go* human→Messages *or* Conferences DAILY/LIVE

IRC Sex Channels Enter the superpacked #sex channel and immediately find yourself caught in the crossfire of ricocheting undergrad hormones. ("I want hot sexy words! Give them to me!!!!" screams Bubbles.) Save your coy coquetry and *hugs* for #ro-

> "Set a mood around any details she has told you, check the email address with a 'who' command, and make some educated guesses about tan lines or winter underwear. Then find yourself spread out on the rug in her den."

Scoring **Cybersex**

mance—#sex and its dozens of variants, from #wetsex to #kinky, is for typing out your most intimate, one-on-one/one-on-ten hard-pumping fantasies.

First you have to find a partner (even here, cybersex mostly takes place in private). Standard tricks include complimenting someone on their nick (handle), asking for some advice on IRC etiquette, and, pretending to be really nervous (this may be easy with a loved one in the next room or co-worker at the next workstation).

Winter underwear

Once you've got someone's attention, set a mood around any details he or she has told you and stick to it. Check the email address with a "who" command and make some educated guesses about tan lines or winter underwear. Then find yourself spread out on the rug in her den. ✓**INTERNET**→*irc* /channel #erotica *or* /channel

> "Standard **tricks** to find a partner include complimenting someone on their nick (handle), asking for some advice on IRC etiquette, and pretending to be really nervous (easy, with a co-worker at the next workstation)."

Downloaded from the DSC Bulletin Board.

#hotsex *or* /channel #kinky *or* /channel #love *or* /channel #netsex *or* /channel phonesex *or* /channel #romance *or* /channel #sex *or* /channel #singles *or* /channel #teensex *or* /channel #truthdare *or* /channel #wetsex

OrgyRoom (echo) "Hi Jenny saw you on here and thought I'd say hi would love to exchange some hot email with you." Or: "Hi Coyote, you really sound like my type of girl (SEX MAD). For now I will just leave you with this to think about. I would love to cover you with whipped cream, from head to waist and lick my way down your body..." Crude, but generally good-natured. ✓**ADULTLINKS** DAILY

People Connection America Online's People Connection is designed like a Cyberspace hotel. After entering through a lobby, Net users choose from among assorted conference rooms. People Connection's chat sites come in three varieties: Public Rooms, which range from broad mixers (The Flirts Nook, The Meeting Place) to directed discussions (Thirtysomethings, Over Forty, Trekkies); Member Rooms, which cater to narrower tastes (Gay in Texas, F Seeking F Mistress, Female Amputee); and finally Private Rooms, created by users for on-site im-

CYBERNOTES

```
"Action: Ride gets
out the whips and
cuffs...
<Ride> Stacy? How
bored did you say?!
;)
<Stacy> hi Ride!
<Stacy> seal: yes :-[
Action: FTD offers
STACY a longstem
rose.
<Sxdevil> hi freckles
<freckles> hi every-
one
Action: Stacy excepts
FTD's gift
<shudder> uh, like,
where's the sex?
<freckles> yeah! i
want some play!
<Sxdevil> shudder: you
need to start it.
Action: Noe hugs r_b
and lands a wet kiss.
<josh> hi all
<Sxdevil> freckles
...you want to play
...play with me...
Action: Noe slams r_b
on the floor and slow-
ly begins to pene-
trate
Action: Sxdevil grabs
freckles gently and
asks her if she would
like to play
<hugeguy> any one in
the mood?
<freckles> i want
some sex!
<shudder> everyone is
in the mood, it's the
sex channel!
<Conan> Let's talk
about sex
<hugeguy> Freckles:
I'll give you some."

—from #wetsex
```

promptu use.

Alienation and intimacy

Each room holds up to 23 people, and users may send private messages to any other chat-zone participant at any time. Live chat is a strange experience, certainly, full of strategies and aliases and disheartening amounts of clumsy pornography. But the unique mix of alienation and intimacy is both thrilling and chilling, and any users looking for like-minded chat pals—or even a one-Net stand—shouldn't hesitate to set up at People Connection and let their fingers do the talking. ✓**AMERICA ON-LINE**→*keyword* people

Fantasies

Cunt (echo) Most of the scenarios in this adult fantasy group play like the hoariest of horny clichés. The traveling-salesman husband is out of town and the hot wife is all alone. The teenage boy is seduced by his best friend's mother.

When they are not narrative, which is about half the time, the messages in this forum cut to the chase, offering explicit propositions that are filled with the typos and solecisms common to the genre. "I live in New Jersey and New York City is my playground for satisfying hot pussies so let's bump." If you love talking about sex without mincing words, this is the place for you. ✓**ADULTLINKS** DAILY

Eros What's your most secret sexual fantasy? Is it the two-lesbians-and-a-turkey-baster thing? Or maybe it's the one about making love to your best friend's mother while her husband and your mother elect each other to office in the bedroom next door.

Whatever gets you off, there's a good chance that someone else

Downloaded from the DSC Bulletin Board.

has dreamt it—or done it. And once they've done it, it seems, they just go ahead and post the event on the WELL's Eros conference.

Quickies and orgies

In addition to the massive conference rooms devoted to sexual fantasy and liberation, there are more specific conversations about virtually every sexual topic imaginable, including anal sex, oral sex, cybersex, masturbation, exhibitionism, quickies, voyeurs, toys, kinks, kissing, orgasm (single), orgasm (multiple), underwear, bondage, orgies, fetishes—you name it.

Messages are usually from the participants themselves, and as a result they contain insights you're not likely to find in sex manuals or more generic pornography. Aching to perform cunnilingus but crippled by TMJ? Dreaming of a woman who can bring you to orgasm by kissing you on the mouth? Get on the WELL. ✓**WELL**→*g* eros DAILY

Fantasies (echo) The long and colorful history of erotic writing—from the Song of Solomon to Sade to *Screw*—is extended by this group. All kinds of fantasies are accounted for—bondage, incest,

sex in public. And the group doesn't limit itself to the literary; the participants are equally interested in having their dreams come true. As one man puts it, "Any special nasty talents you have are greatly appreciated." ✓**AFTERDARK** DAILY

Masturbation

alt.sex.masturbation (ng) Really, when it comes right down to it, this is the only honest alt.sex group on the Internet; when you're sitting at a keyboard imagining ecstasy, one-handed typing is the most common form of pleasure.

This newsgroup hosts a wide range of users, from Danish teens to fortysomething American lawyers. Men and women alike are represented, and the entries range from the erotic to the spiritual (the great tantric group orgasm). ✓**USENET** DAILY

> "Whatever gets you off, there's a good chance that someone else has dreamt it—or done it. And once they've done it, it seems, they just go ahead and post the event on the WELL's Eros conference."

FurryMUCK

On the Net since September 1990, FurryMUCK is home each night to hundreds of

players, many of whom role-play a type of character called a Furry. A Furry is often described as an anthropomorphic animal—an animal with human characteristics such as upright gait, intelligence, human sexual organs, human patterns of behavior, and so forth. Many of the players on FurryMUCK pay special attention to the "and so forth"—the sexual adventuring that brings FurryMUCK both its notoriety and its popularity.

Wolves—Downloaded from CompuServe's Photography Forum.

Log in, wander around the city or the surrounding countryside, and meet and chat with fellow players. Furry has around 150 players logged in on any given evening, half of whom are in all likelihood participating in quasi-sexual encounters with each other.

FurryMUCK is a good place for chatting, but the social dynamics vary somewhat from those of other MUDs and other Internet chat hangouts. It would be a rare FurryMUCK chat session that didn't include someone getting a backrub, chasing a tail (as in the animal kind), or sending a private page to a member of the opposite sex. Since female characters are fair game for random pages and social come-ons, many female players escape this by playing males; many males become more popular by playing females.

There are four distinct chat environments on FurryMUCK:

* West Corner of the Park

West Corner of the Park is the so-called center of the MUCK, located at its geographic center and one room away from the Bandstand, a room any active player can reach simply by typing "bandstand." It's both a major transit route and the main chat area. Theoretically, sexual activity, or "tinysex," as it's called on FurryMUCK, is banned from West Corner of the Park, but in practice, people who don't know the rule often wander in, start fooling around, and have to be chased off.

* The restaurants and cafés

While the heyday of the Cafe Rose is past, others, such as Not Frank's Place and the Club Aero, are very active. Chatting in a virtual café is similar to chatting in a real café. Players will pretend to order items off a menu, and waiters will pretend to bring them, while people chat and welcome newcomers and wave to those heading out. Sexual activity almost never takes place in a Furry restaurant.

* The Underground Nexus

The Underground Nexus is located directly below West Corner of the Park and is a private room, even though anyone can visit. To get there, simply type "nexus." A lot of sex takes place there and in the areas connected to it, such as the Underground Inn and the various Underground Hot Tubs. It's a good place to meet a tinypartner and a very, very bad place to hang out if you're a tinyprude.

* The hot tubs

The Furry hot tubs are home to the explicit hard-X sexual encounters that Furry is famed for. If you're new to FurryMUCK and you're wondering where to go to see total strangers having sex with each other, check out the hot tubs. If you show up and act silly or prudish or offend the other players, you'll quickly find yourself locked out of the hot tubs. If, on the other hand, you'll do most anything you're dared to do, you'll quickly become a very popular player.

There are many characters you'd profit from knowing on FurryMUCK. Lynx and the rest of the wizard corps are the hard-core Furries who are entrusted with running things on the MUCK.

Lynx is stereotypically Cute, as in Extremely, Extremely Cute, and You Better Believe It, Bub.

Then there are the stereotypical Melon-Sized Breasts characters. Some Furries take great pleasure in endowing their characters with extremely exaggerated sexual characteristics. Squeak, for example, has six jiggling breasts she likes to wiggle at people. You'll find a few very amiable, nonsexual, nonaggressive characters at the Room Temperature Banana Detective Agency, located three blocks north of North Corner of the Park, on the northeast corner of the intersection. Characters such as Bojo Pigeon, Cyberskunk, Worgfunk (a rather silly Maine wolf), and Neikrad (a distinguished possum with mad-scientist inclinations) can usually be found there tinkering with MUD gadgets and chatting with anyone who wanders by. None of them will do anything mean or nasty, and they're excellent Furries to ask questions of if you're new. Then there are the aggressive sorts. People like Vulpis and Lochiel will toast your buns off with verbal barrages and spite if you disagree with them in any way.

Wondering what tinysex is like on FurryMUCK? It'll go something like this:

>Lupinus reaches for Carenia's full breast and cups it with one muscular paw.

>Carenia moans with passion and reaches between Lupinus's legs for the throbbing treasure she knows she'll find therein.

>Lupinus responds in kind, lowering Carenia on her back and inserting his pulsating, hairy wand into her dripping…

Okay, enough of that. You get the point.

All it takes to be good at tinysex is an active imagination, the ability to type quickly (and, as they say, with one hand), and the willingness to follow your partner's cues if your partner initiates an action. If you can "get into the spirit of the thing" by acting particularly bestial, you'll be highly sought-after in no time. The only real rule regarding tinysex, other than keeping it out of the Park, is that it must be consensual. And remember, there's more to FurryMUCK than tinysex—really. ✓**INTERNET**→ *telnet* sncils.snc.edu 8888→connect guest guest *Register:* ✓**INTERNET**→*email* fmadmin@sncils.snc.edu

---

alt.fan.furry (ng) There's tension betweeen the zoophiles and the Furries, but is it sexual tension? No topic provokes more debate on this active and rough (watch your back) newsgroup than the is-sex-with-an-anthropomorphic-animal-the-same-as-bestiality debate. The discussions can go off in the most outrageous tangents: "The anthropomorphic character can pay for his half of the dutch date, remember to use a condom before sex, say 'Thank you for a nice evening,' and even send you email later in the week. Show me a normal animal who can," argues one newsgroup poster against the bestiality comparison.

Comics plots

First and foremost, alt.fan.furry is a group for discussing furry comics and cartoons. Look for quite a few posts with spoiler notices at the beginning. Newsgroup members love to post detailed descriptions of the latest comics plot. It's also evolved into an off-site clubhouse for FurryMUCK members to talk about the direction of the MUCK. And if you read the group regularly, you'll never miss a furry convention; notices flood the group. Ahh, looking for erotic furry images? Check out alt.binaries.pictures.furry. ✓**USENET** DAILY

Gay member rooms

If heaven is a mansion with 100 rooms, then gay male heaven can be found in Cyberspace

in the member room section of AOL. Every night the list is dominated by gay-themed rooms covering just about every age, location, fetish, and kink. CyberStuds with screen names like HotJock, GymHunk, BIG14U, and OralJim cruise the rooms with carefree abandon looking for a good time. These rooms are not for the prudish—the emphasis here is on meeting others for mutual gratification, whether through a feverish exchange of Instant Messages, rendezvousing in a private room, exchanging numbers for sexy phone chat or meeting face to face. Of course, AOL's Terms of Service forbid explicit sexual language, but members test those limits every night and, if no one is looking, expand them.

LtherCollar announces he's eagerly submissive, HotLink1 advertises that his link plumps when you cook it, SoxLover wants to smell your socks, and UnZipdGuy tells everyone he's, well, unzipped. Age/location/genitalia-size checks are frequent, as are enthusiastic testimonials to sexual prowess.

The rooms are most active in the evening, but if you sign on during the day you're likely to find quite a number of members taking a respite from their jobs or, more likely, from the prying eyes of

their significant others.

Evening, though, is when the party really rocks and the member rooms, each limited to 23 people, fill up quickly.

Behind the scenes

Some of the rooms are very stable and can be found just about anytime, but most are ephemeral, appearing and disappearing like the dunes of Fire Island. Each room has its own personality, which can change from moment to moment as members come and go. Some are raucous; others—the more bizarre rooms—are eerily quiet as members exchange Instant Messages behind the scenes.

Developing a good member profile is the key if you want to be a player, because chances are that when you enter a room many members will look you up to see whether they're interested in a private chat. But with a little typing skill and a lot of time, you're bound to find that object of your desire.

Stonewall in Cyberspace

Like the Stonewall Inn, Men4Men is where it all started. The longest-running gay-themed room, Men4Men (sometimes called M4M) can trace its history back to the days when AOL allowed only one gay room at a time and monitors unceremoniously closed any additional rooms. Lobbying by die-hard gay members, and the good business sense of AOL, changed that policy, and now gay members enjoy near-total freedom to create any room they want. Gay-bashing, once a problem ig-

> **"Some rooms are very stable; others appear and disappear like the dunes of Fire Island."**

nored by AOL, is no longer tolerated. You've come a long way, baby, and you can thank the veteran members you're likely to encounter in the Men4Men room. They tend to be older, more mature men who are very comfortable with their sexuality. If you're dealing with coming-out issues, Men4Men is a good place to look for support.

Just me and my Calvins

If you're into younger guys, check out YngMen4YngMen. Just about every night, 18-to-25-year-old guys, many of them claiming to be virgins, sit around in their Calvins and chat or fantasize about sex. At times it's like a circle jerk—a love of masturbation jokes is a must here—where stories of lost virginity, sexual conquest, and disastrous dates are freely traded. This is a young room, and frequent age checks serve to intimidate the older set. If you admit to being over 30, you won't find a welcome mat here.

When the wife is asleep...

It's 11:00 p.m...Do you know where your husband is? If he's glued to the computer he may be straddling the fence in the Bi-Men4BiMen room, sometimes called MarriedMen4Men, BiCuriousMen4Men, or some other variation. A haven for the bisexual or those too curious to stay away, this is where a salesman from Florida sets up a meeting with a guy in Chicago, a New York husband takes advantage of his wife's absence, or a college jock explores his longings. A popular topic is how to juggle sexual dalliances with men while still satisfying the wife. Frequent location checks are a sure sign of members interested in face-to-face meetings. But if you're looking for a commitment, you won't find it here.

Stats, please!

Do you give orders? Receive them? Wonder about golden showers? Body piercing? Find others who share your interests in M4M Yes Sir, AOL's ongoing S&M club. Like its real-life equivalent, it's often jammed but intensely quiet. Hang out long enough and chances are your IM window will pop up with a demanding "Stats, please!" When replying, be sure to mention whether you're dominant or submissive, into leather, have any pierced body parts, tattoos, etc. You get the picture.

Location, location, location

Hate the bar scene but want to meet people in your area? Every night members create location-specific rooms hoping to meet others in their area. The offerings change from night to night, so check out the list regularly or create your own room. Name the room simply with your location and interest, such as ArizonaM4M or ChicagoYngGuys4Guys, and soon you'll be chatting up a storm with someone near you. Or at least in the same state.

Nice guys

Bring on the flowers and candy! If you're just not in the mood for raunchy chat, or are looking for a little romance, check out the Nice-Men4Men or the M4MForRomance rooms, a refuge for those with a more traditional approach to dating. Participants here long for candlelight dinners and cuddling by the fire, and generally eschew cybersexual advances. Chat is friendly and unforced as members relax and flirt in an unaggressive setting.

Anything goes

Meet someone who wants to go private in M4M4Private. If hairy chests are your thing, take a look in HairyMen4Men. Fulfill your hazing fantasies in FratDudes4Same. Talk about water sports (and not the Greg Louganis kind) in Gay Water Sports. Wax poetic over feet in GayFootFetish. If after scrolling through the seemingly endless list of possibilities you still can't find your heart's desire, you can create your own fantasy. Anything can happen and anything goes. ✓**AMERICA ONLINE**→*keyword* people→Rooms→Available Room→ Member Rooms

---

Hot hints

Are you a wallflower, even in Cyberspace? Do you wait for an IM that never comes? Try these suggestions and let your online popularity soar.

- Create a screen name with the word **Jock**, **Hunk**, **Hot**, **Big**, **Hung**, or **Stud** in it. Also try to indicate where you live, like **NCHungJock**.

- Reinvent yourself with a detailed member profile. You can be anyone you want. Describe Marky Mark's body and you won't be able to keep up with the IMs. Don't worry about lying because chances are everyone else is lying, too.

- Find people in your area and send them an IM. People love to hear from neighbors.

- Greet everyone who enters a room. The more visible your screen name, the more people will take an interest in you.

- Remember that no one has to know your real name.

Gay sex

The Net is as gay as any big city. Indeed, many of the
attractions of Cyberspace are
urban in nature. There's
anonymity. There's night-
life. There's wide tolerance
of outrageous behavior.
There's a better than average
chance of finding like-minded partners. After the Net-
heads, techies, and college
kids, gays make up one of
the largest and fastest-grow-
ing communities on the
Net. It's as easy to find
someone to share an evening
with in Cyberspace as it is in
any bar (and you don't have
to dress for it). Certainly, the
sex is safe, and sometimes
it's even smart—compare
the hot talk in the IRC
channel **#gaysex** with its
heterosexual counterparts.
What's more, the Net allows
people in the closet to
breathe a little. It allows the
just-curious to be more than
just (it seems everybody
turns gay on AOL). And it
lets the world be promiscuous again.

On the Net

Altlife (echo) The alternative
lifestyles covered by this group are
mostly gay, and mostly involve gay
men. There's Peter, the gay married man looking for a discreet
companion, and Jon, who is in a
similar boat but just wants to talk

through the issue rather than do
anything about it. The topics covered by Altlife are extremely varied, and range from personals
postings to explicit gay erotica to
casual conversation about gay life
in America. ✓**AFTERDARK** WEEKLY

alt.sex.motss (ng) A hairy-
chested man appears in the latest
issue of the closeted, gay, ubiqui-
tous underwear catalog *International Male*. You'd better log on to
alt.sex.motss to find out if this is a
harbinger of a hairy-man come-
back. While you're here, vote on
whether Aquaman is sexier than
Superboy, and find out the proper
spelling of *come* and what to eat to
improve its taste (pineapple juice
and celery seed). You can also
swap dated River Phoenix gossip
and GIFs of the models in *Men's
Health*. No personal ads here;
what's important is the tone,
which hovers somewhere between
goofy and debonair. ✓**USENET**
FAQ: ✓**INTERNET**→*ftp* rtfm.mit.edu→
anonymous→<your email address>
→/pub/usenet-by-group/news.
answers/motss→faq HOURLY

Bi-Sexual (echo) Which region
is more homophobic, the Bible
Belt or Orange County? What's
the proper course of action for a
budding lesbian stranded in rural
Oklahoma? And what about the
plight of Stuart and Amy, the
young married couple who have
both discovered bisexual desires
within the last year? All these
questions and more are addressed
on Adult Link's Bi-Sexual. Interested in true confessions? Well,
then, you might be interested to
know that Roger in Providence
"doesn't mind the feeling of pubes
stuck between [his] teeth." Seeking practical advice? You'll probably want to pay attention to Fast
Eddie's tips for shaving scrotal
hair. Receptive both to practiced
bisexuals and to those in search of
experiment, this group is chatty
and comfortable. ✓**ADULTLINKS**
HOURLY

GayBaths Connoisseurs of sex in
public exchange dirty stories, tips
on avoiding entrapment, and favorite haunts. The fun here
doesn't seem to be as much in the
sex per se as in the risk of getting
caught. Actual gay baths and plain
old-fashioned sex clubs, therefore,
don't get much attention. These

> "To judge from the
> frequent age, loca-
> tion, and underwear
> checks, these boys
> are in their twen-
> ties, live in U.S.
> cities, and wear
> Calvin Kleins."

men prefer highway rest stops and the sort of upstanding gym you might find in a suburban mall, where your boss or his wife might stumble into the steam room at just the wrong, or right, moment. ✓**PRIDENET** DAILY

#gaysex A freshman stumbles in to announce he's finally lost his virginity. Two navy men spray each other down with WD-40. A law student regrets that Richard Posner will never make it to the Supreme Court, and the conversation lapses for no good reason into French. Welcome to #gaysex—part tearoom, part tea party. For serious raunch, go to #jack-off. Sex on #gaysex is campy and the-atrical—stylized flirtation. Come here to swoon over Keanu's new haircut, seek advice on how to ap-proach that volleyball player, or meet the Internet's one and only gay Rush Limbaugh fan. Because bashers regularly attack the chan-nel, the bots are trigger-happy. (One of the channel's cruel plea-sures is watching a newbie hit on a bot; their names are cEvin, Talbot, and Stonewall.) To judge from the frequent age, location, and under-wear checks, these boys are mostly in college or their twenties, live in major U.S. cities or Indiana, and wear Calvin Kleins. ✓**INTERNET**→*irc* /channel #gaysex

#jack-off Eons ago, way back in 1992, most gay IRCers logged onto a channel with the re-spectable name #gblf (an acronym for gays, bisexuals, lesbians, and friends). Those who wished to talk dirty were politely ushered to #gaysex. As the months went by, #gblf got more and more pallid, and as ICRers defected to it, #gay-sex gentrified. Today, #gblf is just another electric memory, and #gaysex is not quite as outré as its name. The one-handed typists

have moved on to #jack-off. A de-ceptive silence may greet you when you join the channel, be-cause the dozen or so chatters are industriously exchanging their happy thoughts in private. If you wait long enough, though, you will be saluted with a private mes-sage of "Hey dude, what's up," or something equivalently butch. But #jack-off, like #gaysex before it, is softening its hard-core. Giggles and conversation break out more often. Also, check out the similar #bisex, #lesbos, #gam (gay Asian males), and #bearcave (furry gay men). ✓**INTERNET**→*irc* /channel #jack-off

---

Lambda Lounge Evening is the best time to check out the Lounge. Every night the room is packed with gay male AOL members quaffing virtual drinks and wink-ing emoticon winks. Everyone seems to know each other, but don't be put off—Lambda Lounge regulars love to party with new-bies. Members joke, flirt, swap lies, and, of course, tantalize each other with sexy innuendos. The room is moderated, though, so don't get carried away. And don't take yourself too seriously either, or you'll leave with a bruised ego. ✓**AMERICA ONLINE**→*keyword* glcf→ Lambda Lounge

The Male Stop (bbs) In New York and looking for a good time? Check out the Male Stop, New York's premier gay male bulletin board, and cruise, cruise, cruise. The Cyberspace equivalent of a very popular gay bar, you'll have free access of 20 minutes daily, or subscriber access of up to three hours a day. When you first sign on, you'll fill out a questionnaire with questions ranging from the color of your eyes to your pre-ferred sexual activity (are you a top or a bottom?). You can then

"browse" other Male Stoppers and the system will tell you how well you match with them. If you like what you see, page them for a chat. The OmniChat feature al-lows for groups to meet, but most members engage one on one. The message boards are also active with topics like "cruising," "the leather board," "dating," and the infa-mous "head to head" board, where members argue topics ranging from politics to NAMBLA. Flam-ing isn't tolerated the way it used to be, and Jason the Sysop will drop you from the service if you harass or insult. There are hun-dreds of gay BBSs across the coun-try—check out the sidebar for a sampling. ☎→*dial* 212-721-4180 →new DAILY/ LIVE

GAY BBSs

Bear Com
703-525-5136
Blue Parrot Cafe
303-321-4281
Carolyn's Closet
612-891-1225
Eye Contact
415-255-5972
Lambda Link
512-873-8299
Lambda Unlimited
813-576-0656
Leather Connection
504-454-0380
Pride Line
206-788-2230
QueerCom
302-323-0535
Risquilly
708-495-6609
Starchat
213-849-4048
10% Connection
312-478-0419
Triangle
904-737-6056
The Wall
718-278-2120

Fetishes

Some men like feet. Some women like spanking. In the world of fetish newsgroups, you don't need to be the least bit shy about what floats your boat, since it's more than likely that you'll find comrades in erotic arms. Like your husband better in diapers? Get a box of Pampers, and slip into **alt.sex.fetish.diapers**. Some fetishists are interested in detailed psychological self-analysis ("I think the reason I like other women's breasts so much is that I had an older sister who used to prance in front of the mirror"); others just want to act out their fantasies in full-throated ecstasy. From **alt.sex.fetish.amputee** to **alt.sex.fetish.fashion**, these are the sexual versions of a special airline meal.

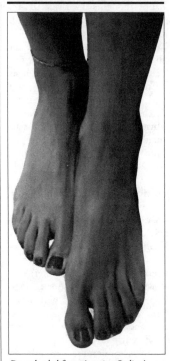

Downloaded from America Online's Mac Graphics & CAD Forum.

On the Net

Across the board

Fetishes "You are normal!" proclaims a posting on CompuServe's Variations II forum. And here, your sexual tastes are never looked at askance—no matter what they might be. Unlike on public venues, the forum moderators Howard and Martha carefully screen all applicants to weed out the merely curious or, worse yet, the condemning. After you have shown what really turns you on you enter a safe world to meet others with the same interests (or as "society" might say, fetishes). There are bulletin boards for adult babies and water sports (urolagnia, klismaphilia, and douching) as well as the general Variations section. Real-time conferences are scheduled regularly for members of each of the boards. Participants can indulge in their favorite cybersex play or exchange trade secrets. Do you know about the Mary Kay product that makes shaving so much easier? Where do you get "nipple adornments" that hurt, but not too much? These are intimate places and people do become very familiar to the point of offering personal, nonsexual advice. But for the most part it's good fetish fun. ✓ **COMPUSERVE**→*go* hsx200→Messages *or* Conferences DAILY/LIVE

Kinky (echo) Take Frank, for instance. A fortysomething suburban professional, married, with two children, Frank loves sucking on long toes. He can't get enough of it, but his wife won't indulge him. She finds it silly. Then there's Marie, a 29-year-old artist who loves to have anal sex while she strokes her cat. The cat doesn't seem to mind, but it makes her boyfriend nervous. So what are people like Frank and Marie supposed to do? They know what they want; they just can't get it. That's where After Dark's Kinky comes in handy. The group is useful in pairing off kinks and letting birds of a feather flock together—

> "Take Frank, for instance. A fortysomething suburban professional, married, with two children, Frank loves sucking on long toes. He can't get enough of it, but his wife won't indulge him. She finds it silly."

uniting infantilists in Indiana, or coprophiles in Kansas. So if your libido is tuned to a narrow band, give it a try. As one participant wrote, "I thought I was the only one...until I found another one." ✓**AFTERDARK** WEEKLY

Bestiality

alt.sex.bestiality (ng) This crowded and diverse newsgroup appears to attest to the fact that large numbers of people extend their human sexuality beyond human boundaries. Mostly devoted to the sexual succulence of man's best friends, the group also investigates the erotic side of horses, cats, hamsters, rabbits, donkeys, dolphins, and snakes. Scott D. of Maryland, for instance, posts a confession of a ten-year affair with his family's golden-retriever bitch, and an aspiring literary talent from Minnesota named R. Rock contributes to the discourse with the "touching tale" about a horse. When the late, great Gilda Radner sang "Let's Talk Dirty to the Animals," she had no idea. ✓**USENET** DAILY

alt.sex.bestiality.barney (ng) The gag alt.sex group to end all gag alt.sex groups, this newsgroup collects detailed stories and fantasies about getting down and dirty with everyone's favorite purple dinosaur (Jurassic Pork, anyone?). To its credit, the group also includes responses from outraged Barney advocates defending the lovable character. Fun for the whole family. ✓**USENET** WEEKLY

Whatever's clever

alt.sex.breast (ng) Subscribers to *Jugs* and other mammocentric magazines will love alt.sex.breast, an erotic newsgroup devoted entirely to the most conspicuous of

> "It's hard to read the anonymous confession 'I can only sleep with women wearing prom dresses' without understanding that sex is not a skin game but a second-skin game."

all fetishes. Like 'em big? Like 'em small? Interested in learning the seven different kinds of nipples? While traffic is mostly male, a few women check in now and then to offer firsthand experience about the topic. ✓**USENET** WEEKLY

alt.sex.cthulhu (ng) Aficionados of the sex/horror author H.P. Lovecraft may recognize Cthulhu, a squidlike personage who is also the star of his very own newsgroup. Although the group is devoted largely to singing the praises of Cthulhu, it occasionally veers into related Lovecraftian territory—necrophilia, decapitation, and other gory obsessions. ✓**USENET** WEEKLY

alt.sex.enemas (ng) That's right. Never has the rear emetic been so celebrated for its erotic potential as in alt.sex.enemas, where the mostly middle-aged subscribers get together to trade stories and tips about rectal fluid injection. Unlike some other newsgroups, this one does not

contain many old messages, and seems to be emptied out regularly. ✓**USENET** WEEKLY

alt.sex.exhibitionism (ng) Not as single-minded as its name might indicate, alt.sex.exhibitionism is a grab bag of an erotic newsgroup, filled with assorted GIFs, stories, and opinion pieces. Anything goes, really, from anecdotes of public sex to discussions of sex in movies. Dominated by male users, the group does have a small but steady lesbian membership (or are they?). ✓**USENET**

alt.sex.fat (ng) Big men and women—that's BM and BW in the group's lingo—have a hard life. The culture deems them unattractive. They get winded quickly. And often, they combat their loneliness by displacing their sexual energies into—gasp!—more eating. Well, the fat need fear no more: Their erotic needs are being cared for by newsgroups like alt.sex.fat. Split evenly between classifieds and erotic stories about obesity, the group protects the erotic rights of the humongous. ✓**USENET** DAILY

alt.sex.fetish.amputee (ng) This newsgroup celebrates the benefits of amputation—not for the handicapped, but for those lucky few who get to have sex with them. A niche market if ever there was one. ✓**USENET** WEEKLY

alt.sex.fetish.diapers (ng) Have you ever made your wife wear Pampers all night long, and begged her to urinate into them rather than get up and go to the bathroom? No? Move along, then. Otherwise, slip out of those briefs and boxers and slip into something more disposable. Deftly combining excremental and infantile fetishes, diaper-wearing has a limited but passionate following that seems to be confined mostly to thirtysomethings—those with children, perhaps, reusing the material of their life for erotic purposes. As Simon, a straight Chicagoan who can achieve an erection only while wearing diapers, puts it, "There's nothing I like better than the freedom of a diaper: you can literally let it all hang out." ✓**USENET** DAILY

alt.sex.fetish.fashion (ng) If sex is a material issue for you, look no further. From fur-covered vibrators to rubber boots, from lycra bodysuits to crotchless wedding dresses, alt.sex.fetish.fashion has got you covered, and postings range from stories about erotic fashion victories to advertisements for particularly complex pieces of lingerie. Fashion slaves may seem like a trivial erotic subculture, hardly the equal of full-blown foot fetishists or bondage devotees, but it's hard to read one young woman's finely textured account of masturbating with leather gloves, or the anonymous confession "I can only sleep with women wearing prom dresses" without understanding that sex is not a skin game but a second-skin game. ✓**USENET** *FAQ:* ✓**INTERNET**→*ftp* rtfm.mit.edu→anonymous→<your email address>→/pub/usenet-by-group/news.answers/alt-sex/fetish-fashion DAILY

alt.sex.fetish.feet (ng) If you think that foot fetishists are relics of a bygone era, it's time to get in-step. Whether spotting podiatric treats in centerfolds—check out the big toe on *Penthouse*'s Miss May!—or otherwise celebrating sole food, the participants in this newsgroup, mostly men in their twenties and thirties, do their best to sustain the cult of the foot. ✓**USENET** DAILY

alt.sex.fetish.hair (ng) A newsgroup that contains two newsgroups within it, alt.sex.fetish.hair caters both to those who experience orgasm while they are getting perms—a substantial percentage of the population, apparently—and to those obsessed with body hair, pubic and underarm primarily. The body-hair contingent dominates the group, with plenty of requests for GIFs of hirsute men and women and stories of ecstasy among the follicles. But it's the haircut segment that manages to provide the most interesting commentary, such as an extended discussion on the political and erotic effects of the Citadel's decision to order a crew cut for ground-breaking female cadet Shannon Faulkner. ✓**USENET** WEEKLY

alt.sex.fetish.orientals (ng) This newsgroup does its best to display the best and worst of the alt.sex format, both debunking and advancing the most pernicious stereotypes about Asian women. Dominated by Western voices—mostly sitcom American college boys who have managed to hook up with an Asian girlfriend some-

> "…an extended discussion on the erotic effects of the Citadel's decision to order a crew cut for ground-breaking female cadet Shannon Faulkner."

where along the line—the group occasionally reflects upon the importance of its fetish. More often than not, though, it's just one more geisha-girl fantasy after another. ✓**USENET** DAILY

alt.sex.fetish.startrek (ng) For the thousands of devoteed Trekkies who found themselves swooning over Lt. Uhuru or putting William Shatner pinups next to their Brando and their Dean, alt.sex.fetish. startrek boldly goes where no pornography has gone before. Interested in the nude film scenes of *Trek* cast members? Curious which character bedded the most aliens? Receptive to speculative pornography about Vulcans? Well, may the force be with you, or something like that. ✓**USENET** WEEKLY

alt.sex.intergen (ng) The middle-aged men who populate alt.sex.intergen go to great lengths to separate intergenerational sex from its less dignified cousin, kiddie porn. Intergenerational sex, apparently, is founded on the belief that children are sexual beings whose desires and allures must be factored into the world's libidinal equation. And kiddie porn? That's just plain sick. If you believe that 8-year-old girls are flowers in early bloom, you might want to join the pedophile movement, or at least contribute to the mix of personal anecdotes and legal briefs that compose this newsgroup. ✓**USENET** WEEKLY

alt.sex.voyeurism (ng) If you're the kind of person who watches *Rear Window* for strategy, this sexually explicit newsgroup is the place for you. Alt.sex.voyeurism users—almost exclusively male and techno-obsessed—offer tips on wiretaps, review the pros and cons of bathroom video monitoring, recommend specific hotel rooms, and trade both stories of sexual espionage and erotic GIFs culled from their excursions. If you're a woman, this newsgroup may be a source of some discomfort: Every time you shower or undress, it seems, some cybergeek has a lens trained on you from across the courtyard. ✓**USENET** DAILY

BackRoom (echo) Anal sex, aka "back-room recreation," is the group's principal focus. The discussion is hot talk. "Drop me a line telling me what you would do if you could have me as your sex slave for one night." "Well, a sex slave for a night....let's see...to get things started, perhaps a good rub-down with some scented oils. Then, as we get more relaxed, I would start to gently kiss and caress your body. Starting at your neck, I would progress down to your firm, round breasts..." Threads become elaborate scenes and, occasionally, powerful pornography. A mix of men and women. ✓**ADULTLINKS** DAILY

Piercing (echo) Do you set off buzzers when you go through the airport metal detector? Are piercings dangerous? Where should you pierce a nipple to minimize the danger of infection? If you have lost sleep musing over these questions, you might want to check out Piercing on AdultLinks, which addresses various aspects of the piercing subculture. With a decided urban slant and a preponderance of subscribers under 25, the group spends much of its time discussing the role of rebellion in piercing, and relating personal anecdotes of increased sexual pleasure. Every once in a while, though, an unlikely piercee appears, such as the Kansas City grandmother who confesses that her recent pierce has enabled "seismic orgasms I would have never

imagined possible, and all from tugging gently on the ring as I am kissed and stroked." ✓**ADULTLINKS** WEEKLY

Tickling (echo) In theory this group is devoted to the finer points of sexual arousal through tickling—"It all depends on what I tickle you with: a feather duster is probably best for your nipples and upper torso. Fingertips, light kisses, and licks would work best on your inner thighs." But something strange is afoot in Tickling. The group often crosses wires with a psychic/prophecies conference, resulting in odd dialogues that were hardly dialogues at all; talk of tongues and pipe cleaners daintily became interlaced with horoscopes and Nostradamus cults. ThrobNet needs to resolve this high-tech version of the Reese's Peanut Butter Cup, but meanwhile, the tickling subgroup seems to be developing quite nicely, supplementing its practical tips with more political discussions (is tickling sadism? Is it inherently invasive?). ✓**THROBNET** WEEKLY

Downloaded from CompuServe's Mac Graphics Plus Forum.

Group sex

You've been friends with Steve for years, and you've always flirted a little with his wife,

Marie. Why wouldn't you? She's married to your buddy, she likes you, and she's cute. So there you are, in a state of constant flirting, calling her for an unexpected lunch date, hugging her for a second too long at parties. But then one day Steve comes up to you and says he needs to talk. You expect to hear that they're having trouble, or that he met someone else. "No, no," he says. "Nothing like that. Marie really likes you, and she and I were wondering if we could, uh, invite you over for, uh..." He stops. He stammers. He flushes bright red. Then it dawns on you. Three hours later, you're sandwiched between the marrieds, accepting Steve's embraces while you unsnap Marie's skirt. And three hours after that, you're too wired to sleep, staying up and detailing your menage for **AdultLinks' 3somes** message board.

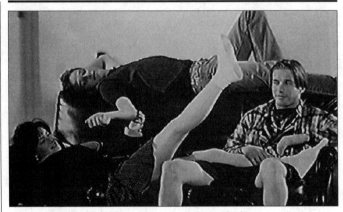

Threesome—*downloaded from GEnie's ShowBiz RoundTable.*

On the Net

3some (echo) Red Rider, a 32-year-old high-school history teacher from the Philadelphia area, is happily married to S., a wonderful woman three years his senior.

They have no complaints about their sex life; in fact, things are so wonderful that the two would like to share their bounty with a lucky bisexual woman. "We have done this before, and found that threesomes done in trust are the most wonderful experience." While there are variations—sometimes the couples are in search of bi men, sometimes two lesbians are seeking a third for "daisy-chaining"—the theme remains the same. In addition to the triangle appeals, the group includes substantial justification of the threesome lifestyle.
✓**ADULTLINKS** WEEKLY

alt.polyamory (ng) First a little etymological lesson. *Poly* means multiple, and *amory* is the act of love, so *polyamory*—if you're still with us—is acting in a loving way with multiple partners, sort of the amateur version of polygamy. Alt.polyamory provides a forum and a sounding board for the polyamorous among us. Much of the newsgroup is devoted to the longings of the monamorous for

deeper experiences. One man asks, "Okay, so I want to go poly. What do I do? Ask my girlfriend if it's okay, and then? Put up signs in bars? Go around hitting on women and then say 'Uh, by the way, there are more'? Go around to my classes and make announce-

> "Okay, so I want to go poly. What do I do? Ask my girlfriend if it's okay, and then? Put up signs in bars? Go around hitting on women and then say 'Uh, by the way, there are more'?"

ments: 'Anyone wanna have multiple relationships with me?'"

Freedom

While other subscribers don't have a tremendous amount of sympathy for these attitudes, the postings sometimes address more important issues from the interior of the polyamorous community—monogamy as a contract or vow, the issue of freedom, the trick of control in relationships ("I find it most difficult to control a relationship with just two people in it, much less three; what's more if I control it I get nothing but what I can think up. If control, like lots of other things, is what you relish, you owe it to yourself to get a golden retriever and forget about trying to 'go poly'"). If you're in a single relationship and want to open up to others, or if you're in the midst of a romantic web and want to share your experience, this is the newsgroup for you. ✓USENET *FAQ:* ✓INTERNET→*ftp* rtfm.mit.edu→ anonymous→<your email address> →/pub/usenet-by-hierarchy/ alt/answers→polyamory-faq WEEKLY

Couples (echo) "It is kind of like dating but more complicated because there are four people involved that have to have common interests, like each other, and be sexually attracted." This is not, in other words, golf. It's people talking about shared group experiences, including how-to, where-to, the special sensitivities that do crop up, and other aspects of couples seeking couples (for instance, amateur videos). In theory, the group is for couples only. You'll be reprimanded if you come on as a lone wolf looking for just a threesome or, egads, a twosome. Strong presence from the South and Southwest United States. ✓ADULT LINKS DAILY

Swing (echo) What makes a swinger? Well, if you take this conference as representative, one of two things: extreme idealism or bitter disappointment. While some of the participants have the fresh-faced eagerness of Karen and Scott ("We are in our early twenties and want to meet another couple for swapping and other arrangements"), others display the resignation of the divorced Memphis man looking for "willing married women" ("Since my wife walked out on me I have decided it is time to live a little"). However you get here, there's plenty of opportunity for recreational sex from Louisville to Waukegan to Tucson. ✓THROBNET WEEKLY

Swingers Howard is unhappy. Well, not unhappy exactly, but committed to a marriage that cramps his style. While he loves his wife deeply, he'd rather be out on the town, meeting young and attractive couples and then returning to their apartment for flesh sandwiches. With the help of AdultNet's Swingers, Howard—along with other aficionados of threesomes, foursomes, and more-somes—can chase his dreams. ✓ADULTNET WEEKLY

Triples (ml) Devoted to "extended, multi-adult, nonmonogamous, intimate relationships," the Triples mailing list marks the spot where David Crosby's "Triad" takes on the feel of a manifesto. Ironically, there's not a whole lot of sex. Instead, subscribers spend their time worrying about the legal and logistical tangles of extended intimacies. One participant, for instance, frets over immigration laws— "Let's assume that you come from a country where polygamy is legal, that you have five spouses, and that you try to enter the U.S."— while another surveys threesomes

in literature from Huxley to Heinlein. If you want hot chat, go somewhere else, but if you're interested in ménages à trois as intellectual propositions, and you want to debate whether they harmonize better with a libertarian or anarchist worldview, just make yourself part of the extended family. ✓IN-TERNET→*email* triples-request@hal. com ✍ *Write a request* WEEKLY

CYBERNOTES

"Hello. It is a real turn-on when two couples that like each other express themselves physically. The actual act is only a climax. If done properly the entire foreplay can excite the anticipation for all and that can be just as erotic. To see your S.O. touching and being touched and to watch as the kisses go from 'Hi' to 'God I want your BODY' is a real turn-on for me also. It generally takes a few dates to watch this evolve—if it happens at all. But when it does it is magic. It is also wonderful to experience the transitions with a partner of your own in front of your S.O. I don't know where you live but if you want, perhaps we can get together and let whatever happens happen."

—from **Couples** on AdultLinks

Sadomasochism

You can take it (or give it) in accord with missionary

convention, or you can add whips, chains, ropes, cuffs, and the attendant mind games—I master, you slave—until the erotic layering overcomes you. In its various S&M newsgroups, bulletin boards, and mailing lists, the Net has charms to soothe the savage beasts among us, whether they be lesbian dominants, gay male submissives, or plain old beat-me, whip-me, thrash-me heterosexuals. And while discussion sometimes tends toward the lofty (high-fa-lutin' philosophical tracts about the ethical boundaries of bondage), there are also plenty of opportunities to get down and dirty by simulating your fantasies in the cybersex world. Heavily trafficked sites include **alt.sex.bondage** and **alt. sex.spanking**.

Downloaded from DSC BBS.

On the Net

Across the board

Agony-Aunt (echo) Doms and subs try to connect with each other in a genial environment. Kinky Karen, "a bisexual lady who has participated in some very unusual sexual encounters such as threesomes and bondage with female friends," is looking to "get some

chitchat going" with Magic Tongue, one of many Australians on the group. Madmax, on the other hand, wants to pursue more specific interests, preferably involving "well-lit and close-up" videos. No matter how earnestly philosophical or graphically violent the observations and discussions might become, the frequent salutation "Hi y'all!" best represents the affable spirit of the group. ✓**ADULTLINKS** WEEKLY

alt.personals.bondage (ng) Open the closet of this newsgroup, and you'll be confronted with rows and rows of straps and whips

and studs. Lots of leather, doms seeking subs, couples interested in trying out tripartite handcuffs with a willing third party. Despite the fairly diverse clientele—men and women, straight and gay, old and young alike—alt.sex.bondage somehow seems unified, and the massive amount of traffic (more than 100 new messages every day) takes on the feel of a juggernaut. Score another victory for the ties that bind. ✓**USENET** DAILY

alt.sex.bondage (ng) From the philosophical (a treatise on the tricky dynamic of both surrendering and retaining control in sex play) to the practical (what kind of rope should a couple use when tying each other up?), the heavily trafficked alt.sex.bondage covers the world of S&M, dominance, submission, leather, and cuffs. The

> **"Open the closet of this newsgroup, and you'll be confronted with rows and rows of straps and whips and studs. Lots of leather, doms seeking subs, couples interested in trying out tripartite handcuffs with a willing third party."**

100-odd messages posted daily are only minimally concerned with personals—for that, see alt.personals.bondage. Instead, the newsgroup splits its attention between journalistic and commercial duties, both discussing bondage issues and advertising products (videos, mostly).

Young and old

If there is a lesson to be learned from the newsgroup's demographics, it's that bondage cuts across all categories, fascinating both young and old, men and women, everyone from the 22-year-old interested in losing her virginity with strings attached to the randy retiree seeking leather-clad teens to punish him. Though some of the practices described seem genuinely dangerous—have you ever had a partner tie you up and then perform oral sex on you while brandishing a straight razor?—the clear-eyed optimism of the group proves that bondage is, as always, a matter of truss. ✓USENET *FAQ:* ✓INTERNET→ *ftp* rtfm.mit.edu→ anonymous→ <your email address> →/pub/usenet-by-group/alt.answers/alt-sex/bondage-faq→part1 *and* part2 *and* part3 HOURLY

#bdsm and #bondage #bdsm (bondage, discipline, sadomasochism) and its sister group, #bondage, are among the busiest net sex IRC channels. #bdsm is open to all, #bondage by invitation only. Many of the #bdsm regulars are also regulars on #bondage, and if you strike up the right relationships on #bdsm, you'll get your invitation into #bondage. Both groups are for serious practitioners. Many members are involved, or claim to be involved, in RL master-slave relationships. Newbies and lurkers tend to be identified quickly and either become participants or are

> **"Jack in Oregon has enjoyed being spanked by his sex partners for as long as he can remember. Since his divorce, though, he can't find a woman who will redden his bottom, and Jack is despairing."**

shut out of the group. Rules are strictly enforced. Do not cross into public scenes—formalized dramas of submission and domination presented with words and the IRC action command—and do not engage in uninvited touching. "Consensual nonconsensual activities," is how one user defined #bdsm manners and practice.

Personal space

Indeed, much of the group's non-sexual conversation relates to rights of personal space. "I fail to see why I should permit anyone to touch me if I do not wish to be touched," says one member. "Even virtual kisses should not be blown," says another. Safe words are a major topic—that is, words that, unlike "stop," truly mean stop! The #bdsm bots are named Hanki and Panki. In a clutch, type /msg panki dcchelp. For gay S&M chat, stop by #gaysm. ✓INTERNET→ *irc* /channel #bdsm *or* /channel #bondage *or* /channel #gaysm

Desade (echo) Serious bondage-and-discipline devotees discuss, well, everything. From Sade-like philosophizing ("Dominance & submission is principally an emotional, psychological power relationship, which strongly resembles the master & slave relationship") to discussion about the use of various devices ("Since it is designed for below-the-waist use, it's seemingly safe vis-à-vis the heart"). The just-curious are in the decided minority here. ✓ADULTLINKS DAILY

Dungeon Throw them in the dungeon! But be forewarned: Once they're in there, they may never want to come out. GEnie's Dungeon offers friendly confines for responsible adults with an interest in consensual S&M, bondage, and dominance and submission. Many D&S email relationships begin here—just posting an interesting message in a topic will get you noticed by more than a few Dungeon residents who'll be interested in exploring email possibilities. Postings are far from tame, and the vanilla among us may not want to read about the finer points of body modifications.

Those enticed by the prospect of dangerous games are advised to enter the Dungeon. A little tip to keep you company as you measure out your rope, or polish your cuffs: "Even a hand spanking can be more intense than a whipping with something like a light deerskin flogger." Request access from the opening menu of the Family & Relationships RoundTable. ✓GENIE→ *keyword* family→Family and Personal Growth Bulletin Board→The Dungeon DAILY

Gay bondage

GL-ASB (ml) Borders and limits fascinate this group. If a slave agrees to surrender his "stop

Sadomasochism **Cybersex**

word," is the violence that follows consensual or nonconsensual? If a whip draws blood and is used on more than one slave, is it the master's responsibility to alert his slaves of the risk of HIV infection, or is the slave responsible for his own safety? Concern with where to draw the line extends to the electronic community itself.

Easily rattled

You might think sadists and masochists would take the occasional flame war well in stride, but in fact people here are easily rattled, and eager to propound rules for appropriate and inappropriate electronic hostility. Gayle Rubin, a scholar who writes about the S&M community and reads GL-ASB, has had to defend her position as interloper, critic, and ally. At times a scumble of nostalgia drifts over the list with discussions about how a dying generation will be photographed, written about, and remembered. But the community of people bound to this group have created an intimate atmosphere where rooms for list members to stay in when travelling are offered as freely as details about members' sex lives. ✓**INTERNET**→ *email* majordomo@queernet.org ✍ *Type in message body:* subscribe gl-asb HOURLY

Spanking

alt.personals.spanking (ng) Jack in Oregon has enjoyed being spanked by his sex partners for as long as he can remember. Since his divorce, though, he can't find a woman who will redden his bottom, and Jack is despairing. "I am looking for a woman of any age in the Portland area for regular spanking experience, the more intense the better. I am willing to drive up to three hours." Although not everyone on alt.sex.personals

is as eager as Jack, all of the participants of this newsgroup find sexual pleasure in the act of spanking, and are trying to find others who share their predilection. Because this is a personals newsgroup, it doesn't offer a tremendous amount of insight into the erotic life of a spanker; most postings, in fact, are open invitations rather than confessions or anecdotes. The traffic is hot and heavy, though, and after a few minutes browsing, any would-be spankers or spankees will be absolutely slap-happy. ✓**USENET** DAILY

alt.sex.spanking (ng) If spankers and spankees decided to secede from the United States and create their own nation, alt.sex.spanking would be their Congress. Old and young, men and women, of all races, creeds and colors, the users of this newsgroup—with the acronym A.S.S.—share one passion: They like to take a slap across the bottom, or to dispense one to a willing partner. Sound fun? Come along. For a group with such a narrow focus, it has an unusually high rate of traffic, and there are brand-spanking-new insights each and every day. ✓**USENET** DAILY

Spanking (echo) Unlike other spanking groups, Spanking is hardly idle chat: Most of the spankers here have a stated interest in bringing their fantasies into reality. As a result, the group tends to divide regionally; South Bend spankees may respond to postings from Indianapolis spankers, but ignore those from Vegas or Burlington. ✓**THROBNET** DAILY

Women

alt.sex.femdom (ng) The first newsgroup for dominant females, alt.sex.femdom serves as a meeting place of sorts. Want a submissive

in the Seattle area? Interested in climbing aboard in Boston? In addition to wish lists, the newsgroup provides a forum for the pressing emotional and cultural issues facing femdoms in the nineties. ✓**USENET**

CYBERNOTES

"Dear A.

"I am 47 years old, and have been into D/S since I was 17 when I was introduced to spanking by an older woman (28).

"For almost three years I have had an email D/S relationship on GEnie and Prodigy with a wonderful woman. We met only once and had a great time doing a lot of the things we had written about.

"I would like to get to know you, and see if we have similar interest in the D/S area. I am mostly dom, but have tried switching and enjoyed playing the bottom much more than I thought I would.

"The reason I am writing is your last post about how physical appearance became overly important to your last friend. I assure you, I am much more interested in your mind and how it affects your body than in your outside shell."

—from GEnie's **The Dungeon**

Part 2

Fans

Music, music, music

Three decades ago Beatles fans had to study the jacket sleeve of *Rubber Soul*, pick up

a copy of a teen magazine, or keep their fingers crossed about Ed Sullivan's booking schedule in order to get more of their favorite band. MTV swept this all away in the '80s, introducing not just round-the-clock Madonna and U2 videos but also a venue for entertainment news and interviews on a daily basis. Now it's the Net's turn. Instead of *Rolling Stone* magazine, there's **alt.rock-n-roll.stones**; *Alternative Nation* on MTV is supplanted by **#altmusic**; and the syndicated *Rocknet* radio interview show gives way to **Rocknet** on AOL. The bands themselves are catching up with their wired fans, making live-chat appearances in the AOL auditoriums, and—in Courtney Love's case—posting scattershot rants to Usenet. Who knows, maybe o+> hangs out in **#prince**.

Bono—downloaded from http://www2.ecst.csuchico.edu/~edge/u2/u2pics.html.

On the Net

Across the Board

Allmusic (ml) Serious music lovers with promiscuous but mostly pop tastes for every style— hippie funk, hip-hop, world music, guitar rock, atonal classical, disco, and so on—gather to dis-

cuss and rebel against a music scene defined by the media (the local college station playlist, MTV's heavy rotation, the latest new music 'zine, and the cover of *Rolling Stone*). One poster sums it all up this way: "Drive whatever excites you into the Allmusic parking garage, but don't expect the attendants to automatically validate your ticket." Participants offer their own view on music events like Kurt Cobain's suicide and Woodstock II. ✓ **INTERNET**→ *email* listserv@american.edu ✍ *Type in message body:* subscribe allmusic <your full name> HOURLY

Music (echo) There's a clique of people on this echo who saturate the ordinary music discussion of everything from MTV to restringing a guitar with sexual innuendo. Look for many conversations to end up with comments like "Aren't

those holes in the LPs rather small?" ✓ **RELAYNET** WEEKLY

Music BB "Because it's a free country, and I can listen to whatever I choose." Whether the freedom to listen to Reba, Elvis, or Shostakovich is what made this country great may be debatable, but fans' devotion to their tunes on this board is not. Predictably, there is some juvenile slamming of the taste of others as well as a healthy dose of teenage mythologizing—the Kurt Cobain–is–God debate comes to mind. But more often people here meet in Jazz, Blues, Rock, and Big Band to worship their idols or just hum along. The timeless "turn that noise off" discussion is replayed with a twist—a 13-year-old praises Mozart while a boomer defends the timelessness of the Moody Blues. ✓ **PRODIGY**→*jump* music

Music, music, music Fans

Music Message Center For a while the AOL "Alternative Rock" in the Music Message Center (formerly associated with Rocklink) was the place for alternative fans, insiders, and even performers to puzzle out the lyrics to the latest Pavement single. Courtney Love still frequents the area, and maintains a number of email relationships formed there and in the forum's real-time component, "Nightclub." In the AOL auditoriums, hundreds of people can join in real-time chat when bands make personal appearances. ✓**AMERICA ONLINE**→*keyword* rocklink→Music Message Center *or* The Nightclub DAILY/LIVE

Alternative

Alternative The best-known hacker hangout on the Net, Mindvox attracts many punk, hardcore, techno, and gangsta-rap fans, who mix quite amicably in this boy-centric forum. If there were a vote, Nine Inch Nails would win the best-band award, although the punk memories here stretch back to the mid-'70s glory days of CBGB. Quite a few discussants frequent New York City–area underground-rock shows—consequently, coverage bests that of any local 'zine. ☎→*dial* 212-989-1550→<your login>→<your password>→forums→ alternative $ ✓**INTERNET**→*telnet* mindvox.phantom.com→<your login>→<your password>→forums→alternative $ DAILY

#altmusic This channel often has nothing to do with alternative music, but the name still attracts a steady crowd of people who identify themselves in part through their love of the latest college-radio bands. Just about any subject is game, especially if it bears on

> **"The wide range here encompasses both Tori Amos, who has never been photographed without vaseline on the camera lens, and L7 who, well, they toss tampons from the stage."**

young love, as in a recent 30 minute soap opera involving a 13-year-old girl named Evangelin: "I am not a goth and I dont want to be one...but I'm in love with a goth. He is always with gorgeous girls that look like vampires." He is also 22. The college guys on the channel fall all over themselves to cheer up indie-rock Lolita, and reach resolution with the advice: "Don't worry, you've got plenty of time to mold yourself into a punk rock-girl queen." ✓**INTERNET**→*irc* /channel #altmusic

alt.music.alternative.female (ng) Just as rock finally goes co-ed—one of alt rock's few genuine revolutions—it seems a little strange to segregate the women of indie rock, including Kim Deal, Courtney Love, and Liz Phair, into their own newsgroup. The wide range here encompasses both Tori Amos, who has never been photographed without vaseline on the camera lens, and L7, who, well, they toss tampons from the stage. A lot of women post here, but strangely enough, it's mostly guys who post about the weepy

acoustic singers. Courtney Love, probably the first *Entertainment Weekly* cover star to venture into a newsgroup, launches a thousand threads whenever she cross-posts a rant against "testerical mathboys." ✓**USENET** DAILY

alt.music.nirvana (ng) It makes sense that the Nirvana newsgroup lends itself to some of the least music-related discussion of any band bulletin board. Although the college-aged participants are generally better versed in rock history than those, say, on the Pearl Jam newsgroup, most discussion centers on touchy reactions to the group's legacy after Kurt Cobain's suicide. One person worries, "Hope no one puts together some kind of 'Kurt Cobain' tour of Seattle or Aberdeen—Yuck!" Another signs her post with an eerie quote from Kurt: "None of you will ever know my true intentions." Many of the angry flames can be interpreted as a kind of early stage of mourning. Maybe "Generation Recycle finally has a Martyr they can parade around on their T-shirts and bedroom walls" is an expression of idealism. ✓**USENET** WEEKLY

alt.music.ween (ng) Ween made their reputation on garbled Led Zeppelin riffs mixed with nitrous oxide, so go with the flow when this newsgroup gets consumed by attempts to discover the meaning of barely audible lyrics like "stroke the lobe." "No," someone insists, "you must be toasted...the lyric is 'stoke the lobe.'" Within a day there are five more messages, each variants to the effect of "that would be 'scope the lobe,' actually." Other worries gripping fans include Dean Ween's recent gig writing a lonely-hearts column for *Sassy* magazine (it's a big sell-out, says Captain Sarcastic of the University of Delaware Math Department) and the possibility that Oliver Stone is a big fan ("yechh!"). ✓**USENET** WEEKLY

Beastie List (ml) The over-educated, young discussants here revere the Beastie Boys as lifestyle gurus for '90s white cool. The real conversations—as opposed to tape trade requests—assume basic cultural literacy in high-testosterone hip-hop (Beastie fans follow rap the way the Beats lusted for jazz) and its white counterparts, hardcore and punk. From this foundation, elaborate threads are built trying to keep up with the latest Hang Ten fashions and deciphering Beastie Boys boasts ("I got more action than my man John Woo" refers to the Hong Kong movie director, not the late-night infomercial realtor). Finally, read the alt.music.beastie-boys FAQ before asking if Dustin Diamond, the guy who plays Screech on *Saved by the Bell*, is really Mike D's brother. ✓**INTERNET**→*email* major domo@world.std.com ✍ *Type in message body:* subscribe beastielist DAILY

Dominion (Sisters of Mercy) (ml) Doubles as a running conversation on gothic rock, which, if you don't already know, fancies the dark side—pierced bodies, mock Satanism, and danceable metal riffs. Spiggy, who also maintains the list archive, will say only this about her appearance. She's recolored with blue-black hair the Jessica Rabbit hard-disk icon to make it look like herself: "I'm not goth, I'm just drawn that way." ✓**INTERNET**→*email* dominion-request@ohm. york.ac.uk ✍ *Type in message body:* subscribe dominion <your full name> HOURLY

Grunge-L (ml) "Grunge" first came into wide circulation to de-

Beastie Boys—from http://www.nando.net/music/gm/BeastieBoys/pics/.

scribe the distorted, unwashed guitar rock that came out of the Pacific Northwest in the early '90s, and that's mostly what people talk about here. Like the term *Generation X, grunge* both offends the people it is supposed to describe and functions as a fairly useful generalization when you're sure that the people who don't really know what it means aren't listening. And they don't seem to be here, so feel free to discuss your alienation from—and disillusionment with—a consumer society controlled by classic-rock yuppies. ✓**INTERNET**→*email* listserv@ubvm. cc.buffalo.edu ✍ *Type in message body:* subscribe grunge-l <your full name> DAILY

Indigo Girls (ml) Don't be surprised to read someone's dream from last night or hear from people stressing over exams in this alternative-folk discussion centered on the music of Indigo Girls, but also covering other womyn folk-music singers and friends like Ani Defranco, Michelle Malone, Michelle Shocked, Kristen Hall, k.d. lang, and Mary Chapin Carpenter. Also includes regular gossip about R.E.M., Matthew Sweet, and other bands from Athens/Atlanta (Indigo Girls' hometown). ✓**INTERNET**→*email* indigo-girls-request@indigo.atlanta.com ✍

Write a request HOURLY

#nin Nine Inch Nails' Trent Reznor is the reigning king of the tortured lyrics and torturous beats that define industrial music, so don't be surprised if you see a typical song lyric like "I'm going to burn this whole world down" being used as a channel subject. One of the surest ways of making friends—besides taking control of the TrentBot that patrols conversation—is to hit a note of loathing about yourself. Torch's search for an uncensored version of "Closer At" is, for instance, occasion to trash "Marion, IN...the lame-ass town that I'm stuck in." Many regulars also use the channel to chat about local clubs that feature industrial or industrial nights. ✓**INTERNET**→*irc* /channel #nin

Pearljam-L Introspective teens and twenty-somethings dominate dicussion of the band *Time* magazine used on its cover to illustrate youthful rage. Heavy debates on lyrics (Is that "can you see them" or "can of Sea Jam"?) and Eddie Vedder's marital status. ✓**INTERNET**→*email* listserv@cornell.edu→ ✍ *Type in message body:* subscribe pearljam-l DAILY

rec.music.rem (ml/ng) Just about any time R.E.M. makes an

More music chat...

Across the board

New Music Discuss your favorite music group or style. ✓**INTERNET**→ *email* majordomo@xmission.com ✍ *Type in message body:* subscribe nm-list

rec.music.misc (ng) Huge catch-all group for any music discussions. ✓**USENET**

rmusic-L (ml) General music discussion. ✓**INTERNET**→*email* listserv@ gitvm 1.bitnet ✍ *Type in message body:* subscribe rmusic-l <your full name> *Archives:* ✓**INTERNET**→ *email* listserv@gitvm 1.bitnet ✍ *Type in message body:* index rmusic-l

Alternative

alt.fan.oingo-boingo (ng) For fans of Oingo Boingo and the work of Danny Elfman. ✓**USENET**

alt.music.alternative (ng) Alternative-music discussion and news. ✓**USENET**

alt.music.enya (ng) For fans of Enya. ✓**USENET**

alt.music.gaffa (ng) For Kate Bush fans. ✓**USENET**

alt.music.nin (ng) For Nine Inch Nails fans. ✓**USENET**

alt.music.pearl-jam (ng) For Pearl Jam fans. ✓**USENET**

alt.music.tmbg (ng) For fans of They Might Be Giants. ✓**USENET**

alt.music.u2/alt.fan.u2 (ng) Two newsgroups for U2 fans. ✓**USENET**

Babble List (ml) For Cure fans.

Elvis Costello—downloaded from http:// east.isx.com/~schnitzi/elvis.html.

For a digest version, use the second address. ✓**INTERNET** ...→*email* babble-request@cindy.ecst.csuchico.edu ✍ *Type in message body:* subscribe babble <your full name> ...→*email* babble-m-request@cindy.ecst.csuchico.edu ✍ *Type in message body:* subscribe babble-m <your full name>

Chelsea (ml) For Elvis Costello fans. ✓**INTERNET**→*email* costello-request@gnu.ai.mit.edu ✍ *Write a request Archives:* ✓**INTERNET**→*ftp* ftp.uwp.edu→anonymous→<your email address>→/pub/music/lists/costello

#depeche Live Depeche Mode discussion. ✓**INTERNET**→*irc* /channel #depeche

Depeche Mode (ml) For Depeche Mode fans. ✓**INTERNET**→ *email* majordomo@cis.ufl.edu ✍ *Type in message body:* subscribe bong

Dominion (ml) For Sisters of Mercy fans. ✓**INTERNET**→*email* dominion-request@ohm.york.ac.uk ✍ *Write a request*

Ecto (ml) For fans of female progressive rock, including Happy Rhodes, Sara McGlaughlin, Tori Amos, and Kate Bush. ✓**INTERNET** →*email* ecto-request@ns 1.rutgers. edu ✍ *Type in message body:* subscribe ecto <your full name> *Archives:* ✓**INTERNET**→*ftp* hardees. rutgers.edu→anonymous→<your email address>→/pub/hr/ ecto

Janes Addiction (ml) For fans of Janes Addiction. ✓**INTERNET**→ *email* janes-addiction-request@ms. uky.edu ✍ *Type in message body:* subscribe *Archives:* ✓**INTERNET**→*ftp* ftp.ms.uky.edu→anonymous→<your email address>→/pub/mailing.lists /janes-addiction

Really Deep Thoughts (ml) For Tori Amos fans. Request either the regular or digest version. ✓**INTERNET**→*email* really-deep-thoughts-request@gradient.cis. upenn.edu ✍ *Write a request Archives:* ✓**INTERNET**→*ftp* ftp.uwp. edu→anonymous→ <your email address>→/pub/music/lists/rdt

SATB-L (ml) For fans of the gothic punk rock band Siouxsie and the Banshees. ✓**INTERNET**→*email* listserv@brownvm.brown.edu ✍ *Type in message body:* subscribe satb-l <your full name>

Tadream (ml) For fans of the German synthesizer group Tangerine Dream. ✓**INTERNET**→*email* majordomo@cs.uwp.edu ✍ *Type in message body:* subscribe tadream *Archives:* ✓**INTERNET**→*ftp* ftp.uwp. edu→anonymous→<your email address>→/pub/music/artists/t/ tangerine.dream

Hippie Funk

rec.music.phish (ng) For Phish

More music chat (continued)...

fans. ✓**USENET**

Spin Doctors Digest (ml) For fans of the Spin Doctors. ✓**INTERNET**→*email* spins-request@world. std.com ✍ *Type in message body:* subscribe spins <your full name>

Jazz

Acid Jazz Discuss the hip-hop jazz band Acid Jazz. ✓**INTERNET**→ *email* listserv@ucsd.edu ✍ *Type in message body:* add <your email address> acid-jazz

Jazz-L (ml) For jazz discussions. ✓**INTERNET**→*email* listserv@templevm.bitnet ✍ *Type in message body:* subscribe jazz-l <your full name>

rec.music.bluenote (ng) Jazz discussions. ✓**USENET**

Pop

alt.fan.madonna (ng) For Madonna fans. ✓**USENET**

alt.music.billy-joel (ng) For fans of Billy Joel. ✓**USENET** *FAQ:* ✓**INTERNET**→*ftp* rtfp.mit.edu→anonymous→<your email address>→ /pub/usenet/alt.music.billy-joel

alt.music.james-taylor (ng) For fans of James Taylor. ✓**USENET** *FAQ:* ✓**INTERNET**→*ftp* ftp.vcu.edu→ anonymous→<your email address> →/pub/misc/music/JT

alt.music.prince (ng) For fans of Prince. ✓**USENET**

Crowded House (ml) For Crowded house fans. For a digest version, use the second address. ✓**INTERNET** ...→*email* listserv@listserv.acns.nwu.edu ✍ *Type in mes-*

sage body: subscribe house <your full name> ...→*email* listserv@listserv.acns.nwu.edu ✍ *Type in message body:* subscribe house-digest <your full name> *Archives:* ✓**INTERNET**→*ftp* ftp.acns.nwu.edu→ anonymous→<your email address> →/pub/crowded-house

Journey-L (ml) For Journey fans. ✓**INTERNET**→*email* journey-l-request@wkuvx1.wku.edu ✍ *Type in message body:* subscribe *Archives:* ✓**INTERNET**→*email* archives@ wkuvx1.wku.edu ✍ *Type in message body:* send index

k-d-lang (ml) For k.d. lang fans. ✓**INTERNET**→*email* majordomo @world.std.com ✍ *Type in message body:* subscribe k-d-lang

Melissa Etheridge (ml) For Melissa Etheridge fans. ✓**INTERNET** ...→*email* listserv@mcgill1.bitnet ✍ *Type in message body:* subscribe mlether <your full name> ...→ *email* listserv@mcgill1.bitnet ✍ *Type in message body:* subscribe mle-d <your full name> *Archives:* ✓**INTERNET**→*ftp* ftp.uwp.edu→anonymous→<your email address>→ /pub/music/artists/e/etheridge. melissa/mail.list

Prince (ml) For Prince fans. ✓**INTERNET**→*email* prince-request@icpsr. umich.edu ✍ *Write a request Archives:* ✓**INTERNET**→*ftp* ftp. winternet.com→anonymous→<your email address>→/user/pnl

Tiger (ml) For Duran Duran fans. ✓**INTERNET**→*email* tiger-request@ acca.nmsu.edu ✍ *Type in message body:* subscribe

Rock

Allman Brothers Band (ml)

For fans of the Allman Brothers Band. ✓**INTERNET**→*email* majordomo@world.std.com ✍ *Type in message body:* subscribe allman *Support:* ✓**INTERNET**→*email* budke@ world.std.com

alt.fan.frank-zappa (ng) For Zappa fans. ✓**USENET**

alt.music.deep-purple (ng) For Deep Purple fans. ✓**USENET**

alt.music.elo (ng) For E.L.O. fans. ✓**USENET**

alt.music.jethro-tull (ng) For Tull fans. ✓**USENET**

alt.music.marillion (ng) For Marillion fans. ✓**USENET**

alt.music.monkees (ng) For fans of the Monkees. ✓**USENET**

alt.music.peter-gabriel (ng) For Peter Gabriel fans. ✓**USENET**

alt.music.pink-floyd (ng) For Pink Floyd fans. ✓**USENET**

alt.music.queen (ng) For fans of Queen. ✓**USENET**

alt.music.rush (ng) For fans of Rush. ✓**USENET**

alt.music.the.police (ng) For fans of the Police. ✓**USENET**

alt.music.the-doors (ng) For Doors fans. ✓**USENET**

alt.rock-n-roll (ng) Catch-all rock discussions. ✓**USENET**

alt.rock-n-roll.acdc (ng) For AC DC fans. ✓**USENET**

alt.rock-n-roll.classic (ng) Ac-

More music chat (continued)...

tive classic-rock discussions. ✓**USENET**

alt.rock-n-roll.metal.gnr (ng) For Guns N' Roses fans. ✓**USENET**

alt.rock-n-roll.metal.heavy (ng) Heavy-metal discussions. ✓**USENET**

alt.rock-n-roll.metal.iron-maiden (ng) For fans of Iron Maiden. ✓**USENET**

alt.rock-n-roll.metal.metalli-ca (ng) For fans of Metallica. ✓**USENET**

Backstreets (ml) For Bruce Springsteen fans. ✓**INTERNET**→ *email* backstreets-request@virginia. edu ✍ *Write a request*

Black Sabbath (ml) For Black Sabbath fans. ✓**INTERNET**→*email* sabbath-request@fa.disney.com ✍ *Write a request*

Blue Oyster Cult/Hawkwind (ml) For fans of the Blue Oyster Cult and Hawkwind. ✓**INTERNET**→ *email* boc-request@spcvxa.spc. edu ✍ *Write a request*

Chalkhills (ml) For Chalkhills fans. ✓**INTERNET**→*email* chalkhills-request@presto.ig.com ✍ *Type in message body:* subscribe chalkhills <your full name>

Digital Graffiti (ml) For Led Zeppelin fans. ✓**INTERNET**→*email* listserv@cornell.edu ✍ *Type in message body:* subscribe zeppelin-l <your full name>

Freaks (ml) For fans of Marillion or Fish (their former lead singer). ✓**INTERNET**→*email* listserv@bnf.com ✍ *Type in message body:* subscribe

freaks <your full name>

Hey-Joe (ml) For Jimi Hendrix fans. ✓**INTERNET**→*email* hey-joe-request@ms.uky.edu ✍ *Type in subject line:* subscribe *Type in message body:* subscribe hey-joe <your full name> *Archives:* ✓**INTERNET**→ *ftp* ftp.ms.uky.edu→anonymous→ <your email address>→/pub/mail-ing. lists/hey-joe

Kissarmy (ml) For Kiss fans. ✓**INTERNET**→*email* listserv@wku vx1.bitnet ✍ *Type in message body:* subscribe kissarmy <your full name>

The Lost Chords (ml) For Moody Blues fans. ✓**INTERNET**→ *email* lost-chords-request@athena. mit.edu ✍ *Write a request*

The Police (ml) Discuss the Po-lice. ✓**INTERNET**→*email* majordo-mo@xmission.com ✍ *Type in message body:* subscribe police

rec.music.beatles (ng) For Bea-tles fans. ✓**USENET**

rec.music.dylan (ng) For Bob Dylan fans. ✓**USENET**

Undercover (ml) For Rolling Stones fans. ✓**INTERNET**→*email* un-dercover-request@snowhite.cis. uoguelph.ca ✍ *Write a request*

The Who (ml) For fans of the Who. ✓**INTERNET**→*email* majordo mo@cisco.com ✍ *Type in message body:* subscribe thewho

Industrial

rec.music.industrial (ng) In-dustrial-music discussions. ✓**USE-NET**

Punk

alt.music.hardcore (ng) Hard-core punk discussions. ✓**USENET**

Other

alt.music.afro-latin (ng) African- and Latin-music discus-sions. ✓**USENET**

alt.music.independent (ng) For discussions about artists singing under the independent la-bel. ✓**USENET**

alt.music.progressive (ng) Progressive-music discussions. ✓**USENET**

alt.rock-n-roll.metal.pro-gressive (ng) Active newsgroup for progressive-rock discussions. ✓**USENET**

rec.music.christian (ng) For Christian-music discussions. ✓**USENET**

rec.music.country.western (ng) Country-music discussions. ✓**USENET**

rec.music.funky (ng) From Funk to Funky music discussions. ✓**USENET**

k.d. lang—downloaded from the Exec PC Bulletin Board.

appearance anywhere, whether it's on *Letterman* or a public-access music show, news and discussion shows up here within hours. When school's in session or there's a new album or tour, this media-watch newsgroup bears fruit on practically a daily basis. Despite the large volume of messages, there is a still an intimate, reflective tone to many threads. People here use R.E.M. to measure their lives, embroidering discographies into personal timelines, as in the case of the guy who started a discussion of the five-year-old album *Green* with a detailed picture of his life when it came out, "smoking a lot of dope, working at Pizza Hut, studying Carl Jung, and starting to come out." On that last point, read the FAQ before posting about Michael Stipe's sexuality if you want to avoid first-degree burns. ✓ **USENET** ✓ **INTERNET**→*email* murmur-digest-request@lynchberg.edu ✍ *Write a request FAQ:* ✓ **INTERNET**→ *ftp* ftp.halcyon.com→anonymous→ <your email address>→/local/ rem/other→rem-faq DAILY

Grateful Dead

alt.music.gdead/rec.music.gd ead (ml/ng) Though Dead elite may treat AOL and The WELL as home, this is the public belly button of online Dead activity. The Dead take the stage some 80 times a year and every show generates its share of "Are you going?" "Do you have tickets?" "Did you party?" "Did they play 'St. Stephen?'" messages. All posts are shared between the newsgoup and the mailing list known as Dead Flames. ✓ **USENET** ✓ **INTERNET**→*email* dead-flames-request@nemesis.berkeley. edu ✍ *Write a request* DAILY

Grateful Dead Conferences

Hey, man, Jerry and company have their very own section on the

Jerry Garcia—downloaded from Compu-Serve's Entertainment Drive.

WELL. No, really. Six linked conferences that give us Deadheads a place to relive our peak experiences. The main one—g gd—lets us talk about the life we lead following the band. Do we feel sexually attracted to Bruce Hornsby? Have we heard any good Deadhead jokes? What drugs did we take at our first Dead show? Even if you can't remember the answers to these questions—a problem that answers the drugs question, if indirectly—the conference will make you feel proud of your tie-dye.

Spillover

We're an entire subculture, big enough to get a second conference devoted to spillover from the first one (g feedback). There's also a

conference devoted to the *Grateful Dead Hour* (g gdh), that weekly radio show that's syndicated across the country, and every radio station that carries the program—from Cupertino to Fargo to New York City—has its own conference room. And that's not all. No way.

There's a tickets conference (g tix), which covers problems like scalping, ticket fraud, and ride sharing. There's a taping conference (g tapes), which not only lists available boots but recommends how to make your own recordings—the kind of equipment to buy, the best place to stand in each venue.

And then there's the coolest thing of all: the concerts conference (g tours), with reviews and set lists from every single show. Remember the Detroit show at the end of July? You were right, dude—they played "Big River" before "Loose Lucy"! I owe you five bucks and a joint. This set of conferences is just incredible. I wonder if Jerry and the rest of the guys know about them. They must be so, uh, grateful. Keep on truckin'. ✓ **WELL** DAILY

> "The editor of the *Golden Road* fanzine is a forum regular, as are most of the Dead inner circle, from soundman Dan Healy to *Dead Hour*'s David Gans."

Grateful Dead Forum This is arguably the best Dead space anywhere on the Net—maybe it's because AOL's president, Steve Case, is a Deadhead. The editor of the *Golden Road* fanzine is a regular participant, as are most of the Dead inner circle, from soundman Dan Healy to *Dead Hour*'s David Gans (who is also a WELL person). Thanks to the elite crowd, little energy is spent on concert and band rumors, and the discussion meanders to the larger personal, philosophical, and merchandizing questions raised by the Dead. ✓**AMERICA ONLINE**→*keyword* dead→Grateful Dead Messaging Forum *or* Winterland: Dead Chat DAILY

What a Long Strange Trip It's Been GEnie's Grateful Dead board cultivates first-person storytelling of the highest order. Make your own contribution to ongoing threads like "a day in the life of a deadhead," "rainbowfamily," and "strange deadhead meets." When one member of this community announced his 25th wedding anniversary, warm replies were mixed with curiosity and amazement that led to heartfelt discussion of what makes a relationship work. ✓**GENIE**→*keyword* music→Music Bulletin Board→WHAT A LONG STRANGE TRIP IT'S BEEN—The Grateful Dead Network WEEKLY

Hippie funk

alt.music.blues-traveler (ml/ng) Many of the Manhattan hippie-funk band's most ardent fans participate in this super mailing list. It's such a tight community that numerous real-life road trips have been arranged amid the usual tape-trade, tour-info, and music-recommendations messages. All messages are shared with the Blues Traveler mailing list.

✓**USENET** ✓**INTERNET**→*email* blues-traveler-request@cs.umd.edu DAILY

HORDE The HORDE concert tour has become one name for the second-generation of Deadhead hippie-funk bands. Best known are the Spin Doctors, Blues Traveler, and Phish. When the history of this music is written, the WELL conference will feature prominently for its central role in bicoastal networking between organizers, promoters, managers, and fans. You're as much a member of the HORDE scene by logging in here as by going to the Wetlands club in New York; this deceptively mellow group is incredibly active. ✓**WELL**→*g* horde WEEKLY

Phish (ml) The stereotypical Phish phan—a sandal-wearing, granola-eating, VW-driving, tape-trading second-generation hippie—is also increasingly wired. This is the main clearinghouse for hippie-funk tour news, bootlegs, and fan connections. Passionate issues include keeping concerts intimate and free of seats, "which interrupt our bodies from moving harmoniously with the kind tunes which emanate from the creator." Even if you don't share a Phish-eyed view of the world, this is still a great place to sell your '82 VW pop-top camper. ✓**INTERNET**→*email* phish-request@virginia.edu ✍ *Write a request* DAILY

Jazz & blues

Blues-L (ml) Blues antiquarians and current concertgoers overlap in the fairly intellectual atmosphere of this mailing list. Recurring questions: Can "white folks" really play the blues? Is a Strat better than a Gibson? What's a good record store in <blank>? Tastes and conversations run toward Chicago and folk blues.

✓**INTERNET**→*email* listserv@brown vm.brown.edu ✍ *Type in message body:* subscribe blues-l <your full name> DAILY

Jazz The WELL's jazz conference provides lists of jazz programs and concerts thoughout the country, a job bulletin board for musicians, and an excellent environment for trading jazz CDs. And the practical services are buttressed by a generous and varied array of discussion topics: not only the ongoing question of how to define jazz (that would be the meta-jazz portion of the group) but best musicians at each instrument, best bands, best albums, and jazz and drugs, among others. In addition, the conference dedicates discussion groups to dozens of individual musicians—Charles Mingus, Pat Metheny, Ornette Coleman, McCoy Tyner, Sun Ra, Bill Evans, Dizzy Gillespie, Jaco Pastorius, and more. For professional players, devoted fans, and even novitiates. ✓**WELL**→*g* jazz DAILY

Pop

Joel (Billy Joel) (ml) Billy the Kid, the Bard of Long Island, Mister Piano Man himself. What matters here? Song lyrics, the Christie Brinkley bust-up, and concert tix. Women and sensitive guys set the mellow tone by sharing personal experiences of how the music brightens their lives. What do you listen to after a nasty breakup, "Honesty" or "Gotta Have Soul"? ✓**INTERNET**→*email* joel-request@ chaos.bsu.edu ✎ *Write a request* WEEKLY

Madonna (ml) When she's in the headlines, this list blisters with defenders who see Maddy as a courageous freedom fighter in the war of the sexes. Usually, though, the young crowd is preoccupied with the Page 6 gossip about new boy- and girlfriends, and tattoos permanent and not. Does she make music? You'd never know it from this list, except when something's freshly released in the interludes between new body piercings (did she really do it there? the list wonders in awe). ✓**INTERNET**→*email* madonna-request@mit.edu ✎ *Write a request* DAILY

#prince These fans of Prince— aka The Artist Formerly Known as Prince, aka TAFKAP—treat IRC as if Prince has the Net in mind when he sings about partying like it's 1999. Jeina, originally from California but now off at school in Peoria, patiently explains to a newcomer that "sometimes we run out of stuff to say about TAFKAP, but we're here every day and always drift back to him eventually." Brode says she is listening to Bootsy Collins's greatest-hits album in her dorm room. FunkaJis complains, "Dang…I think I'm laggin'." ✓**INTERNET**→*irc* /channel #prince

Punk

#punk Nofx enters the channel, looks around, and rudely de-

Billy Joel—from http://www-usacs. rutgers.edu/~rotton/billy-joel.html.

mands, "What's so punk about this?" But everyone is too busy to respond. The conversation is dominated by UPenn students planning a trip to Cabbage Collective's upcoming show in Philly, which irritates Bonkydog "from berzerkley." He wants to talk about recent dates by the bands 3day stubble and Imperial Butt Wizards. After teasing Rogaine for giving out his voice number in an IRC flirtation, 7up acknowledges to Bonkydog that "one of the good things about the West Coast is that good beer is available at almost any venue." Nofx, still not getting any attention, proclaims, "Nirvana sux dick," and is summarily booted from the channel. ✓**INTERNET**→*irc* /channel #punk

Punk-list (Punk/Hardcore Mailing List) (ml) This list eats more of its own heroes than a minimum-wage sandwich maker at Subway. Smile on MTV—sellout! Appear in a Gap jeans ad— sellout! Get your guitar noise played on a commercial radio station—sellout! But underground rock culture—indie bands and labels, mosh pits, 'zines, anarchist politics, runaway squats, vegan diets, and gangrenous piercings— that has managed to avoid the usual trappings of commercial success is fiercely defended and cham-

pioned. This list is as smart and in-bred as a late-night college rock radio show. ✓**INTERNET**→*email* punk-list-request@cpac.washington.edu ✎ *Write a request* DAILY

Rave

alt.rave/NE-Raves/SF-Raves (ml/ng) The pulses of East and West Coast raves beat in these discussions. Promoters and party-goers compare notes on DJ's, drugs, and dances. There's both practical advice on standard supplies and celebration of The Orb, Deee-lite, 808 State, and other rave music stars. Most of all, relive the high of a 7 a.m., undulating, utopian vibe for the benefit of the extended rave community. Check out the more general alt.rave newsgroup for international rave talk. ✓**USENET**→alt.rave ✓**INTERNET**→ *email* listserv@umdd.umd.edu ✎ *Type in message body:* subscribe ne-raves <your full name> …→*email* majordomo@techno.stanford.edu ✎ *Type in message body:* subscribe sfraves

#rave The setting sun is moving across the Eastern Seaboard, darkening a crystal-clear Friday of a three-day weekend. Traffic on #rave is mainly EST people at this hour, home from office and classes waiting for evening plans to get started.

> "My brother has made me promise that if he dies I am to play AC/DC's 'Hell's Bells' at his funeral."

A few participants are aimlessly cruising for last-minute news of a party within driving distance, and they're in luck. Jayvee entices Lulu from Ann Arbor to make the trip to Detroit for a Helmsmen rave that night. Absender, impressed by the high-tech party networking, ends up inviting them both to the Family Groove Kitchen rave the next night (and morning) in Chicago.

"If you come," Absender messages, "I'll be easy to find—wearing this shiny, royal blue, short-sleeved shirt, thin black sunglasses and I'll have this reflector thing with red lights flashing around my belt loop in the front." Such activity gives new meaning to the words *party line*. ✓ **INTERNET**→*irc* /channel #rave

Rock

alt.rock-n-roll.metal (ng) The older crowd here loves its heavy-metal history, and you'll be humbled if you don't know your Metallica and Black Sabbath discographies cold. Touchy-feely talk may not come up very often, but posters are not without sentiment. "My brother has made me promise that if he dies I am to play AC/DC's 'Hell's Bells' at his funeral." Beavis and Butthead would be proud. ✓ **USENET** DAILY

alt.rock-n-roll.stones (ml/ng) Devoted to the most popular rock-and-roll band alive, the newsgroup is a multilane information highway all its own, combining endless personal elaborations of the theme "The Stones make me happy" with the usual fan functions of tour, tape, and tix info. The media's coverage of the Stones is a regular occasion for thick-threaded discussion that reveals the cross-generational character of this list (which is gateway'd in

> "This newsgroup isn't yet splintered into an old school, new flavor, gangsta, female, Native Tongues, Compton, Strong Island, Uptown, Crooklyn, what-have-you subgroup. Think of it as a rare example of rap unity."

both directions with the "Undercover" mailing list). Posts pile up whenever a late-night-show host makes a crack about the age of Mick or Keith. ✓ **USENET** ✓ **INTERNET**→*email* undercover-request@ snowhite.cis. uoguelph.ca ✍ *Write a request FAQ:* ✓ **INTERNET**→*ftp* rtfm.mit.edu→anonymous→<your email address>→/pub/usenet-by-group/news.answers/music/rolling stones-faq→part1 *and* part2 *and* part3 *and* part4 DAILY

Beatles "Will you still be sending me a valentine/Birthday greetings, message online?" When it comes to the Beatles, people tend to get a little crazy. They fight over their favorite Beatle, reminisce not only about the fifth Beatle but the sixth and the seventh, mourn the assassination of John Lennon, and fantasize that the remaining Beatles will reunite. The WELL's Beatles conference has all of this and

more—stories about where participants were when they first heard *Sgt. Pepper's Lonely Hearts Club Band*, passionate debates about the heroism/villainy of Yoko Ono, strange facts about Beatles songs. There's a certain marketplace air to some of the conference rooms—*Beatles for Sale* in the form of memorabilia and bootlegs—but most of the traffic is devoted to pondering unanswerable questions. Who were better, the Beatles or the Stones? What's the best Beatles movie? What's the best Beatles song? And how did Ringo get that hole in his pocket, anyway? ✓ **WELL**→*g* beat DAILY

Bong (Depeche Mode) (ml) *Rolling Stone* hailed the release of a recent Depeche Mode album with the headline REVENGE OF THE EU-ROWEENIES, but don't be misled—DM fans are dangerous. They have, in recent years, torn apart malls where their heroes made in-store appearances, so don't be surprised that this is one intense mailing list. The community here is defined mostly by fan info—album releases, bootleg swaps, concert dates—but it is also the place for sharing your love for songs first enjoyed in the privacy of your own teenage, suburban bedroom or sweet-16 auto. ✓ **INTERNET**→*email* majordomo@cis.ufl.edu ✍ *Type in message body:* subscribe bong DAILY

Dylan Most popular musicians have fans. But no one has quite the cultural cachet of Bob Dylan. While the WELL's Dylan conference spends plenty of time poring over lyrics—why exactly are the eyes of the idol with the iron head glowing?—it spreads its Net over plenty of other topics as well. What's better, acoustic Dylan or electric Dylan? Who won the card game in "Lily, Rosemary, and the Jack of Hearts"? And while these close encounters of the Zimmerman kind often spur participants to rhetorical excess—the man who claims "I have never heard a Dylan cover that I thought touched the original" has apparently never heard Mahalia Jackson's version of "Rainy Day Women #12 and 35"—there's enough in the way of record reviews, collector news, tour information, and fulsome praise of his Bobness's "incomparable, indecipherable voice" to keep Dylanites happy for ages. ✓**WELL**→g dylan WEEKLY

Echoes (Pink Floyd) (ml) There are at least three distinct kinds of Floyd fans, easily identified by their favorite member of the band—Syd Barrett ('60s), Roger Waters ('70s–'80s), and David Gilmour ('80s–'90s) and by their drugs of choice (respectively, LSD/heroin, pot, and straight). What you've got here is a David Gilmour crowd mixed in with some aging stoners. Discussion ranges from *High Times* (which named the '94 tour No. 1 in its Hemp 100 list) to the biographical meaning of song lyrics like "Wish You Were Here." This is also world HQ for Floyd bootlegs and concert info. ✓**INTERNET**→ *email* echoserv@fawnya.tcs.com ✍ *Type in message body:* add echoes HOURLY

National Midnight Star (RUSH) (ml) Three thousand-plus guys reliving memories of getting stoned and listening to "Tom Sawyer" can't be wrong. Daily message volume (which arrives in a convenient but unedited digest package) averages 20–30 pages, alternating between standard fan info ("Q: What is that thing on Neil's chest in the 'Vital Signs' video? A: It's a microphone. A PZM, to be exact. It was used in an attempt to get the drums to be recorded the way Neil hears

Tori Amos—http://www.mit.edu:8001/ people/nocturne/tori/picturelist.html.

them.") and a kind of political grass-roots-movement ("Once and for all, is Seattle's KISW Rush-friendly or not?" "Before we make a big push for an *Unplugged* show, we should decide if we want it"). Lots of north-of-the-border accents here, too—consistent with the band's origins and the mailing list name, taken from a Canadian TV show. Questions often end with "eh?" ✓**INTERNET**→*email* rush-request@syrinx.umd.edu ✍ *Type in message body:* subscribe rush <your full name> DAILY

#pinkfloyd Anything Floydian goes, from a report on the Oslo concert the night before last ("They played 'Marooned'") to the possibility of a new live album. The channel attracts an international crowd, owing to the band's huge popularity in Eastern Europe. Participants are versed in their channel's namesake, able to identify every lyric thrown at them from every age of Floyd. If you ask, "By the way, which one's pink?" someone will answer "Have a cigar" faster than you can ping the server. ✓**INTERNET**→*irc* /channel #pinkfloyd

QMS (ml) The Queen Mail Service community is so tight it even has its own T-shirt. This is also

testament to the large number of Queen collectors who frequent the list. One poster reports on a weekend spent touring rare-record shops in Sydney, only to find that another discussant had cleaned the same shops out two weeks earlier. Members from official Queen fan clubs, like Keep Your Self Alive, Inc. and The Brian May Fan Club, are a strong presence. On the good side, they help dampen the rumors that others spread about the late, HIV-positive Freddie Mercury; on the bad, they tend to toe a humorless, record-company line—even recommending the boycott of an "unofficial" biography. ✓**INTERNET**→*email* major domo@stat.lsa.umich.edu ✍ *Type in message body:* subscribe qms DAILY

Rocknet Rocknet is the Tower Records of Cyberspace—you're not going to learn about any records that aren't already sanctioned by MTV or *Rolling Stone*. Every night at 10 p.m. (EST), music discussants chat in real time about what they're listening to at home while typing. "So what are you listening to?" replaces the standard exchanges of "hi" and heavy panting that fill other live-chat areas on CompuServe. Equally important for these nightly dis-

> **"Feel free to discuss your alienation from—and disillusionment with—a consumer society controlled by classic rock yuppies."**

cussions are the suicides, breakups, and hair-dos from the day's music-related tabloid headlines. ✓**COMPUSERVE**→ *go* rocknet→Messages *or* Conferences DAILY/LIVE

60s_70s_Progrock (echo) Art rock intellectuals (read: never-grow-up record-collecting guys) sustain high-quality discussion of the progressive rock of the late '70s, including Genesis, Yes, King Crimson, Marillion, Jethro Tull, and Pink Floyd. Much of the chatter is sporting in nature. Argument for argument's sake erupts over tongue-in-cheek posts like "Confessions of a Rush Fan." ✓**FIDONET** WEEKLY

Zeppelin-L (Digital Graffiti) (ml) Three questions not to ask here: What's the deal with those four symbols? Didn't Led Zeppelin copy [song title] from [blues artist]? Are there backwards messages in "Stairway to Heaven"? Just about everything else is fair game—including a sporadic phenomenon in which posters agree on a time and IRC channel to meet and discuss a particular album that participants listen to in sync at their own homes. Another quirk is the eerie frequency of posts by guys fondly remembering an early teen infatuation with the first side of the album *Led Zep IV.* One thread, commenting on the trend, wondered whether there could be a hormonal explanation. ✓**INTERNET**→*email* listserv@cornell. edu ✍ *Type in message body:* subscribe zeppelin-l <your full name> DAILY

Other

alt.music.ska (ng) When first stumbling into this active newsgroup, ska fans—whether record collectors, clubgoers, frat boys, or skate punks—must be thinking

Queen Latifah—downloaded from CompuServe's Music Vendor Forum.

that there has been a revolution in pop taste, raising their beloved Might Mighty Bosstones, Specials, and Desmond Dekker to world historical status. Hepcat69, Soopa-Funkay, Twelve-Volt Man, Skeletone, and other users posting under names inspired by ska culture debate the original meaning of the term *rude boy* (is it a natty dresser or a cool street criminal?), trade news of local shows (mostly in London and Northeast America), and deconstruct black-and-white ska fashion. Even though ska is older than reggae, most fans here are younger than those on rec.music.reggae. ✓**USENET** *FAQ:* ✓**INTERNET**→*ftp* rtfm.mit.edu→anonymous →<your email address>→/pub/ usenet-by-group/rec.answers/music/ska-faq→part* DAILY

alt.rap (ng) Of all the pop-music tastes represented on the Net, hip-hop is the most neglected, but it's actually kind of nice that this newsgroup isn't yet splintered into old school, new-flavor, gangsta, female, Native Tongues, Compton, Strong Island, Uptown, Crooklyn, what-have-you subgroups. Think of it as a rare example of rap unity. You're as likely to find a busy thread on the latest Supercat remix as a serious Sugarhill history lesson, a Free Mike Tyson debate, or a report on the state of Japanese

hip-hop. ✓**USENET** *Archives:* ✓**INTERNET**→*ftp* 128.2.41. 20→anonymous→<your email address> DAILY

CountryMusic (echo) Ready to come out of the closet? Pull on your boots and practice your twang. Country music is not just for "bubbas" any more. The regulars in this very active forum show how broad country's appeal has become—an 11-year-old girl, a woman baby boomer who grew up with Motown, a big-city lawyer, and a small-town guy from north of Memphis meet to discuss country music in all its forms. The moderator here encourages diversity in musical taste so you will find no disparagement of that other music, just good conversation about favored musicians and a little friendly sparring about what's "real country" and what's just a cheap pop imitation. ✓**ILINK** WEEKLY

Funky-Music (ml) "Welcome to the Land of Fonk," announces the first message new subscribers get. "Free your mind and your ass will follow. You have been HOOKED UP. You now have a free pass on both the Mothership and the DFLO train. You may board either at any time." Smart, hyperactive fans of everyone from George Clinton to Public Enemy to Prince extend the definition of music so that there's no such thing as "noise." This easygoing attitude also means that discussants are encouraged to try out new topics, from zydeco to Afropop. As the welcome says, "Worst that can happen is that no one will talk about it." ✓**INTERNET**→*email* funky-music-request@mit.edu ✍ *Write a request* DAILY

House Music Scene Raves are the Tupperware parties of the nineties: They are aesthetic and social. If you want to know how to organize a rave, or where the best raves in the Bay Area occur, or if you just want to share your most recent ambient or tribal experi-

REM—downloaded from ftp.sunet. se/pub/music/pictures/r/rem.

ence, then the House conference is your home away from home. And though it is oriented toward the Bay Area club scene, there's still plenty of valuable information for ravers all across the country, and even the world. ✓**WELL**→*g* house WEEKLY

New American Folk (ml) Folk star Christine Lavin is an active participant in this discussion dedicated to the latest music coming out of boho, burbs like Athens, Georgia, and North Hampton, New Hampshire, and New Folk toeholds in New York such as Café Sin-e and the Bottom Line. This is a Celestial Seasonings and decaf latté crowd—fans of artists such as Mary Chapin Carpenter, Indigo Girls, Michelle Shocked, and David Wilcox. Show reviews sometimes turn into discussions of the same concert from the points of view of different participants. Politics, always close to the surface, are lighthearted, leftist, and sometimes lesbian. See also the rec.music.folk. ✓**INTERNET**→*email* listserv@nysernet.org ✍ *Type in message body:* subscribe folk_music <your full name> DAILY

rec.music.reggae (ng) "Selassie vibration meditation causing sensation all over the nation" sums up

the discussion here at its best. The slightly older crowd favors the classic artists over new releases, with many more posts about a Lee Perry concert, Bob Marley video, or Burning Spear single than about what's happening right now with Ninjaman or Mighty Diamonds in Kingston, London, or New York. Maybe there are a few too many industry-heads promoting their own labels, magazines, and concerts lately, but try to look at it as a sign of the newsgroup's growing influence. The monthly update of the FAQ is the most complete guide anywhere to roots-reggae shows on local radio stations around the world. ✓**USENET** *FAQ:* ✓**INTERNET**→*ftp* rtfm.mit.edu→ anonymous→<your email address> →/pub/usenet-by-group/rec. answers/music/reggae DAILY

Movies

The guardians of society were right—talkies are the downfall of American civilization.

The sheer amount of time spent online rehashing, debating and disemboweling movies must have an adverse effect on national productivity. That aside, if you go to the movies alone, or can't talk to your date about the intricacies of *No Escape*, *Ernest Goes to Camp*, or *The Magnificent Ambersons*, the Net provides an outlet. **Rec.arts.movies** is the most active forum, full of up-to-the-minute critiques of late-night cable or the newest blockbuster. Classic-movie fans meet on CompuServe's **Old/Classic Films** forum. And the WELL's "trash 'em" festival is balanced by Prodigy's rather worshipful, star-centered tone. For specialists there are **alt.asian-movies**, **alt.cult.movies** (chainsaw not included), and **alt.fan.james-bond** (Sean Connery, obviously).

Schindler's List—*downloaded from GEnie's Showbiz RoundTable Forum.*

On the Net

Across the board

Movies The movie conference to end all movie conferences, with topics for virtually every wide-release studio film—*Closet Land* to *Cool World*, *Howard the Duck* to *Howard's End*. There are also specialty topics, where you can answer the question, what's the most depressing movie you've ever seen? and criticize the critics. All in all, a golden opportunity to discuss the silver screen. ✓**WELL**→*g* movies DAILY

Movies and Television Styled by the hosts as the "Inferno of Post Modernism," the talk here includes some of the most animated and raucous discussion on TV and movies available online, ranging from *Melrose Place* to Fellini to Japanese pornography. Hint: Ingratiate yourself by bad-mouthing Emma Thompson at every possible opportunity. Also, when posting here, go for a mixture of ten-dollar words and any slightly juvenile insults you may hear from passing schoolchildren. ✓**WELL**→*g* mov DAILY

Movies BB Dare you say it? Many here dare: *Citizen Kane* is really dull! As on many Prodigy boards, the population seems young—many had never seen the films on one man's list, all of which had been made prior to 1980. Gushing girls solicit lists of the ten "cutest" actors, and 14-year-olds swoon over Clark Gable in *Gone With the Wind*. Foreign-film fans best go elsewhere: A discussion of Spanish director Almodovar found no takers, and a favorable review of a new Chinese film was met only with "Do I have to read the bottom of the screen?" Assessments of the latest Schwarzenegger and the newest from Disney clog the airwaves. Another very popular theme is "Have you seen them naked?"—an active compendium of nude scenes. This, of course, leads to deeper discussion: "Is that really her body or not?" ✓**PRODIGY** →*jump* movies bb→ Choose a Topic HOURLY

rec.arts.movies (ng) A blockbuster of a newsgroup. The five-minute frequency of new posts makes it seem like a real-time chat or, if you're bothered by the volume, a 20-screen mall multiplex. Most posts are the online equivalent of moviegoing advice from friends, but discussion is wide-ranging: national self-examinations prompted by the latest *Schindler's List*; parents' advice on how scary the current Disney animation is, Jean Renoir snobs trashing the new Hollywood screen saver. Participants regularly post their reviews to the related rec. arts.movies.reviews. ✓**USENET** *FAQ:* ✓**INTERNET**→*ftp* rtfm.mit.edu→ anonymous→<your email address> →/pub/usenet-by-group/rec. arts.movies HOURLY

Cult Movies

alt.cult.movies (ng) The subject of one post sums up the purpose of the sizable community formed here: "Movies you liked that no other human did." Discussions range from the accidental satire of the big-budget flop *Hudson Hawk* to the badass cleavage in Russ Meyer's D-cup movies to riffs on back issues of the 'zine *Psychotronic*. Beside-the-point posts have plenty of company here, but if you take the time to size up the specialized off-beat, low-budget tastes of the group's active core, you stand to make some pretty interesting new friends. ✓**USENET** *FAQ:* ✓**INTERNET**→*ftp* rtfm.mit.edu→ anonymous→<your email address> →/pub/usenet-by-hierarchy/alt/ cult-movies DAILY

alt.cult-movies.rocky-horror (ng) This gives new meaning to the *Rocky Horror* lyric "Let's do the time warp again." The cult of ritual heckling surrounding this late-'70s gender-bender rock movie still lives in posts like "Attention all New Jersey RIFF RAFFS: The Friday night cast at William Cen-

Rodan—downloaded from CompuServe's ShowBiz Forum.

ters Cinemas in Rutherford, N.J., is looking for a new permanent Riff Raff and Transylvanians." RHPS groups from Austin to Haifa to Boston (well, actually Harvard Square) share stories and make travel plans through this newsgroup. ✓**USENET** *FAQ:* ✓**INTER-NET**→*ftp* rtfm.mit.edu→anonymous→ <your email address>→/pub/ usenet-by-group/news.answers/ movies→rocky-horror-theaters WEEKLY

Other

alt.asian-movies (ng) For about ten years now Hong Kong has been producing the best action movies ever made, with carefully choreographed fight scenes and gangsta epics that would make Schwarzenegger or Scarface wet his pants. Because these movies fall between the cracks in U.S. distribution, this is the best place to find out when the next Chow Yun Fat, Jackie Chan, Jet Li, or Tsui Hark movie is coming to a local Chinatown, film festival, or video store. Weekly rumors concern the Hollywood activity of Hong Kong stars, such as Oliver Stone's recent pitch to Michelle Yeoh, Jackie Chan's friendship with Stallone,

and Quentin Tarantino's worship of John Woo. This group is close-knit, but growing quickly along with the popularity of the flicks. ✓**USENET** DAILY

alt.fan.james-bond (ng) Everyone's got an opinion about who should have been the next Bond, but come here and you'll find much more personal—or obsessive—involvement in the 007 mystique. Discussion is appropriately anglophilic, with regular skirmishes over Bond's relations with

> **"If you take the time to size up the specialized off-beat, low-budget tastes of the group's active core, you stand to make some pretty interesting new friends."**

the ladies and natives (was it racist to ask Quarrel to "fetch" something in Dr. No?). Active participants include some military officers and the co-editor of *Shaken, Not Stirred* (the newsletter of the Ian Fleming Foundation). ✓ **USENET** WEEKLY

H-Film (ml) Geez, everybody's a critic these days. The buzz here is about current films, classics and even Nazi war propaganda. Reminisce about your favorites scene; debate various camera techniques and the quality of the flicks. A recent sweeping statement about the "dumbing down" of the American audience led to spirited exchanges: Were we dumber when we watched Jerry Lewis or when we watch Teenage Mutant Ninja Turtles? Siskel/Ebert-type debate is encouraged—just don't use your thumbs. ✓ **INTERNET**→*email* list serv@uicvm. uic.edu ✍ *Type in message body:* subscribe h-film <your full name> DAILY

New/Recent Films Do you know that *Forrest Gump* was the fourth-fastest film to reach $200 million? Do you care? Whether asking simple questions ("Can anyone tell me what the full name of Hugh Grant's character is in the movie *Four Weddings and a Funeral*?) or venting forthright opinions ("Oliver Stone ranks up there with Bob Guccione as a socially worthless huckster of bad art. At least *Penthouse* is a turn-on"), film fans who aren't shy about their love for the silver screen pack the board.

Ditching Pierce Brosnan

A substantial number of messages are devoted to a cinematic version of Monday-morning quarterbacking—namely, questioning casting decisions. Who should star in *The Bridges of Madison County*? Is Tom Cruise right or wrong for Lestat?

Scarlett and Rhett—downloaded from Exec PC.

And how about ditching Pierce Brosnan and hiring Patrick Stewart as Bond? ✓ **COMPUSERVE**→*go* showbiz →Messages→New/Recent Films DAILY

Older/Classic Films While some of the movies on the message board are probably still in the new releases section at the video store—such as Peter Medak's *Romeo Is Bleeding*—there's a substantial interest in Hollywood's golden age. Participants generally recommend old films or ask other subscribers to help them remember pertinent details—like what exactly was the name of the professor in *The Thin Man*?

Marx Brothers

One fine example was an extended argument on the Marx Brothers' films. Bill: "All I was saying is that the MGM movies revived their career, even if it did set them up for a big fall later on." Steve: "I don't think the financial success of the MGM films has anything to do with this argument. What we're talking about here is the content and quality of their various works, not the political or economic situations revolving around their mak-

ing." Even if you're not interested in the topic, the witty repartee ranks right up there with the courtroom scene in *Duck Soup* ("You'll get 10 years in Leavenworth, or 11 years in Twelveworth, or 5 to 10 in Woolworth's"). Someone give these guys a contract. ✓ **COMPUSERVE**→*go* showbiz→Messages→ Older/Classic Films DAILY

> "Attention all New Jersey RIFF RAFFS: The Friday night cast at William Centers Cinemas in Rutherford, N.J., is looking for a new permanent Riff Raff and Transylvanians."

Television

What were people talking about in your office, or classroom, or coffee bar today?

Seinfeld? *Dave*? *MTV*? Could it be that the real reason people watch television is to talk about it? Clearly, no subject that ever graced a TV screen is too small for detailed discussion on the Net, from the taxi driver in MTV's promo spots (**MTV Online**) to the changing color of Jerry Seinfeld's bike (**alt.tv.seinfeld**) to a three-year-old Richard Simmons infomercial (**alt.tv.infomercial**). The much ballyhooed age of interactive TV may well have already arrived—but on your other screen.

Mad About You—*downloaded from America Online's NBC Online.*

On the Net

Across the board

Entertainment Drive Compuserve's Entertainment Drive boasts more than 50 entertainment companies, including Warner Bros., E! Channel, Disney, CBS, Capitol Records—even Cameron Mackintosh, producer of Broadway shows such as *Cats* and *Phantom of the Opera*. With the corporations come their stars. Celebrity appearances have ranged from the 91-year-old caricaturist Al Hirschfeld to Tom Hanks, who answered questions online from backstage at the '94 Academy Awards. Beck/Smith Hollywood Exclusive and Stein Online are online talk shows that have brought Marisa Tomei, Tim Allen, and Dennis Miller before their wired

fans, but most chat takes place in the Conference Rooms of the Television Parlor or Silver Screen Bar. If you're into scheduled chat-a-thons, check out Overdrive, a Friday-night regular in the Silver Screen Bar at 11 p.m. Eastern that strives for serious analysis of the entertainment biz. ✓**COMPUSERVE**→ *go* edrive→Messages DAILY

rec.arts.tv (ng) TV history and business weigh heavily here, since most current shows usually get their own newsgroup or mailing list. Far-flung fans of *St. Elsewhere* compare notes on local syndication ("WUFT just got through the Peter White rape thing"), CBS detractors debate the networks ten most boneheaded decisions' ("#8 Replacing *Knots* with the superior *Angel Falls*, and then canceling that and replacing *Falls* with the God-bloody-awful *Second Chances*"), and one couch potato sends out an alert for a *Parker Lewis* marathon on cable. Then there are the drive-by postings that set off some of the best threads: "I Hate Willard Scott," "Sara Gilbert

Blows," and "Joan Lunden Makes Me Ill." ✓**USENET** *FAQ:* ✓**INTERNET** →*ftp* rtfm.mit.edu→anonymous→ <your email address>→/pub/ usenet-by-group/rec.arts.tv DAILY

Television Viewers Online AOL's gigantic Television Viewers Online (TVO) covers close to 200 shows. Name a show, any show—even a canceled one. TV Gossip Boards (within TVO) cover it all: MTV's *The Real World*, *Star Trek*, *All My Children* and every other daytime soap, *Saturday Night Live*, *Picket Fences*, the *X-Files*, *Models Inc.*, *Kung Fu*. Don't forget *Be-*

> "Celebrity appearances have ranged from the 91-year-old caricaturist Al Hirschfeld to Tom Hanks."

Television Fans

witched. Most television personalities are discussed in great detail, and without any shortage of opinion.

Conan O'Brien, for instance, is both an "original and daring talent who is always funny" and "the worst talk-show host ever." And, when sitting alone with your favorite TV show (or with people who just don't have the same appreciation for, say, *Mary Tyler Moore* or *Melrose Place*), log on to Television Viewers Online, enter the TV Gossip Boards, and click "The Remote Control" room for live TV-watching parties.

Love triangles

Come here to gush about *The Simpsons* ("I'm constantly amazed at the kind of stuff they cram into each new episode") and *Mad About You* ("Too few shows nowadays deal with couples who really love each other and express that love in very real ways") or, if you're a soap-opera fan, debate love triangles and cliff-hangers. The most interesting section, though, may be the Cable and Syndication message board (buried within the TV Gossip Boards, buried within TVO), which allows tube-heads to dispense wisdom on classic and cutting-edge TV. And really, when it comes right down to it, where else are you likely to find a grassroots campaign to bring back *BJ and the Bear?* ✓ **AMERICA ONLINE**→ *keyword* television DAILY/LIVE

TV BB and TV Network BB "To me Florence Henderson will always be Carol Brady and no one else." If you are an American and don't have a favorite TV show there must be something wrong with you. In the soap section friends meet for a daily dissection of the lives and motivations of TV characters—crying over infidelities or praising how much someone

> **"CBS detractors debate the network's ten most boneheaded decisions ('#8 Replacing *Knots* with the superior *Angel Falls*, and then canceling that and replacing *Falls* with the God-bloody-awful *Second Chances*')."**

has "grown" inside. Teens here get a chance to hone their obnoxious insults on the *Beavis and Butthead* board ("Gay transsexual Nazi Eskimo rabid slugs") or ponder the fate of the *90210* crowd. You can talk about the classics (*Mayberry* to *MacGyver*) or take part in the Letterman (better nice or nasty?) debate. On the Television Networks board you can—theoretically—reach the higher echelons with your programming thoughts; go ahead and lobby for a *Mr. Ed* revival. ✓ **PRODIGY**→*jump* tv bb *and* tv network bb→Choose a Topic HOURLY

TV-L (ml) Heavy soap suds here—especially *All My Children*—but you are also likely to talk about Angela Lansbury's hip surgery, the latest *Star Trek* spin-off, or the likelihood of *Six Million Dollar*

Man or *Hill Street Blues* reunion shows. The soap summaries set off the longest threads, though, whether the subject is the aging of "the Monica/Alan/Sean/Tiffany set on *General Hospital*" or the prospect of Lucas finally screwing up the courage to play a hero on *Days of Our Lives.* ✓ **INTERNET**→ *email* listserv@vm3090.ege.edu.tr ✍ *Type in message body:* subscribe tv-l <your full name> DAILY

Commercials

alt.tv.commercials (ng) An anticommercial tone is set here by people who talk back to the TV and deconstruct soda packaging. Mockery of ad campaigns predominates, with plenty of gleeful attacks on slogans such as "I believe in Crystal Light 'cause I believe in me." But there's also a lively subculture of nostalgia buffs who like to remember the sponsors of old shows (Marlboro for *Dobie Gillis*) and which ads Kate Bush sang. Overall, a fine place for ranting. ✓ **USENET** WEEKLY

---

alt.tv.infomercials (ng) People not only complain about those half-hour late-night ads here but even complain about the products: "What's up with that new smart mop made of whale fibers? That Suzy Homemaker, short-haired blonde lady is Ugh! And the mop Does NOT pick up everything." As with much other Net kitsch, in this newsgroup you'll find the wildly sarcastic and sweetly sincere speaking the same language without any apparent conflict. One dieter will find an informercial self-evidently fraudulent because "to me the best kind of diet is Richard Simmons' 'Deal a Meal,' which then grows into a thread exploring the hilarity of the early-'90s Richard Simmons *Dancin' to the Oldies* ads. ✓ **USENET** WEEKLY

Networks

MTV Online If there's anything besides *Beavis & Butt-head* that can save MTV from 500-channel, video-on-demand oblivion, it's this fantastic experiment on AOL. The younger generation has overrun the show-specific, music, and concert message boards with the kind of buzz that fills a high-school cafeteria at lunchtime. The best stuff is the micro-infatuations with video bit players and third-string VJs. Where else could you find a crowd of people enamored with the promo-spot taxi driver, Donal Logue, who won't shut up about his love of "them videos"? The real-time chat, MTV Yack, hums around the clock with flirtatious chatter and stubborn music prejudice. The MTV Arena is set aside for larger real-time events, such as online appearances by the likes of Daisy Fuentes, Tabitha Soren, and Eric Neis (apparently he can type). ✓**AMERICA ONLINE**→*keyword* mtv→ Message Boards→MTV Online Shows Messages DAILY

NBC Online NBC's area almost feels as though the network were sponsoring a giant Democracy Wall in front of its midtown Manhattan offices, with NBC's head of programming answering the phone every time someone calls to save *seaQuest* from cancellation. (Look for the asterisk next to a post, which flags one of the network's weak-kneed replies.) NBC has also begun bringing Jay Leno and other stars into the AOL auditorium for real-time chat sessions. Fans can enjoy publicity shots, transcripts, and other goodies. ✓**AMERICA ONLINE**→ *keyword* nbc→Message Board *or* Auditorium DAILY

Shows

alt.fan.letterman (ng) Insom-

Beavis & Butt-head—downloaded from CompuServe's ShowBiz Forum.

niacs and would-be television insiders go over the most recent installments of Dave's show with a fine-tooth comb and dissect the performances of celebrity guests. Unlike on most of the alt.fan newsgroups, the show and show business are the center of discussion. Occasional groupie posts (from, say, admirers of Dave's accumulation of speeding tickets) are generally ignored by the amateur analysts who fine-tune their network savvy here. Running tallies track which guests have the rare power to make Dave uncomfortable (Madonna, Sandra Bullock, Richard Simmons, Cher) and which earn his bullying wrath (Howard Stern, Shirley Maclaine). Much overlap and jousting with the alt.tv.talkshows.late newsgroup. "Hey, kids!" ✓**USENET** *FAQ:* ✓**INTERNET**→*ftp* rtfm.mit.edu→anonymous→<your email address>→ /pub/usenet-by-hierarchy/alt/ fan/letterman→alt.fan.letterman_ Frequently_Asked_Questions_(read _before_posting) DAILY

alt.tv.beavis-n-butthead (ng) Huh huh! Quote lists ("Butt-head to Beavis: Did you cut the cheese? /No, I think it came from outside. /What are you, some kind of butt ventriloquist?"), trivia (a running list of the songs that they air-gui-

tar, "duh duh," and headbang to, starting with Black Sabbath's "Iron Man"), and a constant flow of discussion of that day's repeats or—rarely—new episodes. Join in the group celebration of lines like "Dammit, this video's been on for two minutes and this chick's not naked yet." ✓**USENET** DAILY

alt.tv.bh90210 (ng) The young regulars on the *Beverly Hills 90210* newsgroup are evenly divided between naive and cynical. But they are all fans who see the larger world through an Aaron Spelling prism. They are also of two minds on whether Brenda (Shannen Doherty) is missed from the new season—some think her tabloid exploits distracted from the show; others miss the only cast member to take it off for *Playboy*. No surprise that gossipy (read: catty) threads grow quickly, like a catalog of Kelly's bed partners and the burning question of whether the cast are off-camera smokers ("They are," reports one girl who goes to the school where many of the college scenes are shot). A significant minority of the participants are hostile toward the show

> "Join in the group celebration of Beavis and Butt-head lines like 'Dammit, this video's been on for two minutes and this chick's not naked yet.'"

but seem unable to simply turn to another channel or newsgroup: "I surf a lot, so it's always disgusted me the way surfing is depicted on this show. I hope Mr. Sideburns gets deathly ill from that L.A. sewer water. Now, that would be realistic." ✓**USENET** DAILY

alt.tv.game-shows (ng) Remember Ed Grimley, the *Wheel of Fortune*–obsessive Pat Sajack worshiper played by Martin Short on *Saturday Night Live*? The real-life versions mix campy condescension and utter sincerity here in their happy preoccupation with Bob Barker, Monty Hall, Alex Trebac, Wink Martindale, and their comely assistants. Bitchiness does rear its head, as in the sport of tracking Barker's regular problem with remembering contestants' names (and his recent legal trouble with one of the longtime female presenters on the show). ✓**USENET** *FAQ:* ✓**INTERNET**→*ftp* rtfm.mit.edu→ anonymous→<your email address>→ /pub/usenet-by-group/rec. answers/tv/game-shows→canada *and* usa WEEKLY

alt.tv.mad-about-you (ng) Trade Helen Hunt JPEGs, debate whether Paul and Jamie should have a kid ("I don't want to sound like a kid-hater, but children, particularly young ones, are incompatible with living in Manhattan"), and track Paul Reiser's magazine writing. One particularly heartwarming thread concerned two women trying to get hold of a full-length recording of the sitcom's theme music because, says one of them, "Bruce proposed to me after the Valentine episode, and we are both hoping to use it as the cake-cutting music at our weddings." ✓**USENET** DAILY

alt.tv.melrose-place (ng) The two-hour season premiere drew

> "Show writers not only lurk in this newsgroup but sometimes even jump in and defend a happy ending."

more than 200 messages by noon the next day. Emerging consensus: Kathy Ireland should stick to swimsuits, Sidney gets the best lines, and quick, someone get a tape to the poor person who posted the "Help! I set my VCR for the wrong night" message. "Rules for *Melrose Place* drinking games" is a hugely entertaining thread: if Alison looks up and whines 'Uh, Billy'—one drink; If Amanda wears something incredibly inappropriate to the office—two drinks. ✓**USENET** DAILY

alt.tv.muppets (ng) This newsgroup owes its existence to Nickelodeon's decision to air reruns of the late Jim Henson's brilliant half-hour variety-show satire. But many of the posters here are past gratitude and into petitions: "Please write the network and request the Baryshnikov episode where Sam the Eagle tries to make the show 'classy'!!!!" The adoring participants tend to be college students and recent grads who grew up on the show, and cherish it as *The Simpsons* of their childhood. ✓**USENET** WEEKLY

alt.tv.nypd-blue (ng) The most verbally nimble show on network TV attracts the most articulate TV-newsgroup participants. The normal flow of idle chatter often breaks into incisive discussion of the characters and drama, especial-

ly the day after a new episode airs. Show writers not only lurk in this newsgroup but sometimes even jump in and defend a happy ending. During the first season the newsgroup functioned as an informal David Caruso fan club, with female fans reveling in his sensitivity and guys in his macho put downs. When it first looked like Caruso would be leaving the show, posts ran the grief gamut from anger ("His movies suck—what's he thinking?!?") to action (ABS—"Anyone But Smits") to sadness ("They shouldn't kill him on the show—just have him kind of leave"). ✓**USENET** DAILY

alt.tv.real-world (ng) Legend has it that MTV wanted a soap opera but chose a documentary format for *Real World* in order to save money on writers. Well, people take their voyeurism where they can get it, and for a whole generation, it's on MTV. Intricate discussion of *Real World*'s young ethnically correct participants is set off by casual asides such as "For a doctor, Pam sure does dress like a slut," "Puck makes me puke," and "Julie [the cutie from the original New York version] is better looking than Rachel [the cutie from the S.F. series]." Both the show and the newsgroup hit a deep nerve. ✓**USENET** DAILY

alt.tv.seinfeld (ng) "I bet if the producers knew what was going on in this newsgroup, they'd probably make an episode on this alone." Just as on the sitcom, humor is derived from microscopic observations, but instead of Manhattan, the subject is the latest episode and, to a much smaller degree, the tabloid details of Seinfeld's real-life romance. If this newsgroup were a person, it would wear glasses. Come here for intellectual dabbling: Is the famous lost-in-the-parking-garage episode a kind of "Waiting for Kramer," or a metaphor for the drift of Generation X? "No way. These are yuppie wannabes. Remember Kramer's overcoat deal?" One regular poster compiles a "laugh analysis" of which character gets the most laughs per show (George) and which the "most thoughtful teehees" (Jerry). ✓**USENET** WEEKLY

Court TV This is one of the finest places on the Net to play Monday morning quarterback to the nation's tabloid cases. Local color includes the kind of courtroom detail that must occupy most juries, including informal lawyer-specific fan clubs ("I have told my friends for years, if I am ever accused of murder—get me Gerry Spence!") ✓**AMERICA ONLINE**→*keyword* court tv→Message Board WEEKLY

MacGyver (ml) Sure, lots of TV show mailing lists compile quote lists and an exhaustive FAQ, but how many are tight-knit enough to collectively write a script—especially for a show that survives mostly in cable syndication? The appeal of the clever, gadget-based action series here is the grand save-the-world conclusion that comes between the second-to-last and the last commercial breaks, and the rare details of MacGyver's personal history (he was an orphan?!?) that dribble out every few episodes. ✓**INTERNET**→ *email* macgyver-request@cc.gatech.edu ✍ *Type in subject line:* subscribe DAILY

> "If the alt.tv.seinfeld newsgroup were a person, it would wear glasses."

Models Inc. (ml) "Pure, mindless entertainment" sums up the appeal of Aaron Spelling's pulchritudinous *Melrose Place* spinoff, *Models Inc.*, for list members. The mailing list skews away from plot lines and characters and toward the bios of show stars and candidates. What are the chances that sub–*Baywatch*, ex–*Paradise Beach* hunk Ingo Rademacher will get a part? Bet you didn't know that Adam Louder, moody owner of the exclusive Stage 99 nightclub, once opened for the Dead Kennedys. ✓**INTERNET**→*email* ame drano@euclid.ucsd.edu ✍ *Type in subject line:* subscribe modelist *Type in message body:* <your email address> <your full name> DAILY

Soaps

rec.arts.tv.soaps (ng) Once you realize how seriously these people take the "spoiler" injunction against revealing a plot twist—and get past the plethora of show name abbreviations—you're going to start wondering about FAC. Originally it stood for Favorite *All My Children* Character, but now it has come to mean any soap character you want to identify yourself with. Members sign messages to the group with names like Diane "FAC Ted" Heckert and generally look out for that character's best interests. To quote from the FAC FAQ: "[If] someone posts 'I think Tom's trying to force Livia into adopting Jamal,' FAC Livia could respond, 'No, I believe Livia loves Jamal as much as Tom....She took longer to warm up to him because she was afraid he would think she was trying to replace his dead mother.'" ✓**USENET** *FAQ:* ✓**INTERNET**→*ftp* rtfm.mit.edu→anonymous→ <your email address>→/pub/ usenet-by-group/rec.arts.tv.soaps DAILY

More television chat...

alt.fan.conan-obrien (ng) Discuss late-night NBC talk show host Conan O'Brien. ✓USENET

alt.fan.mst3k/alt.tv.mst3k /rec.arts.tv.mst3k (ng) Newsgroup for discussing *Mystery Science Theatre 3000*. ✓USENET

alt.saved-bell (ng) For *Saved by the Bell* fans. ✓USENET

alt.tv.beakmans-world (ng) Discuss the show *Beakmans World*. ✓USENET

alt.tv.brady-bunch (ng) For fans who can't stop singing the theme song. ✓USENET

alt.tv.duckman (ng) For fans of the Duckman. ✓USENET

alt.tv.highlander (ng) For *Highlander* fans. ✓USENET

alt.tv.lois-n-clark (ng) For fans of the latest Superman spin-off. ✓USENET

alt.tv.max-headroom (ng) For *Max Headroom* fans. ✓USENET

alt.tv.mwc (ng) Chat about *Married With Children*. ✓USENET

alt.tv.nickelodeon (ng) Discuss Nickelodeon. ✓USENET

alt.tv.northern-exposure (ng) Follow the adventures of Joel and the residents of Cicely. ✓USENET

alt.tv.prisoner (ng) Discuss the British show *The Prisoner*. ✓USENET

alt.tv.red-dwarf (ng) For *Red Dwarf* fans. ✓USENET

alt.tv.rockford-files (ng) For fans of the syndicated show, *The Rockford Files*. ✓USENET

alt.tv.roseanne (ng) *Roseanne* fans chat about their favorite episodes and the actress. ✓USENET

alt.tv.simpsons (ng) For fans of *The Simpsons*. ✓USENET

alt.tv.snl (ng) For *Saturday Night Live* fans. ✓USENET

alt.tv.talkshows.daytime (ng) Discuss your favorite daytime talk shows. ✓USENET

alt.tv.talkshows.late (ng) Discuss the late-night talk-shows. ✓USENET

alt.tv.twin-peaks (ng) Discuss the TV show *Twin Peaks*. ✓USENET

Blake7 (ml) For *Blake7* fans. ✓INTERNET→*email* blake7-request@ lysator.lui.se

DQMW-L (ml) For fans of *Dr. Quinn Medicine Woman*. ✓INTERNET→*email* listserv@emuvm1.bitnet ✉ *Type in message body:* subscribe dqmw-l <your full name>

Forkni-L (ml) Chat about the sci-fi show *Forever Knight*. ✓INTERNET →*email* listserv@psuvm. psu.edu ✉ *Type in message body:* subscribe forkni-l <your full name>

Highla-L (ml) More discussion about the sci-fi favorite *Highlander*. ✓INTERNET→*email* list serv@psu.psuvm.psu ✉ *Type in message body:* subscribe highla-l <your full name>

LoisCla (ml) Discuss *The New Adventures of Superman*. ✓INTERNET →*email* listserv@trearn.bitnet ✉

Type in message body: subscribe loiscla <your full name>

Mayberry (ml) For fans of *The Andy Griffith Show*. ✓INTERNET→ *email* listserv@bolis.sf-bay.org ✉ *Type in message body:* subscribe mayberry <your full name>

Melrose-Place (ml) For *Melrose Place* fans. ✓INTERNET→*email* ma jordomo@tcp.com ✉ *Type in message body:* subscribe melrose-place

90210 (ml) Chat about the *Beverly Hills 90210* crowd. ✓INTERNET→*email* majordomo@tcp.com ✉ *Type in message body:* subscribe 90210

Quantum_Leap (echo) For *Quantum Leap* fans. ✓FIDONET

rec.arts.sf.tv.quantum-leap (ng) The hub of *Quantum Leap* discussion. ✓USENET

rec.arts.tv.uk (ng) For discussion related to British TV. ✓USENET

seaQuest (echo) For fans of the underwater adventure show, *seaQuest*. ✓FIDONET

Seinfeld (ml) For *Seinfeld* fans. ✓INTERNET→*email* seinfeld-re quest@cpac.washington.eduu ✉ *Write a request*

Space-1999 (ml) For fans of the long-since-canceled *Space 1999*. ✓INTERNET→*email* space-1999-request@quack.kfu.com ✉ *Type in message body:* subscribe space-1999

T-Zone (ml) For *Twilight Zone* fans. ✓INTERNET→*email* tzone-re quest@hustle.rahul.net ✉ *Write a request*

Sci-fi

If Cyberspace did not already exist, sci-fi would have invented it. Hey, wait a minute!

Sci-fi did. William Gibson coined the actual term more than ten years ago in his novel *Neuromancer*. So how surprising is it that science fiction discussions are some of the most developed on the Net? You've got the full range, from Usenet's **rec.arts.sf.*** hierarchy and the three **Sci Fi RoundTables** on GEnie (just try to read it all), each as massive as a galaxy-class starship, to separate mailing lists for Vulcans and Klingons that are as small, sleek, and specialized as a starbase shuttlecraft.

Han and Chewie—downloaded from wpi.wpi.edu.

On the Net

Across the board

rec.arts.sf.fandom (ng) The political nature of the Hugo and other science-fiction awards is a regular theme, but the real use of this newsgroup is planning your next trip to a science-fiction convention (con). Just about every serious American, Canadian, and British con—and there are dozens—is announced here with a list of the featured guests. Participants love to give advice about visiting and running cons. "I want to set up a con suite for people to go when all the other parties die at 3 a.m." leads to a anecdote-filled discussion of the risks (and benefits) of serving alcohol in Glasgow versus Itasca, Illinois. ✓**USENET** WEEKLY

rec.arts.sf.movies (ng) Talk about vaporware. Word of new movies hits this newsgroup before they've even been cast. A recent thread had participants drooling over the possibility that *Jurassic Park II* and *Star Wars IV* would both hit in the middle of '97: "That would make for one great summer!!!!" The rest of the time people rehash *Aliens, Terminator, Robocop,* and the rest of the laser canon with the vigor of a late-night bull session. What are the instructions for the zero-gravity toilet in *2001*? How could Taco Bell ever have won the franchise wars, as *Demolition Man* supposes? Did Deckard (Harrison Ford) rape Rachel the replicant (Sean Young) in *Bladerunner,* or was the rough seduction "just another nod to those trashy '40s detective movies on which the narrative was based?" ✓**USENET** *FAQ:* ✓**INTERNET**→*ftp* rtfm.mit.edu→anonymous →<your email address>→/pub/ usenet-by-group/rec.arts.sf.movies DAILY

rec.arts.sf.science (ng) Private space exploration, cold fusion, personality cloning, and other candidates for the year 2000 edition of the Sharper Image catalog. Speculative science at its best—nowhere else outside of the physics lab do people argue as intelligently about "ways around the Heisenberg uncertainty principle" and other basic assumptions of modern science. The most skillful discussants make the scientific seem absurd and the fictitious sound plausible. As they say on the like-minded Fox TV hit, *X-Files,* "The truth is out there." ✓**USENET** WEEKLY

rec.arts.sf.written (ng) Fan fic-

Sci-fi Fans

tion and published sci-fi overlap without colliding. Many of the contributors struggle with the fact that sci-fi has expanded so much that it's no longer possible for fans to keep up with everything that's published. A large number of semiregular participants therefore rely on reader reviews—both brief and not—posted here for advice on what fantasy, cyberpunk, horror, political, or foreign thread to check out in new releases. At it's best, this newsgroup is a terrific sci-fi book club. A senior editor at Tor Books, one of the most important sci-fi publishers today, occasionally throws his two cents in. ✓**USENET** *FAQ:* ✓**INTERNET**→*ftp* rtfm.mit.edu→anonymous→<your email address>→/pub/usenet-by-group/rec.arts.sf.written/ DAILY

Science Fiction Fandom Concentrates mostly on literature, which means there's heavy traffic for readers of popular authors from Stephen Donaldson to William Gibson to Robert Heinlein. It also means that many of the postings are fans' notes—gushing appraisals of classic works ("Bradbury's *Martian Chronicles* is the most completely imagined science-fiction novel ever"), arguments over originality (should we credit the invention of robots to Karl Capek or Isaac Asimov?), and even clarifications of picayune points in massive epics (how exactly does mind-reading work in Frank Herbert's *Dune*?).

The literary orientation doesn't shut out related media, of course, and there are some fascinating discussions on film and TV, such as a running poll on the best sci-fi film ever. Curious? So far, it's *Blade Runner* by more than a nose, but you're welcome to weigh in. ✓**AMERICA ONLINE**→*keyword* scifi→Science Fiction Fandom Board DAILY

> **" "I have a good plot idea for the *X-Files*,' writes one fan, who proceeds to detail a wild plot that has something to do with paranormal phenomena infiltrating TVs from the inside out. Give it time!"**

Science Fiction RoundTables The full set of Science Fiction RoundTables on GEnie make up one of the biggest chat zones anywhere in Cyberspace, and it seems to be expanding at the rate of the universe itself. Divided into three gigantic bulletin boards—Written Word, Media, and Fandom—the RoundTables have detailed and crowded discussions in progress on everything from Jules Verne to William Gibson to real science, ethics and space exploration, science-fiction pulps, and the economic health of the sci-fi industry.

Want to talk about authors? Well, every author has an individual category, from A (Roger Allen) to Z (Roger Zelazny). Interested in the latest opus by Tappan King or Melinda Snodgrass, or do you just want to ask "what...people think about Buckaroo Banzai, especially the dreadlocks"? Look no further. ✓**GENIE**→*keyword* sfrt DAILY

SF & Fantasy Forum The fo-

rum collects a sketchy, haphazard, and unflaggingly energetic group of posts on various science-fiction and fantasy subjects. "I have a good plot idea for the *X-Files*," writes one fan, who proceeds to detail a wild plot that has something to do with paranormal phenomena infiltrating TVs from the inside out, using boob tubes as transmitters for alien agendas. Give it time!

Sci-fi fans can also speak their piece both on the message boards and in live conferences on the great cultural milestones of their beloved genre—*Star Wars, Star Trek, Highlander,* and even Anne McCaffrey's *Pern* novels—and the forum includes workshops in which published sci-fi authors share their advice on writing effective speculative fiction. ✓**COMPUSERVE** →*go* scifi→Messages *or* Conferences DAILY

SF-Lovers (ml) No, the name of this digest does not refer (specifically anyway) to the incestuous world of cyberpunk authors, Captain Kirk's seduction of green, half-dressed planet princesses, or the late-night action at a science fiction convention. It's lovers of the genre, you see. All science-fiction and fantasy themes are game, and much of the digest material comes from the rec.sf.* newsgroup hierarchy.

Saul Jaffe, the moderator, speaks of the digest as a magazine, and brings a strong sense of decorum to his editorial choices. The flame-free result is really the only human way of keeping up with the hyperactive science-fiction newsgroups for literature, TV, and movies. The digest is still huge, though—monthly compilations available from the immense FTP archive average about 1.25 meg. ✓**INTERNET**→*email* sf-lovers-request @rutgers.edu ✍ *Write a request*

Archives: ✓**INTERNET**→*ftp* elbereth. rutgers.edu→anonymous→<your email address>→/pub/sfl DAILY

SFFan (echo) A fun forum for debating sci-fi history (remember George Lucas's lawsuit against *Battlestar Galactica* for plagiarizing from *Star Wars*?) and the plot twists of current print and screen favorites like *Highlander, X-Files, Pern,* and Terry Pratchett. The participants are willing to follow a winding path from the author Piers Anthony to the British sci-fi comedy TV show *Red Dwarf.* ✓**FIDONET** WEEKLY

Cyberpunk

alt.cyberpunk (ng) No matter if you're drawn to the literary movement, subculture label, or media hype, any thread is likely to careen through that and more. An anti-TV rant against a new Nike ad turns into a discussion of one of William Burroughs's strangest works, *Cities of Night.* Industrial music and William Gibson's rejected *Aliens 3* script are as likely to come up as the proper close-range use of a twelve-gauge shotgun or of public key PGP encryption. Tom Maddox, author of the slim AI classic *Halo,* is said to be a participant. ✓**USENET** *FAQ:* ✓**INTERNET**→*ftp* rtfm.mit.edu→anonymous→<your email address>→/pub/use net/news.answers→cyberpunk-faq DAILY

---

alt.cyberpunk.chatsubo (ng) Devotees of the dark, gritty, and technological world of the cyberpunk genre, as fathered by William Gibson, gather here in the Chatsubo (Japanese for "teacup"; a futuristic bar in Gibson's ground-breaking novel *Neuromancer*) to post their own creative cyberpunk efforts, usually in the form of fiction, poetry, and

X-Files—downloaded from Compu-Serve's Sci-Fi Forum.

roleplaying. The chat here has three rules: give honest and constructive feedback; particpately actively; and treat other authors and characters with consideration. The majority follow these, and the atmosphere is supportive and casual. Some stories have strong adult themes; as one author described cyberpunk: "The future is already here. And you ain't gonna like it." ✓**USENET** DAILY

Isaac Asimov

alt.books.isaac-asimov (ng) There's a lot of talk puzzling out the lineage of Asimov story lines now that they're being farmed out to other science-fiction writers à la the post-Fleming 007 best-sellers. The most soulful participants are making repeat pilgrimages through the Foundation series and wondering out loud about character motivations with the kind of active curiosity that would make a high-school English teacher think she had been transported to a parallel universe. Maybe it's because so many of the group members have shared experiences treading through Asimov's work, but the conversation is extremely polite

and reasoned, even when debating the data storage potential of black holes. ✓**USENET** WEEKLY

Quantum Leap

QuantumLeap (echo) Most conversation follows whatever episode the USA cable channel is up to in its repeats of the sci-fi drama. A small cadre of enthusiasts often acts as a kind of unofficial help desk for the less regular participants who come here to iron out their understanding of Sam Beckett's time travel. There are also several *Quantum Leap* novels and comic books that get treated like extra episodes of the show. ✓**FIDONET** WEEKLY

Star Trek

alt.startrek.klingon/tlhIn-gan-Hol (ng) Charged with the task of devising some alien-sounding Klingon words for use in the *Star Trek* movies, Mark Okrand created an entire warriors' tongue complete with its own grammar, characters, spelling, vocabulary, and usage. At the time of this writing, there are at least several hundred people fluent in Klingon on the Net. Some of the most accomplished frequent the Klingon mailing list (tlhIngan-Hol), where speakers of all levels are welcome. Get involved and you may be drafted for the Klingon Bible Translation Project.

Sexual politics

English is the preferred language for posts to the newsgroup, where sexual politics seen through a macho, honor-bound Klingon eye is consistently the most popular subject. Filled with would-be Klingons, the newsgroup plays out one drama after another: "Obviously, since we can't meet in a bar and challenge each other over mugs of

Blood Ale, what better way of 'butting heads' than to meet in the verbal equivalent, alt.startrek.klingon? You threw down blatantly false statements about honor, and I challenged you to defend yourself with whatever verbal weapons you might have. Honor will be gained when I have soundly thrashed you, and you retract your venomous lies."

And reports about the Klingon versions of *The Dating Game*, which are increasingly popular at *Star Trek* conventions, are posted. ✓**USENET** ✓**INTERNET**→*email* tlhIngan-Hol-request@klingon.east.sun.com) ✍ *Type in subject line:* subscribe DAILY

──────────

Babylon5 (echo) Would Patrick McNee make a better Narn or Centauri? Intersections of the TV and sci-fi continuums make up most of the tangents in this BBS echo for the discussion of the *Babylon 5* TV show that charges along in the wide path cut by *Star Trek*. The tight-knit group of core participants are at work on their own nitpicker's guide (gravity is produced by rotating the station, but is it just one arm that actually moves?), which will no doubt draw on the scientific bent of several key participants (do aliens necessarily have DNA?). If the guide follows the drift of many posts, there should be some interesting sections trying to explain the sexuality of the two strong women characters, Talia and Susan. ✓**FIDONET** DAILY

──────────

rec.arts.startrek.current (ng) The official charter for the newsgroup strictly defines *current* as discussion about shows no older than the last four months, but the restriction breaks down with virtually every interesting thread, from the lighthearted observation that "Picard is always pulling on his

shirt—can't the Federation find him one that fits?" to an intricate analysis of the portrayal of the enemy Romulans over the course of the seven-year *Next Generation* (*TNG*) series. Legend has it that at least one guy from Houston mission control frequents the newsgroup. ✓**USENET** DAILY

──────────

Star Trek (echo) Plenty of critics here. When one fan shared his disappointment that *The Next Generation* didn't make good on its Emmy nomination for Best Drama Series (*Picket Fences* won over *NYPD Blue*), he was soon answered with comments like "The seventh season didn't DESERVE to be nominated in the first place. Get some perspective." The small group of regulars sometimes drift from discussion of current *Trek* TV and movies to BBS shoptalk, boy-girl flirtation, and where-did-you-go stories of vacations away from the keyboard and echo. ✓**RELAYNET** DAILY

──────────

Star Trek Club Classic *Trek* or *Next Generation*? Kirk or Picard? And what's up with Data, anyway? Thirty years after his first big splash, Gene Roddenberry's imagination remains a powerful force in our galaxy. While the forum includes some talk of offshoot projects—*Deep Space 9*, most notably—the vast majority of the discussion (both on the message boards and in the live chat on "The Bridge") focuses on the two TV shows, and their counterpart films. Which *Star Trek* movie is the best? Well, *Wrath of Khan* seems to be in the lead, although a fair number of fans have a soft spot for *The Search for Spock*. *Next Generation* aficionados will be pleased to learn that the forum contains painstaking dissections of almost every episode, including speculation on Deanna and Worf's

sex life. And in answer to the pressing question of William Shatner's toupee, one Trek fan writes that "he is very sensitive about it. During filming of *The Final Frontier*, he was directing for a scene about to be shot in the desert. He tripped on a large rock while talking and fell. His 'piece' fell off and as he got up, all the extras standing on the side started laughing." Bill, please—it's "to *boldly* go where no man has gone before." ✓**AMERICA ONLINE**→*keyword* trek→ Star Trek Message Boards *or* The Bridge DAILY/LIVE

──────────

Trek Conversations here have the fun feel of a bunch of friends watching the show together, talking during the slow parts and real-

"No, as anyone here is happy to point out, the new *Star Trek* series, *Voyager,* is not the first time that a Federation starship has been helmed by a female captain, contrary to the claims of Paramount. There was Captain Garrett of the *Enterprise-C*!"

ly chattering away when it becomes clear that an episode is a dud. Did you see the episode where Wesley goes up to the holodeck after accidentally ingesting LSD? "He spends the rest of the show selling Guatemalan friendship bracelets to the rest of the crew." Who would win a fight between Picard and Kirk? "Picard. A hairpiece saps the wearer's energy, due to the high Tachyon field absorption coefficient of the synthetic strands of hair, coupled with the instability created in the inertial damping field inherent in polymer-based adhesives." ✓WELL→ g trek DAILY

Trek_Voyager (echo) No, as anyone here is happy to point out, the new *Star Trek* series, *Voyager*, is not the first time that a Federation starship has been helmed by a female captain, contrary to the claims of Paramount. There was Captain Garrett of the *Enterprise-C*! During the run-up to the show's debut, most members fretted over names that were floated as possibilities—Patsy Kensit, Lindsay Wagner—especially after Genevieve Bujold walked off the set two days into production. Another large thread was set of by the Gates McFadden Autograph Scandal ("Gatesgate") post. Most respondents reported positive autograph experience with Whorf (Michael Dorn) and Counseler Troi (Marina Sirtis), and one even sympatheized, on the subject of Bujold, with the fact that "*Trek* fandom is singularly unforgiving" to one's private life. ✓**FIDONET** WEEKLY

Vulcan-L (ml) Sorry, Spock, but online Vulcan culture is primitive compared with the elaborate language and warrior code of the Net's Klingon community. But, give it some time; this list and

Jurassic Park—downloaded from GEnie's Showbiz RoundTable.

alt.fan.surak (named after Spock's father) are building a following. Discussants here are at work on a nascent Vulcan-language project that builds on a sizable body of Vulcan-oriented *Star Trek* literature (*Spock's World* and the *Vulcan Academy Murders* are the list's favorites). Expect to find an insistence on logical thought that stays true to the Vulcan reputation. Regular contributors include several students of extraplanetary studies at the Science Academy in the Eridani system (on the planet "which you call Vulcan"), who patch into the Internet through subspace frequencies. As in most *Star Trek* forums, members can't resist speaking in character. Warns one poster about media giant Paramount Pictures, "Do not rely on the Ferengi who rule Paramount. Their paramount concern is gold pressed latinum, not truth…" \\//_ ✓**INTERNET**→ *email* listserv@ ✍ *Type in message body:* subscribe vulcan-l <your full name> WEEKLY

Star Wars

Star Wars Standing head and shoulders above all other sci-fi action movies, George Lucas's 1977 film, along with its two sequels, forever changed the habits and expectations of movie audiences worldwide. In the AOL *Star Wars* discussion, fans are fretting over rumors of new *Wars* films ("The only thing definite about this movie is that nothing is definite"), pointing out inside jokes in other Lucas efforts (in *Indiana Jones and the Temple of Doom*, there's a nightclub named for Obi-Wan Kenobi), and bemoaning the diminished employment prospects of *Star Wars* star Mark Hamil ("Time has not been kind to Hamil…and neither was *Corvette Summer*"). This message board is one big love-in that embraces Luke Skywalker, Darth Vader, Princess Leia, Han Solo, et al. ✓**AMERICA ONLINE**→*keyword* scifi→ Star Trek/Comics/TV/Star Wars Board→Star Wars and Films DAILY

StarWars (echo) There's a sense here of killing time until that next *Star Wars* movie comes out. Meanwhile, there is kitchy '70s *Star Wars* memorabilia to peddle as fine antiques (how much would you pay for a mint-condition white plastic X-wing fighter that seats the Luke Skywalker action figure?), the latest Lucas Arts *Star Wars*-based video games to critique (some find it a bit treasonous to fight on the Empire's side in the DOS smash hit *Tie Fighter*), and even Franklin Mint tchotchkes to wonder aloud about acquiring. A minority talk about the *Star Wars* books—keeping the *Star Wars* myths flickering until they once again light up the big screen. ✓**FIDONET** WEEKLY

Personalities

Cyberspace has a way of inverting and democratizing fame, so that the admirer is

raised up over the admired. Bill Gates may be one of the richest guys in the solar system, but all his gazillions can't shut up even one hooha on **alt.fan.bill-gates**. Dan Quayle may be political history, but a few regulars and a whole lot of weekly participants are having too much fun to give the poor guy a break on **alt.fan.dan-quayle**. There's also **alt.fan.howard-stern**, a newsgroup so rowdy and obnoxious that in contrast it makes its namesake look like a gentleman. At the other end of the spectrum, you have the self-created Net parodies of celebrities like Kibo, king of **alt.religion.kibology**, and Tank Girl, whose ex-boyfriends keep in touch through **alt.fan.tank-girl**.

Howard Stern—downloaded from CompuServe's Entertainment Drive Forum.

On the Net

alt.fan.bill-gates (ng) Nicole wonders if anyone else is aware of the Great Bill Gates Clone Conspiracy Theory. Based on the startling resemblance of a Bill Gates photo in *BusinessWeek* to several of her ex-boyfriends and acquaintances, she pleads: "I want to know if anyone else is on to Bill Gates' diabolical plan, and I want to publicize it before he has me reformatted for knowing too

much..." Replies in this light-hearted newsgroup, populated by the kind of people who read computer-industry gossip columns, are reassuring, and laced with DOS jokes: "Don't worry—he won't be able to make more than 655,360 copies of himself, and they'll be easy to recognize because the names of clones will all be in 8.3 format." One has the feeling that every Microserf (Microsoft employee) is lurking here. ✓**USENET** WEEKLY

alt.fan.dan-quayle (ng) Our Man Dan may have exited from the stage of national politics and late-night monologues, but the

newsgroup lives on, scanning the horizon for a clear shot at the rare bird. In the meantime, other great Republican minds—mostly those of Ronald Reagan and Oliver North—are made the butt of TelePrompTer and malapropism jokes. Also functions as an informal training ground for anti-Rush forces. ✓**USENET** DAILY

alt.fan.howard-stern (ng) Come here to test whether you can be as obnoxious as the man himself. If you complain that Howard hung up on you, the most sympathy you'll get is, "That's just Howard's way of telling you that you have nothing to say." But people do have a lot to say, posting 100 or more messages per day about that morning's show, Howard-centric gossip, and the ongoing sport of attacking the dissenters who regularly come here to complain. Howard Stern offers a free T-shirt to anyone who gets Howard's name mentioned on someone else's call-in show, and posters regularly revel in successful pranks: "One day I was listening to a Christian radio show (which can be good for laughs anyway) and someone got through and asked the host, 'Is it possible that Howard Stern is the second coming of Christ?'" Most on this aggressive, suburban newsgroup think the answer is yes. ✓**USENET** *FAQ:* ✓**INTERNET**→*ftp* rtfm.mit.edu→ anonymous→<your email address> →pub/usenet-by-group/alt. answers/howard-stern→faq DAILY

---

alt.fan.laurie.anderson (ng) This is far from a run-of-the-mill "she's so cool" fan group. Laurie Anderson is a performance artist, not just a smart pop singer, and discussion here extends beyond notices of concert dates and videos. Her fans go to see foreign films as per her lyrics ("Hansel and Gretel are alive and well. She is a cocktail waitress. He had a part in a Fassbinder film"). They discuss her inspiration—a Paul Klee painting led to *Strange Angels*. The group is friendly, recommending their favorite Anderson works to novices and suggesting other artists, visual and musical, that group members might want to check out. They are attuned to the avant-garde of past and present—they even know whether William Burroughs is still alive. Despite pleading from her fans, Anderson has not posted her email address, but she is rumored to lurk here. Too bad her special brand of wit doesn't find itself in

Kate Moss—downloaded from Compu-Serve's Graphics Corner.

---

the postings more often. ✓**USENET** WEEKLY

---

alt.fan.noam-chomsky (ng) The activist Noam Chomsky seems to garner far more postings in this combative newsgroup than the linguist Chomsky. (Although there was a discussion about whether there should be an FAQ because the linguist might be against the canon and codification.) Most of the discussion continues the long-standing battles between left and right. Lefties defend Chomsky against rightest charges of "being a friend of tyrants" or accusations of backpedaling now that the Cold War is over. These loyalists frequently accuse the opposition of not really knowing Noam and send them home to read before they speak. But if you're looking for good political discussion and interesting excerpts by Chomsky himself, the debates here are well attended and well argued. ✓**USENET** DAILY

---

alt.fan.penn-n-teller (ng) Why don't the cyberceleb, *Wired* cover-

boy, *PC Computing* columnist, sometimes magician, and self-confessed porn-consuming NetHead Penn Jillette or the stage-silent Teller post messages here? This might as well be the Waiting for Jillette board. ✓**USENET** WEEKLY

---

alt.supermodels (ng) How do you detect breast implants? "Take her to Colorado, Mexico City, or any other place in a different elevation. The saline implants get air pressure and you can hear a swishing and popping sound." "Just look for the scar. *Playboy* air brushes their photos, but comparing close- and long-range shots, you can usually make your own conclusions." Or maybe you're a leg man: "First of all, Elle's thighs do not touch." Still not your thing? See the related alt.great.ass. paulina, another newsgroup that reads like the letters to the editor of *Playboy*. ✓**USENET** *FAQ:* ✓**INTERNET**→*ftp* rtfm.mit.edu→anonymous →<your email address>→/pub/ usenet-by-group/alt.answers→

> "Getting a hate group is easy, too: Just post enough mean-spirited, unpopular, or generally insane opinions on an otherwise serious newsgroup, and someone will throw one your way."

Personalities **Fans**

Net Personality Groups (ng) Okay. So you want to be famous. So you want to be admired. So you want some…respect. Will you settle for generating a bunch of puzzled questions from newbies who don't know any better? Fine. Short of shooting someone, getting your own newsgroup is the easiest ticket to infamy. Do a little random surfing around the alt newsgroups, and you'll probably come across the alt.fan category. There you'll find your standard gushy-goony groups where "real" celebrities are discussed and/or worshiped. You'll also find fan groups that seem to be about nobody in particular. Or nobody you recognize. Got a friend you think worthy of discussion—or, natch, an enemy? Why not create a newsgroup?

Kibo

The granddaddy of all alt.personality groups is alt.religion.kibology, which was seeded by the eye-poppingly bizarre rants of one James "Kibo" Parry. Alt.religion.

kibology has grown farther and faster than its subject, however, since a number of devotees have taken the liberty of automatically crossposting to alt.religion.kibology the nonsense they post in other newsgroups.

And Parry himself is a regular—a legend in his own group. Alt.religion.kibology has spawned a series of spin-off kibo groups, from alt.exploding.kibo to alt.imploding.kibo to…well, you'll have to do some searching of your own. Kibo has been profiled in *Wired* magazine, *Playboy*, and a number of other publications, sending his tendrils far beyond Cyberspace.

But while Kibo is the first and foremost, he's far from alone. In the alt.fan category, you'll find alt.fan.jen-coolest (which is about not only one particular girl named Jen but all girls named Jen) alt.fan jiro.nakamura, and alt.fan.wal.greenshaw, among others. These groups generally have a few discombobulated posters whose plaintive cry of "What's this newsgroup all about?" can almost be heard above the background static

of the Net.

The stupid, the hated

Meanwhile, the stupid, the hated, and the foul of mouth also have their "fans": anti-choice poster Kevin Darcy continues to march his prolife line in alt.fan.kevin.darcy, surrounded by the jeers of his opponents, and alt.fan.serdar.argic has enough hate traffic to have spawned a T-shirt created by an enterprising "fan." Getting a hate group is easy, too: Just post enough mean-spirited, unpopular, or generally insane opinions on an otherwise serious newsgroup, and someone will throw one your way.

Beware of identity thieves, however. Like that of Kibo, who was outgrown by his own legend, a group that lives beyond its purpose can transform in strange and mysterious ways. Alt.fan.tank-girl was originally an alt.personality group created by friends and ex-lovers of a MU* (social MUD) queen whose handle was Tank Girl. When she lost her Net access, the group was "stolen" by those who were enthusiasts of the indie comic from which she got her name. Tank Girl is gone…long live Tank Girl. ✓USENET

Laurie Anderson—downloaded from Exec PC.

O. J. Simpson

Ask any NetHead, "Where were you online when the Juice got loose?" Everyone seems to have a story—it was that kind of event, a turning point of the Net-eration, so to speak. "I was on ECHO [a New York City BBS and Internet provider] catching up on my Into the Mystic conference when these O.J. messages started appearing from people watching the chase on TV." On AOL, the opening screen announced the getaway-in-progress to all who logged in. Even before the chase, newsgroups like **alt.law-enforcement** were already catching a few O.J. posts a day. But the weekend of the arrest, newsgroups logged minute-by-minute messages. On the **rec.arts.movie group** there were comparisons to *Speed*; on **alt.pave-the-earth**, laments about the limited road options available to O.J.; on **alt.conspiracy**, well, just imagine. **Alt.fan.oj-simpson** was born the night of the Juice's tentative freedom flight, and before the end of the weekend it had spawned offspring like **alt.fan.oj-simpson.drive-faster, alt.fan.oj-simpson. death-chamber, alt.fan. marcia-clark**, devoted to

O. J. mug shot—downloaded from GEnie's Sports RoundTable.

the assistant district attorney prosecuting the case, and **alt.fan.shapiro.ties**, to discuss the Juice's counsel's cravats.

These splinter groups would eventually return to the **alt.fan.oj-simpson** fold, creating a super-group attracting as many as 1,000 messages a day—and perhaps 100 times as many lurking readers. Comprising amateur detectives, lawyers, cops, moralizers, and reporters looking for a quote or hot tip, the group became the center of O.J. speculation, analysis, and, occasionally, paranoia ("Are we being watched? I heard that O.J.'s lawyers are using the Net to see what people think about the case"). The group has made painstaking efforts to stay abreast of the details and developments in the case ("If you are referring to Lange in the GJ testimony, he did not mention a time. Are you basing the 05:00

[7 a.m. minus two hours] on Lange's GJ testimony p.305?"). Then too there has been the effort to go beyond the case itself, with posters trying—mostly in vain— to explore their obsession with Simpson: "Becoming a murderer must be like the unfolding of a deadly blossom in the garden of one's heart. No doubt he knew the seed was buried there. Perhaps he planted it, but how could he imagine the shape of that terrible flower or the way that it feeds upon the spirit?"

AOL members—a fair number of them lawyers—have used the **Court TV Forum** to discuss the day's O.J. events, and play backseat defense attorneys. An O. J. Simpson file area (highlighted with its own O. J. icon) provides access to a large number of trial-related documents. Polls have charted members' rising and falling faith in the Juice.

Bronco screen saver

GEnie's opening menus have directed users to various O. J. discussions. On the **Sports Round-Table**, in addition to passionate O. J. chat, there have been downloads of a Bronco screen saver and a Windows sound file of Judge Kennedy Power clearing the way for a trial. Both got top billing in the summer and fall of 1994.

O.J. talk has been everywhere on CompuServe. The **Speakeasy Forum** carried the initial reactions: "Wow, what a night! A little like the first night of the CNN coverage of the Persian Gulf war." As the story unfolded, members have turned to the **O.J. Simpson Forum** and the **Time Warner Crime Forum**, where the attorneys—not just their arguments but their clothing choices as well—have been the main topics of discussion.

On Prodigy's **News BB**, discus-

O. J. Simpson **Fans**

sion came close in breadth if not depth of coverage to the exhaustive discussion in **alt.fan.oj.simpson**. Messages titled "DNA-Hair," "Another blow to O. J.," "A knife is found," "100% Not Guilty," "Aliens Cloned O. J.," "O. J. Should Fry," "New O. J. Jokes," and "I Just Don't Know" filled the topic. "Too bad I don't live in Calif.," wrote one member, "because I would be the perfect juror. I'm just not convinced that he did it and yet some of the evidence is fairly strong...I can't understand how anyone can really feel sure which way to go."

---

alt.fan.oj-simpson (ng) ✓USE-NET

O.J. Simpson Forum ✓COMPU-SERVE→*go* ojforum

O.J. Simpson ✓COMPUSERVE→*go* speakeasy→Messages→Sports of All Sorts→O.J. Simpson

---

O.J. Simpson ✓GENIE→*keyword* sports→Sports Bulletin Board→Welcome to the Sports RT Bulletin Board→O.J. Simpson

---

O.J. Simpson Case ✓PRODI-GY→*jump* news bb→Choose a Topic→O.J. Simpson Case

---

O.J. Simson on Court TV ✓AMERICA ONLINE ...→*keyword* court tv→Message Board (for discussion) ...→*keyword* court tv→Special/The O.J. Simpson Case (for files)

POLL: O.J. Guilty or Innocent ✓AMERICA ONLINE→*keyword* capital →Message Boards→General Debate→POLL: O.J. Guilty or Innocent

---

The Simpson Case ✓COM-PUSERVE→*go* twcrime→Message Boards→The Simpson Case

---

ALT.FAN.OJ-SIMPSON MESSAGES

Message subjects in alt.fan.oj-simpson, followed by the number of posts

- Judge Ito (3)
- Premeditated or not? (16)
- Bogus Innocence Scenarios? (1)
- Could someone please send GJ transcript? (4)
- Marcia Clark—UGLY? (21)
- Shapiro curses in court? (4)
- Defense down in flames (22)
- Cowling's White Bronco (4)
- Whats in the Will? (15)
- What Shapiro knows about the murders (5)
- Furman, cops, and burnout (24)
- Why does defense want testing? (8)
- Cochran quote (7)
- 10:04 Cellphone Call (4)
- Is Shapiro seeking truth, or seeking to obscure the issues? (17)
- Juror demographics (10)
- Grand Jury Testimony (9)
- O. J. can prove Furman Did it (3)
- "Similar" Unsolved Murder Case Request (1)
- Faking tests (2)
- Chronology (Repost by Request) (1)
- Some thoughts on boredom, tragedy, and O.J. (5)
- Mock trial (3)
- Discovery (7)
- Facts/Rumors/Leaks du Jour (2)
- O. J.'s Blood at Bundy (1)
- Some thoughts—a semifinal wrapup (6)
- Questions—Pictures of the Scene (2)
- Defense down in flames (let's vote) GUILTY (11)
- Mock trial (was Re: 10:04 Cellphone Call) (2)
- What the hell (5)
- Preliminary Hearings Transcript (2)
- DNA Questions (3)
- The knife (6)
- Everybody is leaving (6)
- Mystery Car (8)
- WHAT'S IN SEALED ENVELOPE???? (8)
- WANTED: O. J. CANONICAL JOKE LIST (3)
- Drug abuse
- Insane cocaine creeps
- I did it.
- O. J. the actor vs O. J. the witness
- Prosecution reveals crime sequence
- Who cares?

Pop fiction

As the saying goes, reading is fundamental—and where would the Net be without it? In

a medium as text-based as Cyberspace currently is, it's no wonder that some of the most popular and populated discussion groups focus on the critique and appreciation of the written word, though, to be sure, the Net seems to be more dominated by *Star Trek* than by Shakespeare. Still, if you want to talk about your favorite Tom Clancy novel or complain about the latest John Grisham movie adaptation, the following discussions give you a soapbox on which to stand. Would-be authors will find support groups of their peers, who'll offer gentle criticism and helpful hints (or outrageous pans and acidic comments, though not often, we hope), and dilettantes can even join in interactive prose-writing in a variety of genres, from mystery to science fiction. Write on!

Fabio—downloaded from ftp.u.washington.edu.

On the Net

Across the board

Books (echo) The conference is a sketchy but interesting mix of literary feedback. Because the topic is so general—covering the world of books from cover to cover—it's not unusual to find reflections on

American high realism ("Has anybody else recently read *Age of Innocence* by Edith Wharton? I recently finished it. It was an interesting look at life in the early '20s—how times have changed!)" nestled alongside obsessional musings on the *Star Wars* science-fiction-novel series ("The Han Solo character undergoes some changes in the later books that are entirely inconsistent with the man portrayed in the film, and it's like a burr in my sock to read these books!"). ✓ **INTELEC** WEEKLY

Books and Writing BB Lauren from New York stands up for her choice of *Love Story* as one of the greatest books of all time. Eric lays out his theory that Alex in *A Clockwork Orange* is a Christ figure. Michelle and Cecelia discuss the physical perfection of romance

cover models Fabio and the Bartling Brothers, while Love Ann is disturbed about the increasing incidence of adultery in the same genre.

Teenage boys write science-fiction add-ons and teenage girls join the Babysitters Club. Who says the American public doesn't read anymore? The bulletin board is not a literary salon by any means—a reference to Faulkner as "lame," the preponderance of authors found in grocery-store aisles, and frequent queries in the nonfiction section for books referred to on *Sally Jesse* or *Geraldo* suggest the general tone.

People of all ages are reading here (classics too) and are really engaged in discussing their favorite authors. Books also has a very active Young Writers section, which elicits original prose and poetry. Adults share their creations, publishing advice, and sympathy in the Writing categories. ✓**PRODIGY**→*jump* books and writ ing bb→Choose a Topic HOURLY

Fantasy

alt.fan.douglas-adams (ng) If consciousness is a kind of dense, blurry fog, then the humor of Douglas Adams is an out-of-control lorry that emerges out of that fog against the red, rebounding off of street signs and the occasional pedestrian before crashing through the window of a fish-and-chips shop. Of course, if you've read Adams's five-volume *Hitchhiker's Guide* trilogy, you know this already. Vogon poetry. Pan-Galactic Gargle Blasters. The end of EOEAWKI (Existence On Earth As We Know It) and the answer to the question of life, the universe, and everything.

Alt.fan.douglas-adams, where the *Guide* series and other snarky bits of Adams insanity are discussed, showers readers with incredibly unenlightening points of philosophy, anecdotes of how the number 42 has influenced/ changed/ended their lives, and lots and lots of Favorite Lines. It's moderately trafficked, begging to be read no more than two or three times a week at most, and almost exclusively male; like its cousin alt.fan.pratchett, it has an extensive international following, with posters chiming in from all parts of the Crown and its colonies in addition to the good old U.S. of A.

Not a presence

Unlike on alt.fan.pratchett, however, alt.fan.douglas-adams' icon (whom the alt.fan.douglas-adams fans have nicknamed DNA) is not a presence on the group; a shame, because Adams is known to be something of a computerphile.

> **"Pratchett himself, or a reasonable facsimile, is a regular reader and poster to the group, delivering exclusive reports on his coming books and his brilliantly mundane daily activities. "**

Perhaps it's because he realizes to what degree his most feverish fans are utter raving loons, or perhaps he's simply in the bath. ✓**USENET** *FAQ:* ✓**INTERNET**→*ftp* rtfm.mit.edu→ anonymous→ <your email address> →/pub/usenet-by-group/news. answers→ douglas-adams-FAQ WEEKLY

---

alt.fan.pratchett (ng) Reading alt.fan.pratchett, the gathering place for fans of British pfunny pfantasy writer Terry Pfratchett and other random maniacs, is like sitting in on a barroom conversation about three hours and five pints in: surreal, mind-bogglingly amusing, and so cryptic as to be damned near impenetrable. Of course, the stools in this pub are set rather far apart—say, several thousand miles—but Pterry (as they call him) is a tie that binds enthusiasts from Brisbane to Upper Buckle to the Bronx, regardless of their geographical separation and level of blood alcohol content.

Pratchett's best known works are the Discworld novels (intensely British humor in a fantasy vein, set on a magical world flatter and quite a bit rounder than a slice of ham). Discworld novels come out at the pace of approximately one per year, and are huge sellers in their native England, though somewhat less so here; one ongoing topic is an extended, sulky complaint from American fans to their Brit and Aussie counterparts, who see Pratchett's works months or years earlier.

Neil Gaiman

Pratchett is also coauthor, with comic writer Neil Gaiman, of *Good Omens*, a best-selling novel about the hilarity ensuing when an angel and a devil conspire to thwart the Apocalypse. All of these books get long shrift on the group, as fans provide annotations of Pratchett's pop-culture references, hypothesize as to Pratchett's inspirations, and generally wank about as if they know something.

What's more interesting, however, is the interaction between fans in the *mode* of Pratchett; at any given time, at least a third of the posts on the group are not about Pterry and his works at all, but odd bits of trivia discussed ad absurdum with a glazed, lunatic seriousness. Pratchett himself, or a reasonable facsimile, is a regular reader and poster to the group, delivering exclusive reports on his coming books and his brilliantly mundane daily activities.

The group is fast and frequent, so fairly regular reading is necessary to keep up with the insanity; meanwhile, the gender ratio leans somewhat toward male, and many of these are from Australia or the UK. Expect to see *colour* spelled with a *u* and references to "bollocks." ✓**USENET** *FAQ:* ✓**INTERNET**→ *ftp* rtfm.mit.edu→anonymous→ <your email address>→/pub/ usenet-by-group/news.answers/

Tolkien (ml) One of the most popular writers in the history of our small blue planet, John Ronald Reuel Tolkien spent much of his writing life buried in a medieval fantasy world of wizards and magic rings. The Tolkien mailing list tries to do justice to the power of his imagination. Though some of the subscribers attempt to situate *Lord of the Rings* (or *LotR*, as it is known) within the larger context of English literature (reading Tolkien along with writers like Auden and Hardy), much of the conference has the feel of a cult, and while it's not impossible for a non-Tolkeinite to understand comments on more popular characters such as Frodo and Gandalf, other comments ("Given that Elrond's authority is mandated by the Valar, we can say that Sauron represents power without authority, and Elrond represents authority without power") verge on nonsense to the uninitiated. In short, while this mailing list may be slow going for anyone who hasn't visited Middle Earth, it's an absolute must for anyone who can't kick *The Hobbit*. ✓**INTERNET**→*email* listserv@ jhuvm.hcf.jhu.edu ✍ *Type in message body:* subscribe tolkien <your full name> DAILY

Horror

alt.books.anne-rice (ng) Anne Rice's "ability to make what could be monstrous seem instead intriguingly different" fascinates this young group. They puctuate serious literary criticism with chatter about "vitamin supplements for undead living off undernourished mortals." The film version of *Interview With the Vampire* is a daily thread. Was Tom Cruise the right choice for Lestat after all? Was Daniel significant enough to be

Sherlock Holmes and Dr. Watson—downloaded from Exec PC.

played by Christian Slater? Despite some attention to the witches of the *Mayfair Chronicles*, vampires are the stars of this group. ✓**USENET** DAILY

alt.books.stephen-king (ng) Like Annie Wilkes hobbling Paul Campbell, this group is not about to let the "real" Stephen King get away. Such socially relevant novels as *Gerald's Game* are "not what I am used to reading by King." They prefer *It* ("terrifying; one of the best horror novels I've ever read") or *The Stand* ("to step boldly into the jaws of darkness"). The hottest flames are reserved for those who hint that King uses ghosts on both sides of the keyboard. ✓**USENET** WEEKLY

Anne Rice (ml) Desperate to establish themselves as "true Anne Rice fans" before *Interview With a Vampire* hits the big screen, members are here to discuss Rice's writings—all of her works, not just those about witches and vampires. Despite the moderator's aggressive efforts to keep the list on topic and the steady stream of messages commenting on Rice's writing style—e.g, "Do you think that the third-person style of the first part of *QOTD* enhanced the moral

commentary and debate that Rice is having?"—the list becomes most animated when straying to philosophical questions, such as whether members would accept the dark gift themselves. Get familiar with the acronyms for the titles of the *Vampire Chronicles*. Around this list, the first book in the series is referred to as IWAV. ✓**INTERNET**→*email* listserv@ psu-vm.psu.edu ✍ *Type in message body:* subscribe annerice <your full name> DAILY

S_King (echo) Like scholars of Shakespeare arguing over one line in Act III, Scene IV of *Two Gentlemen of Verona*, the Stephen King experts on this echo search each line for intricate clues to answer the question "Was *The Stand* a parallel universe?" The complete leather-bound volumes of the works of Stephen King (which nearly every poster on this echo surely owns) certainly take up much more shelf space than the Bard's. Thus there is much to talk about. Don't try to compare the master to other, "lesser" lights; do speak your mind about King movie casting, plot subtleties, and character motivation. King's unique, macabre take on life lends itself to philosophical speculation on the end of the world and the meaning of evil. ✓**FIDONET** DAILY

Mystery

Hounds-L (ml) Taking names from the Sherlockian (or is it Holmesian?) canon, Lady Frances Carfax, Thorneycroft Huxtable, Vittoria the circus belle and the other arch and urbane Hounds of the Internet solve mysteries by the minute. Which major star played both Sherlock Holmes and Dr. Watson? (Patrick Macnee.) What is the evidence for the existence of pay toilets in Victorian England? (None, but the counterfeiters in "The Engineer's Thumb" stored their nickel in an outhouse.) There's a Holmes story of the week, but the focus is on digression—from the nasal drops ("like Mother pouring cream down your nose") that sponsored radio mysteries in the thirties to modern computer crime and punishment. ✓**INTERNET**→*email* list proc@beloit. edu ✍ *Type in message body:* subscribe hounds-l <your full name> DAILY

Mystery (echo) "Kathleen felt a warm wetness on her ankle. Looking down, she saw Sirius's tongue taking a second lick, his head protruding from under her chair. Suddenly, she felt overcome by the gesture from this giant Golden Retriever—and a flood of tears rushed down both cheeks. Sirius, overcome in turn by the rush of Kathleen's emotion, crawled somewhat painfully out from under her chair, and laid his head in her warm and now damp lap. 'Damn,' said Harold. We're sitting here wasting time!'" If you agree with Harold, then you might want to avoid this conference. But if you're attached to the idea of writing a round-robin mystery—this is the place for you. In addition to post-ing ongoing contributions to the group's mystery, participants indulge in frequent discussion of reading-group protocol (who was supposed to post a chapter? Why didn't they? What happened to Ellen's July 21 post?). Authors sometimes use the conference to post the itinerary for their book tours. While the quality of the prose varies—it's unlikely that you're going to turn up the new Ross Macdonald online—the round-robin technique generates a tremendous amount of cama-raderie. ✓**INTELEC** DAILY

The Mystery Conference One evening, at about half past ten, a pair of gloved hands switched on the Macintosh computer that sat on Doctor Louis Fremont's ma-hogany desk in his Manhattan study. While Fremont slept—only two rooms away, his right arm protectively encircling his wife Julie—the gloved hands logged into g noir, the WELL's mystery conference, and began to peruse the postings. They seemed to be sets of messages that discussed the great mystery writers Agatha Christie, P. D. James, Ross Mac-Donald, and Dashiell Hammett, as well as newer authors proudly bearing the mystery torch—Walter Mosley, Sue Grafton, Carl Hiassen, James Hall. The owner of the gloved hands noticed that in addition to the author categories, conference participants had plenty to say about mystery bookstores, teen sleuths, true crime. Then, at three minutes past eleven, the screen on Louis Fremont's com-puter went black, and Julie Fremont awoke with a scream. ✓**WELL**→g noir DAILY

Romance

RRA-L (ml/ng) Romance Readers Anonymous has a frantic quality, with message after message men-tioning all-nighters to finish Ju-dith McNaught's latest or one of Harlequin's releases of the month. Conversation sometimes strays to movies and television shows—Arnold Schwarzeneger is not a group favorite, but Alan Alda is. This lively group could go on indefinitely about heros, heroines, and romantic story lines. Many women—yes, it's all women—continue to carry on discussions with each other via email when the rest of the group is ready to move on to other books. ✓**INTER-NET**→*email* listserv@kentvm. kent.edu ✍ *Type in message body:* subscribe rra-l <your full name> ✓**USENET**→ bit.listserv.rra-l DAILY

Pern

The glitter of sunlight off reptilian scales and the slow flapping of leathery wings send

many women (and some men) into a controlled swoon, and no one has been better at capturing draconic romance than Anne McCaffrey, whose *Dragonriders of Pern* books constitute the series with the most female devotees in sci-fi/fantasy fandom. On **alt.fan.pern**, subtle points of dragon anatomy and Pernese technology are debated owlishly by fantasy realists (if that isn't an oxymoron); more lyrical types post filksongs (verses of dragon poetry sans their accompanying music) and bits of short fiction.

McCaffrey herself is aware of the newsgroup and is a distant correspondent with it, receiving the group's questions by Bitnet and responding, via one devoted fan, in bulk digest form. The group has low to moderate traffic, however, with no more than a couple of dozen posts every few days.

True Pern fans with Internet access connect instead to Pern-MUSH, a vividly drawn world that strives to be as close to Pernese reality as is digitally possible: Players can be Holders, Riders, Weyrlings, Harpers, Vintners, and Craftspeople. Affiliations and intrigue abound, and out-of-character action isn't tolerated. The more you know about Pern and McCaffrey's dragons, the better off you are, but the residents are friendly and more than willing to help: One of the kindliest MUSHers is Besander,

Mystical world—downloaded from CompuServe's Photography Forum.

the Steward of Benden Hold, who is quick to greet a new player with a hearty "Welcome to Pern!"

Unlike on most MU*s, there isn't a distinction between "character" and "guest" here: As soon as you connect, you have the option of creating a persona. Just make sure it's one that fits with the motif, and act accordingly—while the denizens will be friendly, they won't embrace you until you've proved that you have staying power. Which means, natch, that you have to stick around for a while.

Seasonal festivals

Social events are highly organized: there are Gathers, which are seasonal festivals, and other, smaller celebrations; there is also much role-playing of mundane activity, such as harvesting, wine-making, and leather-tanning, which are somehow more fun when performed à la MUSH than in RL. If you're brave and diligent, you can even seek out a Dragonrider on Search, and hope to impress a dragon of your own—once you do so, you can fly above the virtual world and fight Pern's deadliest

menace, the mindless, ravening coils of alien fungus known as Thread.

Because of Pern's huge female fan population, the MUSH is the most evenly balanced MU* around, with many, many active female players; average traffic on the MUSH is anywhere from 40 to 60 people at prime hours. If you're a dragon fan, and if you're into structured role-playing in a semi-medieval setting, Pern-MUSH has much to offer. ✓**USENET** (for the newsgroup) *FAQ:* ✓**INTERNET**→*ftp* rtfm.mit.edu→ anonymous→<your email address> →/pub/usenet-by-group/alt.fan. pern/→Welcome* ✓**INTERNET**→*tel-net* cesium.clock.org 4201→create <your character's name> <your password> (for the MUSH)

> "McCaffrey is aware of the newsgroup and is a distant correspondent."

Cartoons & animation

Loony or stoic, violent or heroic, cartoons are as much a part of growing up as, say,

silly squabbling with siblings. The following Cyberspace second homes allow adults who haven't outgrown their love for talking mice, rabbits with attitude, wide-eyed girls in sailor suits, and the occasional giant robot to relive both. Conversations bounce wildly from fond memories of favorite characters, lines, and scenes, to nitpicky recitations of trivia, to—yes!—incredibly stupid arguments. Who's smarter, Beavis or Butt-head? Is *The Lion King* a blatant ripoff of *Kimba, the White Lion*? And if Goofy and Pluto are both dogs, why can't Pluto talk? Discussion is always animated (pardon the pun) and full of the kind of wit and wonder that make cartoons an obsession for children of all ages. Just one word of advice: Don't remind participants that their favorite characters aren't really real. Bugs Bunny, after all, will sing, wisecrack, and blow up Elmer Fudd forever; you'll be around only as long as your RL (real life) access provider lets you…Check **rec.arts.anime**—some of the Net's biggest posters hang out there.

"Be Our Guest"—*downloaded from GEnie's Showbiz RoundTable Forum.*

On the Net

Across the board

alt.tv.animaniacs (ng) One of the newer alt.tv groups, and one with a rabid following, especially after *Animaniacs'* near-cancellation by Fox. Many posters compare the adventures of Wakko, Yakko, and Dot to the classic chaos of the Warner Bros. cartoon heyday; others just love the constant cultural referencing and clever punnery. Light volume, but building, with some of the best FAQ support this side of alt.tv.simpsons, and the gender ratio is good. ✓**USENET** *FAQ:* ✓**INTERNET**→*ftp* rtfm.mit.edu→ anonymous→<your email address> →/pub/usenet-by-group/news. answers/tv→animaniacs-faq DAILY

#anime! Well-frequented by rec.arts.anime regulars, including Enrique Conty and at least one industry professional. Discussion tends to be light and less on-topic than rec.arts.anime postings; usu-ally a good group of 10 to 15 persons can be found late at night. Some of #anime!'s thunder has been stolen by the immense growth of AnimeMUCK, which is #anime! with frills on. ✓**INTERNET**→ *irc* /channel #anime

Disney RoundTable Imagine for a moment that the Disney Empire decided to wage war against the United States. General Mickey would enjoy the support of fervent nationalists (if you think those little people are your loyal children, think again) and an unlimited bankroll (they print their own money, for heaven's sake); Uncle Sam wouldn't stand a chance. Within months we'd all be shaving regularly, and whistling while we worked. Mind you, we're not saying that the takeover is going to happen, only that it could happen, and that if it does, you'd be well advised to dial up GEnie's Disney Conference to await further instructions from the Head Rodent. This imposing set of bulletin boards includes categories for each park, as well as topics on related business ventures, collectibles, and even the gigantic film empire.

Under Disney's spell

For the most part, postings are written by those already under Disney's spell, and even those who dare detract from the Disney vision do so carefully: "I'm excited, but not sold. Why would Walt Disney build a harsh-reality-themed park? Walt Disney is the master of fantasy, not reality. I'd have to see it to believe it. Imagineering is my dream…But there doesn't seem to be be much imagineering in harsh reality. I see Walt in heaven smoking anxiously." While the incredible obedience to the Disney way of life sometimes recalls Jonestown, it'll warm your heart, especially if you're feeling a little Goofy. ✓**GENIE**→*keyword* disney→ The Disney Bulletin Board *or* The Disney Real-Time Conference DAILY

---

rec.arts.anime * (ng) Big sparkly eyes, perky girls in sailor suits, giant robots, psychics, and many-tentacled beasts—it takes a certain sensibility to be a fan of Japanese animation. Anime is the purple-haired, big-eyed monkey on the animation fans' backs, and rec.arts.anime is just one of the means in which they feed the habit.

In the late '80s, when rec.arts.anime came into being, it served as a gray-market connection for the trading of tapes subtitled into English by canny, Japanese-speaking fans. Translated scripts were posted here for distribution, dubbed tapes were offered, and the anime community—that's what they think of themselves as—grew, until, with the recent explosion of commercial English-language distributors, anime has almost entered the mainstream, with consequent

> ## "'I see Walt in heaven smoking anxiously.'"

pluses and minuses. Anime is more readily available, but as with early Hong Kong martial arts flicks, much of it is dubbed, and poorly. Also, the influx of new fans means that the old-timers—the "otaku"—are constantly being inundated with stupid newbie questions.

The more you know…

Like most fan.groups, RAA is arranged as a loose, anarchic hierarchy, based on information. The more you know, the higher you rank. Enrique Conty, an acerbic and articulate poster of staggering volume (he's ranked by sysadmins as the seventh-biggest poster in all of the Net), is perhaps the best-known rec.arts.anime wizard. Others include Hitoshi Doi, who has the advantage of actually being in Japan (and is thus a direct source of new information), and Theresa Martin, a prolific poster of song translations and the best-known female rec.arts.anime'er.

What gets discussed? It helps to remember that many members are not at all embarrassed to treat their favorite characters as "real people"—and, for that matter, tend to identify with them in a manner alien to other animation. fan.groups. Posters will take screen names like C-ko Kotobuki, Ranma, Priscilla Asigiri—the names of their heroes—and defend their animated heroes to the death. Long-running threads are often along the lines of "Who's the cutest babe in <name of series>"; "What would happen if…"; and "Who would win if <x> and <y> got in a fight?" Reviews (of varying quality) are as plentiful as meta-discus-

sions about anime and anime fandom.

RL Gatherings

Rec.arts.anime is one of the most vibrantly social groups around, with regular RL gatherings at fan conventions and local anime screenings. While most posters are male, the female contingent has been growing. Members range in age from high-school students to unrepentant middle-agers, and most are friendly and welcoming of newbies…if you don't yank on their particular peeve-chains.

The group is extremely high-volume, with daily check-ins necessary to avoid unmanageable posting buildup. Last year, it was divided into four linked subgroups: rec.arts.anime (for discussion), rec.arts.anime.info (for FAQs and announcements), rec.arts.anime.marketplace (for legal sales of anime-related items—not tape-trading), and rec.arts.anime.stories (for anime-related fiction written by fans). ✓**USENET** *FAQ:* ✓**INTERNET**→ *ftp* rtfm.mit.edu→anonymous→ <your email address>→/pub/usenet-by-group/rec.arts.anime HOURLY

Toontalk *Ren & Stimpy*, the *Brothers Grunt*, and *Timon and Pumbaa* are the headliners here. While some of the animated characters are created for adults, the talk is often puerile: "Beavis is stupid and Butthead has some common sense. They used to be cool but they've gotten old." Whether you're transfixed by the *Lion King*, amused by *Animaniacs*, or conducting an academic investigation into the motif of cross-dressing in classic Warner Bros. cartoons—Bugs in the dress and Elmer at the altar—this conference is, in the words of breakfast cereal huckster Tony the Tiger, "grrrrreat!" ✓**AMERICA ONLINE**→ *keyword* cartoons DAILY

Comics

So who do we have left to breathlessly idolize? Rock stars

...like Michael Jackson? Olympic athletes...like Tonya Harding? Football players...like O. J. Simpson? Sheesh. Small wonder many of us look elsewhere for jolts of heroic inspiration—the pages of comic books, for instance. And now that comics have emerged from the murk of counterculture into the spotlight of pop acceptability—as proven by the proliferation of comics-discussion groups in Cyberspace—it's even possible to flash your fan credentials with pride. Which isn't to say that a comics fan is a comics fan is a comics fan: In the following groups, you'll meet and chat with hard-core Lycra-and-muscles devotees, enthusiasts of grim and gritty vigilantes, mutant aficionados, furry-animal lovers, underground-comix buffs, and the occasional *Archie* reader.

"Holy diversity, Batman!"

"Yes, Robin. Now shut up and read."

On the Net

Comicbooks (echo) The stars of this conference are the superstrong, the superfast, and the otherwise superendowed, ranging from Alan Moore's Watchmen to the X-Men, from the old Batman to the new Dark Knight. Whether analyzing Professor Charles Xavier's dream that "one day Homosapiens and Homosuperiors will coexist peacefully" or celebrating the naive exuberance of Mighty Morphins Power Rangers, the members of this (almost all-male) club lose themselves in the joy of four-color worlds with clear moral boundaries. ✓ **INTELEC** DAILY

Comics Once upon a time, the world of comics was limited to the likes of *Peanuts, Archie, Superman*. Now, the comics universe has expanded to include graphic novels, computer-generated comics, underground comics and even the lit-crit comics of Art Spiegelman's *Raw*. The WELL's Comics conference covers them all. Hard-core comics readers and casual fans convene to choose their favorite superhero, speculate on the future of classic characters, share opinions on explicit sex and violence. If there is a problem with the conference, it's that it favors the cognoscenti; if you don't know Dori Seda or Alan Moore, or you can't name all the X-Men, you may have a hard time keeping up. But if you follow *Love & Rockets*, and you're interested in a detailed discussion of the character who loses a prosthetic arm at the beginning of "Human Diastrophism," step right up. ✓ **WELL**→*g* comics DAILY

Comics Forum If rec.arts.comics. misc on Usenet is an all-night rantathon of the finest order (and this is meant with grudging respect and admiration), then Comics Forum on CompuServe is its more circumspect fraternal twin.

With a huge population of industry types (ranging from Neil "Sandman" Gaiman to writer James D. Hudnall to indie artist Kyle Baker) and an older, somewhat more discreet reader base, Comics Forum doesn't have RACM's wild flair.

Inside information

Still, there's a fair amount of inside information for fans: Recently Neil Gaiman announced the birth of his beautiful baby girl, Maddy, to a swirl of congratulations and J. Michael Straczynski (creator of TV's *Babylon Five*) fired a photon torpedo at comics journalist Gary Groth, complaining that Groth had misquoted something he'd said on the forum, and swearing never to return. Traffic on the forum is fairly heavy; subcategories on Industry and Collecting are especially well posted. ✓ **COMPUSERVE**→*go* comics→ Messages DAILY

Comics RoundTable Holy Magnitude, Batman! With more than 40 main categories, some 1,600 topics, and an average of 100 messages per subtopic, Comics RoundTable is more like the Library of Congress of Comic Books than like an ordinary online conference. Every comics publisher is represented, every comics character is assigned an individual subtopic—not just Superman and Batman, but Power Man, Hellstorm, Venom, She-Hulk, Flaming Carrot, and Sludge, to name just a few.

Whether you're keeping track of the plot of the latest *Barb Wire* or wondering about the origin of the *Golden Age Green Lantern*, this board will satisfy your appetite. Check out the real-time conference schedule on the RoundTable's opening screen for live discussions in the evening. ✓**GENIE**→*keyword* comics→Comics Bulletin Board *or* Comics Real-Time Conference DAILY/LIVE

Comix No single genre dominates Comix: Fans of underground comix, *Vertigo*, manga and, yes, even the tights-wearing crime fighters are here. Buzz about the next issue of your favorite comic, get the industry's inside dirt from professional writers and illustrators, or get the scoop on works in progress. Comix also throws great face-to-face parties and swap meets in the New York City area. ✓**ECHO**→*j* comix DAILY

rec.arts.comics.misc (ng) Rant city, baby. This is a gathering ground for mavens and manifesto-writers whose seething obsession is sequential art, graphic novels, and similar euphemistic synonyms for comic books. It's one of the largest groups on Usenet, and growing every day—growing so fast, in fact, that it has spawned secondary groups, such as rec.arts.comics.

xbooks, about Marvel Comics' merry mutant brigade, the X-Men, and their 500 associated hero teams; alt.comics.batman (the Darknight Detective), alt.comics.superman (the Man of Steel, post-resurrection), alt.comics.alternative (underground and indie stuff), alt.comics.elfquest (Roger and Wendy Pini's epic tale of tiny, pointy-eared critters dealing with economy-size angst), rec.arts.comics.info, rec.arts.comics.marketplace, and rec.arts.comics.strips.

Fanboys

The main group gets upwards of 300 posts a day: unlike most Usenet communities, RACM is vertically integrated, which means that, in addition to a roiling mass of fanboys (and a very few fangirls), there are owners of comic-book shops, indie 'zine publishers, fan-convention organizers and a few professional artists and writers who read RACM regularly.

One notable celebriposter is Peter A. David, perhaps the most successful comic-book writer of modern times, plotter of *Spider-man 2099* and *The Incredible Hulk*, among other series. Have a theory about how one of your fave heroes will die, be crippled, or come out of the closet? Post it to the Net and watch discussion accrete to it like iron filings to a magnet. Some of the responses will be hostile—keep your asbestos long johns on—but others will be lyrical and imaginative.

Canny references

A densely literate work like *Sandman* has had some fans poring over issues with source material, ranging from Frazer's *The Golden Bough* to the Dead Sea Scrolls, as they try to find all of Neil Gaiman's canny references.

Mainstream superhero works

tend to generate long threads where vets will reminisce about the "good old days, when Purple Penguin was a Real Hero," or argue about RACM's greatest bogeymen.

Reviews

Retailers and first-in-line fans post advance reviews of what to buy and what to avoid. Dave Van Domelen is perhaps the most prolific review generator—his "Rants" regarding different series and his "Timed Release Capsules" generally cover the spectrum from underground to *Archie*.

Here, knowledge of abstruse trivia equals status—gender is not an issue. Be prepared to read this group nightly if you wish to keep up. ✓**USENET** *FAQ:* ✓**INTERNET**→*ftp* rtfm.mit.edu→ anonymous→<your email address> →/pub/usenet-by-group/news.answers/comics/faq→part* DAILY

> "Recently Neil Gaiman announced the birth of his beautiful baby girl, Maddy, to a swirl of congratulations and J. Michael Straczynski (creator of TV's *Babylon Five*) fired a photon torpedo at comics journalist Gary Groth."

AnimeMUCK

Admit it. You've always wanted to wear a white helmet

and drive the Mach 5, burn rubber on poorly drawn highways with your gal Trixie at your side and your little brother Spridle in the trunk. You've always wished you could talk out of sync with your lips, and you dream of having eyes the size of disco balls and twice as sparkly. Which is to say, like a burgeoning number of other apparently normal human beings, you want to be a Japanese animation character. And now—you can. AnimeMUCK is a little more than two years old, and it's grown from being a haven for a small group of real-life anime-enthusiast friends into a huge and thriving virtual community, with a nighttime average of 25 to 50 players online. In AnimeMUCK, you can visit the pomo plasteel towers of MegaTokyo and Macross City, or the wacky suburban chaos of Orange Road and Ranmaland, and you'll meet characters from a hundred different anime series.

Things to do

As in most MUCKs/MUSHs/MUSEs/MOOs, you can't score points on AnimeMUCK, you can't kill anything (except in jest), and

Character—downloaded from Compu-Serve's Graphics Plus Forum.

you can't "win." The only objects here are to create, role-play, and socialize—and not necessarily in that order. Players whose primary goal is to role-play try to stay "IC" (in character) at all times; those seeking just to socialize spend most of their time chatting "OOC" (out of character) about anime-related topics or, more often, about nothing at all.

At night, many characters congregate in ABCB, the central chat area, where the socially inclined can surf through the spam of several dozen characters talking at once, or duck into a private booth with a friend. If you're looking for more structure than that, there are a number of organized activities on the MUCK.

A demon named Tora has organized a Society of Villains, complete with fortresslike headquarters, and has been spurring on the creation of tinyplots (or @plots).

If you're interested in role-playing and would like to be a Devious Bad Guy, look for him. (Heroic Good Guys in training should look for Youshou, bumbling leader of the MUCK Heroez, instead.) A recent @plot involved a fairy-gone-bad named Pfil, who set fires and slayed innocents in the Orange Road area. Beware of her killer roaches.

For those of a less violent inclination, a Miss AnimeMUCK pageant is also in the works, with contestants from several dozen series competing in heated categories ranging from Sailor Suit (being cute in a traditional Japanese schoolgirl uniform) to trivia to Armed and Sexy (posing with weapons, natch). Or you could just ogle.

> "AnimeMUCK has an innocent prudery about itself, and those who stray beyond certain prescribed boundaries (nuzzling in public is okay) are labled H—*hentai*, or perverted. But...people do get married, with full ceremonies presided over by MUCK wizards."

As for going beyond ogling, the question may spring to mind: Is there sex on the MUCK? That is to say, tinysex—fast-paced interactive erotica. The answer? Probably, but not in public. Like most anime, AnimeMUCK has an innocent prudery about itself, and those who stray beyond certain prescribed boundaries (nuzzling in public is okay) are labled H—*hentai*, or perverted.

But…people do get married, with full ceremonies presided over by MUCK wizards or other notables. As for what couples do behind closed doors?—who knows?

Places to go

For those whose motive is creativity, AnimeMUCK is like a living gallery for their works: from programming marvels like the Mecha Battle Arena (a working giant robot combat game—pilot your own metallic monstrosity against player opponents!) and the Dojo (like the Mecha Arena, only focusing on hand-to-hand combat), to the beautifully described landscapes of classic anime like Hayao Miyazaki's My Neighbor Totoro and Laputa: Castle in the Sky, to fun and vaguely insane hangouts of diverse flavors run by proprietors with imagination and a sense of humor.

The Panda Palace is an immense structure that includes a "working" ballroom (where you can train your way up to grandmaster quality), a café, and rooms for 100 characters. A not-quite-operational room that allows characters to play a modified, anime version of the board game Clue should be finished any day now, as soon as the proprietor, in his words, "gets a clue." Mikado's skating rink lets you do everything but bash opponents in the knees.

People to know

The primary wizard of Ani-

meMUCK is Priss. She's somewhat irascible but basically benevolent—not the first person to go to if you have a newbie problem.

If you need help describing yourself or finding a home, look for the Guest Patrol instead (if you sit around long enough in the Anime Bookstore, where you'll arrive if you sign on as a guest, one will probably find you).

Confucius, a professor at the MUCK's university and the owner of a computer store in Ranmaland, is a good person to seek out as well—he's both friendly and knowledgeable. By and large,

however, all of AnimeMUCK's players are affable and helpful; many have a wicked sense of humor and a decided overfondness for puns.

If you're an anime fan, AnimeMUCK is the fulfillment of a surreal fantasy. If you're not, it might be confusing and weird, but should be enjoyable nevertheless.

One thing to remember: The old saw about only one out of ten MU* female characters being real-life women is even more true here. Don't get in over your head. **⁄INTERNET**→*telnet* tcp.com 2035→connect guest guest

---

ANIME VOCABULARY

A.D. Vision: An English-language anime company that concentrates on violent and soft-core-pornographic releases.

AnimEigo: An anime company. [The owner, Robert Woodhead, is a regular poster to the newsgroup rec.arts.anime (RAA).]

Baka: Japanese for *idiot*.

Dubbed: On RAA, usually considered a synonym for *destroyed*.

Hentai (or H, or etchi): Japanese for perverted or pornographic.

Idol: Idolsinger—one of the horde of indistinguishable girlpop stars who rise and fall in Japan's music industry in the space of a year.

Kawaii: Japanese for *cute*.

Macek: Carl Macek, creator of Robotech, owner of Streamline Pictures, and generally despised bête noire of anime fandom.

Streamline: Macek's company, which releases re-edited and dubbed (often horrendously) productions, and which has a spoken policy of being antifan.

Otaku: An anime fan with no other life.

Seiyuu: Japanese for voice actor.

Subbed: Subtitled.

Viz: Publisher of translated *manga* (Japanese comics) and of Animerica, the largest anime fan magazine in the country.

Sports

So you just saw the most incredible catch—Irving Fryar extended over the defender

and stabbing the passing football with one hand. Or maybe it was Shaq muscling into the paint, or Gretzky slapping a shot on goal. Whatever the case, it was one of those defining sports moments, like Bobby Thompson's pennant-clinching homer, and you need to talk to someone about it. So what should you do? Well, call your brother. Call your friends. And then take your enthusiasm to the Net.

As in other media, online sports coverage is dominated by the big games—pro baseball, pro football, pro basketball, and pro hockey. This is most apparent in the array of Usenet newsgroups devoted to individual baseball and football franchises: Whether you want to marvel over the latest Frank Thomas blast (**alt.sports. baseball.chi-whitesox**) or detail Randall Cunningham's injury-plagued past (**alt.sports.football. pro.phila-eagles**), you'll find a ready-made community of like-minded fans.

Stream of chatter

Newsgroups carry scores and news—who got drafted, who got cut, who got injured—but what really keeps them alive is the constant stream of chatter. Bills fans love to make excuses for their always-a-bridesmaid franchise. Indians faithful are content to reprise their half-century lament. The opinions are fast and furious—and unsubstantiated—in the best tra-

Nancy Kerrigan—downloaded from ftp.sunet.se.

dition of sports commentary. "Oscar Robertson is clearly the best ever at his position." "Mike Keenan should be drawn and quartered!" "Mark my words, San Diego faithful, Tony Gwynn will hit .400, and we will all be able to say we saw it happen."

Fanatical fans

While newsgroups are a good starting point, the most fanatical of fans often find their way to mailing lists. On the L.A. Raiders list, hard-core backers of the silver-and-black rhapsodize over the glory days of Ken Stabler and Jesse Hester. And one beleaguered Seattle man uses the Mariners list to lament his team's ongoing mediocrity—"It is hard to follow a team that has been playing as badly as they have this year." Mailing lists

> "You can almost hear the grain of the voices— Golden Age throwbacks showing off their geezer burn with talk of Rogers Hornsby and Bob Feller, wide-eyed kids marveling over Griffey."

don't cover only the major sports; anyone who is still feeling a touch of World Cup fever will get a kick out of the U.S. soccer mailing list, where Alexi Lalas is apotheosized daily.

Other sports

Usenet sports coverage puts new teeth on an old saw—the best things in life are free. But much of the best sports chat belongs to commercial services like AOL's Grandstand, CompuServe's Sports Forum, and Genie's Sports Forum. In addition to extensive discussion of the big four, Grandstand has message boards for a number of other sports, including golf (On the Green), auto racing (In the Pits), and boxing/wrestling (Squared Circle); CompuServe and GEnie offer similar topics. Chat here is slightly more general than on Usenet, and postings tend to be longer.

On Grandstand's baseball message board, for instance, you can almost hear the grain of the voices—Golden Age throwbacks showing off their geezer burn with talk of Rogers Hornsby and Bob Feller, wide-eyed kids marveling over Griffey and Thomas and Belle. And while there aren't any sensual special effects—the crack of the bat on the ball, the thwack of the stick on the puck—it hardly matters. Like the best chat, sports forums are driven, ultimately, by human passion.

On the Net

Across the board

The Grandstand From boxing to baseball, the forum has several sports message boards and live chat. ✓**AMERICA ONLINE**→*keyword* grandstand

Sports (echo) Sports discussion. ✓**SMARTNET**

Sports (echo) Open to all sports discussions. ✓**RELAYNET**

Sports (echo) Chat about sports. ✓**FIDONET**

Sports BB Any and all professional sports discussed. ✓**PRODIGY**→*jump* sports bb

Sports Forum Includes message boards for all professional and many amateur sports. ✓**COMPUSERVE**→*go* sports

Sports RoundTable Categories for all professional and many participatory sports. ✓**GENIE**→*keyword* sports

Baseball

rec.sport.baseball (ng) Baseball discussion. ✓**USENET**

Baseball teams

alt.sports.baseball.atlanta-braves (ng) Discuss the Atlanta Braves. ✓**USENET**

alt.sports.baseball.balt-orioles (ng) Chat about the Baltimore Orioles. ✓**USENET**

alt.sports.baseball.bos-red sox (ng) A forum for Boston Red Sox fans. ✓**USENET**

Bosox Mailing list (ml) A forum for talking about the Boston Red Sox. ✓**INTERNET**→*email* bosox-request@world.std.com ✍ *Write a request*

alt.sports.baseball.calif-angels (ng) Discuss the California Angels. ✓**USENET**

alt.sports.baseball.chicago-

cubs (ng) Chat about the Chicago Cubs. ✓**USENET**

alt.sports.baseball.chi-white sox (ng) For Chicago White Sox fans. ✓**USENET**

alt.sports.baseball.cinci-reds (ng) Discuss the Cincinnati Reds. ✓**USENET**

Cincinnati Reds Mailing List (ml) For Cincinnati Reds fans. ✓**INTERNET**→*email* listserv@miamiu.acs.muohio.edu ✍ *Type in message body:* subscribe cintired <your full name>

alt.sports.baseball.cleve-indians (ng) Stay in touch with other Cleveland Indians fans. ✓**USENET**

alt.sports.baseball.col-rockies (ng) Discuss the Colorado Rockies team. ✓**USENET**

alt.sports.baseball.detroit-tigers (ng) For Detroit Tigers fans. ✓**USENET**

alt.sports.baseball.fla-marlins (ng) For fans of the Florida Marlins. ✓**USENET**

alt.sports.baseball.houston-astros (ng) Chat about the Houston Astros. ✓**USENET**

alt.sports.baseball.kc-royals (ng) Discuss the Kansas City Royals. ✓**USENET**

alt.sports.baseball.la-dodgers (ng) Chat with other Dodgers fans. ✓**USENET**

alt.sports.baseball.mke-brewers (ng) For fans of the Milwaukee Brewers. ✓**USENET**

alt.sports.baseball.mn-twins (ng) Chat about the Minnesota

Twins. ✓**USENET**

alt.sports.baseball.montreal-expos (ng) Discuss the Montreal Expos. ✓**USENET**

alt.sports.baseball.ny-mets (ng) Chat about the New York Mets. ✓**USENET**

New York Mets mailing list (ml) For New York Mets fans. ✓**INTERNET**→*email* mets-request @ccliff.com ✍ *Type in subject line:* subscribe

alt.sports.baseball.ny-yankees (ng) For New York Yankees fans. ✓**USENET**

alt.sports.baseball.oakland-as (ng) For fans of the Oakland A's. ✓**USENET**

Oakland Athletics Mailing List (ml) More Oakland A's discussion. ✓**INTERNET**→*email* athletics-request@maredsous.eng.sun.com ✍ *Write a request*

alt.sports.baseball.phila-phillies (ng) Chat about the Philadelphia Phillies. ✓**USENET**

alt.sports.baseball.pitt-pirates (ng) Discuss the Pittsburgh Pirates. ✓**USENET**

Pittsburgh Pirates (ml) More Pirates talk. ✓**INTERNET**→*email* pirates-request@cats.ucsc.edu ✍ *Write a request*

alt.sports.baseball.sd-padres (ng) For San Diego Padres fans. ✓**USENET**

alt.sports.baseball.sf-giants (ng) Discuss the San Francisco Giants. ✓**USENET**

Giants Baseball Chat (ml) More S.F. Giants discussion. ✓**IN-TERNET**→*email* listproc@medraut. apple.com ✍ *Type in message body:* subscribe baseball-chat <your full name>

alt.sports.baseball.sea-mariners (ng) Chat with other Seattle Mariners fans. ✓**USENET**

alt.sports.baseball.stl-cardinals (ng) For St. Louis Cardinals fans. ✓**USENET**

alt.sports.baseball.texas-rangers (ng) Discuss the Texas Rangers. ✓**USENET**

alt.sports.baseball.tor-blue jays (ng) Chat about the Toronto Blue Jays. ✓**USENET**

Toronto Blue Jays Mailing List For fans of the Toronto Blue Jays. ✓**INTERNET**→*email* jays-request@hivnet.ubc.ca ✍ *Write a request*

Basketball

#nba Live basketball chat. ✓**IN-TERNET**→*irc* /channel #nba

rec.sport.basketball.misc (ng) For any basketball-related topics. ✓**USENET**

rec.sport.basketball.pro (ng) Discuss NBA play. ✓**USENET**

Basketball teams

alt.sports.basketball.nba.at lanta-hawks (ng) Chat with other Atlanta Hawks fans. ✓**USE-NET**

Boston Celtics Mailing List (ml) Discuss the Boston Celtics. ✓**INTERNET**→*email* majordomo@ cisco.com ✍ *Type in message body:* subscribe celtics

alt.sports.basketball.nba.cha

r-hornets (ng) Chat with other Charlotte Hornets fans. ✓**USENET**

alt.sports.basketball.nba.chi cago-bulls (ng) For Chicago Bulls fans. ✓**USENET**

alt.sports.basketball.nba.de nver-nuggets (ng) Discuss the Denver Nuggets. ✓**USENET**

alt.sports.basketball.nba.ho u-rockets (ng) For fans of the Houston Rockets. ✓**USENET**

Indiana Pacers Mailing List (ml) A forum for discussing the Indiana Pacers. ✓**INTERNET**→*email* pacers-request@storm.cadcam. iupui.edu ✍ *Write a request*

alt.sports.basketball.nba.la-lakers (ng) Discuss the Los Angeles Lakers. ✓**USENET**

alt.sports.basketball.nba.mi ami-heat (ng) For fans of the Miami Heat. ✓**USENET**

alt.sports.basketball.nba.mn -wolves (ng) Discuss the Minnesota Timberwolves. ✓**USENET**

alt.sports.basketball.nba.nj-nets (ng) Chat with other fans of the New Jersey Nets. ✓**USENET**

alt.sports.basketball.pro.ny-knicks (ng) For fans of the New York Knicks. ✓**USENET**

alt.sports.basketball.nba.or lando-magic (ng) Chat about the Orlando Magic. ✓**USENET**

Orlando Magic Mailing List (ml) More discussion about the Orlando Magic. ✓**INTERNET**→*email* orlmagic-request@peti.gen.de ✍ *Type in message body:* add

alt.sports.basketball.nba.ph x-suns (ng) Discuss the Phoenix

Suns. ✓**USENET**

Portland Trailblazers Mailing List (ml) For Trailblazers fans. ✓**INTERNET**→*email* blazers-request@cpac.washington.edu ✍ *Write a request*

Seattle Supersonics Mailing List (ml) Chat with other Supersonics fans. ✓**INTERNET**→*email* gilla@carson.u.washington.edu ✍ *Write a request*

alt.sports.basketball.nba.utah-jazz (ng) Discuss the Utah Jazz. ✓**USENET**

alt.sports.basketball.nba.wash-bullets (ng) Discuss the Washington Bullets. ✓**USENET**

Cricket

#cricket Discuss cricket games in progress. ✓**INTERNET**→*irc* /channel #cricket

Football

NFL (echo) Football talk. ✓**FIDONET**

rec.sport.football.misc (ng) For any football discussions. ✓**USENET**

rec.sport.football.pro (ng) NFL talk. ✓**USENET**

Football teams

alt.sports.football.pro.atl-falcons (ng) For Atlanta Falcons fans. ✓**USENET**

Buffalo Bills Mailing List (ml) Discuss the Buffalo Bills. ✓**INTERNET**→*email* buffalo-bills-request@netcom.com ✍ *Write a request*

alt.sports.football.pro.car-panthers (ng) Chat with other

Magic Johnson—downloaded from America Online's Mac Graphics & CAD Forum.

Panthers fans. ✓**USENET**

alt.sports.football.pro.chicago-bears (ng) Discuss the Chicago Bears. ✓**USENET**

alt.sports.football.pro.cinci-bengals (ng) Chat with other fans of the Cincinnati Bengals. ✓**USENET**

Cincinnati Bengals Mailing List (ml) More Bengals discussion. ✓**INTERNET**→*email* listserv@miamiu.acs.muohio.edu ✍ *Type in message body:* subscribe cinbengl <your full name>

alt.sports.football.pro.cleve-browns (ng) Discuss the Cleveland Browns. ✓**USENET**

alt.sports.football.pro.dal-las-cowboys (ng) For Dallas Cowboys fans. ✓**USENET**

alt.sports.football.pro.den-ver-broncos (ng) Fans discuss the Broncos. ✓**USENET**

Denver Broncos Mailing List (ml) More Broncos chat. ✓**INTER-NET**→*email* listserv@lists.colorado.edu ✍ *Type in message body:* subscribe broncolist

alt.sports.football.pro.de-troit-lions (ng) For fans of the Detroit Lions. ✓**USENET**

Detroit Lions Mailing List (ml) More Lions discussion. ✓**INTERNET**→*email* shows@mit.edu ✍ *Write a request*

alt.sports.football.pro.gb-packers (ng) Discussion about the Green Bay Packers. ✓**USENET**

Green Bay Packers Mailing List (ml) More Packers talk. ✓**INTERNET**→*email* packers-request@fullfeed.com ✍ *Write a request*

alt.sports.football.pro.hous-ton-oilers (ng) Discuss the Houston Oilers. ✓**USENET**

alt.sports.football.pro.indy-colts (ng) Chat with other Indianapolis Colts fans. ✓**USENET**

Indianapolis Colts Mailing List (ml) More Colts discussion.

Sports Fans

✓ INTERNET→*email* colts-request@storm.cadcam.iupui.edu ✍ *Write a request*

alt.sports.football.pro.jville-jaguars (ng) For Jacksonville Jaguars fans. ✓ **USENET**

alt.sports.football.pro.kc-chiefs (ng) Talk with other fans of the Kansas City Chiefs. ✓ **USENET**

Kansas City Chiefs Mailing List (ml) More Chiefs discussion. ✓ INTERNET→*email* chiefs-request@mccall.com ✍ *Write a request*

alt.sports.football.pro.la-raiders (ng) For L.A. Raiders fans. ✓ **USENET**

Los Angeles Raiders Mailing List (ml) More Raiders discussion. ✓ INTERNET→*email* majordomo@super.org ✍ *Type in message body:* subscribe raiders

alt.sports.football.pro.la-rams (ng) For L.A. Rams fans. ✓ **USENET**

Los Angeles Rams Mailing List (ml) More discussion about the Rams. ✓ INTERNET→*email* eboltz@acoustica.mrd.bldrdoc.gov ✍ *Write a request*

alt.sports.football.pro.miami-dolphins (ng) For fans of the Miami Dolphins. ✓ **USENET**

Minnesota Vikings Mailing List (ml) Discuss the Minnesota Vikings. ✓ INTERNET→Deborah.Greene@corp.sun.com ✍ *Write a request*

alt.sports.football.pro.ne-patriots (ng) Discussion about the New England Patriots. ✓ **USENET**

New England Patriots Mailing List (ml) More Patriots dis-

cussion. ✓ INTERNET→*email* majordomo@world.std.com ✍ *Type in message body:* subscribe patriots

alt.sports.football.pro.ny-giants (ng) For fans of the New York Giants. ✓ **USENET**

alt.sports.football.pro.ny-jets (ng) Discuss the New York Jets. ✓ **USENET**

Philadelphia Eagles Mailing List (ml) For fans of the Philadelphia Eagles. ✓ INTERNET→*email* rsmith@sol.cms.uncwil.edu ✍ *Write a request*

alt.sports.football.pro.phoe-cardinals (ng) Chat with other fans of the Phoenix Cardinals. ✓ **USENET**

alt.sports.football.pro.pitt-steelers (ng) For Pittsburgh Steelers fans. ✓ **USENET**

Pittsburgh Steelers Mailing List (ml) More Steelers discussion. ✓ INTERNET→*email* steelers-list-request@andrew.cmu.edu ✍ *Write a request*

alt.sports.football.pro.sd-chargers (ng) Discuss the San Diego Chargers. ✓ **USENET**

San Diego Chargers Mailing List (ml) More Chargers discussion. ✓ INTERNET→*email* bolt-backers-request@andrew.cmu.edu ✍ *Write a request*

alt.sports.football.pro.sf-49ers (ng) Discuss football with other San Francisco 49ers fans. ✓ **USENET**

alt.sports.football.pro.sea-seahawks (ng) Chat about the Seahawks. ✓ **USENET**

alt.sports.football.pro.tam

pabay-bucs (ng) For fans of the Tampa Bay Buckaneers. ✓ **USENET**

alt.sports.football.pro.wash-redskins (ng) Discuss the Washington Redskins. ✓ **USENET**

Hockey

hockey-chat (ml) General hockey discussion. ✓ INTERNET→*email* listproc@medraut.apple.com ✍ *Type in message body:* subscribe hockey-chat <your full name>

Hockey-L (ml) All hockey topics welcome. ✓ INTERNET→*email* listserv@maine.maine.edu ✍ *Type in message body:* subscribe hockey-l <your full name>

rec.sport.hockey (ng) Forum for hockey discussions and news. ✓ **USENET**

Hockey teams

alt.sports.hockey.nhl.boston-bruins (ng) For Boston Bruins fans. ✓ **USENET**

Boston Bruins Mailing List (ml) More Bruins discussion. ✓ INTERNET→*email* majordomo@terrapin.umd.edu ✍ *Type in message body:* subscribe bruins

alt.sports.hockey.nhl.buffalo-sabres (ng) For fans of the Buffalo Sabres. ✓ **USENET**

Buffalo Sabres Mailing List (ml) More Sabres discussion. ✓ INTERNET→*email* sabres-request@potter.csh.rit.edu ✍ *Write a request* subscribe

Calgary Flames Mailing List (ml) Discuss the Calgary Flames. ✓ INTERNET→*email* flamesinfo@turq.b8.ingr.com ✍ *Write a request*

alt.sports.hockey.nhl.chi-

blackhawks (ng) For fans of the Chicago Black Hawks. ✓USENET

alt.sports.hockey.nhl.dallas-stars (ng) Discussions about the Dallas Stars. ✓USENET

Dallas Stars mailing List (ml) More Dallas Stars. ✓INTERNET→ *email* hamlet@u.washington.edu ✍ *Type in subject line:* DSTARS

Detroit Redwings Mailing List (ml) List for discussing the Detroit Red Wings. ✓INTERNET→*email* listserv@msu.edu ✍ *Type in message body:* subscribe redwing <your full name>

alt.sports.hockey.nhl.hford-whalers (ng) For fans of the Hartford Whalers. ✓USENET

Hartford Whalers Mailing List (ml) More Whalers chat. ✓INTERNET→*email* whalers-request@access.digex.net ✍ *Type in subject line:* subscribe

alt.sports.hockey.nhl.la-kings (ng) Discuss the L.A. Kings. ✓USENET

Los Angeles Kings Mailing List (ml) More Kings discussion. ✓INTERNET→*email* majordomo@lists.stanford.edu ✍ *Type in message body:* subscribe kings

Montreal Canadiens Mailing List (ml) For fans of the Montreal Canadiens. ✓INTERNET→*email* habs-request@janus.sdsu.edu ✍ *Write a request*

alt.sports.hockey.nhl.nj-devils (ng) Discuss the New Jersey Devils. ✓USENET

alt.sports.hockey.nhl.ny-islanders (ng) Discussion about the New York Islanders. ✓USENET
New York Islanders Mailing

List More Islanders discussion. ✓INTERNET→*email* dss2k@virginia.edu ✍ *Write a request*

alt.sports.hockey.nhl.ny-rangers (ng) For fans of the New York Rangers. ✓USENET

New York Rangers Mailing List (ml) More Rangers discussion. ✓INTERNET→*email* kkeller@nomad.sas.upenn.edu ✍ *Write a request*

alt.sports.hockey.nhl.phila-flyers (ng) For fans of the Philadelphia Flyers. ✓USENET

Philadelphia Flyers Mailing List (ml) More Flyers discussion. ✓INTERNET→*email* seth@hos1cad.att.com ✍ *Write a request*

alt.sports.hockey.nhl.pitt-penguins (ng) Discuss the Pittsburgh Penguins. ✓USENET

Pittsburgh Penguins Mailing List (ml) More Penguins discussion. ✓INTERNET→*email* gp2f@andrew.cmu.edu ✍ *Write a request*

alt.sports.hockey.nhl.que-nordiques (ng) For fans of the Quebec Nordiques. ✓USENET

Quebec Nordiques Mailing List (ml) More Nordiques discussion. ✓INTERNET→*email* nords-request@badaboum.ulaval.ca ✍ *Write a request*

alt.sports.hockey.nhl.sj-sharks (ng) Discuss the San Jose Sharks. ✓USENET

San Jose Sharks Mailing List (ml) More Sharks talk. ✓INTERNET→*email* listproc@medraut.apple.com ✍ *Type in message body:* subscribe sharks-chat <your full name>

St. Louis Blues Mailing List

(ml) Discuss the St. Louis Blues. ✓INTERNET→*email* blues@medicine.wustl.edu ✍ *Write a request*

alt.sports.hockey.nhl.tor-mapleleafs (ng) For fans of the Toronto Maple Leafs. ✓USENET

Vancouver Canucks (ml) Canucks chat. ✓INTERNET→ *email* boey@sfu.ca ✍ *Write a request*

alt.sports.hockey.nhl.vanc-canucks (ng) More chat about the Canucks. ✓USENET

alt.sports.hockey.nhl.wash-capitals (ng) For fans of the Washington Capitals. ✓USENET

Washington Capitals (ml) More chat about the Capitals. ✓INTERNET→*email* majordomo@terrapin.umd.edu ✍ *Write a request* subscribe capitals

alt.sports.hockey.nhl.win nipeg-jets (ng) Discussion about the Winnipeg Jets. ✓USENET

Skating

Skating (ml) Discuss both amateur and professional skating. ✓INTERNET→*email* listserv@umab.umd.edu ✍ *Type in message body:* subscribe skating <your full name>

Soccer

#soccer For soccer talk. ✓INTERNET→*irc* #soccer

Soccer-L (ml) For soccer fans. ✓INTERNET→*email* listserv@ukcc.uky.edu ✍ *Type in message body:* subscribe soccer-l <your full name>

US Soccer (ml) Discuss the U.S. soccer team. ✓INTERNET→*email* us-soccer-request@lermai.lerctr.org ✍ *Write a request*

Part 3

On The Fringe

Bizarre humor

The Net's not all fun and games. There are a lot of serious,

hard working volunteers using the Net to organize and fight for their deepest, most closely held beliefs. To wit: **alt.tv.dinosaurs.barney.die. die.die**, so concerned that the possibility of actually taking up arms is regularly voiced; **alt.devilbunnies**, where vigilant defenders of humanity protect us all from the threat of killer rabbits; and **alt.elvis.king**, a group so pure that Graceland memorabilia is denounced as the handiwork of Beelzebub.

On the Net

alt.aol-sucks (ng) When America Online added Usenet access to its services, thousands of newbies flooded in. In a matter of weeks, Usenet posts from aol.com outnumbered posts from any other domain. And AOLers (known on this newsgroup as "AOLusers"), like all newbies, committed gaffes. The AOL company is bashed here for its corporate paranoia, school-marmish chiding ("We would like to remind you that our Terms of Service prohibit vulgar or sexually oriented language…"), and time-wasting and fee-escalating interface. AOLers themselves are mocked as point-and-click consumers too out of it to know what they're missing, or too Pollyanna-ish to protest. If you're logging on from AOL itself, this newsgroup has the euphemistic name "Flames

Kibo—downloaded from http://www. maths.tcd.ie/pub/images/wee/sindex.html.

and Complaints About America Online." ✓**USENET** DAILY

alt.devilbunnies (ng) A fantasy realm where users interactively construct a new reality online. "Fudds"—self-apppointed defenders of humanity—hunt down bloodthirsty rabbits worldwide. "We are the only thing that stands between a disbelieving human race and horrible, inescapable, fluffy doom," reads the FAQ. A huge, arcane lore has grown up around the battles, the participants and their tribes, and their technology (a "cuteness geometer"?). Patience and a high tolerance for nonsense are required for participation in this highly social environment. Once you're initiated, however, you're free to steer the action in pretty much any direction your fantasy might roam. ✓**USENET** *FAQ:* ✓**INTERNET**→*ftp* rtfm.mit.edu→ anonymous→<your email address> →/pub/usenet-by-group/alt. answers/devilbunnies-faq→part1 <and> part2 DAILY

alt.elvis.king (ng) From Graceland West, in reply to a request for an Elvis fanclub mailing address: "Death to All Drooling Zombie Memorabilia Freakazoid Elvis Fans! Take that 'fan' shit elsewhere, please. This is the place where Elvis's quasi-evil pirate anti-Graceland money-grubbing scientology, Inc., minions are hanging, examining important questions like: 'If The King blows out the seat of his jumpsuit in deep space with a King-sized fart, does it make any sound, and what does it smell like here on Earth?' Let's celebrate E as The King, and not just a cash cow for latter-day wannabe Col. Parkers. This opinion NOT endorsed by Elvis Presley Enterprises, Graceland, Lisa Marie, Lucky 'Michael' Jackson, or L. Ron Hubbard. Elvis (The King) however endorses it wholeheartedly." Much cross-posting to the like-minded alt.elvis.sighting. ✓**USENET** WEEKLY

alt.flame (ng) Postadolescents spew hate in Cyberspace. The group also cultivates a Harvard-Yale-type rivalry with alt.bigfoot, and periodically the two newsgroups invade each other. Pyrrhus never had it so bad. Drop by if you feel the need to call someone stupid. Be careful not to respond

> **"We are the only thing that stands between a disbelieving human race and horrible, inescapable, fluffy doom."**

Bizarre humor On the Fringe

to any posts whose follow-up has been set to misc.test. ✓**USENET** HOURLY

alt.folklore.urban (ng) Did you know Grand Central station is radioactive? Have you heard about the latest fad in Japan—hydrogenated beer, which is green and yields Hindenburgesque inflammable burps? If you enjoy walking the fine line between entertainment and deceit—a practice known on alt.folklore.urban as "trolling"—you will enjoy this newsgroup. Unfortunately, several months ago, James "Kibo" Parry outlawed trolling on a.f.u., and ever since then, the only legends posted here are those whose 'voracity' (no, it is spelled that way) has been confirmed. For example: The more milk you drink, the more mucus your body produces. Rumor (what else) has it that Douglas Adams is a devotee. No smileys allowed. ✓**USENET** *FAQ:* ✓**INTERNET**→*ftp* rtfm.mit.edu→ anonymous→<your email address> →/pub/usenet-by-hierarchy/alt/ folklore/urban DAILY

alt.religion.kibology (ng) A lot of people here claim to look exactly like Penn Jillette. They have important discussions about Darth Vader's middle name ("Space-In"?), compete for longest .sig file, and cross-post to the newsgroup alt.zen, which does not exist. Ludwig Plutonium lectures on the Clown Period of math history. With fearful stamina, James "Kibo" Parry spoofs newbies, e-capitalists, and trekkies. His favorite victims are hapless, serious readers who correct his deliberate errors. A claque of mathematicians, physicists, and pop-culture mavens trail in Kibo's wake, unhelpfully explicating his allusions (Kibo meant to write "Higgs bosom," not "Higgs boson"). Given

the Internet's neither-fish-nor-fowl status as a mass medium, Kibo may either be the most undervalued or the most overplayed comic genius of the late second millennium. ✓**USENET** HOURLY

alt.slack (ng) Not a Generation X thing. Not a Texas art-film thing. Here the concept of slack is a little more, well, organized. Organized into a religion, in fact: the Church of the SubGenius. We can't tell you what slack is, exactly, because we've resisted indoctrination and haven't sent any money to Rev. J. R. "Bob" Dobbs. We do know that your entire life, the Conspiracy has been trying to take slack away from you, and "Bob" will help you get it back. Act now, because in 1998 the world will end and you will want to be on the flying saucers, not left earthbound with all the "pinks." The churchgoers here have a weakness for cascades—series of one-line messages posted in quick succession—and for quoting the Goon Show and They Might Be Giants. ✓**USENET** DAILY

alt.tasteless (ng) Yes, they did use an alcohol swab on John Wayne Gacy when he was lethally injected. Share your fantasies of Beaker getting raped by Gonzo. Inflict hasenpfeffer/roadkill recipes on the squeamish owners of rec.pets.rabbits. The FAQ explains the difference between an ampallang and an apadravya, records that Gandhi drank his own pee, and enlists support in a crusade to restore the word *choad* to modern English. An annual "Tasteless Secret Santa" gift exchange ties the community (on average, 27 years old and 200 pounds) together. As one poster, about to lose Net access, exclaimed, "You're like the inbred family I never had." ✓**USENET** *FAQ:* ✓**INTERNET**→*ftp* rtfm.mit.edu→

anonymous→<your email address> →/pub/usenet-by-hierarchy/alt/ tasteless→Welcome_to_alt.tasteless!_(Monthly_Posting) HOURLY

alt.tv.dinosaurs.barney.die. die.die (ng) According to the Jihad, a group sworn to the destruction of Barney, his message of love is an insidious media virus. A place to draw up battle plans. ✓**USENET** WEEKLY

CYBERNOTES

"A rapidly-reproducing new computer virus was recently discovered by technicians at NASA. It is already quite prevalent on major networks, and has attached itself to many programs people have downloaded. The virus can be spotted by looking for the infected file which is always named 'READ.ME.' On one PC we checked, almost every downloaded program came with a 'READ.ME'! If you own any software with a file named 'READ.ME,' these files could give you a COLD, the FLU, or OTHER DANGEROUS DISEASE if you USE, TOUCH, or LOOK AT THEM. The only way to cure this infection is to send ALL YOUR MONEY TO ME, to TYPE IN ALL CAPS FOR THE REST OF YOUR LIFE, and to STICK PEZ IN YOUR EARS. Thank you for your cooperation. —K."

—alt.religion.kibology

Conspiracies

Interested in joining the kook ecosystem—highly developed

on Usenet, but fundamentally the same all over the Net? Here's what you'll find. First, there are the True Believers, who tend to post anecdotes of personal experience, reviews of things they've read, or grand unified theories of everything. Second, the Scientifics, whose goal is to engage and dissect the topic of discussion, using empirical evidence, scientific method, Occam's razor, and a good amount of skepticism. Third, the Net Bystanders, who, in the course of surfing around, stumble into a kook group and initiate well-meaning conversation, only to be bowled over and torn apart by the other parts of this food chain. In the kook ecosystem, Net Bystanders are plankton. Fourth, there are the Flamers, whose sole interest is in destroying the credibility and integrity of kook groups and their inhabitants. Believe in UFOs? You're a nut! Hunting for Bigfoot? Why not try your butthole, loser! Either because of hardened cynicism or because of a sheer joy in enraging True Believers, Flamers spend at least as

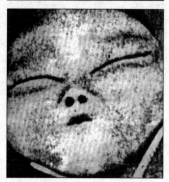

Alien—downloaded from CompuServe's Encounters Forum.

much time on kook groups as the kooks themselves. If you're interested in joining the kook ecosystem, here are some of the best places to drop by.

On the Net

Across the board

alt.paranet* (ng) Believers, skeptics, experts, and amused bystanders jump between the family of paranet newsgroups—alt.paranet.abduct, alt.paranet.paranormal, alt.paranet.science, alt.paranet.skeptic, and alt.paranet.ufo—in ongoing discussions about the possibility of aliens and a world beyond. Discussion on these groups tends to be more scientific and serious than on its newsgroup counterparts. ✓**USENET** DAILY

alt.paranormal (ng) A lightly trafficked newsgroup, mostly because those who believe in the paranormal either (a) focus on spe-

cific interests, like psychic activity, witchcraft, or alien abduction—which have their own newsgroups—or (b) are members of the somewhat more "serious" alt.paranet groups. alt.paranormal mostly has dilettantes talking about personal experiences and dabblers asking querulous or curious questions; the gender ratio is fairly even, and the environment relatively flame-free. ✓**USENET** WEEKLY

alt.tv.x-files (ng) *X-Files* is, after *Star Trek*, the Net's favorite TV show. The Fox series, about two FBI agents who investigate reports of paranormal phenomena, has inspired an online cult. Despite the show's reliance on actual reports of alien abductions and crop circles, most fans in this newsgroup—or X-philes, as they call themselves—spend much more time on the unresolved sexual tension between the two agents, stoic Dana Scully and dashing Fox Mulder, than on the unidentified flying objects. The show's producer and writers speak often in interviews of their reliance on the newsgroup (and the related fan fiction newsgroup, alt.tv.x-files.creative) for viewer feedback, but they don't seem to post. The related IRC channel #x-files fills with *Files*-o-philes when the show airs. ✓**USENET** ✓**INTERNET**→*irc* /channel #x-files HOURLY/LIVE

alt.usenet.kooks (ng) Strange

> **"To be a kook is to be a valued, if often disparaged, member of Cybersociety."**

Conspiracies **On the Fringe**

fixations, odd theories about the universe and its inhabitants, visions of the paranormal and just plain weird, revelations of devious conspiracy—they're all here, just for the asking, on groups ranging from alt.conspiracy to alt.bigfoot to alt.barney.dinosaur.die.die.die to alt.paranet.ufo. The anthropologists of the Net spend most of their time identifying interesting or amusing kooks and kook. groups, and then posting their observations to this high-traffic newsgroup where kook-watchers and their subjects interact in a never-ending war of words, wit, and scurrilous biological comments (because, by and large, true kooks don't like being called kooks). Regular alt.usenet.kooks readers repost nutty statements to the group, and nominate and choose a Kook of the Month. *Kooks* may seem like an unkind word, but it's not meant to be an insult in the classic sense of the term; kooks are as much a part of the Net scene as fanboys, flame-throwers, and would-be wits, and, in fact, there's a fair amount of crossover between these categories. Suffice it to say that to be a kook is to be a valued, if often disparaged, member of Cybersociety. ✓ **USENET** DAILY

Fringes of Reason The conspiracies and crank theories here range from the big ones—UFOs, JFK, ESP, and O.J.—to the modest, such as dowsing, orgone, Satanism, crop circles, vampirism, lycanthropy, Scientology, and the Lennon murder. To even the balance, the conference includes a Skeptics' Corner, but the vast majority of the postings issue forth from those labyrinthine minds that stay up all night worrying about what the Trilateral Commission is going to do next. ✓ **WELL**→*g* fringes DAILY

Crop circles—downloaded from CompuServe's New Age Forum.

Into the Mystic Unlike many similar places in Cyberspace, this one has no back-and-forth flame wars between believers and skeptics. Into the Mystic is for sharing experiences and stories between Thelemites, Catholics, Taoists, Satanists, Discordians, Buddhists, witches, and anyone who believes in ghosts and other strange phenomena. It also functions as a support group for those who have been freaked out or enraptured "on the long road to awakening." Ideas are freely exchanged, and everyone remains respectful of the widely varying beliefs of other members. ✓ **ECHO**→*j* into WEEKLY

Skeptic (echo) These combative skeptics take on the conspiracies, the aliens, and God in the name of rational thought. Challenging them are those willing to argue for the unexplained, the strange, and the mystical, and who have a high capacity for abuse. ✓ **FIDONET** DAILY

Strange and Unexplained (echo) If you look at a puzzle long enough, eventually you'll figure out the answer. This bunch takes crop circles, UFOs, magic, and even the more theoretical enigmas of math and physics, and puts them under the microscope. Believers come here to convince the skeptic, and the skeptics, while

fascinated, try to unlock the puzzles. Be prepared to argue in an informed and logical manner. ✓ **RELAYNET** DAILY

Unexplained Phenomena Strange things happen, and sometimes they happen within earshot of people who subscribe to CompuServe. For instance, 1,700 head of cattle might disappear from a heartland farm, or a 17-year-old

> **"When my wife started coming up with memories and dream recollections that made me suspect she was a possible abductee, I couldn't ignore it anymore. Funny how a thing like that turns your thinking around."**

girl in Palisades Park might suddenly begin to speak fluent Egyptian.

The inexplicable

What can account for these mysterious events? Well, according to CompuServe's Unexplained Phenomena message board, the answer is simple: aliens! Whether disparaging the "growing abductee mentality" or quoting ufologist Richard Hoagland on "large semitransparent structures on the moon," visitors to this forum have a robust interest in the inexplicable, and they're not ashamed to admit it. This is not just a place for speculation on the extraterrestrial and/or paranormal (for that, see CompuServe's Encounters forum). There's also plenty of entertaining chat about the Kennedy assassination, and unorthodox techniques for scuba breathing. ✓**COMPUSERVE**→*go* issues→Messages→Unexplained Phenomena DAILY

Aliens & UFOs

alt.alien.visitors (ng) The group is almost equal parts True Believers, Scientifics, Net Bystanders, and kook watchers—existing, if not in harmony, then in synchronicity. Discussion of crop circles, the "Greys" (insectoid ETs whose activities have been documented, sort of), Erich Von Däniken, and biblical proof of aliens exists side by side with utterly hilarious posts mocking the UFO party line. One ongoing, somewhat paranoid thread concerns whether alt.alien.visitors is now "moderated," i.e., screened for improper—or overly revelatory?—posts. The conclusion anyone might draw from actually reading alt.alien.visitors is: no. If you're a True Believer or Scientific, watch for the posts of Earl Dumbrowski, an even-headed, empiri-

cal researcher and enthusiast of UFOs; if you're more inclined to see the whole thing as a gas, watch for the posts of the so-called Hastings UFO Society, which are allegedly channeled onto the group by a psychic named Madame Thelma. The posts, documenting the activities and beliefs of a UFO club somewhere out in Hooterville, are so strange and well written that you might just believe—for a second—that the UFO Society exists, before you fall down laughing. ✓**USENET** HOURLY

Beyond (echo) When the aliens get here and start rounding us up like cattle, we'd better be organized. Keep a sharp eye on NASA and the Pentagon—they don't really want us to know what's going on. Come here to find out about the meaning of Mars's topology and learn how you can expose the coverups through relentless research and libertarian living. Load your camera and your gun, and keep that telescope lens clean. ✓**ILINK** DAILY

Encounters Forum Associated with the Fox network's *Encounters: The Hidden Truth*, this forum sets out to prove that the world is not an empiricist prison, and that things happen every single day that simply cannot be explained by reasonable scientific minds. The most common phenomenon is alien abduction, generating roughly a dozen messages daily. The subscribers seem dead serious about their lunch dates with aliens; one man says, "When my wife started coming up with memories and dream recollections that made me suspect she was a possible abductee, I couldn't ignore it anymore. Funny how a thing like that turns your thinking around. Encounters also covers ghosts, spiritualism, possession, and spoon bending. (Bob announced his upcoming bending party.) The staff of the *Encounters* television show frequents this forum looking for stories (strange kangaroo behavior in Australia, sidewalk-eating blobs from the sky in San Francisco). ✓**COMPUSERVE**→ *go* encounters→Messages DAILY

UFO-L (ml) Biblical references to UFOs, the recent disappearance of the Mars observer, lost Soviet probes. What can it all mean? This bunch approaches the idea of extraterrestrial life thoughtfully and seriously. A relatively flameless list for the curious and the almost-convinced to figure it all out together. ✓**INTERNET**→*email* listserv@psuvm.bitnet ✍ *Type in message body:* subscribe ufo-l <your full name> WEEKLY

Conspiracies

alt.conspiracy (ng) From the murder of JFK (by the Mafia? The pope? George Bush?)—which also has its own newsgroup, alt.conspiracy.jfk—to the ineffable workings of the Secret Persuaders, alt.conspiracy is perhaps the most "serious" of the "kook" newsgroups. It has the highest ratio of True Believers to kook-watch and Flamer types. Which isn't to say there aren't flames here: Everyone's got an agenda or an idiosyncratic belief, and most of them contradict. Wanna watch irresistible forces hit immovable objects? This is a good place to do it. The "NY News Collective—All the News That Doesn't Fit" posts reprints of articles condemning government activities; the Maoist Internationalist Movement is another regular rant-posting group. Meanwhile, on an individual basis, Brian Redman keeps flames high with his "Conspiracy of the Day" posts, lengthy digressions on topics ranging from the International AIDS

Conspiracy to, yes, the assassinations of JFK and Martin Luther King. Lengthy threads include discussions of the redesign of U.S. currency, the national debt, and ongoing talk about standby subjects like skinheads, the anti-Holocaust movement, and Waco, Texas. ✓**USENET** WEEKLY

Conspiracies (echo) Can a link be established from the framing of O.J. Simpson to Bob Hope's stealing of jokes? If it can be made, these people will do it. If you want to help, come here and explore the tangled web of conspiracies that surround us. Everyone here has a pet theory, and if you are a few facts short, or need a fresh outlook on your favorite secret plot, these seasoned watchdogs will have it for you. Old, tired conspiracies such as Hoffa and JFK are rarely mentioned unless they're tied in with something topical. ✓**RELAYNET** DAILY

JFK assassination

JFK Communist spy, Mafia dupe or black-budget bad guy? Who was Lee Harvey Oswald? You decide. But you have to be able to cite from the Warren Commission Report if you want to make an impression. Thank God these truth-seekers are sometimes willing to joke about their obsession. And they continue to let Bob participate, even though he admits working for the Feds! ✓**PRODIGY**→*jump* books and writing bb→Choose a Topic→Nonfiction→JFK DAILY

JFK Assassination Research Forum According to the official-sounding message at the beginning of CompuServe's JFK Assassination Research Forum, "the purpose of this forum is to facilitate research into the assassination

of JFK, to work together as a cooperative community to determine the facts of the 'crime of the century.'" What this means, of course, is that crank season is now officially open, and that all conspiracy theorists are welcome with open arms. Zionists, the Heritage Foundation, rogue CIA agents, and a Castro-created Manchurian candidate are but a few of the forum members' suspects-for-life. The dialogue can be very contentious and the regulars know their stuff. Posts are filled with code words like "Alpha 66 money man" and "Liberty Lobby." And everyone seems to know someone who was in Dallas that fateful November day. ✓**COMPUSERVE**→*go* kennedy→Messages DAILY

JFK_Assn (echo) Exit wounds, "head spray," the Babushka Lady—every detail of the JFK assassination is pored over and debated among experts, beginners, skeptics, and even firsthand witnesses. A great training ground for the next generation of JFK conspiracists. ✓**FIDONET** DAILY

> "Zionists, the Heritage Foundation, rogue CIA agents, and a Castro-created Manchurian Candidate are but a few of the forum members' suspects-for-life."

(EVIL!)Mud

It's the least stuck-up MUD around. No one who plays on

(EVIL!)Mud gives a damn who you are or what you do in real life. People who play on (EVIL!)Mud do so not because they have some goal to achieve, or because they're trying to make friends or have online sex, but rather because they enjoy sitting around in a town square filled with lava pits being basically weird. And you'll probably meet most of them if you spend some time here—it's a rather intimate group.

(EVIL!)Mud is home to angstful, sarcastic, and just plain odd talk. Its inhabitants include the head wizard, Xibo, archfoe of Usenet's Kibo and Lord of Angst. Xibo has a ready supply of gibes for all occasions—many of them about women. Be prepared to be offended. Xibo has recently become engaged, and you'll often see his intended, Xibeth, online as well.

National hero

Hurin is probably the most famous inhabitant of (EVIL!)Mud. Hurin is Public Enemy No.1 on FurryMUCK and is well known for logging in on FurryMUCK using characters obtained via false pretenses and offending *everyone*. On (EVIL!)Mud, he's kind of the national hero—parts of (EVIL!)-Mud were built to mock Furry-MUCK. When the (EVIL!)Mud mail robot, Paws, crashed and burned two years ago, Hurin brought a used condom to the "funeral" in place of flowers. That's

Door ornament—downloaded from CompuServe's Graphics Plus Forum.

Hurin. Always sensitive and ready with the right gesture. Definitely worth meeting.

Tarrant, one of the other two wizards, is also a Lord of Angst. Much of the building on (EVIL!)Mud owes its creation and guiding spirit to Tarrant's pervading sense of cosmic depression and steady worry. Take a stroll through his abortion clinics or a ride on his Taxicab of Death while you're here. Tarrant can often be found lurking at the bottom of a deep hole. The third wizard, Mobius, is played by Joel Furr, famous Net persona and subject of the newsgroup **alt.fan.joel-furr**. Mobius is the guy who spends most of the time answering newbie questions and helping people get set up. He's also ready to show you around the MUD and help you reach the interesting areas such as West Corner of the Swamp and the Scow.

You'll also meet Legssus, Rosminah, Ahkond, Buzzy, Elminster, Velcromancer, Scolding_Box, Lucifer, McKloud, Tank_Girl, and Codrus. Most, if not all, of these people will be happy to pass the

time with you if you have something to talk about. That's what (EVIL!) is about. A total lack of pomposity and plenty of laissez-faire equanimity.

The main hangout is the Evil Town Square, two rooms north of Limbo. To reach it, type "@tel #3" (you must have your character set up and be established in a hotel room or one of the temporary homes to use this command). ✓IN-TERNET→*telnet* intac.com 4201→create <your character's name> <your password>

> "Much of the building on (EVIL!)Mud owes its creation and guiding spirit to Tarrant's pervading sense of cosmic depression and steady worry. Take a stroll through his abortion clinics or a ride on his Taxicab of Death while you're here. Tarrant can often be found lurking at the bottom of a deep hole."

Gothic horror

It's always midnight on the Net. Beware; Barnabas Collins

has a modem. The idea of living forever or being able to somehow influence the future for good or ill has always been appealing. Plus, we just like to be scared—adrenaline is an aphrodisiac. Thus that Romanian count has spawned a flourishing subculture. The more traditional and subtle (they use understated pallor, live in dank castles, and have pride in their sanguine tradition) head for **Vampyres** to exchange lore and well-crafted stories. The new wave, pierced, painted, and panting, worship at the twin idols of gothic music groups and pop culture (Anne Rice) on **alt.gothic**.

Tom Cruise as Lestat—downloaded from CompuServe's Entertainment Drive.

On the Net

alt.gothic (ng) Discussions of preternatural gloom, the undead, and black hair dye can be found in profusion here; the majority touch on gothic music groups (Bauhaus, Sisters of Mercy, Nick Cave and the Bad Seeds), books, and films. References to Bram Stoker, Edgar Allen Poe, Anne Rice, and the late Brandon Lee (star of the "goth" film *The Crow*) abound.

Most people are in their twenties. They go by names like the Poisoned Black Rose, VampLestat, Blackskull, and Midnight. The "gothic scene" (e.g., industrial nightclubs) in various international cities is a frequent thread. The FTP site holds the FAQ plus a host of related files on gothic culture, dress, and ideology. ✓**USENET** *FAQ:* ✓**INTERNET**→*ftp* ftp.maths. tcd.ie→anonymous→<your email address>→/pub/music/faq→gothic-faq DAILY

alt.magick (ng) Devotees of Wicca, Golden Dawn, Aleister Crowley, kundalini, and other magickal figures and phenomena gather here. Discussions range from helping novices in the "magick business" (as one user described it) get their rituals set to intense intellectual discourses on the supernatural. Resources are excellent: Various FAQs and relevant FTP sites and WWW home pages are posted regularly. ✓**USENET** *FAQ:* ✓**INTERNET**→*ftp* rtfm.mit.edu→ anonymous→<your email address> →/pub/usenet-by-group/alt. magick DAILY

Theatre des Vampires "You seem to…bring out something… in me," Kyrin whispers in her ear, running his tongue across her throat and down the side of her neck teasingly, biting into her soft flesh. Do you like dark and stormy nights? Have the urge to don a white nightgown, grab a candelabra and head upstairs to the forbidden locked door? Does Bela Lugosi make you quiver? Theatre des Vampires, named for Anne Rice's creation, is an active, write-in role-play where like minds meet to create a gothic extravaganza of blood, passion, and danger. Pick an exotic name and nature and slink right in—as steamy as Prodigy gets. ✓**PRODIGY**→*jump* arts bb→ Choose a Topic→Other Clubs→ THEATER DES VAMPIRES DAILY

Vampyres (ml) "'Have vampires lost their fangs?…Are these new-age vampires a betrayal of the ideals of vampirism or just another postmodernist construct?" Vampyres is a very active list—a get-together for philosophers of the dark, writers of lurid tales, and collectors of grave dirt. This is a literate list, not a rehashing of pop vampire books. Regulars with names like Twilite, Baron Gideon Redoak, and Misery exchange fiction and lore and plan their own peculiar events—Bloodstock, for one. There are technical questions ("What do you call someone who makes someone a werewolf?") and deeper queries ("What about vampyres and AIDS?"). This is a friendly (not to say warm) group, and the dialogue and fiction are well worth reading. But one wonders about tag lines like "If vegetarians eat vegetables, I guess that makes you a humanist." Still afraid of the dark? ✓**INTERNET**→*email* list serv@guvm.ccf.georgetown.edu ✍ *Type in message body:* subscribe vampyres <your full name> DAILY

Net-tripping

Should you mix cough syrup and Prozac? What was the

last really bad drug experience you had? And what about Timothy Leary, dearie? Mostly white-collar and largely collegiate, the Net's drug users have tried everything from pot and coke to ecstasy and crystal meth, not to mention a whole host of prescription drugs with names like *Star Trek* characters (Darvon, Percocet) and side effects like special effects. And while there are plenty of reports from the experiential front ("Does ecstasy affect your libido? Man, oh, man, let me tell you about it"), there are also topical discussions about American society's obsession with drugs—how a pill becomes an outlaw, what constitutes illegal search and seizure, why the anti-pot lobby is so strong, even whether warrants can be issued on the basis of information obtained over the Net.

Woodstock yuppie—from http://sfgate.com/examiner/woodstockhome.html

On the Net

alt.drugs (ng) Want to learn how to spot a narc? Need to know your rights if you're arrested for drug possession, or what combinations of drugs can be most harmful? If so, this busy newsgroup has the answers. The majority of subscribers here are college students and recent grads whose motto is "Just Say Know." Though the occasional antidrug message is posted, most threads deal with the practical, political, and educational issues surrounding legal and illegal drug use: "Can I take cough syrup when I'm on Prozac?" "How can I build my own smoking device?" "Does eating hemp seeds make you test positive for cannabis use?" Of course, the drug-legalization controversy is an ongoing theme. Check the FTP site for 4.7 megabytes of compressed text relating to drugs. ✓USENET *Archives:* ✓INTERNET→*ftp* ftp.hmc.edu→anonymous→<your email address>→/pub/drugs HOURLY

alt.psychoactives (ng) This Usenet group distinguishes itself from alt.drugs by dealing not so much with the politics as with the science of drug use. Chemists, psychiatrists, authors, and students discuss the various psychotropic drugs and their effects on the brain. Some threads deal with the clinical application of drugs, such as the therapeutic uses of LSD, thorazine, and antidepressants. Other threads are decidedly more recreational in nature: "DMAE makes me stinky! What can I do about it?" ✓USENET WEEKLY

alt.smokers (ng) "I am a nonsmoker, but nothing turns me on more than a woman who smokes," writes one member of alt.smokers. The overwhelming majority of subscribers here are smokers. This is one of the few places left they can safely wax poetic on the pleasures of lighting up. And they do. Topics include how "antismokers have turned smokers from individuals into a subclass" and how second-hand smoke affects pets. One popular thread keeps a tally of confirmed celebrity smokers. Also

> **"Inspired by the works of Timothy Leary and Terence McKenna, Lerilanders attempt to 'change the rules of their reality' by periodically engaging in the synchronous use of meditation and psychedelics."**

look for frequent updates from FOREST, the Freedom Organization for the Right to Enjoy Smoking Tobacco. ✓**USENET** WEEKLY

Drugs The WELL's drug symposium covers all aspects of drug culture: dosages, side effects, penal codes. The group also includes huge rooms on Fetal Alcohol Syndrome, drug testing, legalization, and sex while stoned, as well as smaller discussion groups on more arcane substances such as woodrose, yohimbe, datura. There are plenty of seasoned drug users willing to share their wealth of experience. ✓**WELL**→*g* drugs DAILY

Leri-L (ml) The founder of Leri-L describes this list as "the only virtual community dedicated to consciousness expansion through psychedelics, metaprogramming, alternative living, all the wrong politics, and net-tripping. It's quite a family." Students and freethinkers of all ages frequent this "electronic commune."

Inspired by the works of Timothy Leary and Terence McKenna, Lerilanders attempt to "change the rules of their reality" by periodically engaging in the synchronous use of meditation and psychedelics. The results are posted to the list in the form of stories, poetry, and personal revelations. ✓**INTERNET**→*email* ma jordomo@pyramid.com ✍ *Type in message body:* subscribe leri-l *Archives:* ✓**INTERNET**→*ftp* ftp.pyra mid.com→anonymous→<your email address>→/pub/leri DAILY

Mind This conference attempts to probe the nooks and crannies of mental experience. How do psychedelics work? What do humans do better than machines? What do machines do better than humans? Who are the most extraordinary thinkers currently working in the consciousness field? The partici-

pants range from academics to hobbyists to full-blown crackpots—one man's theory, that the brain is powered by ordinary table salt, and that the secrets to cognition lie in the sodium chloride crystal, is so foolish it's almost brilliant—and there's even a section on the Shadow, that pseudo-superhero who has the power to cloud minds. ✓**WELL**→*g* mind DAILY

Mind-L (ml) This mailing list explores "the whole range of technologies that work directly or indirectly on your mind." Subscribers discuss consciousness-altering software, sensory-deprivation tanks, lucid dreaming machines, electronic stimulation hardware, and many more "tools for exploration."

Be prepared for high-tech jargon such as "Transcutaneous Electrical Neural Stimulation" (electronic acupuncture) and "Hemisynchs" (audiotapes that produce frequencies designed to confuse the conscious mind). Another popular topic is "smart drugs"— the natural amino acids that reportedly increase energy and memory. ✓**INTERNET**→*email* list-proc@apocalypse.org ✍ *Type in message body:* subscribe mind-l <your full name> *Archives:* ✓**INTERNET**→*ftp* asylum.sf.ca.us→anonymous→<your email address>→/pub/mind-l DAILY

talk.politics.drugs (ng) This is a college-educated drug crowd; illegal searches and seizures get lots of airplay, as do concerns about wiretaps and attempts to find constitutional justification for legalization. By far the most common topic, though, is marijuana laws—National Organization for the Reform of Marijuana Laws has a presence on the newsgroup, and most of the subscribers seem outraged that the government hasn't at least ac-

knowledged the relatively minor effects of the drug: "Should our laws be such that an adult should go to prison for consuming marijuana at home? Should the users be exposed to brutal, profiteering drug dealers? Should the users have their houses broken into by SWAT teams with faulty warrants, looking for a few joints?" ✓**USENET** *FAQ:* ✓**INTERNET**→ *ftp* rtfm.mit.edu→ anonymous→<your email address> →/pub/usenet-by-group/talk.poli tics.drugs DAILY

CYBERNOTES

"You write about your friend not being the same again after a psychedelic experience. You can't figure it out, and your friend seems to have gone ga-ga.

"Psychedelics in high (and sometimes even low) doses can have the effect of totally dissolving reality. This means that everything experienced during such a trip can be seen as the 'absolute truth' by the tripper.

"Because this 'truth' is mindblowingly different from your average reality, it can have severe effects on the psyche. In actual fact, some of the things you mention your friend saying I recognize from my own trips. Especially the faces melting to reveal the real face."

—**alt.psychoactives**

Techno-culture

Who needs cyberpunk fiction when the Net gives you the

real thing—death threats made over newsgroup spams, hackers so dangerous that they can tap the FBI agents sent to get them, and scarily simple techniques for reading someone else's private email? And the magazines that cover Net culture best also occasion some of the most interesting discussion of what this all means. *Mondo*, still one of the most active centers of cyberpsychedelics, pushes the Net as a kind of smart drug. Meanwhile, *bOING bOING* excels at worst-case scenarios for new technology (what will unscrupulous police departments do with photomanipulation?), and the futurists at *Wired* expand the "You will" line from those AT&T ads into a kind of *Martha Stewart Living* lifestyle guide for the cyberyuppie set.

On the Net

Hacking

alt.2600 (ng) *2600* is the name of the premiere phone-phreak 'zine; the title refers to the frequency of a tone that used to unlock Ma Bell's diagnostic services. The newsgroup may as well be called alt.crime. Share technical tips for counterfeiting postage stamps; follow the exploits of Kevin Mitnick, a hacker so dan-

John Plunkett's Cyber Rights logo—from CompuServe's EFF Forum.

gerous that he has been able to phone-tap the FBI agents who can't catch him; build your own universal garage-door opener; pirate cable; steal Internet passwords.

Inundated with dumb questions from would-be scam artists, the regulars have switched over to a moderated newsgroup (alt.hackers). The twist is that instead of actually having a moderator, discussants simply know how to forge the "control message" that authenticates moderator posts.

The frauds cooked up here are even more clever than they are childish—which is saying a lot—and they often score useful anticorporate points. ✓**USENET** *FAQ:* ✓**INTERNET**→*ftp* rtfm.mit.edu→ anonymous→<your email address> →/pub/usenet-by-group/alt.2600 →alt.2600_(Newsgroup_for_the_ Hacker_Quarterly)_FAQL DAILY

alt.hackers (ng) *Hacker*, in the popular media, is synonymous with computer criminal, but in this newsgroup and most pro-

grammer subcultures, the term is an honorific for a top-notch, irrepressibly curious programmer. "Hacking," according to the FAQ, "is not about breaking things."

The rule for posting here is that every message—especially requests for help—should include a hack, whether it's a "grad-school food hack" on how to eat for a week on $5 ("eggs, rice, bread, and Coke") or a performance tweak to a Motorola beeper. The group is designated as "moderated" (although there really is no moderator) to filter out posts from people who don't know how to circumvent the restriction. "There are at least four different trivial ways" to post, explains the FAQ, "so if you try one and it fails, don't start whining. Start hacking!" ✓**USENET** *FAQ:* ✓**INTERNET**→*ftp* rtfm.mit.edu→ anonymous→<your email address> →pub/usenet-by-hierarchy/alt/an swers→hackers-faq DAILY

Hacking/Cracking Unauthorized computer break-ins are the province of a talented (and socially uncomfortable) few, aggressive techno-nerds who spend the night picking away at high-tech gateways, looking for information, profit, and, above all, power. The WELL's hacking conference spends much of its time clarifying exactly what it is that hackers do: Are they trafficking in "forbidden knowledge in a technological society" (topic 31), challenging the liberal notion of intellectual property (topic 47), or merely trying to improve the world of the future (topic 96)?

While the conscientious portion of the hacker community carefully clarifies its particular moral code, the rest of the participants in the conference just go about their business, discovering and then disclosing how to thwart Caller ID, or break into the company payroll, or bollix the boss's Sharp Wizard. In case you're caught, the conference also contains a fair amount of legal news on pertinent hacking cases—updates on what's happening to those hackers who broke into CBS, or the man who was caught releasing viruses onto the Internet. ✓**WELL**→*g* hack DAILY

Media

bOING bOING The magazine with the annoying name and a bird's eye view of the future—*bOING bOING*—has produced an electronic conference every bit as high-strung, neurotic, and underground as its namesake. Though the content has been referred to as "brain candy for happy mutants," it keeps the mind at attention, training its hyperactive gaze on impossible inventions, real-life robocops, photo manipulation, and virtual reality, among other topics. As one discussion topic explains, "Conspiracies: real and imagined, they're all the same to us." ✓**WELL**→*g* bb DAILY

Mirrorshades This fairly small conference is devoted to cyberpunk, a literary genre with subcult status and its own vocabulary. Hard-core cyberpunks and tourists in the land of cutting-edge synthetic humanity are advised to check it out. People here worry aloud about the imbrication of circuitry and other machine elements into the delicate state we call human existence. ✓**WELL**→*g* mirrorshades WEEKLY

Mondo 2000 Magazine *Mondo 2000* pushes relentlessly toward the future, borne along on a wave of cyberpunk, smart drugs, virtual reality, hypertext, raves, robots, cybernetics, and cryptography. While the trendiness can sometimes become overwhelming—

more than a 1,000 messages on neo-feminist dogma?—this conference also has more tender moments, such as a touching discussion devoted to the great jazz innovator Sun Ra. The most rewarding topics are those that understand their own insignificance and press on anyway, such as a spotter's guide to the amusement parks of the world—there's something immensely satisfying in learning that there's extensive use of Smellovision in the Hello Kitty theme park in Kyushu. ✓**WELL**→*g* mondo DAILY

Wired The coolest and hottest guide to the technology of the future, *Wired* magazine plugs its readers in to future-minded artists and writers such as Douglas Coupland, Laurie Anderson, Nam June Paik, and William Gibson, as well as offering coverage of developments in computer technology. Like the magazine, the WELL's *Wired* conference fuses aesthetics and hard-core future-spotting, posting detailed updates in hardware and software and hosting highly rhetorical debates about refashioning criminal justice in the computer age, fixing fees for interactive TV, and determining the ethnic makeup of the Internet. ✓**WELL**→*g* wired DAILY

Other

GRANITE (ml) Gender and New Information Technologies is an international forum using the Internet to study the Internet. Posters may find discussion of the relationship of gender to technology design for everything from microwaves to pantyhose ("obviously designed by men to aggravate women and run at the least touch"). The real import of GRANITE is in providing a forum for debate on how the information superhighway serves the

needs of men and women. Hot topics include the possible restriction of sexual materials online and the purpose/ethics of restricted-sex lists. GRANITE actively seeks the participation of more women. ✓**INTERNET**→*email* listserv@hearn. nic.surfnet.nl ✍ *Type in message body:* subscribe granite <your full name> WEEKLY

news.admin.misc (ng) "Dirtbag Lawyers Plan More Internet Advertising". This is the Net's superego, the Netiquette HQ for tracking newsgroup spams—messages indiscriminately posted to every newsgroup—such as the notorious Canter & Siegel green-card ads and more recent examples like MAKE.MONEY.FAST. Regular proposals for "Good Net Neighbor" standards are floated, and the effect of commercial-service connections to the Internet is monitored (apparently CompuServe did not at first correctly follow the threading protocols for posts). Other hot issues include whether to file police reports automatically when death threats are posted to newsgroups. ✓**USENET** *FAQ:* ✓**INTERNET**→*ftp* rtfm.mit.edu→ anonymous→<your email address>→ /pub/usenet-by-group/news.admin.misc DAILY

> "There's something satisfying in learning that there's extensive use of Smellovision in the Hello Kitty theme park in Kyushu."

Part 4

Net Op-Ed

Abortion

Today's Chancellorsville and Gettysburg are battlefields in Cyberspace with "pro-life"

and "pro-choice" embroidered in the opponents' banners. There are several dedicated abortion sites, including **alt.abortion.inequity** and RelayNet's **Abortion** echo, but verbal scuffles in unrelated Net areas—such as **alt.music.pearl-jam** or **comp.sys.mac.advocacy**—break out regularly. They all tend to be fairly barren and unpleasant. Wear your battle gear. Experience shows that constructive debate on the issue requires a moderator, which is precisely why FidoNet's **Abortion** echo has become a haven of reason and respect. Which doesn't mean that there is no room for the highly emotional aspects of the abortion debate. When a teenager shares the bitter story of her recent abortion, all—whether pro-this or pro-that—rally to console her.

On the Net

Abortion (echo) Teenage Andrea signed herself on to Fidonet's abortion forum as a novice pro-lifer. She received three welcome messages. One to "keep an open mind," one welcome from "another who opposes the killing of children," and a third, which reminded the poster of the second message

Abortion clinic blockade—downloaded from CompuServe's Photo Forum.

that everybody opposes the killing of children, but many "also oppose the erosion of our liberties"—including the right to abortion. Most debate is polite, with a slight tendency toward sanctimony on all parts. ✓**FIDONET** DAILY

Abortion (echo) This abortion forum is likely to contain statements like "God is awesome" but occasionally provides some interesting legal and moral debates. A wide spectrum of men and women relate their personal stories of making an agonizing decision. Is anyone listening? It is hard to tell—but the large number of postings show that lots of people are willing to give their two cents. ✓**RELAYNET** DAILY

Abortion Is Brutal This discussion percolates within the domestic-issues message board of AOL's Capital Connection, but there are always several abortion discussions going on concurrently in the forum. As the title might indicate, it's not exactly objective: The AOL

header proclaims that "when someone tells you that abortion is a matter between a woman and her doctor, they're forgetting someone," and the someone they're talking about isn't Bryant Gumbel. The conversation tends

> "Stupid Jack and Stupid Jill went up their little hill / Stupid Jack and Stupid Jill forgot their little pill / Now Stupid Jack and Stupid Jill have a baby they must kill."

Abortion Net Op-Ed

> ## "God invented fundamentalism because he had a robust sense of humor."

toward extremism, and the rhetoric inflames whenever possible. A man named Job, in fact, attacks "feminazis" with a string of questions that insist that abortion's horror is boundless: "Was slavery a Southern issue about which the North should have minded its own business? Was the Holocaust a German issue, so outside interference was uncalled for?"

Still, there are occasional moments of rapprochement—deep in the heat of an argument, one man apologizes to his adversary for calling him a bigot, and the accused responds that "to apologize as you have done is a rare thing in these forums, and I admire you for it." Can't we all just get along? ✓**AMERICA ONLINE**→*keyword* capital→Message Boards→Abortion Is Brutal WEEKLY

alt.abortion.inequity (ng) The inequity appears to be that the abortion decision rests mainly with women. This newsgroup is essentially a few men (the same names are always present) sitting around debating the sentience of the zygote and the viability of the fetus outside the womb. When threads are entitled "The Overpopulation Myth Is Bull Pucky," it shouldn't be surprising that although there is vociferous ongoing debate, there is little movement on either side. ✓**USENET** DAILY

Potpourri These two message boards consider abortion in the context of spiritual thought and religious regulation. Representatives of any and all religions are invited to contribute their views, and while there's a fair amount of unregenerate dogma from both sides of the fence—"Stupid Jack and Stupid Jill went up their little hill/Stupid Jack and Stupid Jill forgot their little pill/Now Stupid Jack and Stupid Jill have a baby they must kill" versus "God invented fundamentalism because he had a robust sense of humor"—there are also interesting speculative discussions.

Referring to the biblical Hagar, one man says, "So, here we have a raped slave who finds herself pregnant with a child, who is likely to live his life at odds with the rest of society, and—in the name of the Lord—she is denied the right to not have this child. Does that sound familiar to all you who have followed some of the arguments here?" ✓**GENIE**→*keyword* religion→Religion & Philosophy Bulletin Board →Potpourri *and* Potpourri II DAILY

talk.abortion (ng) "We've been subjected to 21 years of being told that a woman has a right to do with her body as she wishes," writes one exasperated man. "Can you present any compelling reasons why she should *not* be allowed to control her own body?" queries an equally annoyed man.

Count on it. The abortion debate here is not pretty, and some of it is even quite volatile.

On the other hand, its obnoxiousness is not entirely unentertaining either. Why shouldn't a woman be allowed control of her body, for instance? Well, you know, "in the U.S. no one controls his/her own body totally. You can be called to jury duty..." Day in, day out, these gladiators sling rhetoric at each other. Never a dull moment. ✓**USENET** DAILY

Church & state

Go somewhere else for spiritual peace and metaphysical

tranquillity, CompuServe's **Politics and Religion** discussion is for slugging it out over school prayer, **talk.origins** is for settling scores between creationists and scientists, and FidoNet's **Holy-Smoke** is for the kid in you who always wanted to know whether dogs go to heaven.

On the Net

Church&State (echo) "Hey Crackpot, didn't the 1961 Supreme Court's School Prayer decision allow for a moment of silence?" And the response? "Hey Dimwit, school prayer is school prayer, no matter what else you might call it." So goes a typical day in this volatile conference, where the issues rarely change (school prayer, creationism, the occult, the morality of politicians, and the "virtues" of liberals and conservatives) but the passions stay roused. Rarely does discussion transcend the level of an emotional street-corner argument—many a post here begins with the words "I feel." ✓**FIDONET** HOURLY

Ethics/Debate Religion is a powerful force in political and moral decision-making. What is the scriptural justification for "pro-life" killers? Was Albert Schweitzer a conventionally religious man? And what about suicide? These message boards contain postings from the devout to the skeptical, with local stops in between—from Steve's lament over the incompatibility of spirituality and science ("A belief

Pope John Paul II—from CompuServe's Reuters News Pictures Forum.

in God negates a belief in evolution. One cannot serve two masters") to Ruth's question about the place of guns in godliness ("Is it Christian to defend yourself with firearms?"). ✓**AMERICA ONLINE**→ *keyword* religion→Religion & Ethics Message Center→ Ethics *and* Debate DAILY

HolySmoke (echo) The Holy-smoke conference exists for the sole purpose of provoking discussion on matters of faith. Is God real? Is religion valid? If so, why? And if not, why not? Jesse—the True Believer—says, "They survived over 40 years on manna and water." Carl—the Skeptic—says, "Don't be an idiot. There's no known food that even comes close to the manna described." ✓**FIDONET** DAILY

Politics and Religion Much of the message board is devoted to the irreconcilable differences between evolution and creation, or the equally problematic gap between faith and verifiable fact. The debate is surprisingly learned and respect-

ful. ✓**COMPUSERVE**→*go* issues→Messages→Politics & Religion HOURLY

Politics and Religion This conference covers a fairly narrow corridor of topics: Operation Rescue's scare tactics, the ins and outs of cult awareness, the infamous Branch Davidians, the conflict between liberal ideals and religious demands, and the role of religion in political office. But within those limits, the opinions are measured and compelling: When one man suggests that "any honorable Christian would always be a failure as a secular president," Bill (no, no...another Bill) responds that "[as] a 'born again Christian'—one of those awful people who actually takes the Bible seriously—I also maintain that I would rather be 'ruled' by an honorable and competent unbeliever than by an incompetent and/or dishonorable 'Christian.'" ✓**GENIE** →*keyword* religion→Religion & Philosophy Bulletin Board→Politics and Religion DAILY

talk.origins (ng) The great debate between evolutionists and creationists. In this corner, the Grubaugh Polar Configuration model, the "indisputable truth of fossilized remains," and the fact that "research has fixed the point at which man emerged from other forms of life." In the other corner, the word of God. And that, in short, is the problem with this newsgroup, which is less a discussion than it is a collision of faiths, one in scientific research, the other in spiritual documents. Polemics notwithstanding, there's still some fascinating material, such as an attempt to reconcile the biblical account of the Flood with available geological evidence. ✓**USENET** *FAQ:* ✓**INTERNET**→*ftp* rtfm.mit.edu→ anonymous→<your email address> →/pub/usenet-by-group/news.answers/talk-origins DAILY

Civil liberties

Electronic privacy is rapidly becoming the principal civil-rights issue for the middle class, whether it's the database at your local video store, your medical history, or your email at the office. The Electronic Frontier Foundation (with official Net presence in CompuServe's **EFF Forum**, and supporters and critics in **comp.org.eff.talk**) is the cyber-ACLU. But there's still plenty of discussion of offline troubles, like racism (**alt.discrimination**) and free speech (**alt.society. civil-liberty**).

Rosa Parks—downloaded from Reuters News Picture Forum.

On the Net

alt.censorship (ng) The discussion is about censorship in all its manifestations. Should tabloid media be restrained? Should newspapers be prohibited from printing the names of rape victims? What about employers who monitor personal email on company systems? Or race hate spread by computer mail? One of the most compelling issues discussed here is the role of moderators. As one man writes, "If I believe my message is such that it merits placement in front of every Usenet reader, why should someone else's opinion that my belief is wrong take precedence?" ✓**USENET** DAILY

alt.discrimination (ng) Along with the usual commonsensical exposure of injustice ("Mistreatment is wrong"), there's a tremendous amount of new idiocy—complaints by male victims of affirmative action, a revisionist complaint that *"Schindler's List* falsifies history!"* and even a posting that tries to give new teeth to the old saw that girls can't do math. ✓**USENET** DAILY

alt.society.civil-liberty (ng) The newsgroup raises a number of issues that outrage civil libertarians, from the disappearance of newsstands in New York City to illegal searches and seizures to school prayer. Some of the most interesting discussions are about AB138X, California's notorious no-smoking code. ✓**USENET** *FAQ:* ✓**INTERNET**→*ftp* rtfm.mit.edu→ anonymous→<your email address> →/pub/usenet-by-hierarchy/alt/so ciety/civil-liberty DAILY

comp.org.eff.talk (ng) Discuss the activities and goals of the EFF. ✓**USENET** DAILY

comp.society.privacy/alt.privacy (ng) Governments, businesses, even fellow citizens want information about you. The average American fills out 45 forms a year, and is kept track of by some 25 businesses and institutions. The bulk of that information ends up in computer data banks. Who has access to these databases? Could a hacker enter your records? Could your credit report fall into the wrong hands? These concerns and many more (Net users worry that other Netters can trace them; a man rigs his ex-wife's answering machine) are discussed here. True, sometimes the stories leave you hungry for a how-to guide. ✓**USENET** DAILY

EFF Forum The "digital revolution" is transforming our lives, traditions, and institutions. We may need an entirely new way of thinking regarding law, medicine, advertising, even personal identity. That's precisely the ambitious mission of the Electronic Frontier Foundation—not only to catalog those new concepts but to exert some critical control over them. This forum functions as an EFF storefront. For instance, after one woman complains that a new policy at her husband's company violates his electronic privacy—"The company may audit, access, and, if necessary, disclose any transaction such as phone usage, voice mail, and email messages, using corporate resources"—forum members respond, explaining that the company has not only the right but the obligation to manage its electronic resources. ✓**COMPUSERVE**→*go* effsig→Messages WEEKLY

soc.rights.human (ng) The group discusses human-rights abuse throughout the world. ✓**USENET** WEEKLY

Current events

Just as CNN came into its own during the Gulf War and the Russian coup attempt, the

Net also matured during these crises, with real-time IRC chat originating from ground zero in areas like Tel Aviv and Moscow (see the list of country IRC channels on page 185). CompuServe's **Hotspot** has recently served as a conduit for debating U.S. policy toward Haiti and Cuba. Regular radio talk-show fodder is also on-line, most notably in the **Simulchat** that accompanies the NPR afternoon show, *Talk of the Nation*. The Net is also becoming a standard organizing tool for political activists, as evidenced in the **alt.activism.death-penalty** newsgroup.

Cuban refugees—downloaded from Reuters News Picture Forum.

On the Net

Across the board

alt.activism.d (ng) A gathering place for activists of all stripes. Hence there are plenty of discussions that seem to be parties of one. In addition to these lone voices, there are plenty of topics that blossom into interesting discussions—a long and compelling explanation of the ins and outs of Vietnam draft dodging ("There was a brief exemption for married men with children, but the Congress got a clue when the sales of condoms dropped <grin>"); a daunting report, complete with "actual statistics," that claims that capitalism does not benefit the American worker ("The U.S. is becoming a polarized society—the rich are getting richer; the workers are getting less and less of what they produce"); and even a 200-plus message thread on the Senate's treatment of the NEA. ✓**USENET** *FAQ:* ✓**INTERNET**→*ftp* rtfm.mit.edu→anonymous→<your email address>→/pub/usenet-by-hierarchy/alt/activism DAILY

Current Events Shocking news ripped from today's headlines! While CNN takes you around the world in 30 minutes, the WELL's current-events conference brings the world to your doorstep in an ongoing stream of electronic reaction. Interested in talking about Michael Jackson's child-molestation charge? Want to discuss the shooting of doctors in front of abortion clinics? Need to shoot your wad on Nixon's death, or the Bobbitt trial, or the O.J. murder trial? While it's useless to try to predict new topics, here's a good rule of thumb: If it happens, wait ten minutes, and someone will have opened a conference room on the WELL. ✓**WELL**→*g* current HOURLY

CurrentEvnt (echo) Much of this conference is ripped-from-the-headlines boilerplate—O.J., Rush, Clinton. What distinguishes it, though, is the reactionary tone of its postings. "What's the difference between evolution and astrology?" asks one man. "Well, evolution is a pagan myth promoted by secular humanists, and astrology is a pagan myth promoted by secular humanists." Another participant charges that Ted Kennedy is a—

> **"Here's a good rule of thumb: If it happens, wait ten minutes, and someone will have opened a conference room on the WELL."**

gasp!—communist. Misanthropy and antiliberal sentiment run high, and everyone is concerned about the moral dissolution of our society. ✓**RELAYNET** DAILY

Marginal Issues What exactly is a marginal issue? Well, from the looks of this bulletin board, most forms of bigotry qualify; the board contains an alarming amount of homophobic and racist rhetoric. Gay men, explains one woman, are making America into a "21st-century Sodom." And as for African Americans, "Those people don't have music, it's called 'rap.'" ✓**COMPUSERVE**→*go* politics→Messages→Marginal Issues DAILY

NEWS BB Got a soapbox? Head right on over to the NEWS BB. Meet a "Principal Native Fundamentalist American" (not an Indian) and an advocate of the impeachment of "Billary." The less than moderate nature of the board is also seen in the WORLD news section—Holocaust deniers, anti-Castroites and both vehement PLO supporters and opponents

> "Got a soapbox? Head right on over to the NEWS BB. Meet a 'Principal Native Fundamentalist American' (not an Indian) and an advocate of the impeachment of 'Billary.'"

dominate the discussions. Even discounting these voluble souls, the tone here is somewhat right-wing and can sometimes get very nasty. So if you want to exercise your constitutional right to mouth off—do so with impunity. ✓**PRODIGY**→*jump* news bb→Choose a Topic HOURLY

Politics The WELL's political conference is the place to let all your polemic hang out. Want to complain about California term limits, or the Bush administration's War on Drugs? Got a flea in your underwear about China, or BCCI, or NAFTA? Or do you just want to do that call-in radio thing where you vent your underinformed views about national health care, or President Clinton's reputed incompetence on the international front, or Rudolph Giuliani's unexpected liberal leanings? Go ahead and yak. It's a free country. ✓**WELL**→*g* pol DAILY

Politics (echo) Like most of the politics and opinion conferences, the busy, noisy Politics is a boy's club, a place for men of all stripes to convene and opine. The tone is often strident, and rarely generous, and there's the definite sense that participants are just searching for more and more powerful rhetoric with which to discredit their opponents. ✓**RELAYNET** HOURLY

talk.politics.misc (ng) Subtitled "Political discussions and ravings of all kinds," talk.politics.misc lives up to its name. Why don't more women own guns? Does capitalism benefit the American worker? What should be done about Whitewater? While the hot topics are the same as elsewhere on the Net—more than 600 subscribers posted responses to an essay entitled "Is Health Care a Right?"— there's an entertaining

diversity, with brief but impassioned discussions on Scientology, Prozac, pornography, and Nixon's anti-Semitism. ✓**USENET** *FAQ:* ✓**INTERNET**→*ftp* rtfm.mit.edu→anonymous→<your email address>→/pub/usenet-by-group/talk.politics.misc HOURLY

Animal rights

Animal_Righ (echo) If you love animals—not as pets but as fellow creatures upon this earth who deserve their dignity every bit as much as human beings—you'll love this conference. There's not a tremendous amount of fur flying, since most of the participants are preaching to other converted, but there's plenty of insight into what makes hard-core animal-rights activists tick. Never rhetorically shy, the participants go right for the jugular, and when one man says that the euthanizing of old greyhounds reminds him "of the Holocaust when the Jews were gassed then put into a big holes dug for mass burial," only a few other writers object. The conference tackles a wide variety of topics, from the macro (the philosophy of animal rights) to the micro (Mandi writes Simon to tell him that his decision to care for a hurt bird warms her heart). ✓**RELAYNET** DAILY

Death penalty

alt.activism.death-penalty (ng) In addition to a small amount of news, both national ("Nebraska reinstates the death penalty") and international ("Killer beheaded in Riyadh"), alt.activism.death-penalty offers shouting from both sides of the fence. Some of the facing-off is nothing more than old loggerheads made new; the law-and-order types who feel that crime won't stop unless the state acts with mortal impunity ("Quite frankly, I get sick of the anti-DPers whining about the poor criminal, while I stand around having to console yet another family of a murder victim") versus those whose stomachs turn at the prospect of sanctioned killing ("How can the state kill under any circumstance?"). But the newsgroup also includes more textured issues: whether televised executions are an atrocity or an effective expansion of capital punishment's deterrent power, what should be done with the statistics about racial bias in death-penalty convictions, the irony of many pro-lifers' support for capital punishment. There are a few nuggets for bumper-sticker entrepreneurs: "Guns don't kill people—the state kills people." ✓**USENET** DAILY

Domestic policy

Education Eddie, a former gang member who cleaned up his act, knows why schools are failing in their attempt to discipline our kids: "When the psychologists and the ACLU took away the ability to punish, they took away the ability to control what, after all, are no more than unsocial animals until they get trained—our dear, darling children." Eddie's opinion quickly comes under fire, with parents objecting that punishment should occur in the home, or that negative reinforcement is no reinforcement at all.

CompuServe's education message board ranges far and wide. Discussions of socialism in schools leaks into a full-blown debate over bastardy in colonial America and then expands again to incorporate gender stereotypes, Jungian psychology, and the flaws of the crime bill. When they stay on target, the postings can be provocative; questioning whether the government is

Bosnian devastation—downloaded from http://www.math.hr/links/war.html.

doing everything it can to help qualified students attend college, or bemoaning diminishing economic opportunities for high-school graduates. An ad for "secretary" will attract huge numbers of persons with decades of experience at firms which have downsized or gone under, and your basic H.S. grad simply isn't in the running"). ✓**COMPUSERVE**→*go* politics→Messages→Education DAILY

Health Care Postings in this forum cover a fairly narrow spectrum of issues: How do the competing American plans compare with other systems worldwide? Is universal coverage socialist? And what of the specific economic facts of the plan? The detailed considerations of economics are fascinating, even if presented as rigid polemics. But in navigating the Sargasso Sea of risks and rewards, participants sometimes sounds like high-school debaters, engaging in mental calisthenics that don't transcend the commonest common sense: "Should we outlaw cigarettes? Then why not beer? Then why not anything with cholesterol? Where does it stop?" Not here, apparently. ✓**COMPUSERVE**→*go* politics→Messages→Health Care HOURLY

Hotspot: USA Are our cities

hurtling toward certain civil war? Should Cuban immigrants in the post–Cold War era be granted the status of political refugees? And what is the government doing for the American farmer?

On CompuServe's Hotspot: USA message board, Americans of all races, creeds, colors, classes, ages, and regions sound off about the issues that stick in their craw. Whether it's a young woman writing to complain about the blocking of RU-486 ("Reproductive freedom is not and will never be a threat to good government, and it is owed unconditionally to the women of any intelligent nation") or a middle-aged man criticizing government disease-control policy ("FDA inaction is increasing the spread of antibiotic-resistant bacteria"), the bulletin board accommodates a wide spectrum of political views.

Hot spots

The true hot spots, however, seem to be health care and abortion rights; one man even goes so far as to suggest that abortion-clinic bombings are not the work of anti-abortion activists but rather

> "Reproductive freedom is not and will never be a threat to good government, and it is owed unconditionally to the women of any intelligent nation."

arson scams, or pranks. ("Innocent until proven guilty' is supposed to be the doctrine followed, but it doesn't seem to apply for right- wing Christians.") Never a dull moment. ✓**COMPUSERVE**→*go* crisis→ Messages→Hotspot: USA DAILY

Talk of the Nation Simulchat
The afternoon chat in the Talk of the Nation Forum's Control Room starts off with the same topic as on that day's radio program (should you own a gun at home?), but the 45 participants online are soon barreling along on their own separate track. You don't really need to be listening to the radio to participate in this open marriage of on-line and on-air. Only when the radio show takes a break for a news update and returns with a new topic does the online chat downshift for the switch to the second hour's subject. Moderators are lightly trained volunteers who sign an agreement to report all users who curse. ✓**AMERICA ONLINE**→*keyword* npr→Talk of The Nation→The Control Room

International

GeoPol (ml) You've got the whole world in your hands. The vast world of Cyberspace is the perfect place to discuss geography and politics—on GeoPol anything that happens just about anywhere is fair game. Although there are a fair number of scholars on this list—political scientists, geographers, historians—there are also a lot of activists and public-policy strategists from many different countries. This creates very vivid exchanges about pretty much everything—U.S. welfare policy, AIDS, the Rwandan revolution, the Islamic revolution, the oil market, gays and lesbians and po-

litical violence, and what have you. ✓**INTERNET**→*email* listserv@ukcc.uky.edu ✍ *Type in message body:* subscribe geopol <your full name> WEEKLY

Hotspot: Haiti Though CompuServe's Haiti message board serves a relatively small group of Haitian-policy enthusiasts, the discussion is both factually responsible and powerfully opinionated. Is U.S. policy toward Haiti supporting democracy? As on most policy bulletin boards, there are more knots tied than untied, and there is more territory claimed than conquered. But even if you are not a diligent reader of international-policy journals, you can still drop into this bulletin board to offer your opinion. ✓**COMPUSERVE**→*go* crisis→Messages→Hotspot: Haiti WEEKLY

International Issues Forum
Large, but not unwieldy: The hundred or so messages posted daily to the forum are sorted into a number of more specific message boards. While the Political Viewpoint board seems overly concerned with labels and terms—what do you call liberal?—the Domestic Issues board includes some surprisingly well-informed posts on crime, health care, and child care. Other boards, such as International Issues, fare less well—there's the sense of having bitten off too much to chew, of lumping together everything from Gaza to Cuba, extradition to female circumcision. The most compelling attractions are perhaps the specialty message boards—Campaign '94 has a folder for each state and invites residents to post their thoughts on elections, and Pending Legislation has passionate ranting about crime and health care. ✓**AMERICA ONLINE**→ *keyword* issues HOURLY

War War! What is it good for? Impassioned political and philosophical discussion. The WELL's war conference puts its finger on a variety of global hot spots—Bosnia-Herzogovina, Somalia, Lebanon, Azerbaijan, Haiti—and pushes, trying to clarify why human beings sometimes feel the irrepressible urge to take up arms against another group of human beings and duel to the death. In addition, conference participants check in with updates on war technology, reviews of military books and films, and personal anecdotes from combat situations. √**WELL**→*g* war WEEKLY

Second Amendment

Gun Politics/SRA Jack says, "Hurry, hurry, all amendments must go! Order now, while you can still get some!"—and that seems to be the dominant feeling on CompuServe's Gun Politics message board. Along with the usual disparagement of the Brady Bill and the frequent use of firearm jargon—"They offer the P94 in 9mm and .40 for civilian sale without the laser light"—the bullet-heads on the Gun Politics message board seem most interested in defeating gun-control arguments with reductio ad absurdum.

> **"All you gun supporters don't mind the prospect of accidental shootings because you already have holes in your heads."**

Gun—downloaded from gipsy.vmars.tuwien.ac.at.

To wit: "One of the anti-gunners' arguments is that our Founding Fathers did not foresee the advancement of technologies of the next 200 years. They would have us believe that the Second Amendment limits us to black-powder muskets and the like. Of course, that might also limit and ban radio, TV, electronic communication, and modern printing presses." And maybe even personal computers. √**COMPUSERVE**→*go* outdoors→Messages→Gun Politics/SRA HOURLY

RTKBA (echo) The mysterious abbreviation of the title stands for the gun-control clause of the Second Amendment, "the right to keep and bear arms," and that's what they talk about here, arms and the man—although this bulletin board has a higher number of women than other pro-gun sites.

Usual arguments

The RBA faithful truck out the usual arguments against gun control—"I want the option to be able to protect myself and my family if the need arises," "Why should one part of the Bill of Rights be any more or less valid than another?"—while occasionally going on for scintillating wordplay (*assumption* becomes "ass/u/me-tion"). There's an incredibly high frequency of posts, in part because participants

love to discuss local legislation, as well as very specific gun-related problems. If there's anything surprising about RTKBA, it's the creeping presence of violent paramilitary forces—one man refers to "a post from some new militia bunch (allegedly) that calls for an armed 'raid' on Congress," and another subscriber advises that "the best bet is to live in a small town and get the local government to go sovereign." √**FIDONET** HOURLY

talk.politics.guns (ng) This newsgroup has a double-barreled appeal—in addition to posting passionate debate, it offers a cross section of America that does away with common stereotypes: There are urban hunters and rural pacifists, Republican gun-control supporters and Democratic riflemen.

Rhetorical shells

On talk.politics.guns, the various pro-gun and anti-gun postings square off and fire rhetorical shells at one another. "If we accept the Brady Bill, we allow the feds to dictate law enforcement." "I would much rather see people like you beaten, raped, and murdered than give up my Second Amendment rights." "All you gun supporters don't mind the prospect of accidental shootings because you already have holes in your heads." √**USENET** HOURLY

Environment

The same technological progress that has enabled us to spoil and destroy the planet,

ironically, is helping us perhaps to appreciate its fragility. Thirty years ago there were the first big-blue-marble photos from outer space, now there is the incipient reality of a global village based on the Net. America Online's **Network Earth**, tied in with the Turner TV program, hews to practical therapies, while the WELL's **Whole Earth** charts the eco-avant-garde.

Air pollution—downloaded from America Online's Mac Graphics Forum.

On the Net

Ecology (echo) Is the rise in ocean levels caused by global warming or increased pumping of the world's aquifers? Are zoos a valuable resource for ecologists or just another example of man's wanton and irresponsible treatment of his surroundings? And what of this sociology question, which seems inspired by Disney's latest animated smash: "Could the violence between lions and hyenas be called hate if you attempted to put it into human terms?"

The Ecology conference brings together men and women concerned about the future of our planet, and the relationship between society and the environment. The posts are usually quite serious, but there's a satisfying amount of rhetoric (of two new methods of waste disposal, one subscriber writes that "both ideas have been turkeys and real money sponges") and even a little irony (an extended flap over the revela-

tion that the cofounder of an international ecological organization still drives a car, claiming, "If I miss a train, I have to wait an hour for another one, so it cuts into my family time").

Ultimately, there's an embattled air about the proceedings: When you're fighting against avaricious corporations and apathetic societies, you realize more than ever that it's not easy being green. ✓**FIDONET** DAILY

Environment Need to dispose of used motor oil? Want to know more about bovine growth hormone? How about teak harvesting? The conference covers all this and more—and along the way manages to articulate some fascinating theories about the way that environmental responsibility represents a fertile crossbreeding of spiritual and economic concerns. ✓**WELL**→*g* env HOURLY

Environmental Forum The fo-

rum divides environmental issues into national and global topics. The former helps explain what ordinary citizens like Donna ("I try

> "And remember, online conferences are ecologically airtight (except for the electricity use, the radiation from your monitor, and all the electromagnetic fields generated by the get-together)."

to recycle but sometimes my neighborhood doesn't help me with regular pickups") and Saul ("Are there any environmental harms to email?") can do to improve their environment.

As for the latter, the Global Action and Information Network uses this forum as a base, publishing regular news releases and updates on environmental breakthroughs, and encouraging all kinds of green activism. Live conferencing happens in the Environmental Chat room. ✓**AMERICA ONLINE**→*keyword* eforum→EcoMessaging Center *and* Environmental Chat DAILY

Network Earth Online Affiliated with TBS's Sunday-night TV show, AOL's Network Earth Online worries about what happens when human society loses sight of the relationships that protect and preserve our planet. Less lament than therapy, Network Earth offers a variety of solutions, from organic gardening to environmental games to energy-rating your own home.

Depressing news

That doesn't mean there's no depressing news, of course, and Network Earth participants aren't hesitant to point out that we are squandering our resources at unprecedented rates, that our synthetics have kicked the breath out of the natural world, and that we must "live with the effects of our previous, unrestricted uses of mainly organochlorine compounds."

Those having trouble shaking the world-gone-wrong nightmares from their heads are advised to check out this recent suggestion, made by a lapsed environmentalist: "For four and one-half billion years, life has survived on our planet. We must be egotistical to

think that the actions of a humanity and its relatively few pounds of biomass are going to destroy our biosystem." ✓**AMERICA ONLINE**→ *keyword* network earth→ Message Boards *and* Conference Hall WEEKLY

talk.environment (ng) "I want to be green/recycle my mail/I'm hoping to be/a friend to the whale." It's just a song, of course, but it accurately summarizes the dominant sentiment on this newsgroup, which speculates on both the small (recycling your newspapers) and the large (nuclear power) things that we can do to clarify our responsibility to the earth.

Subscribers are the usual suspects—younger activists who worry that the world will not bear their weight, as well as older activists who want to provide for the future. And remember, online conferences are ecologically airtight (except for the electricity use, the radiation from your monitor, and all the electromagnetic fields generated by the get-together). ✓**USENET** DAILY

Whole Earth This conference is the nerve center of the WELL, housing a huge set of discussions relating to the *Whole Earth Review*. In addition to critical assessments of other publications and commentary on the *Whole Earth Radio Show*, the conference plows a fairly wide furrow through the environmental avant-garde, whether it regards the environment of a forest, below sea level, or inside your head.

This conference hosts thoughtful debates on a wide variety of topics—from virtual cultures to mathematical bioeconomics, from Luddites to Biosphere 2, from Loompanics to public radio. ✓**WELL**→*g* we HOURLY

CYBERNOTES

"If the poles were to melt and life continued to exist, it would take centuries. Guess what, the time between major ice ages is about 200 centuries.

"Trick is, nobody said the whole polar cap has to melt to cause serious flooding around the world. A minor temperature change of 1 to 3 degrees could see huge amounts of flooding, moving the melt line about 100 miles north and south.

"Well, one degree hasn't done it! As a matter of fact, just recently, an article stated how much the levels should have risen and they had risen slightly more. It was postulated that the overage was due to the increased pumping of the world's aquifers, which caused the seas to rise.

"Are you aware of the ocean's ability to be a heat sink and a reflector of solar radiation? The increased surface areas will act as a balancing agent."

—from **FidoNet's Ecology**

Political ideologies

Is Bob Dole insane? Is Dan Quayle really that dum? And is there any truth to the rumor

that Bill Clinton is releasing a pop song with the words "It's my party, and I'll exploit it for personal financial and sexual gain if I want to"? If you're fascinated by major-party politics, these electronic party lines are for you. Most commercial services have a White House Forum, and CompuServe sports one forum each for the Democratic Party and the GOP. While sentiments don't always rise above the petty—Republican traitors! Democratic pinheads!—local races tend to receive serious discussion and debate. If you love organized politics but can't bring yourself to kowtow to the majors, take heart: There are also discussion groups devoted to anarchy and libertarianism.

Ronald Reagan—downloaded from byrd.mu.wvnet.edu.

On the Net

Across the board

alt.politics.elections (ng) It's the great American ritual, the behavior that repeatedly reaffirms and reshapes our national identity. No, not watching O. J. on Court TV. Elections. There's something elegant about purely theoretical arguments for proportional representation or term limits, and the intellectual marrow of the matter inspires some truly innovative pro-

posals—one man suggests that officeholders be reimbursed for their service based on approval ratings. But the newsgroup's strongest asset is its ability to collect the opinions of election watchers, who are almost like sports fans in their devotion to unbridled rhetoric and their belief in themselves as armchair Nostradamuses.

As one man says of the Virginia senatorial race featuring noted perjurer Oliver North, "I think North will do to Virginia Republicans what George McGovern did to the national Democratic Party: leave it divided and ineffectual for a good long while." ✓**USENET** WEEKLY

White House Forum Is Bill Clinton linked to gangland slayings? Should the White House be renamed the Sleaze House? Is it true that Bob Dole and Hillary had lunch last week, and that Hillary even ordered dessert? All these questions and more are handled with great passion and a bare

minimum of tact on AOL's White House Forum. Encompassing both domestic policy and international affairs, the White House Forum also has two special message boards devoted to Current Legislation and Media Watch.

The former is pretty much filled by questions and answers about universal health care and the crime bill. The latter offers forum participants a chance to fire away at media figures. As one man asks in an open letter to Cokie Roberts, "As the daughter of a former Democratic legislator from Louisiana, a graduate of the liberally politically oriented Wellesley, not to mention your cozy relationship with NPR, how do you hope to convince your audience that you don't allow such influences and/or biases to creep into your reporting?" Cokie doesn't answer. ✓**AMERICA ON-LINE**→*keyword* whitehouse→Message Boards DAILY

White House Forum Serves up

a bouillabaisse of facts, questions, and opinions on the federal government. Trying to get a handle on President Clinton's personality? Curious about Whitewater? Or maybe you just want to complain about the lack of attention devoted to Chelsea Clinton? When the forum moves into issues, it settles on many of the same worn posts that can be found in other newsgroups and discussion forums. It is perhaps most interesting for its presidential trivia: Charles offers the tantalizing tidbit that "Coolidge pulled out of the race for a second term after he lost his 'cool' when his wife 'disappeared' with her Secret Service escort for several hours." ✓**COMPUSERVE**→*go* white house→Messages DAILY

White House RoundTable Bob Dylan once pointed out that even the president of the United States sometimes must have to stand naked—that and other trivia are confirmed on GEnie's White House Bulletin Board. While the traffic is a little light for a forum dealing with the future of our nation, the topics cover all the important aspects of federal government, from the judicial branch ("Whatever his flaws, Clinton seems to have chosen rock-solid personnel for the court"), to legislative matters (lots of talk about "the conceptual failure of gun control") to international affairs, environmental policy, welfare reform. And there are a number of less formal sections of the Bulletin Board: personal questions about the first family, discussion of D.C. architecture, and even a category devoted to the historical White House—does Dolly Madison's ghost still roam the halls, dispensing snack cakes and sage advice? ✓**GENIE**→ *keyword* whitehouse→ White House Bulletin Board *or* White House Real-Time Conference

WEEKLY/LIVE

Anarchy

alt.society.anarchy (ng) Ah, anarchy. "People can have total freedom and total choice, and the strong-arming of individual spirit will end decisively." Much of alt.society.anarchy seems to have its origins in the overenthusiasms of college life—ignited by Nietzsche and whatever other deep thinkers appear to support "the breakdown of all institutions so that people are free to live as they choose." There's a decent amount of discussion about techno-anarchy, and in response to the suggestion that computers will make people "almost godlike" by disarming society's apparatus of detection and punishment, one young man cannot contain his glee: "I am a wholehearted fan of the individual superpower concept. It will make people much harder to push around." ✓**USENET** DAILY

Democratic

alt.politics.clinton (ng) Like them or hate them, the first boomer president and his wife (Heather? Valerie?) have forever altered the face of American politics. For the first time ever, we have a president not shaped primarily by the Good War, a powerful, active first lady, and a White House redecorated with questions of generational angst—antiwar activism, drug use, open admission of sexual misconduct. On alt.politics.clinton, the FOB (Friends of Bill) and SEOBs (Sworn Enemies of Bill) dig in and fire off, and the close quarters generate the kind of unyoked rhetoric that spices up the best political newsgroups. Those posting are mostly young adults, and the tone of messages ranges

from snotty ("I have great respect for the office of the president of the U.S., which is why I have no respect for the lying, incompetent excuse for a president who currently occupies that office") to clever ("This Halloween, Clinton is planning to wear a really outrageous costume—he's going as a two-term president") to flat-out cruel (Robert Reich is described as "a troll" and "a Marxist midget"). All in all, a crash course in how a Bill becomes a target. ✓**USENET** DAILY

Democratic Forum What is a Democrat? Well, someone who believes in welfare, for one thing ("In the richest nation in the world, it is our obligation to support those whose misfortunes enable the rest of us to be successful"). Someone who despises Pat Buchanan ("His red-meat rhetoric brings out the worst in people, inspires fear and loathing"). Someone who resists being a slavish ideologue by gently needling rad-lib oracles like Noam Chomsky ("Is he still mad at himself for being Jewish, or has he calmed down his anti-Israel diatribes?"). And, above all, someone who posts on CompuServe's Democratic Forum.

Issues range from domestic economy to crime to international affairs, and the opinions come from all over the country—from the D.C. insider who suggests that Bill Clinton is "quietly assembling one of the more impressive administrations of the last 30 years" to the Oregon man who disparages his state for deeming it "'unnecessary' to offer women breast reconstruction after breast cancer." There are dissenting voices, of course, but they're usually drowned out within a day or two, and the Democratic way of life ascends again. ✓**COMPUSERVE**→*go* democrat→Messages DAILY

Libertarianism

alt.philosophy.objectivism (ng) While objectivism has existed in some form since the mid–19th century, most adherents to this philosophy trace the term to the influential 20th-century novelist Ayn Rand, known for her leaden prose style and her devotion to a brutally realistic view of social morality.

But even if you don't have your dog-eared copies of *Atlas Shrugged* and *The Fountainhead* on hand, there's plenty here to occupy you, from disquisitions on other objectivist philosophers (David Kelley, Leonard Peikoff) to specific applications of objectivist thought to social matters such as health care, redistribution of wealth, and the rendering of legal opinion. Skeptics should note that the group isn't always so high-minded, and that a number of postings occupy themselves with the important question of how to pronounce *Ayn*. ✓ USENET *FAQ:* ✓ INTERNET→*ftp* rtfm.mit.edu→ anonymous→<your email address>→/pub/usenet-by-hierarchy/alt/answers/objectivism→faq DAILY

alt.politics.libertarian (ng) Give me libertarianism or give me death. Or something like that. Why do we need birth certificates—are we people or "subjects"? Why don't we have very, very short term limits? All in all, governments in general take a beating, and virtually every administrative action is seen as an attack on personal liberties.

To its credit, the newsgroup does sometimes attempt to reconcile the libertarian hard line with real-world concerns. For instance, after one post insists that taxation equals extortion—"Taxation is unjust, and only despotic governments tax, and, since all govern-

Ayn Rand—from http://www.rpi.edu./~pier1/phil/objectivism.html.

ments tax, all governments are despotic"—dozens of other participants wonder aloud how a libertarian government would raise money. ✓ USENET *FAQ:* ✓ INTERNET →*ftp* rtfm.mit.edu→anonymous→<your email address>→/pub/usenet-by-group/alt.answers/libertarian DAILY

Ayn-Rand (ml) The discussion bills itself as "a moderated discussion of objectivist philosophy." For the uninitiated that means this list addresses questions like "Do rights exist?" "Who can judge another citizen?" "When is coercion wrong?" There is much activity here, in long postings—recently about how to support a government without the unreasonable intrusion of taxation.

At times the list does chapter-by-chapter analysis of objectivist works, accompanied by essays from new scholars, and all other discussion is put on hold. The members always welcome new blood and new ideas for creating the anarcho-capitalist state. ✓ INTERNET→*email* listserv@iubvm.bitnet ✍ *Type in message body:* subscribe ayn-rand <your full name> WEEKLY

Republican

Republican Forum The Grand Old Party has its very own CompuServe forum, and while it's slightly less bustling than its Democratic counterpart, the Republican Forum has substantial traffic in issues ranging from the defense budget to health care to the crime bill. Because the party is still smarting over having lost the presidency, most of the messages are undisguised broadsides against the Clinton administration.

And while some participants texture their rage by considering the shifting identity of the GOP—"I am absolutely outraged," writes one man, "by the traitors in the Republican Party who have betrayed the American people by their votes for a crime bill that does nothing more than hand the Democrats billions to buy more votes with"—others forgo insight for cheap shots, such as the man who persists in calling Hillary Clinton "Hitlery." The forum also offers separate message boards for East, Midwest, West, and South. ✓ COMPUSERVE→*go* republican→Messages DAILY

> **"Charles offers the tidbit that 'Coolidge pulled out of the race for a second term after his wife "disappeared" with her Secret Service escort.'"**

Rush Limbaugh

The country's most popular Republican after Ronald Reagan inspires some of the best

right-center-left clashes on the Net, with legions of Rush-for-president followers and a smaller cadre of Flush Rush critics going toe-to-toe on a show-by-show basis. Judge for yourself whether Rush emerges better or worse for the wear after bruising battles in **alt.fan. rush-limbaugh** or Relay-Net's **RushLimbaugh** echo.

Rush Limbaugh—downloaded from Exec PC.

On the Net

alt.fan.rush-limbaugh (ng) "Sporting" may be the nicest way to describe the voluminous discourse here, where Flush Rush detractors commit drive-by attacks. Rush-for-president acolytes post lengthy "amens" to recent Rush sermons. Media junkies from across the political spectrum come here to debate the bias of radio, TV, and print. Above all, though, the fray is about issues; gun control, birth control, private property, personal privacy, free speech, free health care, flag burning, and flag waving—you name it. ✓**USE-NET** HOURLY

Rush H. Limbaugh Like its subject, CompuServe's Rush Limbaugh message board is bloated, with hundreds of posts each day dissecting the phenomenon of America's windiest windbag. While there are plenty of Rush supporters, there's also a large anti-Rush contingent that insists on detailing his lies and distortions (dubbed RushRongs by the bul-

letin board): "How his inaccuracies can go unchallenged by such a large segment of the population, how people can delude themselves into respecting him as a worthy adversary, is so mysterious that perhaps this group should be absorbed into 'Unexplained Phenomena.'" Is he racist? Will he run for office? Didn't he meet his wife online? And why is Garry Trudeau attacking this nice man? ✓**COM-PUSERVE**→*go* issues→Messages→ Rush H. Limbaugh HOURLY

RushLimbaugh (echo) Not since Richard Nixon has a single figure so polarized the political opinion of the nation. And not since Richard Nixon has a figure of this stature taken on such sophomoric nicknames. America, meet Rush Windbag, and Rush Dimbulb, and Rush Lamebrain, and Rush Limburger. There are even more conceptual monikers: Baby HUAC, anyone?

This Rush bulletin board doesn't waste too much time talking about Rush himself—the newlywed, the media power, the om-

nivore—choosing instead to concentrate on the issues in orbit around the man.

Corrosive rhetoric

Want to know about Clinton's alleged deceits? Fretting over the prospect of socialized medicine? Worried about women without husbands? Well, you'll find enough corrosive rhetoric here to last you a lifetime.

And while there are plenty of broadsides against Democrats and other "mealy-minded liberals," those of the mealy minds aren't afraid to fight back, to offer evidence that Limbaugh is giving the facts the bum's rush, and even to get in a few zingers of their own: "Giant sucking sound? Neocon foot on its way to the mouth." ✓**RELAYNET** DAILY

> "How people can delude themselves into respecting Rush Limbaugh as a worthy adversary is so mysterious that perhaps this group should be absorbed into 'Unexplained Phenomena.'"

Part 5

Coffee House

Idle chatter

Want to talk about your new shoes? Need to ask about how to spot during weightlifting?

Just trying to hang out and make new friends? Welcome aboard, motormouths. In addition to the pure generic character of CompuServe's **CB channels** and GEnie's **Real-Time Chat**, there are also growing numbers of virtual chat environments. In AOL's **LaPub**, for instance, participants pretend that they are in a neighborhood bar, and the illusion comes complete with bartenders, tabs, and regulars. Norm!!

Cheers—*http://www.maths.tcd.ie/pub/images/wee/sindex.html.*

On the Net

Across the board

Adult Issues One of the most satisfying sites online for detailed adult discussion, examining "everything from foster parenting to adoption; from pregnancy to parenting teens to grandparenting, and other family relationships." Although sex as a topic is excluded on this restricted channel, there are postings on issues of sexuality such as false sexual-abuse charges and rape. The postings are almost all articulate and levelheaded, addressing a small but quirky set of issues—sexuality and religion, marital fidelity, even adult bedwetting and incontinence. ✓**GE-NIE**→ *keyword* family→Family and Personal Growth Bulletin Board→ Adult Issues WEEKLY

Chat Lines With up to 45 chan-

nels of generic conversation, GEnie's real-time chat zone is skeletal but effective. It is relatively anonymous—only your alias is displayed, although participants have access to your service account name and monitors keep scatology to a minimum. As a result, the flirting that goes on is friendly: As one woman says, "Hugs all around."

On any given day, you might stumble into a heated argument about the role of Ron Wood in the Rolling Stones ("Saw him live and he was doing more than Keith, who seems to sleepwalk through the show while he dreams of his Connecticut estate"), witness the beginning of a beautiful relationship ("Cute handle, Little Sister: How old are you?"), or experience the delightful randomness that characterizes chat at its best ("I will continue to talk about the kind of hat I am wearing. It is a fedora, and a very nice one at that"). ✓**GENIE**→*keyword* chat

The Exchange "I have been on

Prozac for a few months, and I have noticed that my sex drive is diminishing. Has anyone else had this problem?" "I've heard that Prozac boosts your sex drive—and how great was it when you were despondent, anyway?" While this little exchange about the libidinal

> "Experience the delightful randomness that characterizes chat at its best ('I will continue to talk about the kind of hat I am wearing. It is a fedora, and a very nice one at that')."

effects of Prozac is racier than most of the material on The Exchange, it's representative of the informality and intimacy of this set of bulletin boards. With six main headings—Communities Center, Interests/Hobbies, Crafts/Sewing, Outdoor Activities, Collector's Corner, Home/Health/Careers—The Exchange organizes postings on subjects ranging from stay-at-home parents (that's SAHPs to you) to spelunking to numismatics. The Communities Center is a highlight, with individual folders devoted to various strategies of self-definition—not only gender but ethnicity (African American, American Indian, Asian) and even occasional speculations on regional character. ✓**AMERICA ONLINE**→*keyword* exchange WEEKLY

General Band While most of CompuServe is rigidly broken down into forums and services on specific topics, the CB channels, especially those in the General Band, are anything but focused, and members like them that way. People hop from channel to channel with handles like City Slicker, Fire Bear, and Princess Lily, enjoying the company of CB friends who mix a little bit of serious chat with a whole lot of silliness—laughing, exchanging hugs and kisses, and bopping each other over the head.

Holodeck

Although the General Band offers 36 channels, members consistently gather in only a few—The Holodeck, with a *Star Trek* theme (channel 7); Teen Only (channel 17); The Bear Cave, where many of the chatters have handles with "bear" in the name (channel 18); Village Elders, where chat is in theory more mature than on the teen channel (Channel 22); and

> "College men compare car stereos, bragging about removable faceplates, graphic equalizers, subwoofers, and four-figure price tags."

Game Play I and Game Play II, where real-time word and trivia games are held. Part of the fun here is in joining or forming private group discussions. (See the FAQ for instructions on how to do it.) You may even be involved in multiple, private discussions at once! Channel 2's "Welcome Newcomers" offers assistance to CB newbies. ✓**COMPUSERVE**→*go* cb→CB General Band

#hottub #Hottub is clubby; you have to work a little if you want to belong. I got kicked off several times, because I asked about this strange word in the topic line, *Xney*, and it turned out to be this guy's name in the encryption program rot-13. Hey, that's cool. They told me to get a clue, but once I told them they were vicious they let me stay. It was neato. College men compared car stereos, bragging about removable faceplates, graphic equalizers, subwoofers, and four-figure price tags. A young woman who'd eaten too much pizza with her vodka wondered if she was going to vomit. William Bennett should meet these people. ✓**INTERNET**→*irc* /channel #hottub

LaPub Sometimes you want to go

where everybody knows your screen name. And when you do, you might try AOL's LaPub, a virtual bar "hosted most days from noon, and every night starting at 8 p.m. until at least 2 a.m." It's full of tavern ambience, with a community of regulars and friendly debates over favorite beers.

Taco Night

Technology has not yet enabled beer to be delivered over the Net, but there are special events like Taco Night, Hot Tub Night, and LaToga night. In the "cellar," patrons can recall (and even download) "memories" of past parties—transcripts of that time Maria and Jen did the dance of the seven veils—man, were they drunk.

Like all online meeting places, LaPub produces experience at one remove, but the barroom conceit makes it a little stranger than most. Some people actually seem to be drinking at home during their login time, and it's not uncommon for someone logged on during the late shift to attempt intoxicated speech ("So what I'm shayying…").

And while one regular refers to himself as a "cyber-space alcoholic," there's no word on whether AOL has considered founding a recovery program to help people who can't stop pretending that they are drinking. ✓**AMERICA ONLINE**→*keyword* lapub→ENTER LAPUB

Prodigy Chat Of all the chat services, Prodigy's Live Chat has the furthest to go. While its basic outlines seem to mimic AOL's People Connection—themed rooms, the ability to send private messages to other users—poor design greatly limits its effectiveness. Screen nicknames can be changed only once each day, message display is sluggish, and the instant-message screens are incredibly unwieldy. Suggested categories range from hobby clubs to romance-ad fare like Big Beautiful Women. So far, though, Prodigy users don't seem too entranced with the service, and while one woman confessed that she was "totally addicted to chat," it's going to take some time and some serious retooling to float this boat. ✓**PRODIGY**→*jump* chat

Speak Easy Forum A new catch-all for those little odds and ends of conversation not covered by any other forums. If you want to share your thoughts on games, gadgets, travel, pets, environment, you name it—this is the place, especially if your thoughts tend toward the cursory. In the history section, a woman provides a little lesson on Dartmoor, the wild heart of the West Country, while over in Family Matters, one man advises another on the malleability of gender ("Mark—after a course of hormone injections, you could indeed breast-feed in public, or anywhere else. Those nipples on your chest just need a little help to become functional").

While it's unlikely that Speak Easy will change your life, it may very well provide you with some interesting minutiae, such as a recent study conducted by the University of Loughborough that suggests that lone sleepers get better rest than those with bedmates. ✓**COMPUSERVE**→*go* speakeasy→ Messages WEEKLY

Confessions

Life Stories Whether you subscribe to theories of the monomyth or not, our lives are given shape—even meaning—by stories, that tricky business of what happens when, to whom, and how. The WELL's Life Stories conference presents narratives on a wide

David Letterman—from http://www. cen.uiuc.edu/~j18287/late.news.html

variety of topics, everything from real-estate deals gone bad to the loss of loved ones to cancer. Usually a single participant will post an extensive story and then readers will respond, asking questions and sharing insights.

When one woman related an account of working as a topless dancer—fighting with the management, withstanding overwhelming misogyny—the response blossomed into a fertile discussion of distaff sacrifices in contemporary America. Not all stories are this successful at generating response—"My Life With the Opposite Sex: A Comedy," a long and somewhat tedious account of life and love in the sedentary middle class, sat flat for weeks. Those are the breaks, though; if you have a story, compose it and post it, and see what happens. ✓**WELL**→*g* life DAILY

True Confessions If you have any interest in birth, death, love, joy, sex, fear, anger, money, or pets, you'll want to read this. All true! All confessions! Only on the WELL. ✓**WELL**→*g* tru DAILY

Pen pals

soc.penpals (ng) The conversations don't take place here, but it's

where they begin. "Married with three sons (only one still home)" seeks pen pal. "Looking for New Age music lovers," "Still looking for Asian female," "Gay Hungarian pen pals?," and the very simple "Looking for friends" are but a few of the posts. Lots of people connecting for both email and snail-mail relationships. ✓**USENET** DAILY

Virtual pubs

alt.callahans (ng) The forerunner of the other alt.pub.* groups, Callahan's is a virtual-reality saloon based loosely on the books by Spider Robinson. The VR concept is taken more seriously here than in the similar alt.pub.coffeehouse.amethyst—various extras in Callahan's include a hot tub, a pizza machine, and a dance floor. Strangers are "friends we've just met," and everyone is welcomed and made to feel at home. People share serious, painful experiences

> "Some people actually seem to be drinking at home during their login time, and it's not uncommon for someone logged on during the late shift to attempt intoxicated speech ('So what I'm shayying...')."

in their lives just as often as they chat about upbeat things, and everyone's posts are respected. "Callahanians" often get together in real life; friendship, romance, and "even a marriage or two" have resulted from these parties.

And unlike your real friends, Callahanians will remember your birthday—an almanac is kept, and people you've never even met will send you electronic mail for the happy occasion. Stop by the IRC channel on Wednesday evenings for live get-togethers. ✓**USENET** ✓**INTERNET**→*irc* /channel #callahans *FAQ:* ✓**INTERNET**→*ftp* physics.su.oz. au→anonymous→ <your email address>→/mar/callahans HOURLY/ LIVE

---

alt.pub.coffeehouse.amethyst (ng) Hang out, have a cup of espresso or tea (no alcohol allowed), and talk. Unlike some alt.pub.* groups, this one has no specific theme, no fictional characters; you play yourself in third person, the Cyberspace equivalent of you in RL surroundings are creative and casual, and numerous files containing biographies of the users conventions of the group (e.g. basic descriptions of the "room," etiquette for posts, etc.) are available for FTP. ✓**USENET** *Archives:* ✓**INTERNET**→*ftp* physics. su.oz.au→anonymous→<your email address>→/mar/amethyst *FAQ:* ✓**INTERNET**→*ftp* rtfm.mit.edu→ anonymous→<your email address> →/pub/usenet-by-group/alt.pub. coffeehouse.amethyst→ADMIN:_ Amethyst_Coffeehouse_Frequent ly_Asked_Questions DAILY

---

alt.pub.dragons-inn (ng) Gather with friends who know you only as the adventurer you play online— a fictional character inside The Dragon's Inn, a public house in the city of Generica sometime during the Middle Ages. Anyone who's

played Dungeons and Dragons will feel at home here, but no dice are rolled and there's no dungeon master.

Collective story

Instead, any adventures your character undertakes are part of a "collective story," and the plot depends on the imagination of all concerned. Introductions with full character descriptions are the norm. Plenty of relevant files concerning history, characters, etiquette, etc., can be found in the FTP sites. Other role-playing VR groups include alt.pub.clovenshield (a similar D&D/medieval atmosphere) and alt.pub.havens-rest (futuristic space and science-fiction adventures). ✓**USENET** *Archives:* ✓**INTERNET** ...→*ftp* rtfm.mit.edu→ anonymous→<your email address> →/pub/usenet-by-group/alt.pub. dragons-inn ...→*ftp* ftp.netcom.com →anonymous→<your email address>→/pub/mrhyde/APDI *FAQ:* ✓**INTERNET**→*ftp* rtfm.mit.edu→anonymous→<your email address>→ /pub/usenet-by-group/alt.pub.drag ons-inn DAILY

> "Unlike your real friends, Callahanians will remember your birthday—an almanac is kept, and people you've never even met will send you electronic mail for the happy occasion."

Local scenes

Eastcoast Horace Greeley's biggest nightmare, the WELL's Eastcoast conference celebrates the region more colloquially known as "a bunch of big cities all sandwiched together at the top right of the United States." Though the conference is dominated by New York City—much like the East Coast itself in this respect—participants don't hesitate to discuss other cities as well: Boston, Baltimore, Philadelphia, Washington D.C. Topics range from advice for those who are moving to critiques of museum exhibits to laments about commuting. And, as always, there's a lot of talk about the weather; as one Philadelphia woman explained in the summer "the weather is too brutal to do anything but stay inside and type." ✓**WELL**→*g* east DAILY

Midwest If the midriff of the nation—that chunky region bounded by the Canadian border, the Mason/Dixon line, the Rockies, and the Ohio-Pennsylvania border—were to secede, its daily newspaper might look a little something like the WELL's Midwest conference, which does its best to fight the image of Midwesterners as gentle giants, cornfed rubes who wouldn't know culture if it smacked them in the face.

There are plenty of postings from Detroit to Topeka that celebrate local music scenes, museums, and fine restaurants. Despite the slight chip on the shoulder of the participants—many of the topics, such as "Great Midwesterners through history," seem designed specifically to combat stereotypes—there's a homey feel to the conference, and much of the business conducted here is charmingly small-town ("Mac needed in Chicago," "Please help with one-way van rentals to Mil-waukee"). ✓**WELL**→*g* midwest DAILY

New Orleans (ml) You might not be able to go home again, but you sure as hell can try to make yourself feel better by talking about it. A librarian from Hawaii, a DJ from Santa Monica, and a computer programmer from Waltham, Massachusetts, chat daily with those lucky enough to still be down on the bayou on the laid-back New Orleans list.

This down-home list has everything that makes the city great (and notorious): politics, music, gossip, food, and booze. Between debates on newly legalized gambling and the Saints' fall lineup you can find recipes for crawfish, stuffed filet mignon, Bananas Foster, or Bread Pudding, as well as tips for the hottest new bars and best bands.

Old neighborhood rivalries might surface in a jovial manner, but the real loyalty of all here is to their city. Hating commercialization and change, the regulars band together to help preserve the creole feel. Don't ask for directions to the N.O. Hard Rock Cafe here—these people only frequent Tippitina's. ✓**INTERNET** ...→*email* mail-server@mintir.new-orleans.la.us ✍ *Type in message body:* subscribe new-orleans (for individidual messages) ...→*email* mail-server@mintir.new-orleans.la.us ✍ *Type in message body:* subscribe neworleans-weekly (for weekly digest) ...→*email* mail-server@mintir.new-orleans.la.us ✍ *Type in message body:* subscribe neworleans-digest (for daily digest) DAILY

New York Online (NYO) (bbs) "Hip Hoppin', Slammin', Funkified, Jazzed-out, and all around happenin'," says one member about the BBS that *The Village Voice* called "Hacklyn"—punning

> **"Offline get-togethers for concerts in Central Park, Indian dinners on East 6th Street, or parties are frequent."**

off of Spike Lee's *Crooklyn*. But chatters, not hackers, hang out on NYO—some 20 people on any given night. From its Subway board, where people are talking about their fave street musicians and least fave advertisements, to the New York Tales, where people describe their homes, their 'hoods, and their lives in New York City, members have an opinion about everything.

And judging by the activity in the board's Kiosk conferences—each conference is based on a separate periodical such as *El Diario, Spin, Wired, Vibe, The Forward, The Village Voice, Sun City, The New Yorker,* and the *Amsterdam News*—an opinion about everyone else's opinion. From the moment you enter on the Macintosh version (Windows available but not as good) you are welcomed to an acid-jazz beat (literally—the BBS runs on First Class Software, which offers audio as well as pretty graphics).

Happening

As you move through NYO, you'll hear as much as you see. "On-air guests" arrive weekly. Chuck D (Public Enemy's frontman), Bootsy Collins, and US3 have dropped by in the past. But even without the celebs, the public chats are happening. Most of the action takes place in the Free For All Station or Flavor Station, but the

Music Station is a popular live-chat area as well.

Offline get-togethers for concerts in Central Park, Indian dinners on East 6th Street, and farewell parties for members leaving the system are frequent. Omar and Peta are your guides on this journey through a virtual community in New York City. It doesn't get much better than this. ☎→*dial* 718-596-5881 DAILY/LIVE

San Francisco In the WELL's San Francisco conference, the Bay Area becomes one big coffeehouse (as if it weren't already). The visitors, who represent a wide range of ages, economic and ethnic backgrounds, and neighborhoods, talk candidly about the shape and rhythms of the city—its newspapers, parking, government—and in general the discussion is evenly split between celebration and lament. Where's the most popular place to take visitors, or to repair your car? Who has the best pizza? What's your favorite love story about the city? And, on the other side: When the big one comes, where will you go to loot? Don't you just hate those panhandlers? And what about that sudden infiltration of Argentinian army ants? ✓**WELL**→*g* sanfran DAILY

#texas College kids across the Lone Star State tease, guzzle beer, and offer to FedEx each other SuperMonsters with barbecue sauce from Freebird's. The screen scrolls by furiously with op wars, the details of last week's party, where Pokey fell asleep—but then he always falls asleep—and cheap shots at Aggies. You feel sorry for the lost child who logged on to say, "Hi all I am stoned," because the right drug for this channel is speed. ✓**INTERNET**→*irc* /channel #texas

IRC chat

Hundreds of conversations are going on simultaneously

throughout the world of IRC—more college-dorm, perhaps, than world. Wanna join? Just choose a channel. Down the hall at **#bored**, a group of friends are whining about life in general (and seem to be enjoying themselves). Over at **#abortion**, people with that freshman-like energy and "clarity" grapple with the issue—starting, of course, from square one. There's a game of stud poker going on next door at **#studpoker**—the game, in fact, never stops. Don't they ever go to class? Ditto about the **#jeopardy** dweebs.

Orientation is happening at **#penpals**, where people are determined to make a friend, and there are frat parties (not just Thursday night) at **#hottub**, **#sex**, **#netsex**, **#phonesex**, **#wetsex**, and all the "unofficial" frats that come and go. Extracurriculars are a great way to meet people—just check out **#karate** or **#astronomy**. Cliques are natural—Asians hang out with Asians on **#asian**, Muslims with Muslims on **#islam**, goths with goths on **#gothic**, Bostonians with Bostonians on **#Boston**, and the older crowd with each other on **#30plus** and **#40plus**. And, of course, IRC specializes in nonstop, anything-goes, just-can't-stop-myself-even-if-there-is-no-point chat. Try **#talk**, **#talk2me**, **#happy**, and **#callahans** for a sampling.

Earth—downloaded from galaxy.uci. agh.edu.pl. For astronomy chat, see #astronomy.

On the Net

#abortion Abortion debate. ✓INTERNET→*irc* /channel #abortion

#ad&d Discussion and role-play related to Advanced Dungeons & Dragons. ✓INTERNET→*irc* /channel #ad&d

#africa English and several African languages spoken here. ✓INTERNET→*irc* /channel #africa

#altmusic Some alternative-music discussion and a lot of general chatter. ✓INTERNET→*irc* /channel #altmusic

#amiga Amiga computer discussion and questions. ✓INTERNET→*irc* /channel #amiga

#amigager German-language discussion about Amiga computers. ✓INTERNET→*irc* /channel #amigager

#anime! Anime discussion. ✓INTERNET→*irc* /channel #anime!

#applellgs Discuss and ask questions about Apple II computers. ✓INTERNET→*irc* /channel #appleiigs

#asian For Asians. ✓INTERNET→*irc* /channel #asian

#astronomy Astronomy talk. ✓INTERNET→*irc* /channel #astronomy

#aussies For Australians. ✓INTERNET→*irc* /channel #aussies

#australia More Australians. ✓INTERNET→*irc* /channel #australia

#aynrand "The Objectivism Channel," for libertarian debate. ✓INTERNET→*irc* /channel #aynrand

#bawel For Indonesian speakers. ✓INTERNET→*irc* /channel #bawel

#bdsm Bondage talk and play. ✓INTERNET→*irc* /channel #bdsm

#bearcave For gay male bears and their admirers. ✓INTERNET→*irc* /channel #bearcave

#beijing Chinese- and English-language discussion. Participants mainly from Beijing. ✓INTERNET→*irc* /channel #beijing

#biblestud Religious discussion about the Bible. ✓INTERNET→*irc* /channel #biblestud

#bisex For bisexuals. ✓INTERNET→*irc* /channel #bisex

#bondage Bondage talk and play. ✓INTERNET→*irc* /channel #bondage

#bored General chatter and whining. Lots of regulars. ✓INTERNET→*irc* /channel #bored

#boston For Bostonians. √INTERNET→*irc* /channel #boston

#brasil For Brazilians and Portuguese speakers. √INTERNET→*irc* /channel #brasil

#buddhist Buddhist discussion. √INTERNET→*irc* /channel #buddhist

#callahans Where alt.callahan newsgroup readers hang out. √INTERNET→*irc* /channel #callahans

#camelot Home base for people who like to wage war on other IRC channels. There's an Arthurian theme. √INTERNET→*irc* /channel #camelot

#canada Ostensibly for Canadians—lots of others hang out here as well. √INTERNET→*irc* /channel #canada

#cheers A virtual bar—"where everyone knows your name." √INTERNET→*irc* /channel #cheers

#china For Chinese speakers and students. √INTERNET→*irc* /channel #china

#chinese For Chinese speakers. √INTERNET→*irc* /channel #chinese

#christ Christian discussion. √INTERNET→*irc* /channel #christ

#christian Christian discussion—all denominations. √INTERNET→*irc* /channel #christian

#c-64 For Commodore-64 questions and discussions. √INTERNET→*irc* /channel #c-64

#conquest Discussion about the fantasy game Conquest. √INTERNET→*irc* /channel #conquest

#cricket For fans of the sport cricket. Mostly European users.

Amsterdam—downloaded from America Online's Mac Graphics & CAD Forum. For Dutch chat, see #dutch.

√INTERNET→*irc* /channel #cricket

#crossdres For transvestites. Channel is private. √INTERNET→*irc* /channel #crossdres

#darkrealm For gothic and vampire discussions. √INTERNET→*irc* /channel #darkrealm

#depeche For Depeche Mode fans. √INTERNET→*irc* /channel #depeche

#disney Disney talk, or discussion about anything even remotely related to Disney. √INTERNET→*irc* /channel #disney

#dutch For Dutch speakers. √INTERNET→*irc* /channel #dutch

#egypt For Egyptians. Arabic is often spoken here. √INTERNET→*irc* /channel #egypt

#england For the British. √INTERNET→*irc* /channel #england

#erotica Sex talk and play. √INTERNET→*irc* /channel #erotica

#espanol For Spanish speakers. √INTERNET→*irc* /channel #espanol

#eu-opers For European IRC server administrators. √INTERNET→*irc* /channel #eu-opers

#filipino For Filipino speakers and students. √INTERNET→*irc* /channel #filipino

#40plus For IRCers who are 40 and older. √INTERNET→*irc* /channel #40plus

#42 Private channel for Finnish speakers. √INTERNET→*irc* /channel #42

#francais For French speakers. √INTERNET→*irc* /channel #francais

#france For French speakers and students. English spoken as well. √INTERNET→*irc* /channel #france

#freenet Finnish-language channel. √INTERNET→*irc* /channel #freenet

#F.U.C.K. One of the raunchier channels. √INTERNET→*irc* /channel #F.U.C.K.

#gam For gay Asian males and their friends. √INTERNET→*irc* /channel #gam

> "Over at the IRC channel #abortion, people with that freshmanlike energy and 'clarity' grapple with the issue—starting, of course, from square one."

#gaysex Gay sex talk and play. ✓**INTERNET**→*irc* /channel #gaysex

#gaysm Gay S&M talk and play. ✓**INTERNET**→*irc* /channel #gaysm

#gb For British users. ✓**INTERNET** →*irc* /channel #gb

#germany For German speakers and students. ✓**INTERNET**→*irc* /channel #germany

#gothic Gothic topics discussed. ✓**INTERNET**→*irc* /channel #gothic

#hanzi For chatting in HZ Chinese Code. ✓**INTERNET**→*irc* /channel #hanzi

#happy General chatter. ✓**INTER-NET**→*irc* /channel #happy

#heart General chat—lots of Taiwanese users. ✓**INTERNET**→*irc* /channel #heart

#heathers Campy talk—named after the movie *Heathers*. ✓**INTER-NET**→*irc* /channel #heathers

#hk For Cantonese speakers and students from Hong Kong. ✓**IN-TERNET**→*irc* /channel #hk

#hkfans For Hong Kong students. ✓**INTERNET**→*irc* /channel #hkfans

#hmong For Hmong students. ✓**INTERNET**→*irc* /channel #hmong

#hotsex Sex talk and flirtation. ✓**INTERNET**→*irc* /channel #hotsex

#hottub Everyone's sitting around in a hot tub. Campy and often flirtatious banter. ✓**INTERNET** →*irc* /channel #hottub

#iceland For Icelanders. ✓**INTER-**

Trent Reznor—downloaded from http:// www.scri.fsu.edu/~patters/otherpics.html. For Nine Inch Nails chat, see #nin.

NET→*irc* /channel #iceland

#india For Indians and Indian students. ✓**INTERNET**→*irc* /channel #india

#iran For Persian speakers and Iranian students. ✓**INTERNET**→*irc* /channel #iran

#ireland For the Irish. ✓**INTERNET** →*irc* /channel #ireland

#islam Islamic discussion. ✓**IN-TERNET**→*irc* /channel #islam

#israel For Israelis and Jews. ✓**IN-TERNET**→*irc* /channel #israel

#italia For Italian speakers. ✓**IN-TERNET**→*irc* /channel #italia

#jack-off Sex talk, particularly gay sex talk. ✓**INTERNET**→*irc* /channel #jack-off

#japan The place for Japanese speakers. ✓**INTERNET**→*irc* /channel #japan

#jeopardy Ongoing *Jeopardy* games. ✓**INTERNET**→*irc* /channel #jeopardy

#jesus Discussions sometimes about Jesus and sometimes not.

Come with a sense of humor. ✓**IN-TERNET**→*irc* /channel #jesus

#kampung For Malaysian speakers. ✓**INTERNET**→*irc* /channel #kampung

#kana For Finnish chat. ✓**INTER-NET**→*irc* /channel #kana

#karate Karate talk. ✓**INTERNET** →*irc* /channel #karate

#kinky More sex talk. ✓**INTERNET** →*irc* /channel #kinky

#korea For Korean students and speakers. ✓**INTERNET**→*irc* /channel #korea

#kuwait For Kuwaitis. ✓**INTER-NET**→*irc* /channel #kuwait

#laos For Laotian speakers. ✓**IN-TERNET**→*irc* /channel #laos

#lesbos Lesbian flirting and play. ✓**INTERNET**→*irc* /channel #lesbos

#limbaugh Rush Limbaugh–like debate. ✓**INTERNET**→*irc* /channel #limbaugh

#linux Linux questions and discussion. ✓**INTERNET**→*irc* /channel #linux

#love Flirting and idle chatter. ✓**INTERNET**→*irc* /channel #love

#macintosh Macintosh discussions and questions. ✓**INTERNET**→ *irc* /channel #macintosh

#malaysia For Malaysians. ✓**IN-TERNET**→*irc* /channel #malaysia

#martial_a For martial-arts enthusiasts. ✓**INTERNET**→*irc* /channel #martial_a

#melbourne For Australians from Melbourne. ✓**INTERNET**→*irc*

/channel #melbourne

#mindvox For members of New York's MindVox community. Always active. ✓ **INTERNET**→*irc* /channel #mindvox

#moscow For Russians or those interested in Russian events. ✓ **INTERNET**→*irc* /channel #moscow

#movies Movie discussions. ✓ **INTERNET**→*irc* /channel #movies

#mtg Talk about the game Magic: The Gathering. ✓ **INTERNET**→*irc* /channel #mtg

#nba Basketball chat. ✓ **INTERNET**→*irc* /channel #nba

#netsex Sex talk and play. ✓ **INTERNET**→*irc* /channel #netsex

#newcastle For Britons from Newcastle. ✓ **INTERNET**→*irc* /channel #newcastle

#nicecafe Generic chat. ✓ **INTERNET**→*irc* /channel #nicecafe

#nin For fans of the musical group Nine Inch Nails. ✓ **INTERNET**→*irc* /channel #nin

#nippon For Japanese speakers. ✓ **INTERNET**→*irc* /channel #nippon

#norway For Norwegians. ✓ **INTERNET**→*irc* /channel #norway

#os/2 OS/2 questions and discussions. ✓ **INTERNET**→*irc* /channel #os/2

#pakistan For Pakistanis. ✓ **INTERNET**→*irc* /channel #pakistan
#palestine For Palestinians and those interested in Palestine. ✓ **INTERNET**→*irc* /channel #palestine

#penang Malaysian users chatting in English, usually. ✓ **INTERNET**

Deanna Troi—downloaded from lajkonic.cyf-kr.edu.pl. For Star Trek chat, see #startrek

→*irc* /channel #penang

#penpal Idle chatter. ✓ **INTERNET**→*irc* /channel #penpal

#perl Discussion about the Perl programming language. ✓ **INTERNET**→ *irc* /channel #perl

#phonesex More sex talk and play. ✓ **INTERNET**→*irc* /channel #phonesex

#phreak For phone phreaks and computer hackers. ✓ **INTERNET**→*irc* /channel #phreak

#pinkfloyd For Pink Floyd fans. ✓ **INTERNET**→*irc* /channel #pinkfloyd

#poker Ongoing games of poker. ✓ **INTERNET**→*irc* /channel #poker

#polska For Polish speakers. ✓ **INTERNET**→*irc* /channel #polska

#prince For fans of the musician formerly known as Prince. ✓ **INTERNET**→*irc* /channel #prince

#punk For punk-rock fans. ✓ **INTERNET**→*irc* /channel #punk

#rave For rave fans. ✓ **INTERNET**→*irc* /channel #rave

#report Discuss major world events. ✓ **INTERNET**→*irc* /channel #report

#romance For flirting and cybersex. ✓ **INTERNET**→*irc* /channel #romance

#root Computer discussion for system administrators. ✓ **INTERNET**→*irc* /channel #root

#russian For Russian speakers and those interested in Russian events. ✓ **INTERNET**→*irc* /channel #russian

#seattle For Seattleites. ✓ **INTERNET** →*irc* /channel #seattle

#seoul For Korean speakers and students. ✓ **INTERNET**→*irc* /channel #seoul

#sex More sex talk and play. ✓ **INTERNET**→*irc* /channel #sex

#siam Thai-related discussion, in both English and Thai. ✓ **INTERNET**→*irc* /channel #siam

#silly Idle chatter. ✓ **INTERNET**→*irc* /channel #silly

#singapore For Singaporeans. ✓ **INTERNET**→*irc* /channel #singapore

#singles Single and looking? Stop by to flirt. ✓ **INTERNET**→*irc* /channel #singles

#soccer For soccer fans. ✓ **INTERNET**→*irc* /channel #soccer

#spanking More play of the disciplinary kind. ✓ **INTERNET**→*irc* /channel #spanking

#startrek *Star Trek* talk and role-play. ✓ **INTERNET**→*irc* /channel #startrek

#starwars For *Star Wars* fans. ✓**INTERNET**→*irc* /channel #starwars

#studpoker Ongoing games of stud poker. ✓**INTERNET**→*irc* /channel #studpoker

#sweden For Swedish speakers. ✓**INTERNET**→*irc* /channel #sweden

#taipei For Chinese speakers from Taiwan's capital, Taipei. ✓**INTERNET** →*irc* /channel #taipei

#taiwan For Taiwanese speakers and students. ✓**INTERNET**→*irc* /channel #taiwan

#talk Generic chat. ✓**INTERNET**→*irc* /channel #talk

#talk2me More generic chat. ✓**INTERNET**→*irc* /channel #talk2me

#teens Teen talk. ✓**INTERNET**→*irc* /channel #teens

#texas For Texans. ✓**INTERNET**→*irc* /channel #texas

#30plus For IRCers who are 30 and older. ✓**INTERNET**→*irc* /channel #30plus

#tibet For Tibetans or those with an interest in Tibet. ✓**INTERNET**→*irc* /channel #tibet

#truthdare An ongoing game of Truth or Dare. ✓**INTERNET**→*irc* /channel #truthdare

#turks For Turkish speakers and students. ✓**INTERNET**→*irc* /channel #turks

#tw For Taiwanese users. Discussion is mainly in English. ✓**INTERNET**→*irc* /channel #tw

#12step Sunday night meetings at 8 p.m. for people in recovery.

From CompuServe's Graphics Corner Forum. For erotic chat, see #wetsex.

✓**INTERNET**→*irc* /channel #12step

#twilight For fans of *The Twilight Zone*. ✓**INTERNET**→*irc* /channel #twilight

#unix For UNIX questions and discussions. ✓**INTERNET**→*irc* /channel #unix

#usa General chat for Americans. ✓**INTERNET**→*irc* /channel #usa

#vampire For vampire lovers. ✓**INTERNET**→*irc* /channel #vampire

#viet For Vietnamese speakers. ✓**INTERNET**→*irc* /channel #viet

#vietnight For Vietnamese speakers. ✓**INTERNET**→*irc* /channel #vietnight

#warung For Malaysians. ✓**INTERNET**→*irc* /channel #warung

#wetsex Sex talk and play. ✓**INTERNET**→*irc* /channel #wetsex

#wicca Wiccan discussions. ✓**INTERNET**→*irc* /channel #wicca

#www World Wide Web questions. ✓**INTERNET**→*irc* /channel #www

#x4war For playing the Chinese

Talkers

If you're looking for an endless stream of chatter, unham-

pered by role-playing requirements but with more atmosphere and stability than an IRC channel, venture onto one of the Cyberspace hangouts known as "talkers"—part frat party, part playground. Internet users can telnet to talker sites, log in with a handle, move between "rooms," and, of course, type-talk to each other.

Dax—downloaded from lajkonic.cyf-kr.edu.pl.

To talk, just type what you want to say (on a few sites, you must begin each comment with a double quotation mark). If you need help or would like more access privileges, ask around for what's known on talkers as a "superuser." While most people on talkers are in their early twenties, many teenagers log in from all over the world. Some are older. A 41-year-old father with the handle Cypher logs in a couple of times a day to what are collectively known as the "Rivendel sites": Deep Space 9, Dragon's Lair, Gamma-Quadrant, and Cyber Eden (the first talker in the U.S.). His 11-year-old son drops by sometimes too.

Cypher, like most people who hang out on talkers, has a circle of about 15–20 friends whom he chats with regularly. While members of the stable and friendly Rivendel talkers often choose handles in keeping with the sites' sci-fi and fantasy names, discussion rarely, if ever, is related to the theme. In other words, someone with the handle Picard on DS-9 probably won't discuss *Star Trek*.

On the other hand, Coffee House talker, despite its genteel opening description, is filled with hyperactive teens set on spewing every insult they can think of. For more adult discussion, drop by Tele-Chat, with rooms like "adult," "party," "hottub," "crackhouse," and "motel." Ahh, there's even a room called the "toilet."

The Hotel

A fair number of techies hang out on The Hotel, and those who speak Estonian might want to drop by Estonia. Foothills, with its numerous command options, is perhaps the most popular—200-plus people on each evening. But don't be surprised if you can't see more than 50 (type "swho" on Foothills and ".who" on most others to get a list of people on the talker). The others are in private rooms engaged in conversation or cybersex.

And, if you've always wanted to spend an evening in virtual Greenwich Village, stop by The Village. The subway will pull into Astor Place and you can head to the Limelight, Ray's Pizza, Soho, Washington Square, a deli, or back to the subway. People will smile at you and say "ciao" here.

Coffee House ✓INTERNET→*telnet* eleven.uccs.edu 2525

CyberEden ✓INTERNET→*telnet* rivendel.slip.umd.edu 5000→<your handle>→<your password>

Deep Space 9 (DS-9) ✓INTERNET→*telnet* rivendel.slip.umd.edu 3000→<your handle>→<your password>

Dragon's Lair ✓INTERNET→*telnet* rivendel.slip.umd.edu 7777→<your handle>→<your password>

DS-Gamma-Quadrant ✓INTERNET→*telnet* rivendel.slip.umd.edu 6000→<your handle>→<your password>

Estonia ✓INTERNET→*telnet* anna.ioc.ee 4002→<your handle>→<your password>

Foothills ✓INTERNET→*telnet* marble.bu.edu 2010→<your handle>→<y or n>→<your gender>→continue

The Hotel ✓INTERNET→*telnet* games.infinet.com 7200→<your handle>→<your password>

Jurassic Park ✓INTERNET→*telnet* squid.code3.com 4782→guest→guest

Skull ✓INTERNET→*telnet* skull.cc.fc.ul.pt 3000→<your handle>→<your password>

Tele-Chat ✓INTERNET→*telnet* ns.speedway.net 8888→<your handle>→<your password>

The Village ✓INTERNET→*telnet* 129.49.31.56 5000→<your handle>→<your password>

BayMOO

Quiet and gently nutty, the MOO by the Bay is distinguished primarily by its many cool

interactive rooms: There are rooms that automatically turn your typed speech into fractured Franglish ("C'est quoi time? Merde, it's cinque o' clock!") or into jumbled gibberish, transposing verbs and randomly assorting nouns; there's an improv room that scores your ability to think—and type—fast, as you create instant limericks or other bits of doggerel; and there are galleries of ASCII art, painstakingly created pictures made of characters and spaces typed just so. You can even speedily see the MOO's sights through one player's deftly programmed WarpTour of the MOO, which zips your character from room to room, giving you just enough time to see the sights, wave, and disappear. New players should check out Davey Jones' Locker (apparently a reference to the dead pirate, not the live Monkee), where rooms full of tips and hints about the MOO and its features are listed and extensively described. You can hang out at the Hippie Haight, or visit the Hotel California, where you can check out any time you want.

Bay Bridge—downloaded from America Online's Mac Graphics & CAD Forum.

BayMOO is smaller in both size and population than some other MOOs (an average prime-time on-line crowd consists of 20 people or so), but the denizens tend to be friendly. A number of them are software programmers themselves, which accounts for the MOO's wild variety of features.

Poke around: Hidden exits will lead you to some very strange places indeed, including a working Tarot Parlor, where Madame Moreau will read your future in the cards.

Fresh blood

The average age of the resident population is about 25, and most of them are male, but—and this is BayMOO's best feature—Bay attracts new guests all the time, who provide the MOO with fresh blood and life. Guest privileges are more than generous: Guests can change their names and descriptions, and even build up to two objects each.

And if you're a guest, it won't be long before someone hails you by page and gives you a welcome to the MOO. An amiable, entertain-

ing place to visit, and a sociable place to settle down. ✓**INTERNET** →*telnet* mud.crl.com 8888→connect guest

> "There's a wild variety of features. Poke around: Hidden exits will lead you to some very strange places indeed, including a working Tarot Parlor, where Madame Moreau will read your future in the cards."

DeepSeas

In any society, you will find those who by dint of age, experience, or simple irritability

consider themselves the upper crust, the veterans, the diehards. In MUDding parlance, these individuals are called dinosaurs, or more simply, dinos. Dinos are longtime MUDders, people who were MUDding when the first TinyMUD went up in 1989. These days, you can find most of the MUDding dinos—often called (though never by themselves) the Random Gang—on **DeepSeas**.

Everyone hangs out in room #274, the SnnnOctopus's (Beer) Garden. Just type @tel #274 or navigate to ocean location 0, 0, 18 and type "enter seastation" and then go up one move and north one move. Newbies get killed a lot on DeepSeas—usually because they're annoying. Being killed doesn't mean anything, really—it just means you get sent to your room and get paid 50 pennies insurance. You can come right back. You may want to set a command to return you to the Beer Garden as soon as you've been killed (@akill me-@tel #274).

Every so often the subject of SAT or GRE scores comes up and it turns out that the average SAT score of the people who hang out on DeepSeas MUSH is somewhere around 1550—rather smart people. While at times the place can seem like a career-placement service—job opportunities, especially in the computer-science field, are always being exchanged—socialism, libertarian-

Flipper—downloaded from America Online's Scuba Forum.

ism, David Letterman, Santa Cruz, body-piercing, bunnies, Christianity, and Internet happenings are among the many other topics of conversation. If you don't enjoy a healthy dose of technogeek talk and feel awkward listening to people discussing their high salaries, DeepSeas may not be the best place for you.

Real name

If you hang out here long enough to become accepted, you'll find people often ask where you live, what your name really is (as opposed to your MUD name), what you do for a living, and so forth. Similarly, you can expect to find this information out about others, often without asking. Everyone on DeepSeas knows where everyone else lives and works and, quite often, what restaurant they prefer to run out to for a quick snack.

When the DeepSeas MUDders travel around the USA or, for that matter, the world, they often plan their itinerary around visits to other DeepSeas MUDders. Not long ago, a group of DeepSeas MUDders converged on New York City

> "Someone will wander into the Beer Garden and vent his angst about delays in traffic and everyone will commiserate and then offer their own recent traffic difficulties."

for a taping of *Late Show with David Letterman,* flying in separately, staying at the same hotel, hanging out with New York and New Jersey members of the group, and in general being very weird.

Lollipops

Socializing on DeepSeas frequently centers on what's going on in the real lives of the members. Someone will wander into the Beer Garden and vent his angst about delays in traffic and everyone will commiserate and then offer their own recent traffic difficulties. Another chatter will mention that she was turned down for health insurance and everyone else will chime in and four hours later the discussion will have evolved from health insurance to lollipops to candy to the New England Candy Company factory in Massachusetts to NECCO wafers to sulfur to toxic waste and back to health care again.

During the course of the discussion, dozens of players will come in, greet everyone, wait a minute or two to grasp the course of discussion, then start adding their two cents.

Prime time

Lunchtime is prime time on DeepSeas—it runs for four hours (Eastern time, Central time, Mountain time, and Pacific time), with a fairly frenetic course of discussion that dies down only after the Pacific-time-zone people go back to work. Then there'll be a lull, with moderate levels of chatting until the evening comes, when the participants with nothing to do will log in from home and spend the rest of the evening amiably yakking about life, dinner, what's on television, why they wish they had a date, why they know it's just as well they didn't have a date since they'd just act

nervous and geeklike, and so on.

DeepSeas is not the sort of place where you'd be going if MUDding for you includes a healthy dose of simulated sexual activity. It's not that the Random Gang members hate tinysex. They just think it's laughably pathetic.

Inhabitants

Among the many that regularly inhabit DeepSeas are Hugh, a super-bunny character from California who gives everyone updates on what his eccentric co-workers are up to; Woodlock, an angstful guy from Michigan who worships David Letterman; Nihilistic-Kid, a card-carrying Socialist from New York City who genuinely believes that a workers' revolution is coming in the USA; Shiro, a card-carrying Libertarian from Colorado who genuinely believes that any form of taxation is theft and that government is total evil; Tourmaline, a female math Ph.D. student from Purdue who builds lots of odd MUSH devices and leaves them lying around; Ozy, a Microsoft employee in Washington who is more irritable than most; phi, who rules the Boston-area science-fiction-fandom scene with an iron hand; ashne, the alt.sex.bondage devotee who manufactures nipple clips in Boston; and Shadow, the MUD's token airhead.

Touchy people

The MUD changes from time to time, but the members don't—touchy people who get along great with each other but really don't like new company. Over the years, quite a few MUDs have run at Oklahoma State University that were home to the Random Gang: TinyHELL, TinyHELL II, Asylum, Chaos, DreamScape, Space Madness, and the current MUD, DeepSeas MUSH. Space Madness lasted the longest—nearly two

years. DeepSeas, the present incarnation, has been up since February 1994.

The Random Gang is often referred to by its quasi members as "Random and Moira MUDders." Random (Russ Smith) and Moira (Jennifer Smith) are the husband-and-wife wizard-team who provide the MUDs that the Gang hangs out on.

Holding court

Moira is often involved on other MUDs and is only occasionally on DeepSeas, but Random, under his DeepSeas name of Marc Spencer, is often logged in and holding court. Formerly one of the most irascible MUDders, always ready with a bitingly sharp wit and a ready jibe, Random has mellowed—rarely will he @toad (destroy) annoying newbies. ✓**INTERNET**→*telnet* muds.okstate.edu 6250→connect guest guest *Register:* ✓**INTERNET**→*email* deepseas-request@muds.okstate.edu ✍ *Email request to register a character* <your character's name> <your password>

> "Formerly one of the most irascible mudders, always ready with a bitingly sharp wit and a ready jibe, Random has mellowed—rarely will he @toad (destroy) annoying newbies."

LambdaMOO

Nestled deep in the silicon heart of XeroxPARC's massive

UNIX core is what some have called the Mother of all MOOs, a digital world whose thousands of inhabitants reside in, and continually expand, the odd chambers of a sprawling gothic mansion. This is LambdaMOO, one of the oldest and largest MOOs—MUD Object Orienteds—in existence.

Like most MOOs, Lambda has no specific motif; it's a virtual theme park where jungle paradises, baroque salons, and streamlined futurescapes squat uneasily side by side. Its sheer size makes it worth a visit. Its sheer size also makes it nearly impossible to fully explore for a hapless newbie who's just been dropped into the MOO's closetlike antechamber.

On the plus side, it's not unusual to find hundreds of players connected to Lambda at any given hour of the night; exiting the guest antechamber dumps you immediately into the Living Room, the MOO's primary chat area, so finding a sociable group is easy.

Delays

On the minus side, the presence of so many MOOsers simultaneously often results in frustrating delays between typing a command and watching it occur on screen. Before you connect, you'll be warned of the number of seconds of lag the MOO has developed. Anything more than three seconds is guaranteed to drive you to smash your monitor, so keep your eye on the lag indicator and go read a magazine until the waiting

MOO cow—downloaded from Compu-Serve's Computer Art Forum.

time drops down to something humane.

Once you've been on for a while, you'll become aware of the turbid politics of this macroscopic virtual society, and be able to take part in some of Lambda's many meta-debates.

Digital democracy

Lambda has become large enough to spawn something like a digital democracy, with an "architectural review board" of elected player-characters and frequent referenda on MOO law, ethics, and enforcement. Should building quotas be imposed? What rights should guests receive? And how should antisocial types (the so-called dillweeds) be punished?

The turning point for Lambda occurred some months ago, when a character named Mr. Bungle utilized one of the MOO's weird objects, a Voodoo Doll, to serially terrorize MOO denizens, forcing them to commit acts of grotesque perversity: shoving steak knives into their own rectums, performing graphic sex acts, and the like.

The P.O.'d victims called these acts virtual rape, and demanded that Bungle be "toaded"—in other words, killed. One of Lambda's wizards eventually did bump him off, but not before Haakon, the MOO's archwizard, decided to put such punishment in the hands of the proletariat. Enter the great MOO review: Players now have the option of voting on changes in MOO policy, which—if they receive twice as many yes as no votes—the wizards will then implement.

Filibuster

If you like to filibuster about justice, fairness, and the virtual way, then LambdaMOO is probably for you. If you like to hang out in hot tubs and engage in tinysex, the MOO might be to your fancy as well. On the other hand, on one recent trip to Lambda this cybertourist was subjected to two hours of nitwitted discussion as to whether Ernest (of *Ernest Goes to Camp*) was funny or merely stupid; it degenerated eventually into catcalls of "You're a faggot!" "No, YOU'RE a faggot!"

What's to do on the MOO? Well, for instance, if you're lucky and stubborn, you may be able to find Dr. Bombay's full-scale I Ching garden, a peaceful arboretum of forking paths that will, if explored properly, eventually deliver you a hexagrammic augury of the future.

Lambda's natives are moderately friendly toward guests (though to be sure, you'll run into the occasional surly dillweed lookin' for a live one to abuse), so don't be afraid to ask for help. Nicely. A plaintive request in the Living Room should do the trick. The step-by-step tutorial for new players is also recommended. ✓**INTERNET**→*telnet* lambda.parc.xerox. com 8888→help

MediaMOO

Tucked into a deep digital pocket of MIT's Media Lab, MediaMOO is more than just a

place to chatter and build. According to archwizard (they call them janitors here) Amy Bruckman, MediaMOO is a full-fledged research facility, where those interested in alternative media congregate, discuss ideas, exchange FTP sites for papers, and socialize. The MOO is large, containing multitudes, but tends to be slow off-peak; a regular poetry night, however, generated its own off-MOO newsletter.

The MOO also has parties in its very own Ballroom, where people can choose an off-the-rack costume to wear (or describe one of their own), and a beautifully rendered Theater, with a working stage with lights, a curtain that can be raised or lowered, and other neat features. When wandering around MediaMOO, ignore the greetings of otherwise idle characters. Some Media-Wags have installed automatic wave-and-smile programs on themselves, to provide the facsimile of being awake while disconnected.

Three train systems, The Thin Blue Line, the Flame Train (work in progress), and the Peace Train, will take you just about anywhere

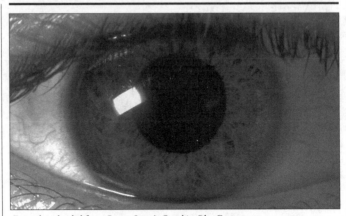

Eye—downloaded from CompuServe's Graphics Plus Forum.

you want to go in the MOO. You can also zip into a nearby computer terminal to descend directory by directory to the ROOT level of the MOO (where you might also want to visit the MOO's Haunted House).

In the libraries, which are serviced by interactive, audio-animation librarians, there are book reviews written by other players, notes on building (designing your own additions to the MOO), and other interesting reading material. A religious area is home to an ashram, pagoda, and synagogue, which is described in devoted detail.

More mature

Not all of Media's residents are "media researchers," but they do tend to be older and more mature than those found in most MU* environments.

Discussion can be intellectual, occasionally dizzyingly so, but there are more than enough residents willing simply to shoot the proverbial bull. Just find a group of people and go with it.

The ratio of men to women here is also better than at most MOOs, possibly because of its relatively academic environment, but don't assume that this is an object-oriented relative of FurryMUCK —it's not.

MediaMOO is definitely worth exploring. ✓**INTERNET**→*telnet* purple-crayon.media.mit.edu 8888→ connect Guest

> "Discussion can be intellectual, occasionally dizzyingly so, but there are more than enough residents willing simply to shoot the proverbial bull."

Fine arts

The muses gather on the Net. This new medium provides

for the rapid exchange of ideas about dance, theater, music, and the visual arts. Self-consciously cutting-edge (or "downtown") types disparage the art market and outdo each other with "difference" on **Avant Garde**. The WELL's **Arts conference** makes the most of the Net to bring together people with new ideas, while **Artcrit** takes a look at visual arts. Prodigy's **Arts BB** combines technical advice, art history, and chat. While the professional musicians and discographers on **CLASSM-L** dissect the Ring Cycle, the **Mozart** echo allows for lots of levity along with the love of music—gee, it's tough getting your tuba on the bus. The theater talk on the Net divides into several camps—starry eyed girls on Prodigy, teachers and amateurs on **Astr-L** and the **Theatre Discussion List**, and Equity members and Equity aspirants on **Performance**.

On the Net

Avant-garde

Avant Garde (ml) "She said she was an anarchist...but." Absolutely the worst thing you can say about someone on this mailing list is to accuse him of pandering to

Ricardo Muti—downloaded from DSC BBS.

the tastes of the bourgeoisie, the "Curator Class,"—or heaven forbid—economic necessity. All the really hot and nasty debates here concern the selling, or selling out, of art. To combat the serious nature of art discussion there are treatises on Groucho Marxism and calls for philosophy experiments on the space shuttle. Let's "bring down capitalism" with mixed media. ✓**INTERNET**→*email* majordomo@world.std.com ✍ *Type in message body:* subscribe avant-garde WEEKLY

Classical music

Classm-L (ml) All is silent in the concert hall; you gaze about nervously, watching for cues. Was that the adagio or the allegro? You wonder: "Do I clap now?" You will never experience this type of culture anxiety in Classm-L, the mailing list for classical-music afi-

cionados. Regulars trade Canadian jokes and debate the modernizing of classic operas (*Don Giovanni* in Air Jordans?). People here really do know their stuff and are willing and able to discuss the finer points of comparative recordings of Mahler's Second for days. But you don't have to be an expert discographer to feel welcome; you just really have to love music. ✓**INTER-NET**→*email* listserv@brownvm.brown.edu ✍ *Type in message body:* subscribe classm-l <your full name> DAILY

Mozart (echo) "This reminds me of something an enlightened wag (I forget who) said about Wagner. 'It has its great moments, but they're separated by interminably tedious hours.'" If you can be lighthearted about your requiems, cantatas and enjoy poking fun at really big opera stars, Mozart is the classical-music forum for you. The regulars—music teachers, music players and music lovers—favor one-liners over pensive evaluations of a work. Even discussions about funding for the arts or cranky conductors are witty—18th-century goof Wolfgang Amadeus would have loved these guys. ✓**ILINK** DAILY

Performing arts

Astr-L (ml) The Theatre History Discussion List brings together historians, actors, directors, and audience. Topics range from a discussion of fatal circus accidents to when and why theaters began bringing down the lights. A voice from California wonders whether Madonna plays the same social role as Mae West ("trampy and tough"). Subscribers are eager to provide advice on everything from lighting design to what to do with a bad case of stage fright in an amateur player. ✓**INTERNET**→*email* listserv@vmd.cso.uiuc.edu ✍ *Type in*

Fine arts Coffee house

message body: subscribe astr-l <your full name> DAILY

Dance/Theater "Fame—I want to live forever" is the incessant cry of young girls in the Dance and Theater sections of Prodigy's ARTS bulletin board. Aspiring dancers and actresses post myriad questions about drama schools, pointe shoes, and publicity photos and talk endlessly about parents who don't believe in them and their "dedication to the craft." More mature theatergoers discuss the merits of their favorite shows and hotly contest casting decisions. Young and would-be thespians live out their footlight fantasies in one of the many role-playing clubs, enacting scenes from *Phantom, Cats, Les Mis,* or *Annie.* ✓ **PRODIGY**→*jump* lifestyles bb→Choose a Topic→Theater *and* Dance HOURLY

Performance Performance is the virtual green room for New York's performing-artists scene. Actors, directors, musicians, playwrights, and dancers swap experiences and review the latest show at BAM (if you don't know what that stands for, don't bother). Participants look to each other for encouragement, critiques, and camaraderie. Even if you haven't been on stage since sixth grade, it's a great place to learn about good shows and the fine art of performing. ✓ **ECHO**→*j* performance WEEKLY

rec.arts.theatre.misc (ng) Not a wide-eyed groupie among them, these players, playwrights, directors, graduate students, and the occasional angel expertly view the stage from both sides of the proscenium. The regional theaters of Canada, Australia, and Middle America share the spotlight with New York and London. Hot threads: Are labor unions destroy-ing the stage? Do you have to like Brecht to love his work? Was Camille Paglia right about Shakespeare's *Cleopatra*? Also contest announcements, some with good cash prizes, and shameless hustles for backers. (Eat your heart out, Max Bialystock!) ✓ **USENET** ✓ **INTERNET**→*email* stagecraft-request@zinc.com ✍ *Write a request Archives:* ✓ **INTERNET**→*ftp* world.std.com→anonymous→<your email address>→/RAT-archive *FAQ:* ✓ **INTERNET**→*ftp* quartz.rutgers.edu→anonymous→<your email address>→/pub/theater→rec-arts-theatre-faq* WEEKLY

The Theatre Discussion List (ml) A professor from the University of Crete asks list members for the best drama schools in the United States, and how to help a professional-actor friend find better dentures. A techie from North Carolina offers his best suggestion for getting that one-of-a-kind bug-zapping sound without having to employ moths as extras. Directors, actors, designers, and playwrights meet here to talk about the serious business of putting on a show on Broadway, Off Broadway, or nowhere near Broadway, without taking themselves too seriously. ✓ **INTERNET**→*email* listserv@pucc.princeton.edu ✍ *Type in message body:* subscribe theatre <your full name> WEEKLY

Visual arts

Artcrit (ml) "Are seascapes reactionary?" How can modern art be explained to a skeptical populace? More to the point, should it be? Artcrit is aptly named—it is where artists meet critics. There is no discussion here of whether it is better to use oil or tempera. This is a philosophical place, grappling with ideas of progress and art, "green theory" and commodifica-tion. People here want to explore why they, and their predecessors, chose to become artists. Responses to a working artist's post about class background showed the breadth of readership—ages 20 to 80, privileged and poor, all with the urge to create and to talk about it afterward. ✓ **INTERNET**→*email* listserv@vm1.yorku.ca ✍ *Type in message body:* subscribe art crit <your full name> WEEKLY

Arts Of all the WELL's arts-oriented conferences, this is the most general, with such topics as "Dance" and "Fine Art Photography" and the slightly more directed "Sports and Art" and "Virtual Reality and the Artist," which has drawn a whopping 500-plus postings to date. The Festival of New Mime in Philadelphia has its own conference room, as does the Mucho/Arts event in Fort Mason. Painters, dancers, sculptors, and performance artists notify other users of openings and events, while others wonder what the museums of the future will look like. Creativity isn't dead; it's only changing, and this is one of the sites of the transformation. ✓ **WELL**→*g* arts DAILY

> "Hot threads: Are labor unions destroying the stage? Do you have to like Brecht to love his work? Was Camille Paglia right about Shakespeare's *Cleopatra*?

History

Hey—it was a long time ago. Get over it. There are multitudes of Net users who emphati-
cally do not agree. Scholars, students, and buffs unite to discuss everything that was once under the sun. Beware—these people aren't just talking ho-hum names and dates; this is about sex and politics and life itself. There are forums for every era (**Mediev-L** to **alt.war. vietnam**), every culture (**Islam-L** or **Amwest-H**), and every specialty (**H-Labor**, **H-Idea**). In general the newsgroups and echoes are less "scholarly" than the mailing lists, but all welcome any sort of interested posts. Couch generals meet in **Milhst-L**, **soc.history. war. misc**, **H-Diplo**, and **Milhistory** on FidoNet. Those who want to relive history can get together in CompuServe's **Living History Forum**, **alt.history.living**, and **rec.food.historic** to talk about 14th-century fashion, how to load a musket, or what Columbus ate . See how many flames you can gather by praising General Sherman on **Civil_War-F** or **alt.war.civil. usa**. Got a hankering for tea, crumpets, and discreet scandal? Head over to **Victoria**. BYOT (bring your own theory) to

SS women—downloaded from ftp.u.washington.edu.

the very entertaining **alt. history.what-if**. What if everything you learned in school was wrong?

On the Net

Across the board

History (echo) This History conference is all over the map—but if there's anything that happened sometime before yesterday (i.e., history) that you want to talk about you will find someone here to chat back. You might learn why there are Cuban-Chinese restaurants in New York City. (Sugar plantations in Cuba used contract Chinese labor.) It is a serious-minded group and tempers are kept in check even over potentially inflammatory issues like American isolationism in World War II and Japanese concentration camps. ✓**RELAYNET** WEEKLY

History (echo) A close-knit group of regulars place themselves in the role of famous leaders— conjecturing why the Nazis never invaded Switzerland or whether Richard III really had murder in his blood. Those on this active newsgroup appreciate the "facts," but they also encourage speculation. ✓**INTELEC** DAILY

soc.history (ng) Soc.history is actually two conferences—a forum for amateur historians and a political battleground. Topics are varied, from Nazis and the economy to the Post-Columbian pandemic and the necessity of using the A-bomb in World War II. Marshaling their facts and citing "the experts," posters stay generally friendly. But then there's the rabid political character of the group. Ancient Greek history is fodder for a bitter debate over Macedonia and Armenians; Muslims and Turks commit verbal atrocities daily in a constant, ugly reliving of the past. ✓USENET *FAQ:* ✓INTER-NET→*ftp* rtfm.mit.edu→anony-mous→<your email address>→/pub/usenet-by-group/soc.history DAILY

American

alt.war.civil.usa (ng) For some, Gettysburg is more familiar than the Gulf War. All the old contro-versies are here, but much of the debate slides over into the pres-ent—to the issues of contempo-rary guilt "imposed" on the South. The effects of 130 years of brood-ing are quite clear. "States rights" are referred to in the present tense and the Confederate flag remains a rallying point. ✓USENET *FAQ:* ✓IN-TERNET→*ftp* rtfm.mit.edu→anony-mous→<your email address>→/pub/usenet-by-hierarchy/soc/answers/civil-war-usa→faq DAILY

alt.war.vietnam (ng) "Napalm bomb" could accurately describe the flame wars that ignite in alt.war.vietnam. It is not just the class of '68 butting heads with the ROTCs—several generations of ill will meet up here. These people definitely do not see the war in In-dochina (or the Cold War) as over. (When is the last time you called someone "commie pinko scum"?) Simple questions like "What if the U.S. hadn't entered Vietnam?" quickly devolve into name-calling and dogma-slinging. There is also a sharp divide between the "been there" and the "others." Many par-ticipants have complained that the discussion has deteriorated to at-tacks on a single individual—and are attempting to correct this. For now, let it just be said that Presi-dent Clinton probably should choose to discuss the 1960s and the Vietnam War in another fo-rum. ✓USENET WEEKLY

Amwest-H (ml) No query is

> "These people defi-nitely do not see the war in Indochina (or the Cold War) as over. (When is the last time you called someone 'commie pinko scum'?)"

turned away here. Amwest-H members chat amicably with well-known scholars about the evolu-tion of country music and how mean Billy the Kid really was (pretty doggone nasty). Could there have been a "Dr. Quinn, Medicine Woman"? What kind of music did Indians really play? And what about gays and lesbians in the old West? ✓INTERNET→*email* listserv@ umrvmb.umr.edu ✍ *Type in message body:* subscribe amwest-h <your full name> DAILY

Civil_War (echo) The talk here (with a perceptible Southern ac-cent) is generally among amateur Civil War "buffs," not historians. Topics range from the minutiae of war (how many people died from bayonet wounds)—and Monday morning generaling (Lee lost a battle because he had a head cold, not because he misplaced his bat-talions)—to higher-level discus-sion of slave abuse and Indian pol-icy. Like most Civil War groups, this BBS is at least half populated by people who proudly proclaim, "I am of Southern blood," and have obviously never gotten over

the burning of Atlanta. While this provides a close community for the former "Rebels," it can occa-sionally drag discussion back 150 years to sectional partisanship. ✓FI-DONET DAILY

H-South (ml) Although it was designed as a scholarly list, H-South also provides a great deal of "Southern hospitality" to new-comers and regulars (even offering travel tips). Because H-South is not limited to "history" but also embraces culture, a wide variety of topics are discussed and remi-nisced about by the large contin-gent of Southerners on the list. Recent threads included the sexual abuse of slaves, whether Maryland was a "Northern" state, voodoo, and barbecue. ✓INTERNET→*email* listserv@uicvm.uic.edu ✍ *Type in message body:* subscribe h-south <your full name> DAILY

Cultural

Artifact (ml) Bob believes that the invention of the vacuum cleaner changed the gender basis of rug cleaning. Alana thinks it was always a woman's place to get the dirt out. Artifact is the home of online discussion of material culture—the real stuff (or junk) of history. Museum curators, histori-ans, preservationists, and the just plain insatiably curious come to-gether on this active list to discuss the evolution of vacuum cleaners, manhole covers, tombstone de-sign, and techniques for preserving faux-marble facades. If, like a re-cent poster, you want to chat about the origins of gift wrapping, this is the place for you. ✓INTERNET→*email* listserv@umdd.umd.edu ✍ *Type in message body:* subscribe artifact <your full name> WEEKLY

Folklore (ml) Aesop, Uncle Remus, and the Brothers Grimm would have all subscribed to this active, unmoderated list. The Folklore list provides information and insight about folk culture worldwide, but it also helps modern minstrels perfect their tale-telling skills. A mother and bard from New Hampshire asks whether it is okay to tell bedtime tales with bad witches in them. A Wiccan from New Mexico provides new alternatives. The discussion is as much about cultural discovery as about historical or literary interpretations. ✓**INTERNET**→ *email* listserv@tamvm1.tamu.edu ✍ *Type in message body:* subscribe folklore <your full name> DAILY

---

rec.food.historic (ng) Nutritionists, historians, geographers, and the curious with good appetites engage in interesting and unusual discourses about what people eat, and why. Long threads speculate on how and why certain spices became popular—why the tomato was thought poisonous and what Scandinavians ate before the potato came from the New World (herring). Friendly and funny, rec.food.historic is a place to find new (old) recipes (the 18th-century way to make catsup or the Bayou variant of fry sauce) and other food for thought. Perhaps because of its homey subject matter, this newsgoup has the feeling of a close bunch of friends chatting over a good meal. ✓**USENET** WEEKLY

European

Mediev-L (ml) Jay asks, "Could people in the Middle Ages swim?" Did the erudite scholars of the medieval list jump on him and beat him soundly for asking such a silly question? No—they spent a week debating and discussing the query. Charlemagne could swim;

most sailors could not (they preferred to drown quickly). One reader suggested that it must have been uncommon or else the dunking test for witches would have been senseless—and another week was spent on the topic of witches and how to spot them. Someone else wondered when people began swimming for pleasure rather than to save their lives. Sure, a lot of those on Mediev-L can quote in Latin, but they'll speak in English too. Newcomers welcome. ✓**INTERNET**→*email* listserv @ukanvm.bitnet ✍ *Type in message body:* subscribe mediev-l <your full name> WEEKLY

Victoria (ml) A list dedicated to the Victorian era—repressed sexuality, rooms full of frilly knick-knacks, demure young maids, and Dickens, right? Wrong. Victoria is the most active history list on the Net and it's terrific. There have been long threads about whether *The Piano* did/should accurately portray Victorian life and whether young people with pasty skin and black clothing are the conscious inheritors of the Victorian gothic past. What does it mean to be well bred? What did it mean before Darwin? Victoria is never just an exchange of information. Sit down and have some tea and gossip; Queen Charlotte's divorce (A.D. 1820) or Prince Charles's affairs—it's all allowed here. ✓**INTERNET**→ *email* listserv@ ubvm.usc.indiana. edu ✍ *Type in message body:* subscribe victoria <your full name> HOURLY

Living history

alt.history.living If you've always wanted to wear thigh-high black leather SS boots or enjoy imagining yourself as Rhett Butler—but in that pink hooped number Scarlett wore to the pic-

nic—there are other places on the Net for you. But if you are serious about trying to re-create the past—uncomfortable shoes and all—alt. history.living is a good place to meet like-minded individuals you might one day face across a battlefield. Most participants are men playing soldier, who are also very concerned about authenticity—leading to earnest debates. The place of women in battle, the value of "amateur" history, and just how to "be" when you are acting out history are discussed with fervor and intelligence. WEEKLY

Living History Forum How did men and women do laundry in 1198 A.D.? These people are serious about living as history—even to doing without spin cycles. The Society for Creative Anachronism gathers here to play lords, ladies and lance victims. ✓**COMPUSERVE**→ *go* living→Messages DAILY

Military

MilHistory (echo) Debates here are long and extremely detailed. Here "amateur" historians tackle the subjects on which professionals hedge. You need to know the

> **"Sit down and have some tea and gossip; Queen Charlotte's divorce (A.D. 1820) or Prince Charles's affairs—it's all allowed here."**

facts here—but no other qualifications are required. Modern military technology and the Pentagon budget are also fair. Like most military-history lists, this one has a good number of ex-servicemen on board—the discussion sometimes reflects the divide between them and civilians. ✓ **FIDONET** DAILY

Milhst-L (ml) Diverse souls meet here—an ex-colonel and a teenager discuss WWII battle plans; a military librarian posts a tidbit about a Civil War general's ground-breaking use of the insanity defense. The list entertains discussion about things nobody could possibly remember, like the dietary requirements of medieval crossbowmen. There are many ex-servicemen on this list, which makes for a friendly rivalry and fosters a tendency toward reminiscence. Newcomers and noncombatants are welcome. ✓ **INTERNET**→ *email* listserv@ukanvm.bitnet ✍ *Type in message body:* subscribe milhst-l <your full name> DAILY

soc.history.war.misc (ng) Battle strategy, favorite generals, and lethal weapons are the subjects of the group. There are many ex–military men here, and your credibility rises with trench experience. This is especially evident when the arcane discussion of castle sieges is replaced by modern issues—women in the military is a particular favorite. But not all are part of what one participant called the "He Man Woman Haters Club," and real debate is allowed and encouraged. ✓ **USENET** DAILY

Other

alt.history.what-if (ng) Professional historians refer to speculative history with the phrase "If my grandmother had wheels she'd be a Greyhound bus." But this news-

Abraham Lincoln—downloaded from byrd.mu.wvnet.edu: pub/history/.*

group and its denizens are a whole lot of fun. What if the south had won the Civil War? Or if the Nazis had won World War II? What if Jesus had never lived? There are serious, well-reasoned questions about Ceasar's effect on the Roman Empire as well as fantasy speculations about Atlantis and other "lost" civilizations. The group is always polite, mostly interesting, and sometimes frightening in its profoundness. I mean, what if Elvis were still alive? ✓ **USENET** DAILY

alt.revisionism (ng) Revisionists are historians of a sort, unregener-

ate polemicists who suggest that Nazi war atrocities were exaggerated by self-serving Jews looking to reap the benefits of a planet's pity. While the newsgroup wanders into related topics—general anti-Semitism, "identity" Christianity (the theory that God's favor is reserved for the direct descendants of Adam)—it spends a great deal of time haggling over factual questions of the Holocaust. Was it really 6 million? Weren't some of the Jews common criminals? ✓ **USENET** DAILY

Dinosaur (ml) This list is not about Barney, and everyone here

> **"Jumping into the brave new world, the mailing list H-Rhetor has debated whether a verbal 'rape in Cyberspace' did/could take place."**

knows exactly how Spielberg got it wrong. Dinosaur welcomes experts and novices alike—all that is required is a fondness for the Land of the Lost. ✓**INTERNET**→*email* list-proc @lepomis.psych.upenn.edu ✍ *Type in message body:* subscribe dinosaur <your full name> WEEKLY

Elenchus (ml) Ever wonder whether Jesus' healing power has a modern medical counterpart? Elenchus provides answers from doctors, anthropologists, and theologians. Is there a historical Christ or Socrates? Got a question? Ask it. The members of Elenchus are not intellectual snobs. ✓**INTERNET**→ *email* listserv@uottawa.bitnet ✍ *Type in message body:* subscribe elenchus <your full name> DAILY

H-Idea (ml) Intellectual history has been called the cocktail-party field—and reading the list will certainly give you some juicy, erudite-sounding tidbits to drop over the canapés. You won't, however, get simple answers here. Ask about modern life in Athens and follow a trail of ideas in the ensuing discussion that includes Byron, Hitler, Catherine the Great, and architec-

ture. Don't be frightened away; list members decry pretentiousness and snobbishness. ✓**INTERNET**→ *email* listserv@uicvm. uic.edu ✍ *Type in message body:* subscribe h-idea <your full name> DAILY

H-Rhetor (ml) If you know your semiotic lingo you will feel right at home. Recent threads have evaluated the rhetorical styles of current politicians and how the rhetoric of science always suggests "truth." Jumping into the brave new world, H-Rhetor has debated whether a verbal "rape in Cyberspace" did/could take place. ✓**INTERNET**→*email* listserv@uicvm. uic.edu ✍ *Type in message body:* subscribe h-rhetor <your full name> WEEKLY

H-Russia (ml) A good place to make contact with scholars, writers, and retired spies in the former Soviet-bloc countries. H-Russia also provides a translated-news service from Moscow, with daily updates from the republics. Join the members in their efforts to analyze the updates and make sense of the process of history in the making. ✓**INTERNET**→*email* listserv@uicvm. uic.edu ✍ *Type in message body:* subscribe h-russia <your full name> WEEKLY

H-State (ml) One of the busiest history lists around. Participants are eager to discuss anything that touches on the history of "the state"—social welfare policy, past and present, crime and punishment, public education, etc. The list has a strong international base, which makes for good cross-cultural comparisons of social programs and social needs. H-State is friendly to newcomers. ✓**INTERNET**→*email* listserv@uicvm.uic.edu ✍ *Type in message body:* subscribe h-state <your full name> DAILY

CYBERNOTES

"I don't think that among scholars there has really been any doubt about the '60s as a direct descendant of the Romantics (however, television does occasionally bowl me over with its brilliant flashes of insight). Add the fascination with the occult and it is early 19th century all over again. I see the Age of Victoria as a backlash against a great number of cultural excesses. If you think that Prince Charles's marital problems are spectacular, have a look at George IV and Caroline of Brunswick. Mrs. Fitzherbert = Camlia Parker-Bowles. Like wow. And after William IV, the Brits were aching for someone to restore some sort of respectability. I shall probably not live to see young Harry ascend the throne, unless Charles breaks his fool neck playing polo, but I would be willing to bet that in 30 to 40 years the U.K. will do another turnaround. I could be wrong, but historians do tend to think in cycles.

—from **Victoria**

Literature

Alarmists think the Net spells the death of the bound, page-by-page form that books have had since scrolls and parchment passed out of favor. Even moderate thinkers admit that the computer age has touched off a crisis of faith in devotees of literature. With so many screens and windows, and so much multimedia gadgetry, a regular old book seems, well, regular and old. No sizzle. No vim. No verve. But as these newsgroups and mailing lists demonstrate, the Net can also be a powerful force in the preservation of literature. While many of the Usenet lit sites and mailing lists are dominated by academics—and many of the academics do little to combat the stereotype of the nattering intellectual myopic—there's also plenty of opportunity for the lit critic who wants to condemn Erica Jong for her self-indulgence, or celebrate Stanley Elkin's indefatigable energy. Literary parties on the Net are nothing if not eclectic—Gilgamesh standing alongside Carol Gilligan, Job rubbing elbows with Joseph Wambaugh, Tyrone Slothrop smoking in the corner.

Mark Twain—downloaded from CompuServe's Archive Forum.

On the Net

Across the board

Books Here you'll find some of the most voracious readers anywhere, trying to tackle the canon of Western Literature while they're still alive. They rant and rave over James, Dostoyevsky, Joyce, Pynchon—all the "serious" writers of today and years gone by. Populated by writers, editors, and critics, the Books conference is also a source of industry gossip. Conversation is deep and borders on literary criticism, so the easily intimidated should lurk first and ask questions later. ✓**ECHO**→*j* boo DAILY

Literary (ml) If you are kept awake at night by apocalyptic visions of Shakespeare's bald pate overrun with circuitry, take heart in this mailing list, which proves not only that readers of fine literature are alive and well but also that technology can aid and abet their pursuits. Thanks to the synthetic community of mailing lists, bibliophiles can debate the reputation of Saul Bellow, recommend favorite novels, and even address more arcane matters. If you're interested in an extended conversation about the linguistic basis for sexual identity in Proust's *Recherche*, this mailing list—textured and thoughtful—is the place to go. ✓**INTERNET**→*email* listserv@bitnic.cren.net ✍ *Type in message body:* subscribe literary <your full name> DAILY

The Literary Forum Gossippy, prone to drift wildly off topic, CompuServe's Literary Forum will frustrate any reader or writer who might describe himself as serious. A thread titled "Literary market" contained advice on how to keep visiting in-laws from smoking indoors. The "Romance/Historical" section is ruled by ladies who have queened and duchessed themselves, in a sort of role-playing game called "The Keep." Under the category of research methods, a writer struggling to perfect her leprechaun dialect was advised to learn Gaelic off an Enya CD. A

> **"If you're interested in an extended conversation about the linguistic basis for sexual identity in Proust's *Recherche*, this mailing list is the place."**

rear guard of literary hardheadedness is snapping bitterly in a corner of the "Poetry/Lyrics" section. Surrounded by what they call "heartfelt quick-draw poetry," they veer in tone between curmudgeonly and virulent. "You want advice on how to fix your poem?" one beleaguered Hallmark-hater asked. "Burn it." After you read poems that rhyme *budgie* with *fudgie*, you'll agree. ✓**COMPUSERVE**→*go* literary→Messages HOURLY

rec.arts.books (ng) That was Burroughs in the Nike commercial, and no, J. D. Salinger and Thomas Pynchon are not the same person. This baggy newsgroup debates matters such as whether Yeats was an obscurantist, who belongs on a list of the top ten poets of this century, and the delicately inflected ambiguities in *Go, Dog, Go*. Amateurs, alone and in networks, post reviews on everything from sci-fi to Michael Ondaatje, although sometimes one suspects the handiwork of a publishing house's paid flunky. Several camps—sci-fi & fantasy, secretive postmodern novels, poetry, and long fat British books—coexist peacefully but fairly hermetically. On the evidence here, American readers are not as stick-in-the-muddish as the *New York Times* Book Review. If you rant about academic cabals, for instance, you will politely but firmly be advised to read Jonathan Culler and Terry Eagleton and then to try again. ✓**USENET** *FAQ:* ✓**INTERNET**→*ftp* rtfm.mit.edu→anonymous→<your email address>→/pub/usenet-by-hierarchy/rec/arts/books HOURLY

American lit

AmLit-L (ml) This mailing list attracts mostly academic users, which has both benefits and drawbacks. The benefits are that aca-

demics generate a uniformly high level of discourse, with detailed and often fascinating meditations on American literature. How is Beat poetry related to the projective verse of Charles Olson and the Black Mountain School? What were the factors involved in fixing the literary reputation of African-American poet Melvin Tolson? But the same intellectual rigor that produces diligent investigations of these issues also gives rise to a self-importance that is sometimes stultifying. If you can overlook the arch tone and the pretension, you'll find that the heavier material is offset by a number of lighter entries—graduate students confessing their weakness for (gasp!) popular authors, professors relating humorous classroom anecdotes, ordinary citizens celebrating the simple pleasure of reading good literature. ✓**INTERNET**→*email*

> "Woe unto the subscriber who confuses Catherine, Heathcliff's inamorata, with Cathy, her daughter, in *Wuthering Heights*. It suggests a preference for the vilified Olivier-Leigh film, which rendered the distinction moot."

listserv@mizzou1.missouri.edu ✍ *Type in message body:* subscribe am lit-l <your full name> DAILY

Twain-L (ml) "Clothes make the man. Naked people have little or no influence..." Mark Twain is America. Almost everyone knows Huck and Tom or can quote a pithy statement or two. On this active mailing list, academics and amateurs meet to interpret Twain's work and worship at his oracle. These people love Twain and want him on their side. Thus a recent thread about Twain's meeting another 19th-century wit, Oscar Wilde, sparked a long discussion about Twain and his probable opinion toward homosexuality. Those who saw Twain as liberal cited his acceptance of Walt Whitman (Twain was "a sexual libertarian"); the other side pointed toward his "moral" family life ("Twain was an honorable man"). Sometimes the list is academically trendy—how Huck's raft spawns homoerotic friendship. Sometimes it is just an exchange of favorite stories. Whichever, it is one of the most entertaining lit lists on the Net. ✓**INTERNET**→*email* listserv@ vm1.yorku.ca ✍ *Type in message body:* subscribe twain-l <your full name> WEEKLY

British lit

Bronte-L (ml) Although they're hardly Harlequin types, this rarefied crew is a testament to the origin of the romance novel—the Brontë sisters on the Yorkshire moors. Seasoned world travelers meet Ph.D. candidates. Professors seek advice on college syllabuses. Gentle appreciation, travel tips, book reviews. Passionate discussion on the ideal film cast for *Jane Eyre*. Occasional pilgrimages to Haworth, the Brontë home. No flames generally, but woe unto the subscriber who confuses Catherine, Heathcliff's inamorata, with Cathy, her daughter, in *Wuthering Heights*. It suggests a preference for the vilified Olivier-Leigh film, which rendered the distinction moot. ✓ **INTERNET**→*email* majordo mo@world. std.com ✍ *Type in message body:* subscribe bronte <your full name> DAILY

FWake-L (ml) "And so they went on, the fourbottle men, the analists, unguam and nunguam and lunguam again, their anschluss about her whosebefore and his whereafters and how she was lost away." What is there to say about a group of people who spend time trying to figure out what was probably a big practical joke? Actually, FWake-L is a very friendly list—congratulations flowed in from around the world for a daughter born on Bloomsday. In the sprit of Joyce, FWake-L welcomes all manner of enthusiasts and helps them "catch up." When down to business, members take a paragraph of the book at a time for analysis. But that's not all— then they go through the "levels" of the text, which means constant speculation on whether the different versions resulted from intentional flashes of brilliance or are typos! You really have to be Joycean for this, but there seem to be plenty such folks about. ✓ **INTERNET**→*email* listserv@irlearn. ucd.ie ✍ *Type in message body:* subscribe fwake-l <your full name> WEEKLY

ModBrits (ml) These scholars of modern British literature (Joyce, Wilde, Woolf, Conrad., etc.) are a tad hip and not overly cerebral. Here, in addition to discussions of the subtext of *To the Lighthouse*, you will find information on how to run a *Ulysses* scavenger hunt ("a pin for her drawers"). A recent long thread sought opinions on texts that crack you up and times that you have trouble keeping a straight face while in class. The list goes beyond literature: Regulars suggest singing World War I's greatest hits to better immerse yourself in the ambience of the writers you love. ✓ **INTERNET**→*email* listserv@kentvm.kent.edu ✍ *Type in message body:* subscribe modbrits <your full name> WEEKLY

Kid lit

KidLit-L (ml) When you think of great characters from literature, you may think of Stephen Dedalus and Victor Frankenstein, Faust and Sethe, but you probably don't think of Curious George. After reading this mailing list, you may amend your canon to include the mischievous little monkey. Kids' books sit at the root of any reader (and any writer), and this mailing list tries to cover them all, from tried-and-true classics (*Goodnight, Moon*; *Runaway Bunny*) to less successful attempts by ambitious celebrities (Bobby Darin, Julie Andrews, Whoopi Goldberg). Postings range from recommendations ("John Bellaires is the author for scary and well-written!") to more theoretical discussion of the purpose of children's literature. Popular authors like R. L. Stine occasionally drop in to offer their insights. ✓ **INTERNET**→*email* listserv@ bing vmb.cc.binghamton.edu ✍ *Type in message body:* subscribe kidlit-l <your full name> DAILY

Mythology

alt.mythology (ng) Scholars, elves, and writers of role-playing games meet to puzzle out arcana. The Hollywood blockbuster *Mask* tossed off a reference to the Norse god Loki; here you can read about Loki's two wives and three no-good children (one is a giant wolf, thankfully chained to a rock until the end of the world). Finding answers is what motivates this group. Must ghouls feed on corpses? What was the meaning of the word *Crotoan*, carved on a tree at Roanoke, the only clue to what happened to the abandoned British settlement there? Was Joseph Campbell an anti-Semite? Does Clinton's campaign rhetoric count as a bona fide "rags to riches" myth? ✓ **USENET** DAILY

"I wonder if we are not stretching the idea of Twain's libertarian views on sex a little far. After all, when Twain himself had the opportunity to write about someone who really could be considered a sexual libertarian, Shelley, he pilloried him ('A Defense of Harriet Shelley'), and he castigates the English nobility in 'A Connecticut Yankee' for their loose sexual conduct. Twain also seems to have lived a life of absolute devotion to his own wife. Apart from his own private musings about the anomaly of sexual desire (who has not mused as much?), Twain was, in this as in every area of his life, essentially an honorable man."

—from **Twain-L**

Writer's forum

Crewrt-L (ml) "What don't we do on this list? Flame. Call names. Bait people for politics, sexuality, religion. Post really terrible writing and get outraged when someone gently mentions that quality. Use pseudonyms." What do they do on this list? Quote from Philip Larkin's *Aubade*. Wonder about the most effective ways to teach character development to high-school students. Digress into polemics about the limited political power of fat women, or the ascendant stardom of Ken Griffey, Jr. While the traffic is largely academic, there's enough variety to accommodate subscribers from any walk of life. ✓**INTERNET**→*email* listserv@mizzou1.missouri.edu ✍ *Type in message body:* subscribe crewrt-l <your full name> DAILY

Techwr-L (ml) Technical writers are a species all to themselves: highly organized, obsessive, precise. Unlike ordinary people, they lose sleep over hyphenation, formatting, and how to translate certain technical terms into French. Their newsgroup does the same: encouraging protracted discussions about punctuation and spelling, as well as offering job listings. If you're not a technical writer, you may still want to subscribe, primarily for the fascinating linguistic discussions. For instance, after one woman on the list began to investigate the etymological origins of the word *dirt*—which can be traced through the Norse *drit* to the Old English *dritan* and the Old Norse *drita*, both of which mean "to defecate"—dozens of other subscribers objected, insisting that such crassness was hardly appropriate for a technical-writing mailing list. ✓**INTERNET**→*email* listserv@vm1.ucc.okstate.edu ✍ *Type in message body:* subscribe

Jack London—downloaded from CompuServe's Archive Forum.

techwr-l <your full name> DAILY

Words-L (ml) Originally a forum for discussion of the English language, this mailing list has become a minefield of digressions: nightclubs in Amsterdam, regional cuisine, the architecture of North Carolina State University, the literary value of books on tape. At this point, anything goes, and the chaotic nature of the list works against sustained interest. But perhaps the entropy is only illusory. As one subscriber writes, "Chaos is but unperceived order." ✓**INTERNET**→*email* listserv@uga.cc.uga.edu ✍ *Type in message body:* subscribe words-l <your full name> DAILY

Writers (ml) In addition to providing a forum for issues related to writing—everything from the tricky dodge of inspiration to the practical matter of survival—this mailing list fancies itself part of a warm and fuzzy world, an electronic community that supplements its occupational counsel with far less formal discussion of the "Oscars, the lunchboxes we had as kids, buttered cats and gravity, Tori Amos and whether *Picket Fences* and *Northern Exposure* are too similar." If you write professionally, or as a dedicated

hobbyist, or if you have just recently begun to consider the merits of humorous doggerel, this mailing list will accommodate your needs; one warning—since the participants are writers, this list will choke your mailbox unless you prune regularly. ✓**INTERNET**→ *email* listserv@vm1.nodak.edu ✍ *Type in message body:* subscribe writers <your full name> HOURLY

Writers The modem is mightier than the sword. The WELL's writers' conference takes on all aspects of the writing life. What editors have good reputations? Do most writers use computers? Is it normal to feel depressed after writing a book? In addition to chatty discussion, the conference offers practical advice on freelance opportunities, self-publishing, and even book signing (never personalize; it's a waste of energy and rarely appreciated). Because writers always write with a split brain—they are both absorbed in the moment and at one remove, both writing and watching themselves write—the conference is incredibly self-conscious. Many of the postings are devoted to determining how electronic media and Net participation have affected prose. ✓**WELL**→ *g* wri HOURLY

Philosophy

What is the meaning of life? No, this is not a rhetorical

question. At least it's not for those people who spend their time on and off the Net pondering deep matters. There are two levels of posting to the philosophy sites; extremely analytical and musing. The WELL's **Philosophy** conference entertains both questions about the specifics of Heidegger's epistemology and—more often—average-guy ponderings on truth, happiness, and other headaches. Professors and philosophy groupies can chat about their favorites on **Nietzsche**, **Kant**, or **Derrida**. All this lofty thought comes down to a practical level in the WELL's **Ethics** conference, where you can seek relief for your particular moral dilemma—or tell someone else what to do. For pro-opponents of the death penalty, assisted suicide, or plain old infidelity, there is no better place to hone your arguments.

Nietzsche—downloaded from Reuters News Picture Forum.

On the Net

Across the board

Ethics There are problems with ethical debate: It takes up lots of space and time and is often as painstaking as satisfying. That's where the WELL's Ethics confer-

ence comes in. Let's say you're developing an argument to justify making jokes that disparage your own ethnic group, but you're hung up on the problem of insider rights versus outsider rights. Or let's say you're musing about the problem of cheating on a quadriplegic spouse. The kind and thoughtful participants in the ethics conference have already sketched out the contours of the problems, and all you have to do is dive right in and pick a stance. Whether it's the death penalty, euthanasia, or infidelity, the complexities have been parsed and packaged. The Ethics conference also includes a special topic on electronic ethics, as well as the immensely enjoyable "Silly Ethical Questions." Right and wrong have never been so much fun. ✓**WELL**→*g* ethics WEEKLY

Philosophy These categories try to tackle philosophical issues that

intersect with both religion and politics. Most of the discussion revolves around ethicists of various shapes and sizes, everyone from Aristotle to John Stuart Mill to Ayn Rand. Because the chat incorporates both practiced philosophers and interested neophytes, the quality of the comments varies; in a discussion on Ayn Rand, the reactions range from the canny ("Two big problems dogged Rand: first, her views were politically offensive to both conservatives and liberals, and second, not unlike the followers of Marx and Freud, many of her disciples spent, and spend, more time cleansing 'the party' than attempting to present her ideas in any practical framework") to the catty ("Of course she was a better writer than Kant—who isn't?"). And because of the diversity of background, a feelgood vibe pervades the whole discussion: As one man says to a young woman, "Wish you well in school!" ✓**GENIE**→*keyword* religion →Religion & Philosophy Bulletin Board→Philosophy WEEKLY

Philosophy The philosophy practiced on the WELL's conference runs the gamut from very formal analysis (point-by-point treatments of Heidegger, Popper, Nietzsche, etc.) to very informal discussion (endless and colloquial musing about happiness, suffering,

> ## "Long threads speculate on what Friedrich would have thought about mass-produced pornography."

truth, knowledge, and so on). While hard-core philosophy buffs may find the level of conversation pitched a little low for their tastes, if you've ever taken a philosophy course, or wish you had, or know someone who did, you may find pearls of wisdom gleaming in this conference. ✓**WELL**→*g* phil DAILY

---

talk.philosophy.misc (ng) What does philosophy say about predicting the future? What are Descartes's ideas of God? How was time measured before the beginning of the universe? These as well as more scholarly philosophical questions are contemplated on talk.philosophy.misc. The newsgroup's greatest strength is its ability to move from academic discourse to good, long existentialist tales of the rogue kind. ("Existence cannot be defined, it can only be experienced. The mind is incapable of true expression or true knowledge.") ✓**USENET** DAILY

Philosophers

Derrida (ml) Deconstruction—that tricky critical process that is the secret weapon of literary critics everywhere. Simply perform an intellectual operation, and voila! Truth collapses. Epistemology is thrown into flux. The very fabric of language, and even thought itself, rips along the bias. This mailing list, full of courage and folly, attempts to fix the critical thought of the deconstructionists, led of course by French phenomenological renegade Jacques Derrida. "Did the phenomenological reduction put the Cartesian subject in parentheses? How does the Nietzschean notion of supplementarity compare to the similar concepts unearthed in Rousseau? And what can be done about the equivocal ontological status of the signature?" While much of the list is impenetrable, professional academics looking for their Derridean fix will find it here, and there are even moments of occasional clarity that demonstrate why Derrida, for all his willful opacity, is something more than a charlatan. ✓**INTERNET**→*email* listserv@cfrvm.bitnet ✍ *Type in message body:* subscribe derrida <your full name> DAILY

Kant (ml) "I must say I find the intrinsically shifting and wiggly relation between positivism and Kant fascinating." Believe it or not this holds true for quite a number of souls. This is heady stuff—is there free will? Is it possible to know anything as "truth"? Kantians from around the world frequent this list to address questions such as these. Sometimes postings require translation from Philosophese to English. Get past that little drawback and this list will make you really think about what you know and how you know it—or even if you know it. ✓**INTERNET**→*email* majordomo@world. std.com ✍ *Type in message body:* subscribe kant WEEKLY

Nietzsche (ml) Ever remark to yourself, "God is dead, but did Friedrich himself have to go?'" If your answer is yes, then this is the place for you. This active forum engages in intricate evaluations of whether Nietzsche moralized, and what he thought about truth—quotations get you extra points. But the list moves beyond the dry rehashing of his complete works. Long threads speculate on what Friedrich would have thought about mass-produced pornography, which thinkers of our time would admire, and what art he'd hang on his walls. This makes for very interesting reading! ✓**INTERNET**→ *email* majordomo@world. std.com ✍ *Type in message body:* subscribe nietzsche WEEKLY

Part 6

Identity

Ethnic bonding

Ernesto has never been to Spain, but his parents are

native Madrilenos, and he's worried about the increasing vehemence of Basque terrorism in the Spanish capital. Susan has studied Chinese language and literature, and she wants to discuss the classic novel *Dream of the Red Chamber*. And Jean-Claude weighs in with opinions on all things French, from the nation's health-care system to its rich culinary tradition (zee onion pie? *C'est magnifique!*). These are only a few of the topics people like to talk about on the Net's rich array of ethnic- and national-identity discussion sites. First and foremost, of course, there are the 50-plus **soc.culture** newsgroups. From the Arabic and the Nordic to the German and the Thai, the newsgroups are lively chat sites (often in their respective foreign language) for ethnic minorities within the United States as well as participants from overseas, with foreign students dominating discussion. "Israel and Syria must come to terms with one another." "Iranian stereotypes have reached absurd levels of negativity." Most commercial services

Louis Farrakhan—downloaded from CompuServe's Archive Forum.

also offer numerous opportunities for ethnic chat— the WELL, for instance, has an immensely detailed and satisfying **Irish/Celtic** conference—and there are dozens of mailing lists and bulletin boards on which political and cultural debate bloom. As one woman says, tongue at least half in cheek, "It's like Epcot, but without all the annoying rides and overpriced food."

On the Net

Across the board

The Cosmopolitan As part of AOL's Campus at a Glance, The Cosmopolitan offers an opportunity for international students (or anyone who feels like a student at heart) to post messages about international events, to reflect on the problems of foreignness in the United States, or merely to converse in the language of their choice. Itching to talk about your recent breakup in Ivrit? Want to review the latest movie blockbuster in Thai? Or are you merely interested in practicing your high-school Spanish? No problemo. ✓**AMERICA ONLINE**→*keyword* bull moose→Campus at a Glance→The Cosmopolitan WEEKLY

Country and Language IRC Channels An international tour on IRC is more Eurail pass than Orient Express. It's not witty banter over cocktails that chink lightly as countryside rolls past. It's more of a budget-rate all-night train ride, shoved into a compartment of six with slobbering drunk soccer fans. In #india, conversations shift from Hindi to Urdu to English and back. But urbane it isn't. "Are you a homo?" is practically a refrain; college-boy macho does not respect international borders.

Another disappointment will be familiar to real-world travelers: There's a little bit of USA in every corner of the globe. Grateful Dead albums are traded in #israel, in #italia there's a debate about O. J. Simpson, and almost everyone in #ireland is dialing from Seattle.

Online French

The French do not much frequent #france. You'll find them in #francais, *bien sûr*, languidly discussing how they plan to smuggle a mysterious something past Customs. Thanks to Minitel, online French is practically a separate dialect. "*Qui est-ce?*" turns into "*Ki s?*" for example. But then, no visit to Paris, virtual or real, would be complete if you weren't humiliated for your clueless college French.

If you speak the language, try #polska, #russian, #chinese, or

Ethnic bonding Identity

#dutch. #Espanol is lively, but consumed by bot wars. Douglas Adams jokes fly by on #israel, where they good-naturedly steal each other's nicks and arrange a pizza party in Manhattan. #England mocks BBC radio ("Is that a lump of shite, or is it radio 1?") and has revived the ancient joke of adding the words "in bed" to every sentence. The #aussies seem happiest—or at least the most drunk. They call each other "wanker" and say things like, "Imagine for just one sec that I'm a blonde floozy." And if, in a burst of affection, one Aussie calls another a "fucking lard-ass piece of shit," you'll know you've witnessed the kind of authentic moment the serious traveler lives for. ✓**INTERNET** *irc* SEE LIST OF IRC CHANNELS ON PAGE 185

Cultures BB With topics like Latin America, Eastern Europe, and Asians, Cultures is where Prodigy members come to meet others of the same ethnicity. The busiest topic on the bulletin board is African American, which has more mature discussion than the other topics. Whether its single Asian Americans meeting in the Asian topic or activists discussing racism in the African American topic, the board is more clubby than provocative. A lot of younger Prodigy members use the Cultures BB to trace their family roots. ✓**PRODIGY**→*jump* cultures bb→ Choose a Topic WEEKLY

Africa

Africa-L (ml) "You should all remember that when they first came to our lands and said 'Let's pray' they spelt the word *pray* with an *e* i.e. *prey*." Africa-L is an intensely political and left-leaning mailing list and an interesting place to get cross-cultural perspectives of Africa in the 20th century. ✓**INTER-**

> "The #aussies seem happiest—or at least the most drunk. They call each other 'wanker' and say things like 'Imagine for just one sec that I'm a blonde floozy.'"

NET→*email* listserv@vtvm1.cc.vt.edu ✍ *Type in message body:* subscribe africa-l <your full name> WEEKLY

African American

AFAM-L (ml) A scholarly list for those devoted to the study of African American culture that has evolved into a very active place to talk about the here and now of African American life. A news release about the firing of the head of the NAACP sparked immediate debate about the specific incident, the history of the organization, and its current direction. The news that the Fox network had canceled five black-oriented shows led to a weeklong discussion of media images and media power. AFAM-L is an essential gathering place for scholars, activists, and anyone else interested in the African American experience. ✓**INTERNET**→*email* listserv@mizzou1. missouri.edu ✍ *Type in message body:* subscribe afam-l <your full name> DAILY

Afro-American Culture & Arts Forum The Salon, a general chitchat board, is the most active

section in the forum. It's where parents discuss how to deal with a teen "indefinitely homebound" (a nice euphemism for grounded) and where everyone picks apart the media image of the single black mother. Recent immigrants link up in Caribbean Meeting to talk about the old country. The forum also includes serious political talk about Rush and O.J., occasional accusations of "blacker than thou" posturing, and a group that periodically shares its favorite items from *Weekly World News*— like the one about the 50-foot Jesus terrorizing a small town. The big draws are the culture topics— art, history, film, theater, and music. ✓**COMPUSERVE**→ *go* afro→Messages <or> Rooms DAILY/LIVE

AGE-L (ml) Topics such as the South African budget and Mandela's presidency, the pros and cons of American forces in Haiti, and how best to assist in Rwanda are all analyzed in great detail from a startling number of different perspectives on this list. Its multinational membership also spawns interesting debate about the shared backgrounds of Africans and African Americans. ✓**INTERNET**→*email* listserv@uga.cc.uga. edu ✍ *Type in message body:* subscribe age-l <your full name> WEEKLY

ASA-L (ml) Provides an opportunity for African American students worldwide to share ideas, strategies, and humor. Predictably much more active during the school year, the list members are young, smart, and impassioned. Keeping abreast of international developments, the ASA-L often creates networks for relief work and political action. Students also get a chance to form friendships with their counterparts in other countries, and to check out opportunities for travel (e.g., Mark from the States discusses the club scene with a new friend in Cairo). The chat is often fun—how about a long discussion that re-evaluates fairy tales from a modern perspective? ✓**INTERNET**→ *email* listserv@ tamvm 1.tamu.edu ✍ *Type in message body:* subscribe asa-l <your full name> WEEKLY

BlackExperience (echo) This bulletin board is one of the best places in Cyberspace for African American chat, from the impact of *Brown* v. *Board of Education* to the history of rap. Discussions tend to be provocative and political. To wit: "If a black man were to find a cure for AIDS, would people say that he was a white man?" A popular gripe is the depiction of blacks in the media, from *The New York Times* and *The Wall Street Journal* to shows on the Fox network, including *In Living Color, Martin,* and *Living Single.* ✓**RELAYNET** DAILY

---

soc.culture.african.american (ng) This can sometimes sound like a neoconservative group. The African Americans here can be more acute critics of black politics than any talk-show right-winger. But politics takes a backseat to the topic of all topics—the relationship between men and women. In a recent discussion about love and marriage—"What is it about marriage that women want so desperately?"—more than 100 people weighed in.

Stay around the group long enough, and you'll grow accustomed to the monthly "What is racism?" or its sibling discussion "Is that really racism?" After one participant (not an African American) asked, "Could it be that the funny looks you get in the elevator are more about being male?" an exasperated regular wrote back: "I really think you need a vacation from this group." Perhaps as many

Two Asian girls—downloaded from America Online's Mac Graphics & CAD Forum.

as half the regulars on this newgroup are not African American. ✓**USENET** DAILY

American

soc.culture.usa (ng) A German Turk recently doubted there was much point in a newsgroup called soc.culture.usa, because "the mighty USA does not have a culture; instead it has a self-made culture." His doubt is forgivable.

Soc.culture.usa is a grab bag of politics and pseudoscience, not focused any more closely on the United States than any other newsgroup. Bosnia's partition, the Cuban refugee crisis, and Senate filibusters have equal airtime here. This is a good place to cull data on American folk beliefs about race and language, but the closest it came to self-conscious "culture" was when a woman requested a GIF of an Alaskan totem animal for a tattoo she was planning.

Of recent concern to America's self-made culture: whether the *Lion King* was plagiarized, whether mosquitoes carry AIDS, and whether Connie Chung represents a setback in Chinese-American relations. ✓**USENET** DAILY

Asian

soc.culture.china/soc.culture. hongkong/soc.culture.taiwan (ng) No, they aren't the same. And in fact, that's one of the most frequent topics in these three newsgroups—the distinctions, and political hostilities, between the "three Chinas."

Soc.culture.china is dominated by Chinese students doing study-abroad programs in the States. Most are taking the time to freely post antigovernment messages, safely out of reach of rolling tanks; of course, Tiananmen and its lingering aftereffects are a high-volume topic.

Pinyin phrases

Much conversation is conducted with embedded pinyin phrases; watch out. Soc.culture. hongkong, on the other hand, is more evenly balanced between Chinese Americans with Hong Kong roots and Hong Kongese in America to study; it also draws a certain number of non–Hong Kongers who are fans of Hong Kong film or music. A recent flame-post attacking Hong Kong–pop pretty boy Andy Lau set off a firestorm against the original poster.

Cantonese Star Names

Don't expect to talk about Hong Kong movies after a single viewing of *The Killer*, either—the fans here know what they're talking about, and will use the original Cantonese versions of movie and star names just to drive you mad. Soc.culture.taiwan is one of the Asian newsgroup family's most contentious members. TIs (those demanding Taiwanese Independence) square off against WSRs (those Wishing to Stay a Republic), lobbing bazooka blasts across the Net with the regularity of shots fired in a free-fire zone along the Maginot Line during World War II. If you don't care about Taiwanese politics, there's still discussion of Little League baseball scores and pop singers, as well as the movies of Ang Lee. ✓ **USENET** *FAQ:* ✓ **INTERNET**→*ftp* rtfm.mit.edu→ anonymous →<your email address> →/pub/usenet-by-group/news.an swers/hongkong-faq→part 1, part2, part3 *and* part4 WEEKLY

---

soc.culture.filipino (ng) Mostly news about the Philippines, with a fair amount of it regional enough so as to be incomprehensible to the non-Pinoy; some discussion of Filipino American issues, though mostly in relation to "heritage" and "tradition." The Net equivalent of an atomic bomb landed on SCF recently when Filpop star/Broadway babe Lea Salonga (of *Miss Saigon* and *Aladdin*) began posting here. Her fans, as is apparent from the thicket of gushing posts following her own, are legion.

It's not clear whether she's been driven into lurk mode by the uproar or she's dropped her account. About 95 percent of soc.culture. filipino members are Filipino, and there are even numbers of men and women. The age range is di-verse since a number of postcollege and older Filipino Americans seem to use the group as a place for public correspondence. ✓ **USE-NET** *FAQ:* ✓ **INTERNET**→*ftp* rtfm.mit. edu→anonymous→<your email address>→/pub/usenet-by-hierarchy /news/answers/filipino-faq→part1, part2, part3, *and* part4 WEEKLY

---

soc.culture.indian*/**rec.music.indian***/**alt.culture.karnatka** (ng) Hundreds of messages a week pour into the mammoth Indian newsgroups (in particular, soc.culture.indian), where Indian traditions, politics, and culture are celebrated—and just as often attacked.

The community includes young Indians querying about schools in the U.S., undergrads debating the tradition of arranged marriages, angry activists calling for the dismissal of Amnesty International from India. Whether they're about Bengali literature, Hinduism, or vegetarianism, the discussions are usually very informed—many would seem almost scholarly if not for their emotional undertones.

The group is at its best when covering cultural topics. When a woman asked about the influence of Mozart on Indian classical music, someone else mentioned the relationship between Czech, Gypsy, and Indian music, which a few messages later became a discussion about Czech author Milan Kundera's novel *The Unbearable Lightness of Being*.

Break away

Political debates, however, feed the strong centrifugal forces in soc.culture.indian—people are always petitioning to break away with a new newsgroup—not unlike in India itself. And there are already several other Indian newsgroups: Read Indian news in misc.news.southasia; request spe-cific information about journal articles, visas, Internet access, and the like in soc.culture.indian.info; join the often personal discussions by Indian Americans about preserving culture and living in the U.S. in the newsgroup alt.culture.us.asian-indian; engage in political debate in the rather quiet alt.india.progressive (most political discussions happen in soc.culture. indian); get into a flame war in the volatile alt.culture.karnataka, which also has an inordinate number of members seeking a marriage partner—"Alliance invited from well educated brahmin guys from good south Indian family for a brahmin girl"; join the usually more lighthearted soc.culture.indian.telugu, where discussions often cover movies, music, and recipes, with the occasional travel companion, roommate, or babysitter sought; or turn to rec.music.indian. classical and rec.music.indian.misc for endless music conversation. ✓ **USENET** *FAQ:* ✓ **INTERNET**→*ftp* rtfm.mit.edu→anonymous→ <your email address>→/pub/usenet- by-group/soc.culture.indian

> ## "The Net equivalent of an atomic bomb landed on SCF recently when Filpop star/ Broadway babe Lea Salonga (of *Miss Saigon* and *Aladdin*) began posting here."

→[soc.culture.indian]_FREQUENT-LY_ASKED_QUESTIONS HOURLY

soc.culture.japan (ng) Out of all of the major soc.culture Asian newsgroups, soc.culture.japan is the only one that seems largely dominated by non-Asians. Quirky discussions of cultural difference (why are there fewer bald men in Japan than in the U.S.?) prompted by questions from returned tourists or exchange students are common.

The handful of regulars posting from Japan are entrusted with a sort of guru status; they're asked to deliver Solomonic decisions who's right and who's wrong about various aspects of Japanese culture. A fair amount of spillover from the newsgroup rec.arts.anime comes here; men outnumber women and posters are older on average than those on some of the other soc.culture Asian newsgroups. ✓USENET *FAQ:* ✓INTERNET→*ftp* rtfm.mit.edu→anonymous→<your email address>→/pub/usenet-by-group/soc. answers/japan→refer ences DAILY

soc.culture.korea (ng) If you're reading this newsgroup, you'd better know Korean politics, culture, and language fairly intimately. If you're posting to this newsgroup, you'd probably better be Korean. Soc.culture.korea can be disorienting for new posters, since regulars have no qualms about posting anecdotes, jokes, and other material with enough Korean-language content to make it a frustrating pursuit for non-Koreaphones. Nonreaders of Korean can find themselves ignored, and sometimes abused. Males dominate, but females are well represented—the ratio is about three to one—and most users are young. ✓USENET WEEKLY

Afghan man—from America Online's Mac Graphics & CAD Forum.

Asian American

AAGPSO (ml) The Asian American Graduate and Professional Students Organization mailing list carries some of the most intellectually heady discussion available on the Net—though not always; dumb jokes and sly, inside remarks are also sent to the list in large numbers. Still, if you like your Asian American issues with a double helping of Derrida, find someone to invite you to join AAGPSO—it's members-only, and in the interests of preserving a sense of flame-free security, the policy is that an AAGPSO member must recommend a would-be list member. But don't get your hopes up: The current members are wary of increasing the list's size from its current hundred or so. The list can be guaranteed to send you a dozen or two pieces of mail a night. It skews slightly more male than female, with a decidedly older crowd than soc.culture. asian.american. One RL get together has occurred; it was a great success, and more will be planned. ✓INTERNET→*email* (by invitation only) DAILY

soc.culture.asian.american (ng) Believed to be the grand-daddy of identity newsgroups, soc.culture.asian.american has managed to barrel on through years of flesh-searing flame wars to survive to this day as one of the most exciting and vitriolic newsgroups on the Net. Topics include English-only legislation, immigration questions, the media portrayal of Asian Americans (any recent movie, TV series, or, for that matter, comic book with Asian American characters is likely to get a thorough going-over), issues of violence and cooperation between races, interracial dating, and... well, interracial dating.

Sometimes these discussions function as mere triggers for the fusillades that follow between the two armed camps that dominate the group. The primary factional breakdown is simple: Non-Asians who consider the group to be a place for all who admire or concern themselves with Asian American issues versus Asian Americans who consider the group to be a haven for intra-Asian discussion and bonding. The fact that some of the former are also active in another group, called alt.sex.fetish.orientals, has been a source of much irritation among the latter.

On the plus side for those seeking interesting conversation, soc.culture.asian.american is moderately well represented by both sexes, the ratio being about three males to two females. The age skews toward the collegiate. Most people are truly concerned with the issues here, and they post what they feel and think with passion. They're also pretty regular about it: A few hundred new posts a night is not uncommon. Regional RL get-togethers by soc.culture.asia.american members in the Bay Area, in Boston, and in New York are common.

Shouting contests

Posting hints: Avoid any discussions dominated by crossfire between Bryan Wu (one of the newsgroup's original members, and an almost maniacally obsessive poster) and Brian Robinson, his equally post-happy soc.culture. asian.american nemesis. These often degenerate into you're-stupid/no-you're-stupid shouting contests. Also ignore posts placed by Dwight Mishima (né Dwight Joe), an almost legendary individual whose frothingly hate-filled rants against those of Chinese descent and inane system of classifying persons by race, culture, and genetic background have caused him to be the only person with a full subheading in the soc.culture.asian.american FAQ. (Joe himself is known to be Chinese.) ✓USENET *FAQ:* ✓INTERNET→*ftp* rtfm.mit.edu→anonymous→<your email address>→/pub/usenet-by-group/soc.culture.asian.american→ FAQ_for_soc.culture.asian.american DAILY

Australian

soc.culture.australian (ng) Imagine that you've captured an Australian and you can ask him anything you want. "As a black American, how would I be treated as opposed to a white American?" "How do Ozzies feel about the queen?" You're probably thinking of visiting Australia, aren't you? So drill him: Where do I stay? What do I see? When do I go? And, of course, what about Oz beer? Discussion sometimes becomes very serious—"I have another question before I actually move in late October: Are the *Star Trek* series readily available in Australia and if so, what season are they on?" ✓USENET *FAQ:* ✓INTERNET→*ftp* rtfm.mit.edu→anonymous→<your

email address>→/pub/usenet-by-group/soc.answers/australian-faq→part1, part2, part3, *and* part4 WEEKLY

Canadian

soc.culture.canada (ng) While U.S. citizens just can't resist posting about their border-crossing experiences, Canadians dominate the group with discussion about domestic politics, the environment, the country's bilingualism, trade relationships, and the highly charged debate over Quebec's sovereignty. Too often for most members, a man named Laurence, who hated the time he spent in Canada, jumps into the conversation with anti-Canadian comments. But for every Laurence post, there are many more enthusiastic posts about Canada. ✓USENET *FAQ:* ✓INTERNET→*ftp* rtfm.mit.edu→anonymous→<your email address>→/pub/usenet-by-group/soc.answers/canada-faq→part* WEEKLY

European

European Forum Doom-mongering Europeans worry that Americans "kill for fun, sport, and revenge." You can agree that the worst is true or instead ask, "Are we dysfunctional, or do we just need good haircuts?" In this wide-ranging, neighborly forum, members also volunteer to translate "baking soda" and "condensed milk" into German, find an apartment in Stockholm for someone's wife and kids, walk each other through the French scuba-permit bureaucracy, and ask which are the best seats in Prague's Strahov stadium for the upcoming Pink Floyd concert. Be prepared for threads to bounce in and out of English. ✓COMPUSERVE→*go* eurfor→Messages DAILY

Mideur-L (ml) A mixture of contemporary political debate, historical discussion and ethnic bonding. List members here include scholars from around the world and middle Europeans in and outside the borders of their countries. Emotions run high here during talk of current strife—Tatiana writes about Bosnian partition to a Serb, "I am pregnant as it is, so there is no need for chetniks to come here and rape me." Slovaks complain about the media's "pro-Czech" stance. Scholars step in every once in a while to moderate discussions of how hate builds throughout time—anti-Catholicism, anti-Semitism, anti-...But there is also an element of ethnic support here—as a young American seeks prayers in Croatian to ease his dying grandfather's mind. ✓INTERNET→*email* listserv@ubvm.cc. buffalo.edu ✍ *Type in message body:* subscribe mideur-l <your full name> WEEKLY

UK Forum An American reading the Politics group on CompuServe's UK Forum might think she'd stepped into a parallel universe, where the Clinton health plan has passed and is running as smoothly as the post office; where Social Security is—for some reason—called National Insurance, and where elected officials actually participate in political discussions on the Internet. Don't worry: It's not the future; it's just Britain. In Rover's Return Pub, Brits and Merchant-Ivory victims pretend to be drunk and fondle each other boozily. Recently, forum members met offline in Manchester, London, and Los Angeles. Tourists share tips—such as the Dylan Thomas house in Wales and the hedge mazes at Hever Castle—or arrange to rent a converted barn in Cornwall. John Cleese's name pops up in nearly every thread.

✓ COMPUSERVE→*go* ukforum→Messages DAILY

Latin American

soc.culture.mexican (ng) Conducted mostly in Spanish, soc.culture.mexican addresses issues related to America's giant Southern neighbor. And those, of course, range from NAFTA to Mexican elections to the World Cup. Not all of the discussants are interested in Mexico's relationship with America—there's also a substantial amount of conversation about Mayan culture, the Mexican stock market, Mexican punk music, Mexican baseball, and the spread of the Net through the Yucatán. But coming to terms with the United States is an ever present concern, and at least one subscriber can't restrain himself from asking a pressing questions about American public restrooms: "¿Por que los banos publicos en los Estados Unidos son disenados de tal forma que siempre hay una ranura en las puertas, de tal forma que la pobre victima (o sea el que esta ahi sentado) no puede disfrutar de un poco de privacidad?" ✓ USENET *FAQ:* ✓ INTERNET→*ftp* rtfm.mit.edu→anonymous→<your email address>→/pub/usenet-by-group/soc.answers/mexican-faq DAILY

Middle Eastern

il.talk (ng) Discuss Israel and the Jewish community in the United States. Worried about Jewish attrition through intermarriage? Want to know about the Peter Gabriel concert in Tel Aviv? If there's a problem with il.talk, it's that the generic character of the group doesn't exactly encourage extended discussion—threads don't get very long and many of the discussions are about the indirection of the group itself. Political debates tend

> **"In a duel of quotes, both the agnostics and the devout claim the poet Abu al-Alaa. And everybody claims the finest recipe for Muloukhiyyah soup."**

to waken the group. ✓ USENET DAILY

soc.culture.arabic (ng) Everything is up for grabs in soc.culture.arabic. Edward Said compares Arafat to Mandela, and immediately two camps form to claim each leader has been insulted. In a duel of quotes, both the agnostics and the devout claim the poet Abu al-Alaa. The more it's explained, the murkier Frank Zappa's religion becomes—he could, it is pointed out, be both a Muslim and a Jew. And everybody claims the finest recipe for Muloukhiyyah soup. Women's rights and Bosnia are emotional subjects; these threads show no sign of petering out. Arabs have cottoned to the Net: Arabic-language software is traded avidly, and Muslims in non-Arab countries can even place matrimonial ads through a listserv program at Georgia Tech. ✓ USENET DAILY

soc.culture.iranian (ng) Maligned here in the United States, what with the shah and the ayatollah, the Iranian/Persian culture is one of the most fascinating in the world—a reasonably well preserved relic of ancient times as well as a vibrant modern force. This

newsgroup not only clarifies cultural and political issues pertaining to Iran but also grapples with the distance between ancient traditions and contemporary practice (many of those posting are American college students).

There are also a fair number of non-Iranians who have respectful questions about the culture. Issues range from the institutional oppression of women in contemporary society to reflections on the Armenian conflict, from reviews of Farsi word processors to listings of Iranian get-togethers from across the country.

One caveat: Much of the material is transliterated from the Farsi, and postings like this clarification of the authorship of the Iranian dramatic classic *Shahre Ghesse*—"Mofid did not write many of the songs in that play (such as 'mAdaram zeynab khAtoon, gees dAreh ghad-e kamoon' and the final song 'kheyr nabeeny hamoomy'). He did not write the central story of each animal having a job and 'feel oomad tamAshA kone, oftAd-o dandoonesh shekast'"—won't make a tremendous amount of sense if you don't share the tongue. ✓ USENET *FAQ:* ✓ INTERNET→*ftp* rtfm.mit.edu→ anonymous →<your email address>→/pub/usenet-by-group/soc.answers→iranian-faq DAILY

soc.culture.israel/soc.culture.jewish (ng) These two newsgroups cover all things Jewish—from the Israeli economy ("The tax on the bourse is the greatest thing to happen in years") to the Lubavitcher worship of Rebbe Schneerson ("What it most resembles, in religious practices, is the Catholic veneration of saints as the interceders with God"); from Jewish views on abortion ("In Orthodox law, it's required to save the life of the mother") to anti-Semitism in Batman movies ("Is Danny Devito's Penguin a cruel caricature?"). Subscribers weigh in with opinions, share personal anecdotes and spiritual counsel, and give pointers (six-pointers, that is) about Jewish life in the United States and in the world— will Yiddish ever return as a living language? What is the best way to remember Kristallnacht? ✓**USENET** *FAQ:* ✓**INTERNET**→*ftp* rtfm.mit.edu→ anonymous→<your email address> →/pub/usenet-by-group/soc. answers/judaism DAILY

soc.culture.lebanon (ng) In some ways, this newsgroup is exactly that—a news service, with informative postings about Lebanon's role in the crazy quilt of the Middle East, and especially its volatile relations with Syria and Israel. The group is dominated by American college students, and like many American college students, they tend to be both impassioned and naive, and demonstrate an almost palpable desire to put things right. As one student from Amherst College writes, "The point I am desperately trying to make is don't try and have it easy by blaming everything on Israel. I hate Israel for what they have done to Palestinians and others at different times—but I also hate Assad for what he has done to us." The group also has its lighter moments—nostalgia for Grandma's Lebanese cuisine, for instance. ✓**USENET** *FAQ:* ✓**INTERNET** →*ftp* rtfm.mit.edu→anonymous→ <your email address>→/pub/ usenet-by-group/soc.answers/ lebanon-faq→part1 *and* part2 DAILY

soc.culture.palestine (ng) This may be small consolation, but the nation without a country at least has a newsgroup. In this newsgroup, even after "the handshake," every hot button gets pushed—Is-

Native South American girl—from CompuServe's Photography Forum.

raeli cruelty to Palestinians, the absence of Palestinian self-control, the ignorance of the international community. PLO stalwart Yassir Arafat looms largest, with Israel a close second, and even when the postings seem to treat scholarly questions—"Are Jews monotheists or polytheists according to Islam?"—the political undercurrents are unmistakable. ✓**USENET** DAILY

Native American

soc.culture.native/alt.native (ng) If you're a New Age pale face looking to learn ancient tribal wisdom, go away. The consensus here is that only a huckster would try to teach Indian spirituality to a white person, and the hucksters who make money at it infuriate Indians. Issues of trust and authenticity matter here.

A woman who can't decide whether she should give to a relief charity posts the names of the board of directors. Others then check the list, confirming that they went to school with X, or knew Y on the rez (reservation). In the ongoing feud between the national and state chapters of the American Indian Movement (AIM), a dirty and effective weapon is the smear campaign—once you allege that X is not a "real" Cherokee, the ru-

mor never quite dies. The moderators work hard to include news from unwired places such as Chiapas, but they can also be a bit officious, adding long-winded comments to others' posts. Expression is freer on alt.native. ✓**USENET** *FAQ:* ✓**INTERNET**→*ftp* rtfm.mit.edu →anonymous→<your email address>→/pub/usenet-by-group/ alt.native→FAQ:_Soc.Culture. Native DAILY

Other

Esper-L (ml) Invented in the first years of the century by Polish oculist L. L. Zamenhof, Esperanto is an artificial international language that attempts to bridge the gaps between continental tongues by relying on words common to European languages. It's like a Venn diagram of Western cultures, a hokey-pokey in which each country puts something in and shakes it all about.

College French

While Zamenhof's ambition was admirable—one activist group calls his invention "The First Foreign Language for All Mankind" —Esperanto hasn't exactly caught on like wildfire.

However, this language without a country lives on in this mailing list, where you'll spend much of your time trying to use your college French, or high-school German, to extract a few nuggets of meaning. In the meantime, here's a phrase that will help you the next time someone cues a Mariah Carey CD at your Esperanto get-together: "Ri kantas egete bone sed ne sufice bone." ("She sings pretty well but not well enough.") ✓**INTERNET**→*email* listserv@vm 3090.ege.edu.tr ✍ *Type in message body:* subscribe esper-l <your full name> WEEKLY

More ethnicity chat...

soc.culture newsgroups

soc.culture.afghanistan
soc.culture.african
soc.culture.argentina
soc.culture.asean
soc.culture.austria
soc.culture.baltics
soc.culture.bangladesh
soc.culture.belgium
soc.culture.berber
soc.culture.bosna-herzgvna
soc.culture.brazil
soc.culture.british
soc.culture.bulgaria
soc.culture.burma
soc.culture.caribbean
soc.culture.celtic
soc.culture.chile
soc.culture.colombia
soc.culture.croatia
soc.culture.cuba
soc.culture.czecho-slovak
soc.culture.ecuador
soc.culture.esperanto

soc.culture.europe
soc.culture.french
soc.culture.german
soc.culture.greek
soc.culture.hongkong.entertainment
soc.culture.indonesia
soc.culture.italian
soc.culture.jewish.holocaust
soc.culture.laos
soc.culture.latin-america
soc.culture.maghreb
soc.culture.magyar
soc.culture.malaysia
soc.culture.mexican.american
soc.culture.misc
soc.culture.mongolian
soc.culture.nepal
soc.culture.netherlands
soc.culture.new-zealand
soc.culture.nigeria
soc.culture.nordic
soc.culture.pakistan
soc.culture.palestine

soc.culture.peru
soc.culture.polish
soc.culture.portuguese
soc.culture.puerto-rico
soc.culture.punjab
soc.culture.quebec
soc.culture.romanian
soc.culture.scientists
soc.culture.singapore
soc.culture.slovenia
soc.culture.somalia
soc.culture.soviet
soc.culture.spain
soc.culture.sri-lanka
soc.culture.swiss
soc.culture.tamil
soc.culture.thai
soc.culture.turkish
soc.culture.ukrainian
soc.culture.uruguay
soc.culture.venezuela
soc.culture.vietnamese
soc.culture.yugoslavia

IRC channels

African
#africa
Asian
#asian
#beijing
#china
#chinese
#filipino
#hk
#hmong
#indo
#indonesia
#japan
#korea
#laos
#malaysia
#nippon
#penang
#saigon
#seoul
#singapore
#taipei
#taiwan

#tibet
#viet
#vietnight
#siam
Australian
#aussies
#australia
#melbourne
#newcastle
Canadian
#canada
#quebec
European
#belgium
#bosnia
#dutch
#espanol
#francais
#france
#england
#germany
#iceland
#ireland

#italia
#norway
#polska
#sweden
#turks
Latin American
#argentina
#brasil
Middle Eastern
#egypt
#iran
#israel
#kuwait
#palestine
Russian
#moscow
#russian
Southwest Asian
#india
#banglades
#pakistan
U.S.
#usa

Gay and lesbian forum

The Gay and Lesbian Community Forum, the largest and most complete resource for

the gay community available on the Net, was launched in May 1991, on AOL. Stay up-to-date with the **National Gay and Lesbian Task force**, the **Gay and Lesbian Alliance Against Defamation**, and other community organizations. Learn the implications of recent legal decisions and legislative initiatives. Download the newsletter for information on upcoming events and conferences, as well as points of interest in the forum. There's even a map, updated weekly, of all the gay topics that spring up on other message boards. The boards are extensive and include the full range of gay and lesbian concerns—from homophobia in the workplace to religion to the merits of body shaving.

Spirituality board

Topics on the Spirituality board range from Catholicism to Buddhism as members exchange thoughts, concerns, and insights on the spiritual life of the gay and lesbian community. Check out the Religion and Gays folder for Bible citations to fire at Bible-thumping fundamentalists.

Community Issues board

Discuss boycotts or find a room-

Downloaded from America Online's Gay and Lesbian Community Forum.

mate on the Community Issues board. In the Dialogue between Gays & Straights folder you'll find gays and straights engaging in a surprisingly intelligent discussion without any flames from bashers or religious zealots. And, don't miss the teens discussions—on the Community Issues board and the Gay Message Board.

Teens who need support or Teen Issues board

Grab a Kleenex because only the coldest heart could remain unmoved by the stories of teenage homosexual angst and isolation on these two boards. Unquestionably the most important message boards in the GLCF, they provide a sanctuary for teenagers to discuss, anonymously, the loneliness and pain of growing up gay. Here gay teens need never feel alone. How do I come out to my parents? What will my friends think? Why am I this way? Thoughtful and concerned members respond promptly and sensitively to all inquiries and provide information

about local gay youth organizations. Anyone, except maybe Reverend Phelps, would be inspired by the courage and heart expressed here.

Arts & the Media

The Arts & the Media boards are fantastic resources. Discuss gays and lesbians, or the lack thereof, in the arts and media. Tip: Browse the Celebrity Talk! folder to find out who is and who isn't. Other sub-topics include the Lesbian Writers folder, about and for lesbian writers; the Gay Books/Book Clubs folder, with book suggestions; the Gay Films folder, for the latest information and criticism on ground-breaking gay films; and, of course, a folder devoted to k.d. lang worship. Curiously, the Barbra Streisand folder is not very active. What does it all mean?

Gay, Lesbian, and Bisexual Message Boards

The Gay, Lesbian, and Bisexual Message Boards cover the gamut of topics. Are you a gay bodybuilder? Exchange workouts in the Bodybuilders folder. Love pets? Check out the Dykes With Dogs folder. Into Karate? Chat away in the Martial Arts folder. Hobbies, relationships, travel, dating, work, sports—just about the whole range of human experience is here, from the gay point of view.

Heart to Heart board

Meet new friends or someone special by placing a personal ad in the Heart to Heart message board. ✓**AMERICA ONLINE**→*keyword* glcf
DAILY

Gay pride

If the Net population is doubling every year, the gay

Net population may well be doubling every month! The explosion in gay users has a lot to do, of course, with the prurient possibilities of the Net. But the wired gay community is finding something else out in Cyberspace: information, sanctuary, and pride. It's an inclusive neighborhood: gays, lesbians, bisexuals, teens, the HIV-positive, straights. From the MOTSS (a Net coinage meaning members of the same sex) groups—**soc. motss** along with local **MOTSS** groups—to the **Bears** mailing list to **Moms and Gay Dads**, the Net is a permanent Gay Pride parade, with hundreds of thousands of people chanting, dancing, kissing, and chatting their days and nights away.

On the Net

Across the board

Alternative Lifestyles Just what is "Prince Albert piercing"? Someone here knows and cares. A gathering place for swingers, voyeurs, cross-dressers, S&M practitioners, and gays and lesbians. Complaints about the Prodigy police are frequent, and many postings are tagged with "This is not a solicitation." Innuendo is the key

Stonewall March—downloaded from spdcc.com/pub/swall_25.

to success: You can be subtle ("Do you prefer satin or silk next to the skin?") or blatant ("I'd love to meet you for a LONG neck at the HARD Rock Cafe"). People do connect here. There is also a fashion forum and clothing exchange among the cross-dressers, a participatory lesbian-ranch serial, and lots of chat about favorite American gladiators and opera divas. ✓**PRODIGY**→*jump* lifestyles bb→ Choose a Topic→Alternative Lifestyles DAILY

bit.listserv.gaynet (ng) Not as chatty as you might expect, given its volume. Most of the posts here are one-shots: news items, informational queries, announcements. You'll hear the upcoming-events schedule of the Gay and Lesbian Utah Democrats, a notice of the closing of the New York hustler bar Rounds, and a pointer to alt.tv.northern-exp, where Don McManus, the actor who plays a

gay ex-Marine, has delurked. The occasional minidebate over oral sex or gay bookstores soon expires from inattention. ✓**USENET** HOURLY

Gay (echo) This group is a general meeting place for gay men. With a nationwide clientele, the messages are oriented more toward conversation than toward personal meetings. Interested in the formative gay experiences of other men? You'll find them here. Need advice on the best ways to masturbate while you are performing oral sex on your partner? Read on. While straight men or lesbians occasionally drop by to browse, the population of the group is fairly homogenous. ✓**THROBNET** DAILY

Gay Alliance Like old friends, the posters (mostly male) drift quickly into teasing and banter. A thread about personal ads turned into a debate over formalwear, then into a Chip-and-Dale-esque duel of manners, eventually won by a gloating but scrupulously polite boy from Charleston, N.C.

Tomatoes

It's friendly here—one man was offering tomatoes from his garden that he didn't have time to can— and safe enough for serious topics, such as gay parenting, to be debated honestly and at some length. A more typical debate, though, was over the young cashier at someone's local gourmet food store

> "There is lots of chat about favorite American gladiators and opera divas."

(yes, he is a parishioner, but he's also a "practicing alkie"). ✓**COMPUSERVE**→*go* hsx 100→Messages→ Gay Alliance HOURLY

Gay and Lesbian This forum's members are not big on socializing, but they like vigorous debate of public issues. They'll spew venom back at Andrew Holleran for his dissing of "queers." The recent Helms amendment to cut federal funds to schools that were tolerant of homosexuality provoked scores of posts. ✓**WELL**→*g* gay DAILY

Gay and Lesbians You have to jump through several administrative hoops to win entry to this private forum. But if you think they're hiding a raunchy fantasyland behind the bureaucratic barriers, you'll be disappointed. The pickup scene here isn't any steamier than CompuServe's open forum, Gay Alliance—i.e., not steamy at all. When a confused 20-year-old asked for help here, he was flooded with sensible, generous, and slightly do-goodish advice. Men flirt under the personae of "Lady Bracknell" and "Ernest"; lesbians brag about their cats. The main function of this forum's added privacy seems to be to shelter people who are not yet ready to come all the way out of the closet. ✓**COMPUSERVE**→*go* hsx200→Gay and Lesbians DAILY

Gay Private Members of this intimate community, apparently flameless, share the stories of their lives in New Age diary entries, free-verse poetry, and prayers. Might seem corny at first, but keep reading; it can be quite moving. Women and men, in a friendly balance, talk about the not-so-well-intentioned psychiatrists they survived; how they have learned to enjoy tantric sex, without orgasm; the joy they feel for friends in their

> ## "'I find most gay literature just WAY too tragic! I really really just want to read a plain ole boy meets boy, boy loses boy, boy gets boy back story (insert girl here for lesbians!).'"

forties who are finally coming out; and the struggle of a person with AIDS whose family has abandoned him (gaypriv members are helping him move into a hospice). Now and then the conference gets together off line in San Francisco for dinner in the Castro. ✓**WELL**→*g* gaypriv DAILY

Gay/Lesbian/BisexualRelationships "I was teased UNMERCIFULLY in high school. Whole lunch rooms of farmers' sons standing up, throwing food at me, calling me faggot while the faculty just stood there and watched, calling it 'just being kids.'" Postings here are extremely personal, and there's as a broad palette of topics—Gay and Lesbian Parenting, Coming Out, Peer Pressure, Gay Images in Media, Gay Sex. One straight man's comment, "I have a 14-year-old son who has told me he thinks he might be bi or gay—he does not know yet," brings a barrage of advice from uncloseted gay men and women who thought their own parents dropped the ball or stepped up magnificently. A gay

man disparages "specialty" literature: "I find most gay literature just WAY too tragic! I really, really just want to read a plain ole boy meets boy, boy loses boy, boy gets boy back story (insert girl here for lesbians!)." And a lesbian writes about the difficulty of knowing if an affectionate female friend intends sexual signals: "You've got to bring out that person's ideas on homosexuality and then come out. Unfortunately, I've never been able to find out if a friend's interest was romantic until AFTER I came out to her." Ultimately, the concerns here—self-respect, excitement over sex, naïveté and wisdom—are the same as those found on a good hot message board. ✓**GENIE**→*keyword* family→ Family and Personal Growth Bulletin Board→Gay/Lesbian/Bisexual Relationships DAILY

Gaylink (echo) Gaylink readers were in a fine tizzy over a recent cache of nude GIFs of Wil Wheaton, the hunk of *Star Trek: The Next Generation* ("Prepare to be boarded!" one man exulted). Unfortunately, Gaylinkers don't often get so worked up. This group is more international and more closeted than other groups, and these factors lead to a certain obtuseness. Canadians insist on remembering the battles they won during the War of 1812. A man from Saskatchewan and a man from Holland discover that they both live in regions of the world known for being flat. They even debate fundamentalist Christians here. ✓**FIDONET** DAILY

Gender Alternatives/Gay Lifestyle/Lesbian Lifestyle None of these channels permits obscene or sexually explicit language; monitors lurking in the background will escort offenders and bashers off channel, but these monitors seem much less obtrusive than AOL's "Terms of Service" enforcers. In fact, in spite of the rules, some of the men on channel 33 clearly feel the best way to win friends and influence people is to repeat the size of their endowment in a once-a-minute mantra.

Other men catch up with long-distance, platonic friends, but mostly in private. When we eavesdropped on them, the lesbians on channel 34 were having a livelier night of it, trading Clinton jokes ("What does Bill say to Hillary after sex?" "I'll be home in 20 minutes"). The transvestites and transgendered people on channel 13 have logged on to talk with their friends, not to perform. On all channels, ages range from teens to seniors, but from a scan of their CompuServe profiles, most here are in their thirties. ✓ **COMPUSERVE** →*go* cb→Adult Band I *or* Adult Band II

Local MOTSS Groups For love-hungry singles, the Internet is tantalizing: At a stroke you meet hundreds of new men and women who are witty, caring, literate, technologically hip, and by and large very far away. Even if you're not looking for a date, it's easy to get lost in an international newsgroup like soc.motss or in the bubbly but impersonal corridors of AOL. One solution is to whittle down your playing field by geography.

Microversions

Microversions of soc.motss have sprung up across America (and elsewhere) in either mailing list or Usenet newsgroup formats. On pdx-motss, for instance, Portland, Oregon–area gays and lesbians arrange joint outings to hear lectures by gay historian (and Portland local) Allan Berube, to get tattooed together at the nude beach on Sauvie's Island, and to

square-dance at the Methodist church downtown. The local slant also makes pdx-motss an ideal weapon for fighting the antigay Oregon Citizens Alliance. See sidebar for newsgroup and mailing list addresses. WEEKLY

panix.user.queer Compare the impact of #2 and #3 clippers on your buzzcut, hear a prostitute explain why she doesn't like to shower with her clients, and agree to disagree on whether Camille Paglia is like okra (i.e., a matter of taste). Casting themselves as surly, trenchant Manhattanites, the Public Access Unix gay community voted themselves "queer" instead of "MOTTS," but most aren't as scary as that might sound. Home base for some of soc.motss's and soc.bi's most voluble Net celebrities. ✓ **INTERNET**→*telnet* panix.com→ <your login>→<your password>→ News→ panix.user.queer DAILY

soc.motss (ng) The mother of all gay newsgroups. I defy you to read it every day and keep your job. It is bloated, cliquish, self-important, contentious, and brilliant. "Motss" stands for "members of the same sex"; the name was chosen because back in 1983 when the group was started it was innocuous. Today the word "MOTTS" has crept into every corner of Cyberspace. The community here is real. Get-togethers take place regularly in many U.S. cities; GIFs and bios of frequent posters are available by FTP.

Cute flirting

Stories of coming out or personal hardship will get a warm response, and there's cute flirting over border collies, leather gear, and the names of tropical storms, but don't be lulled into false security. If you claim any knowledge of art, music, or literature here, you may be tak-

---

CYBERNOTES

"Since my posting re: the date from hell with 'Chuck Of The Broken Hand,' I've been stood up for a date with a totally different person. At least this one had an original excuse, which he emailed me not quite two hours before our date on Friday evening. No phone call. Just the email message [Comments to myself in brackets]:

'I just bought a house, and a friend offered to lend me his truck today so I can move some big things over there, and I know this is going to make me sound like a flake...'

[Too late. You already sound like a flake.]

'...but this is the only time he can lend me his truck, and it'll be free (except for gas), so I have to cancel out for tonight, and let's reschedule for some time real soon now.'

[Uh-huh. Like Labor Day, 1996.]

Truck rentals, incidentally, run from about $20 to $75/day."

—from **Bears**

ing your life in your hands. A small but snippy group of self-appointed mandarins will attack; quietly but quickly add them to your kill file, and move on. ✓**USENET** *FAQ:* ✓**INTERNET**→*ftp* rtfm.mit.edu→anonymous→<your email address>→/pub/usenet-by-hierarchy/soc/answers/motss→faq HOURLY

Bisexuals

BiAct-L (ml) Elaine, the "list dominatrix," leads her troops in the fight against bi-ignorance. Add your two cents to Coming Out Bi, a pamphlet under development; sign up for FOX-TV's open auditions for a real-life bisexual couple; or find out how to enroll your local queer activist group in your state's Adopt-a-Highway program. Recent campaigns have included educating the parents' group PFLAG and telephoning support to Visa, under attack from the religious right for contributing to Gay Games IV. ✓**INTERNET**→ *email* listserv@brownvm.brown.edu ✍ *Type in message body:* subscribe biact-l <your full name> DAILY

Bisexu-L (ml) When you sign up for this mailing list, you get a stern Netiquette lecture, including this warning: "Posts made solely to titillate or arouse are inappropriate." Too bad. This group could use a little danger. Friends chat mildly about what to do with kitty's hairball, or they boast about their skill at making chocolate truffles. When a really interesting question does surface—e.g., was there more same-sex hugging on TV in the 1970s than there is now?—it goes unanswered. ✓**INTERNET**→ *email* listserv@brownvm.brown.edu ✍ *Type in message body:* subscribe bisexu-l <your full name> HOURLY

Bithry-L (ml) For people who live

ACT-UP—downloaded from spdcc. com-pub/swall_94.

bisexuality—not just play it online. This is a smart, active list perhaps a little too caught up in postmodern, academic queer/feminist theory. Long threads frequently digress into other issues—a recent musing about human nature and love wound up with a critique of evolution and its implications for bisexual identity—passing through illness and genetics, gathering 20 or so posters along the way. Bi women will find the list especially interesting. ✓**INTERNET**→*email* listserv@brownvm. brown.edu ✍ *Type in message body:* subscribe bithry-l <your full name> DAILY

soc.bi (ng) Even the news that Jesus wants them to repent elicits mostly giggles from this crowd. The boys here juggle their crush on Eric of the comic book *The Crow* with their fondness for the net.woman with "the most beautiful hair on soc.bi." This newsgroup is willfully giddy, as only undergraduates can be. They quote *Monty Python* sketches from memory, pronounce on whether the lyrics to the Crash Test Dummies' latest hit are or are not je-

june, and wonder whether it's harder to come out to your parents as pagan or as gay. The group also meets for real-time parties and picnics in New York's Central Park. ✓**USENET** *FAQ:* ✓**INTERNET**→ *ftp* rtfm.mit.edu→anonymous→ <your email address>→/pub/ usenet-by-group/soc.bi HOURLY

Lesbians

Girls Ladies 18 and over chat and network. Gossip about the women on *American Gladiators*, recruit for your bowling league, or reminisce about the silver medal you won in the Games in '94. Friends, rather than lovers, are in demand, but nonetheless, you can catch single ladies suggestively and enviously counseling their married counterparts about what to bring (poetry) and not bring (swimsuits) on camping trips. The board is heavy on introductions; one suspects that the more interesting conclusions take place in private through email. Many of the women are posting from south of what they call the "Manson/Nixon" line. ✓**PRIDENET** WEEKLY

> "Of course, rules are made to be broken: Caught in the act, one offender asked in her sweetest and most faux-naif voice, 'Is *wet* a sexual word?'"

#lesbos The U.S. girls under-19 soccer championship is on television, but you've got no one to watch it with. Sail to #lesbos. Bots named Elektra, Ophelia, and Isis protect this island from the depredations of horny net geeks (HNGs). Public netsex is frowned upon; in fact, newbies are advised to choose a nickname that's not overtly sexual, to keep the HNGs at bay and to strike the proper #lesbos attitude of flirty but cool.

Of course, rules are made to be broken: caught in the act, one offender asked in her sweetest and most faux-naif voice, "Is *wet* a sexual word?" In this brave new world, sexual is what you make of it. Heidi, for example, is mad about her wife, Duffer, and boasts they are "the two cuties of the channel," yet they've never met offline: Heidi lives in Australia, Duffer in the U.S. √**INTERNET**→*irc* /channel #lesbos

Moms (ml) What is better than one mommie? The subscribers to this list have an answer—two. Moms is for lesbian couples with families or those considering starting one. This list is an oasis of support in a world where the idea of any different family structure sends school boards and the papacy into head spins. Legal, emotional, and biological advice is freely shared.

Should you have an anonymous donor or a friend? How do the non-bio mom get legal rights? How important are male role models? Will insurance pay for insemination? Who do you tell a child are the real parents? Moms also offer help to other members with troublesome older kids—gee, just like "normal" parents everywhere. √**INTERNET**→*email* majordo mo@qiclab.scn.rain.com ✍ *Type in message body:* subscribe moms <your full name><your email ad-

Bears—downloaded from spdcc.com/ pub/MOW93.

dress> DAILY

Sappho (ml) Do the words to "MacArthur Park" make sense? What is a bi-dyke—a mythical creature, "wishful thinking," or an oxymoron? The very vocal members of Sappho, a women's-only list, are happy to answer such questions. This is not a pick-up scene, but rather a gathering place for thirty- and fortysomething lesbians and "womyn-centered" bisexuals to meet and discuss issues of sexual identity. Although this is generally a friendly list, the undercurrent of tension between bi's and lesbians may make it a difficult place for those insecure in their identities. Members of this list often get together in real life for lunch. √**INTERNET**→*email* sappho-request@ mc.lcs.mit.edu ✍ *Write a request* HOURLY

Men

Bears (ml) A "bear" is a burly, hairy, cuddly gay man. Typically, a bear has a Santa Claus figure, a Grizzly Adams wardrobe, Walt Whitman facial hair, and an Allen Ginsberg libido. Bears prowl about looking for other bears to rub fur with, to see if they can start a forest fire together. If you can stand the puns, check out this

list. Bears seem to have mental energy to spare: They toss off essays on everything from piercing to New Age tchotchkes, and they identify themselves to each other with an arcane system of "bearcode" devised by two ursine astrophysicists. The community is if anything too generous: One list member had to politely ask his fellow bears to stop sending free porn videos to his work address. Bears often take road trips to visit each other; the reports of these group encounters, when posted, can be fur-raising. √**INTERNET**→ *email* bears-request@spdcc.com ✍ *Write a request* DAILY

Chubbies Full-figured men and their fans exchange mash notes and GIFs. Get a full report of the German Girth and Mirth Club's Hamburg get-together (scavenger hunts and boating on the Elbe), and details about signing up for Convergence, the annual large

> "Many posters are newbies, unsure whether they're ready to come out, unclear about the details of safe sex, so the place is the online equivalent of a gay dive bar— where the painfully naive meet the long-since jaded."

men's convention. Not for anyone timid about flesh or the fleshly. ✓**PRIDENET** DAILY

Gay Dads (ml) A few of the men here chose to become fathers after living for years as out gay men. They want to know at what age they should come out to their child, trade titles of gay children's books, and share the joys of staying up till 2 a.m. to the tune of "Rock-a-Bye, Baby" instead of "I Will Survive." Most, however, are men who married before they were comfortable with their gay identity, hoping marriage would straighten them out. These men are more concerned with their relationships with their wives than with their children, despite the group's name. Bisexuals welcome. ✓**INTERNET**→*email* majordomo@ vector.casti.com ✍ *Type in message body:* subscribe gaydads HOURLY

Politics & debate

alt.flame.faggots (ng) The name says it all. When this newsgroup first appeared in 1993, indignant cyberqueers signed on, cowed the homophobic enemy, and imposed a spirited debate over how best to arrange kindling to ensure a nicely blazing campfire. That thrill is now gone; the gays and lesbians don't bother anymore, and the bozos have come slouching back. Often cross-posted from alt.fan.rush-limbaugh, these messages should probably be ignored, unless you need to boost your adrenaline level. ✓**USENET** DAILY

alt.politics.homosexuality (ng) Before you enter the fray, check the .sig file of the debaters: generally speaking, those who quote Nine Inch Nails are not on the same team as those who quote Saint Paul. In the rare, quieter mo-

ments, gay politics are discussed, including the pros and cons of gay marriage. But essentially this newsgroup is a battlefield: hand-to-hand combat between gays and the religious right. You hear all sorts of neat facts: Simon LeVay, the gay neurologist, is actually Anton LeVay, former leader of the Satanic Church. Same-gender sex is impossible, because of the American Heritage Dictionary's definition of the word. One of this group's regular homophobes actually managed to get himself banned from alt.flame. ✓**USENET** HOURLY

alt.sex.homosexual (ng) As alt.sex newsgroups go, this one is pretty straight (pun intended). Despite a smattering of postings about homosexual erotica, this group is mostly informative, with detailed discussion and debate about gay-rights developments worldwide. The only place in the alt.sex world you're likely to read about jailed Italian activists. Many posters are newbies, unsure whether they're ready to come out, unclear about the details of safe sex, so the place is the online equivalent of a gay dive bar— where the painfully naive meet the long-since jaded. If you're new to cyberqueer culture, try one of the "MOTTS" groups instead, preferably a local one. ✓**USENET** DAILY

Homosexuality-Ethics and Religion Folder One of the longest-running, most active and most flame-prone of all the topics, where members argue the religious objections to homosexuality with Bible citations, insults, and threats of damnation. The threads rarely go anywhere or reveal anything new, which makes you wonder why anyone bothers, but some thoughtful posts by reverent gays and non gays alike keep it worth-

CYBERNOTES

"My lover who is the non-bio mom is very threatened by the idea of our daughter getting to know her father, and getting confused about who her 'real' parents are (US!)...The only candidate for the position of consistent loving male is her father. He would like this role."

"When I see my daughter with her dad(s) hugging and kissing her, bathing her, dressing her, and she's laughing and just in heaven, I am so glad for her that she will grow up with a positive image of what men CAN be. We were at a party in the Castro last weekend, and it was so adorable to see all these big leather fags fighting over who got to give Liv her bottle, who got to hold her next (no one wanted to do the diaper, but oh well! %^)) and my friend Laura said to me 'I don't know who is getting more out of this, the baby or the boys!' I say if your daughter's father wants to give that love to her, why not?"

—from **Moms**

> **"Supermarket to see and be seen in? The Christopher Street D'Agostino's in New York!"**

while. If you want to read hate-speech thinly veiled as the Gospel of Love, this is the place. ✓**AMERICA ONLINE** *keyword* ethics→Ethics & Religion Message Center→Debate →Homosexuality DAILY

Other

Gay-LIBN (ml) This list has the dirt. A fair amount of the traffic is shoptalk—requests for or recommendations of lists of books in specific fields, such as gay consumer health or gay South African literature—but these are people who've staked their careers on being savvy and helpful (which are the supermarkets to see and be seen in? The Christopher Street D'Agostino's in New York, the Prudential Center Star in Boston, the 6:30 a.m. farmers' market in Lawrence, Kansas), and it shows. ✓**INTERNET**→*email* listserv @vm.usc. edu ✍ *Type in message body:* subscribe gay-libn <your full name> DAILY

Gayteen (echo) A young man wakes up with an erection after dreams about cross-dressing, but he's afraid to dress in drag, because his mother is threatening him with a psychiatrist. Another boy won't rule out suicide, but he's decided to wait and see if things improve. These kids flirt, advise, and help one another. One boy even agreed to pass a message to the cute elevator operator at Six Flags amusement park in Dallas next time he

visited. For some, Gayteen is cyberqueer chic; for others, it may be a lifeline. Very few women, lots of Canadians. ✓**FIDONET** HOURLY

Khush (ml) This list is struggling to define itself, starting with its embattled name. *Khush* is the Hindi/Urdu word for "happy." Lately, movie directors and activist groups have been using the word as if it were a direct translation of the English word *gay*. Some Southeast Asians are unhappy to have to lean so heavily on a foreign loan word, but the native term *hijra* causes even more trouble, since it designates a specific Indian community—of eunuchs, transvestites, hermaphrodites, and hustlers—that has no parallel in the West. Nestled within the anthropological debate, you'll find advice on Hindi movies with same-sex flair, close links to *Trikone* magazine, and announcements of the upcoming Mr. and Ms. Gay Asian Pacific Alliance pageant. ✓**INTERNET**→*email* khush-request@husc3.harvard.edu ✍ *Type in message body:* subscribe khush <your email address> WEEKLY

Out in Linguistics (ml) Why have some gay men begun to refer to themselves as "myn"? How come the letter "l" always seems to come first in abbreviations like "lbg" ("lesbian, bi, gay") or "lgb" ("lesbian, gay, bi")? If you're dying to understand these linguistic phenomena, or why the title page of *The Daughters of Egalia* says "Translated from the Norwegian" rather than simply "Translated from Norwegian," come here to find out, and to exchange bad puns with other "homophones." An almost equal number of wim and menwim gather here. ✓**INTERNET**→*email* majordomo@lists.stanford.edu ✍ *Type in message body:* subscribe outil DAILY

LOCAL MOTSS

ba.motss (ng) Bay Area residents. ✓**USENET**

ba-sappho (ml) Bay Area lesbians. ✓**INTERNET**→*email* ba-sappho-request@labrys.mti.sgi.com ✍ *Write a request*

dc-motss (ml) Washington, D.C. residents. ✓**INTERNET**→ *email* majordomo@vector.casti. com ✍ *Type in message body:* subscribe dc-motss

fl-motss (ml) Florida residents. ✓**INTERNET**→*email* fl-motss-request@pts.mot.com ✍ *Write a request*

la-motss (ml) L.A. residents. ✓**INTERNET**→*email* la-motss-request@flash.usc.edu ✍ *Write a request*

ne.motss (ng) New England residents. ✓**USENET**

NE-Social-MOTSS (ml) Northeast residents. ✓**INTERNET** →*email* majordomo@plts.org ✍ *Type in message body:* subscribe nesm

nj-motss (ml) New Jersey residents. ✓**INTERNET**→*email* majordomo@plts.org ✍ *Type in message body:* subscribe nj-motss

oh-motss (ml) Ohio residents. ✓**INTERNET**→*email* oh-motss-request@cps.udayton.edu ✍ *Write a request*

pa.motss (ng) Pennsylvania residents. ✓**USENET**

pdx-motss (ml) Portland, Oregon, residents. ✓**INTERNET**→ *email* pdx-motss-request@agora. rain. com ✍ *Write a request*

Transgender issues

It's the Net at its most valuable—nowhere is being the man or woman you want to be

easier than here. From the solace sought and offered on **alt.sex.trans** to the rage expressed on the **Transgen** list to the lifestyle tips in TV, the Net addresses the sexual passions and identity confusions of cross-dressers and transsexuals—quite possibly as well as or better than literature or the analyst's couch. Check out one of the largest of these havens, the **Transgender Community** on GEnie, for confessions and anecdotes filled with humor and drama.

Dana, a transvestite—downloaded from America Online's Gay and Lesbian Forum.

On the Net

alt.sex.trans (ng) Light traffic, but with an unusual poignancy. Most of the postings, in fact, are cries for help—men who can't stop wearing their wives' clothes and can't stop worrying that they are consigning themselves to an afterlife filled with sulfur and brimstone. The group also serves as a forum for discussion of transsexual practices, and even accommodates the occasional personal ad. ✓**USENET** WEEKLY

Gender Issues Discuss crossdressing and gender reassignment in a safe setting. You'll also find information on upcoming conferences and conventions. ✓**AMERICA ONLINE**→ *keyword* glcf→Message Boards→ Gender Issues WEEKLY

Transgen (ml) Although some people pour their hearts out—in diarylike entries, in letters to parents who will never read them—this is not always a nurturing environment. Hormones, natural and artificial, run high. Alison, a male-to-female transsexual whose surgery went wrong, became outraged when she was not allowed to post a 56K description of her case. Tom, a female-to-male transsexual beginning to experiment with male aggression, tries to shame male-to-female members of the group. The list may be more useful as a source of information or as an arena in which to practice a new identity than as a support group. ✓**INTERNET**→*email* listserv@ brownvm.brown.edu ✍ *Type in message body:* subscribe transgen <your full name> WEEKLY

The Transgender Community GEnie's transgender message board attempts to articulate some of the risks and rewards of the TG lifestyle. There's a good deal of talk about TG in the media, whether it's Patrick Swayze crossdressing for Hollywood or a man confessing his desire to document his own sex reassignment on *Oprah*. There's celebratory conversation about The Look (how does RuPaul do it?). There are lists of clothing stores that don't stigmatize TVs. And then there are personal confessions, hundreds and hundreds, about public outings, forced feminization, hormone treatments, closet cross-dressers. The message board isn't restricted to transvestites and transsexuals, but respect for the lifestyle is absolutely mandatory—while there's plenty of self-deprecating humor, no cheap shots are tolerated. ✓**GENIE**→*keyword* family→Family and Personal Growth Bulletin Board→ The Transgender Community DAILY

TV (echo) ThrobNet's TV offers chat, fashion tips, and sympathy for cross-dressers across the United States. The group is dominated by urban black transvestites, and the *Paris Is Burning* crowd has remade the echo into a land of snap divas and shoulder pads. Still, there seems to be room for cross-dressers of all stripes, and the group is very receptive to new voices. ✓**THROBNET** WEEKLY

Men's issues

"I enjoy being a guy." A whole lot of male talk on the Net centers on two issues—penis

size and how tough men have it in the modern (read: increasingly woman-dominated) world. Actually, public versus private makes a great deal of difference in the content of Men's Issues forums. The very open newsgroup **soc.men** is the most vicious in its anti-woman/anti-world postings, so if you want to flame about your ex, politics, or gun control, go there. FidoNet and Prodigy's **Men's Issues** have their share of bathroom humor and chick hating but also move on to the joys of parenting, the reaffirmation of masculine pride, and car repair. But it is on the private, male **For Men Only** that guys can afford to be "sensitive" a lot of the time. Fathers fighting deadbeat-dad images congregate on **Free-L** and **alt. dads.rights**.

Father and son fishing—downloaded from CompuServe's Graphics Corner.

On the Net

Across the board

For Men Only Confidential to men: How many times a day do you have a question or a comment that just isn't appropriate for mixed company? This private forum restricted to men and their needs is the place to go when you

want to gush about the joy of fatherhood without seeming weak ("I cannot describe the incredible feeling of seeing my mannerisms and features mixed with those of my wife in a newborn baby boy") or address the highly equivocal (and highly trafficked) topic of fathers and daughters. A wide emotional range is exhibited here in addition to interest in stereotypical subjects—the male view of sex, the simple pleasures of a close shave or a football game, and even penis size. Insert dick joke here. And then go on to read about the cultural constraints of masculinity, or the strange power of fatherhood. ✓ **GENIE**→ *keyword* family→ Family and Personal Growth Bulletin Board→For Men Only DAILY

Men's Issues It's guy-talk here, though women are welcome, too. A hodgepodge of topics include "the art of mooning," baseball, how to install a car stereo, how best to come out of the closet, and whether penile enlargement is a

myth. Part support group, part "bitch" session (in many senses), part nasty beer brawl, part sexual braggadocio, with a healthy dose of *MAD* magazine humor. The posters include a confused teenager who worries about losing his

> "It's guy-talk here, part support group, part 'bitch' session (in many senses), part nasty beer brawl, part sexual braggadocio, with a healthy dose of *MAD* magazine humor."

virginity, a young woman asking what men mean when they say, "I love you," and an older man considering throwing it all in who gets advice on his mid-life crisis. ✓ **PRODIGY**→*jump* lifestyles bb→ Choose a Topic→Men's Issues HOURLY

Mens_Issues (echo) The battle of the sexes is as evident here as it is on other gender-based conferences—women are frequently labeled "the enemy." But there are other issues that are typically discussed in polite tones—the use of corporal punishment in parenting, for one—and men's-movement types often connect for soul-searching. Skip, a Vietnam vet, tells Jay, a civilian, why he feels that he could rely on women in combat. ✓ **FIDONET**

Mens_Issues (echo) Boys will be boys. If you have a review of the best "exotic dancing" spots in your hood, send it on in to Mens_Issues—it will become part of a national compendium. Recently Sean asked if in a public restroom looking at another man's "penus" [*sic*] made anyone "feel gay". He got very few answers to this, but his request for a survey on organ size (before the moderator stepped in) was large (so was the average cited in the responses). This men's-issues forum does occasionally deal with delicate issues—say, how do you talk to a partner about HIV testing?—but for the most part it is just a bunch of Joes trying to figure out if you still open car doors for women. Pass the beer nuts. ✓ **NORTH AMERICA NET** DAILY

soc.men (ng) A support group for men who feel victimized by affirmative action, nasty "XXs," and lite beer. Threads here tend to reinforce the male stereotype—guns, sports, and a preoccupation with

John Wayne Bobbitt—from CompuServe's Reuters' News Picture Forum.

circumcision and castration. Soc.men's tone is sometimes belligerent (because of testosterone?): "Your post was such a swill of unsubstantiated and light-years from context ideological crap that it's hardly worth responding to." But many men are doing the bonding thing—if only through mysogyny. Besides the unique discussions, there are a significant number of posts that are crossposted to both the men's and women's newsgroups. ✓ **USENET** HOURLY

Fathers' rights

alt.dads-rights (ng) Elsewhere single mother Murphy Brown might have a greater following than the single dad on *My Three Sons*, but not here. Alt.dads-rights attempts to combat what many ex-husbands see as the unflattering picture society paints of them. Disgruntled divorced dads share their personal stories and offer each other advice, battle plans, and sympathy. Although some do seem mainly to resent the outflow of cash ("A woman will track you down just out of spite"), most really seem concerned with access to their children. Men vent their anger at social roles and a court system that in their eyes favors women—and just as quickly, ex-

wives defend themselves against the image of dead-beat moms. ✓ **USENET** HOURLY

FREE-L (ml) Discussion on FREE-L (Father's Rights and Equality Exchange) ranges from pragmatic legal advice for divorced men who want more time with the kids to vituperative attacks on feminists, family courts, and "father bashing." Fathers with non-U.S. citizen exes help each other deal with the international courts. The recent call "What we need is not a Gandhi but a John Brown to lead the movement" conveys the general tenor of the discussion—a sense of being wronged. ✓ **INTERNET** →*email* listserv@indycms.iupui.edu ✍ *Type in message body:* subscribe free-l <your full name> DAILY

> "This men's-issues forum does occasionally deal with delicate issues— say, how do you talk to a partner about HIV testing? —but for the most part it is just a bunch of Joes trying to figure out if you still open car doors for women. Pass the beer nuts."

Women

I am woman, hear me roar (or flame, or speak, or type). The Net is a male-dominated

world, but women are trying to make it their own with women's forums catering to every interest—for instance, women and religion, medicine, politics, philosophy, the sciences, computer technology, history, and geography. There is often a measure of a good kaffeeklatsch—women talking to each other about their work, love, sex, and the nightly news. Sure, male malcontents pop up every now and then, asking for trouble by stating that all feminists are lesbians. Go to **alt.feminism** if you are ready to butt heads with these Rush fans. For real discussion of modern feminist issues try the **MS forum** on Echo, **soc.feminism** (moderated), or the **WMST-L** (women's studies mailing list). **STOP RAPE** and **alt.talk.rape** provide survivor support as well as a good deal of political discussion. CompuServe's **U.S. News Women's Forum** runs the gamut—from the glass ceiling to troublesome teens. For a good time, dial North America Net's **Women** or **FEMREL-L**, where female wit prevails.

Hillary Clinton—downloaded from Exec PC.

On the Net

Across the board

soc.women (ng) If you ignore the cross-postings from those groups with the dreaded word *feminism* in their title, soc.women is a very different—casual and warm—place to be. The group has far fewer lurking male malcontents, and the men who do post query why boys have to go to the drugstore to buy tampons, or they leave sexist jokes that die without a response. There are no crusaders.

Downhome chat

Au contraire. This is down-home chat with the girls (no disrespect intended or felt here) about the "business" of being women, with a good deal of joking about shaving legs, the ordeal of housework (Jeanne from Oregon says she doesn't find it demeaning, just "utterly unnecessary"), and the other "species"—with animosity toward none. ✓**USENET** HOURLY

U.S. News Women's Forum

There are an awful lot of people named Mike, William, Peter, John, Steve, etc., on this forum devoted to women's issues. Some post things like "The trouble begins when a woman disobeys her husband," but others just hang out, making friends with the opposite sex. By and large this forum provides intelligent mature, discussion of issues like domestic violence, abortion, and breast-feeding in public.

Banter

Women here also indulge in general banter, get some advice on love, or discuss how to avoid being "frustrated at 40." Groups of pals seem to fix a locus for their get-togethers—the Women and Work section contains more talk about one woman's pool parties than about pay equity. The sysop is very good at stimulating discussion with posers like "Are men and women really that different intellectually and emotionally?" or "Just what the heck does sex mean anyway?" There is something to interest any woman here—and someone to talk back. ✓ **COMPUSERVE**→*go* women→Messages DAILY

WMST-L (ml) WMST-L's moderator warns newcomers that this is a forum for the serious discussion of women's studies by professionals—not a Q&A forum about the basic tenets of feminism. But for the initiated, WMST-L is a very lively locale for a higher-level discussion of absolutely anything related to women and their lives. The genesis of the American obsession with body size ("dislike of fat women") recently brought together biologists, psychologists, historians, and the personal experiences of list members living in the Twiggy world. The use and meaning of the term *lady* got equal play. Why is it "Avon ladies," "Women marines," "Male nurse"? This is definitely not a general support session or assertiveness-training course, but thanks to a common commitment to things female it's one of the best places on the Internet to find interesting discussion. ✓ **INTERNET**→ *email* listserv@umdd.umd.edu ✍ *Type in message body:* subscribe wmst-l <your full name> DAILY

Women (echo) ILink's Women conference is distinguished from its Feminism conference by its tone and its gender balance. There are more women here and they are talking to each other instead of being forced to defend themselves to men. Topics are as broad as

Janet Reno—downloaded from CompuServe's US News & World Report Forum.

women's lives. It is especially interesting to see what women say to each other about censorship and pornography. In one thread an ex-stripper discussed her motivation (economic) with an antiporn advocate (exploitation) and performer of "erotic arts" (expression). Family issues are also heavily covered. Fierce debates over public and private schooling and day care, for instance, provide survival strategies for modern mothers. But all is not serious on Women—the friends on the conference are also there to affirm women's power. Why else would a long thread sing the praises of Mrs. Peel of *The Avengers*? ✓ **ILINK** DAILY

Women (echo) "Sigh. Well, if anyone's interested in my favorite tofu recipe, just post me." So ended the mouthwatering discussion of the tuna casserole with potato chips scrunched on top from our collective past. Everyone introduces herself on the Women conference, and that's about as serious as things get. The female moderator of this conference is very visible—in a sort of Algonquin Roundtable of pop culture. Gender issues do rear their heads, including dating advice and the date's aftermath. ("What does the smirk mean?") But expect to be

accused of cheating if you read a book on the psychology of the opposite sex. Some feminists may not appreciate the moderator's dismissal of sexual harassment (it appears that the most "radical feminist" among frequent posters is named Bill). Women's wacky take on life makes it a pleasant place to hang out, to be a woman, and even to talk to men. ✓ **NORTH AMERICA NET** DAILY

Women The Women's Issues section on Prodigy suffers from the same problem that most online women's forums do—nasty male interlopers. They post absurdities—such as that women never really wanted to vote ("Elizabeth Cady Stanton was a lesbian"). One male anti-abortionist updates a graphic fetus "death clock" daily. Another attributes the abortion rate to women's natural "lustful ways and promiscuity." Others try, very unsuccessfully, to pick up

> "A man asks: 'What did [a woman in a well-known sexual harassment case] think when he asked her up to his room?' A woman responds: 'I can think of several things—a private conversation, for one.'"

chicks. The women here, however, are tough and attempt to make the board their own in spite of this less than ideal atmosphere—for instance, warning the uninitiated not to answer suspicious postings like "seeking hose for muscular legs" and the "clitoris size survey." Women here can put aside differences to share their stories—as in a recent thread about abortion and emotion. Sometimes a fun place, Prodigy's Women topic also provides a place to pose important questions, like "What is all this about the Wonder Bra?" ✓**PRODIGY** →*jump* lifestyles bb→ Choose a Topic→Women's Issues HOURLY

Feminism

alt.feminism (ng) It's not really feminism that's being discussed here but rather a certain male view of what feminism is—á la the feminazis of Rush Limbaugh's fevered fantasies. When threads with titles like "NOW in All Out War Against American Family" or "Why Should Men Be Blamed for Domestic Violence" are the most active, one knows that serious discussion of feminism is not likely to be found anywhere. Except for a few women, Women Avengers of sorts, noone bothers defending feminism here. And you can hardly blame them. Given the general tone of the debate, there's likely to be little if any common ground— let alone any conversions. A handful of men do attempt to add a note of moderation, but if what you're looking for is a place to meet men and complain about women, alt.feminism is the locker room of the Internet. Or if you are a feisty woman, jump right in. The battles are there waiting. ✓**USENET** HOURLY

Feminism (echo) A man asks: "What did [a women in a well-

Virginia Woolf—downloaded from CompuServe's Archive Forum.

known sexual-harassment case] think when he asked her up to his room? A woman responds: "I can think of several things—a private conversation, for one." This feminism conference is preoccupied with its gender balance and attempts to alleviate the predominance of antifeminist and anti-woman postings by suggesting broader discussion topics. Real dialogue on women's issues can be found here, although many disillusioned women wonder why they are still "hanging around" fighting or hoping for some more of their kind to show up. ✓**FIDONET** DAILY

Feminism (echo) ILink's Feminism conference is for the most part a continuous dialogue arising from men's efforts to understand or to provoke women. Unlike on many of the men's rights forums masquerading as feminist discussions, these damned women do talk back. Here statements like "*Playboy* is feminist" or "*Better Homes and Gardens* exploits men" do not go unchallenged. Men still do seem to define the topics under discussion—why women hate pornography (do they?), the unfairness of gay rights, etc. But the level of response is intelligent and women themselves occasionally find the space to discuss their own

issues, like the importance of physical appearance to oneself and society. "Mary Kay—for me or them?" ✓**ILINK** HOURLY

Feminism (echo) What does one say when someone calls all feminists lesbian half-men/half-women and all profeminist men gay? Suggest a dose of cyanide? Take two aspirin and check the board in the morning? Or take 'em on? This is a group of men and women who are trying to talk about living together in the modern world, but they constantly have to deal with a particularly nasty set of male provocateurs. But these men and women are not shy and do get down to real discussions of relationships, abortion, and affirmative action. The large contingent of profeminist men in this conference makes it unique. ✓**SMARTNET** WEEKLY

Feminist (ml) Librarians are so common on the Internet that they get not one but two terrific women-oriented lists. This list is the domain of the American Librarians Association Feminist Task Force. Where LIBWAT focuses on issues of gender and technology, Feminist is geared to a more general discussion of women's issues—abortion, equal pay, sexual harassment. But it is not just theory here. Sharon from Ohio offers her story of harassment at work and is inundated with strategies and sympathy. Because many participants are librarians, the list often feels like a reading group. Discussions are long and intelligent, and often about books of interest to feminists. Reading *The Morning After* sparked a long and heated debate among women and men on the issue of date rape. ✓**INTERNET**→*email* listserv@mitvma.mit.edu ✍ *Type in message body:* subscribe feminist <your full name> WEEKLY

Women **Identity**

MS Jane said she became a feminist not by choice but by upbringing; Liz, in the aftermath of date rape; Marcia, when a Southern minister shamed an unwed mother in front of the congregation. There's a long thread entitled "what is feminism," but it is agreed that whatever the subtleties, feminism is a good thing. This very busy forum provides women (and a few like-minded men) the chance to discuss how to be a feminist in the modern world. Women assist each other in dealing with sexism in the workplace and on the street. Feminists of all stripes debate how best to deal with violence and pornography. Women support each other through problems with lovers, family, and friends. The forum intentionally retains a sense of humor to disprove all those cranky images. The "to shave or not to shave" thread was especially good. The conference, sponsored by *Ms.* magazine, is private. You must email the current moderator to participate. ✓**ECHO**→ms DAILY

---

soc.feminism (ng) soc.feminism is a moderated newsgroup and thus probably the only group with *feminism* in its name that has a majority of postings by women. Through real debate between actual feminists the group shows that not all feminists are a scary monolith of male-bashers. "Many of the posters do not line up in alphabetical order and follow anyone's party line," declares one frequent participant. The moderated newsgroup enables women (and some men) to debate the many issues within feminism—(NOW's pro-gun-control stance and women's need to protect themselves, date rape, breast cancer, Camille Paglia and postfeminist theory) without having to defend feminism's right to exist every step of the way. Equal

rights for women are a given here —the rest is up for intelligent, and courteous, debate, as well as comfortable talk with like-minded women. ✓**USENET** *FAQ:* ✓**INTERNET** →*ftp* rtfm.mit.edu→anonymous→ <your email address>→/pub/ usenet-by-group/news.answers/ feminism HOURLY

Professions

FEMJUR (ml) You had better have your facts straight because FEMJUR is no place to put forth a shoddy argument. This active list, populated by lawyers, legal scholars, and the ordinary jury pool, meets for "discussion and information about feminist legal issues." Up-to-the-minute information on Congress and the Violence Against Women Act, antiracketeering laws and abortion protests, or the manslaughter appeal of a woman who killed her rapist, come immediately over the wires. On FEMJUR there is always intelligent discussion—whether in the form of legal advice, comments on a brief, or general theorizing. It is the best feminist argument in town—and open to anyone with something to contribute. ✓**INTERNET**→*email* listserv@suvm.acs.syr. edu ✍ *Type in message body:* subscribe femjur <your full name> WEEKLY

LIBWAT (ml) Marion the Librarian, move over. One thing the subscribers to Library Women and Technology don't say is SSSHHH-HHH!!! LIBWAT is a forum for exchanging information on the rapidly developing technical world beyond the card catalog, but because librarians spend so much time on the Internet the list has evolved into a spirited discussion of general issues about gender, technology, global information, and even cybersex. LIBWAT often provides papers on pertinent topics—de-skilling of technology and sex typecasting in jobs, or flaming and gender on the Internet. The dialogue is usually hefty and intelligent. The list is theoretically for librarians, but its content will interest a much broader techno-savvy audience. ✓**INTERNET**→*email* listserv@ubvm.cc.buffalo.edu ✍ *Type in message body:* subscribe libwat <your full name> WEEKLY

SWIP-L (ml) "Maybe I am a Pythagorean at heart," remarked one poster to the Society for Women in Philosophy, a moderated list with 600 subscribers of both sexes. Do not be fooled, however. Just because its members might know what it is to be a "Pythagorean at heart," do not expect this list to spend much time on the intricacies of Hegel or Hume. Instead you'll find discussion of current feminist philosophers, and conversation (active but never flaming) that takes a philosophical approach to current women's issues. Equal pay for equal work, for instance. Or gender stereotypes in advertising, which are debated with the big picture of ethics, dialectics, and political theory in mind. Men also take an active part in SWIP discussions—with their own insight into the philosophical foundations of maleness. ✓**INTERNET**→ *email* listserv@cfrvm.bitnet ✍ *Type in message body:* subscribe swip-l <your full name> DAILY

WISENET (ml) The Women in Science and Engineering Network can provide the formulae for the volume and surface area of a prolate spheroid, but it is more likely to offer insight and advice about how to get on in a world still predominantly male. The topics pursued on WISENET are usually gender-based on a practical level.

Candice Bergen—downloaded from CompuServe's ShowBiz Forum.

How to "deal with the XYs" in your lab that ignore your input, for example. Or—more philosophical—is the culture of science in some sense "male"? A recent debate covered the tendency of newscasters to ask male scientists about the hard facts and women scientists about how science makes them feel inside. Women professionals gain support and timely and intelligent conversation here—slide rule optional. ✓**INTERNET**→*email* listserv@uicvm.uic.edu ✍ *Type in message body:* subscribe wisenet <your full name> DAILY

Religion

FEMREL-L (ml) "Come for the theology, stay for the pie" pretty much sums up this very active discussion (up to 100 messages a day). FEMREL-L describes itself as "an open discussion of women, religion, and feminist theology"—*open* being the operative word. Recent threads have ranged from re-gendering the Book of Genesis to child-rearing to the evolution of FDS, the feminine deodorant spray (opinion held it a generally bad idea). Both men and women are active in discussion of "feminist" issues like the opening of the Citadel military academy and abortion—and oddly enough they

seem to like each other. There are no flames here, but there is an earring exchange program. Almost anyone could wander in here and feel at home—as long as you're good-natured, a bit quirky, and interested in discussing both the origin of the patriarchy and the word *pfiffle*. ✓**INTERNET**→*email* listserv@mizzou1.missouri.edu ✍ *Type in message body:* subscribe femrel-l <your full name> HOURLY

WMSPRT-L (ml) If you have an 18-inch python skin and you would like to learn how to preserve it for your pagan altar you have come to the right place. Women's Spirituality and Feminist Oriented Religions is a relatively active list (check for new posts daily or weekly, perhaps depending on planetary alignment) of "Pagans, neo-Pagans, Goddess worshipers, and feminist Christians of both genders." The active discussion ranges from the morality of buying African animal handicrafts to how to deal with "those pesky electric experiences that move you to a higher plane." Advice is freely given on planning pagan ceremonies, channeling and raising ecoconscious inner (and real) children, and how to deal with your mother (Earth and earthly). Feminists should be warned that this is a "Wild Woman" inner-voice list. Issues like abortion are discussed in "spiritual" terms. Although the readership is divided, the discussion is not dogmatic. ✓**INTERNET**→ *email* listserv@ubvm.cc.buffalo.edu ✍ *Type in message body:* subscribe wmsprt-l <your full name>

Support

alt.talk.rape (ng) A college woman wonders whether what happened last night was rape. A young man wants to know what constitutes going too far. This is a very active newsgroup, but its content is difficult to categorize. It is part support group, part legal discourse, and part heated male/female debate. The verbal violence of some of the postings reflects a troubled social dynamic. Here men and women rarely agree—saying that "no doesn't always mean no" on a board where many readers are rape survivors understandably inflames passions. Other exchanges focus on the legal rights of both victims and accused. Survivors and friends of survivors form close bonds, discussing vulnerability as well as treatments of the trauma of rape and sexual abuse. The newsgroup is not an easy place to be—but its very unease reflects its importance. ✓**USENET** DAILY

Menopaus (ml) A very active support group and discussion forum. The list may be limited in its audience, but the conversation ranges far beyond hot flashes. There are real controversies in the "treatment" of menopause, and the difference between chemical and holistic approaches is extensively debated—sometimes with a little heat. Women also share experiences and offer advice. Gwen gingerly asks if any other women find that their heels hurt, and the response is overwhelming—cures, and sympathy, and a sense that although her symptoms may not be textbook, they are real. There is a doctor who monitors the group and actively contributes his medical expertise. ✓**INTERNET**→*email* listserv@psuhmc.hmc.psu.edu ✍ *Type in message body:* subscribe menopaus <your full name> DAILY

STOPRAPE (ml) The "Sexual Assault Activist List" does provide networking for support groups, but it also serves as an active forum for discussion about issues re-

lated to society and sexual violence. There seem to be two camps here—divided, not surprisingly, by gender. Because of the volatile nature of the subject matter, flaming is not infrequent. STOPRAPE is more "dogmatically" feminist than many lists—seeing in for example, gangsta rap and the sexual bartering in the movie *The Piano* a very hostile world facing women. Men who come to the list are defensive ("How can anyone defend Lorena Bobbit?") and argumentative ("No doesn't always mean no!"). Other issues related to sexual abuse (false-memory syndrome, multiple-personality disorder, etc.) are covered with less animosity. ✓**INTERNET**→ *email* listserv@brownvm. brown.edu ✍ *Type in message body:* subscribe stoprape <your full name> WEEKLY

Other

GENDER (ml) GENDER is a hotline for the discussion of gender and communication. As its rather broad title suggests, the group often boils down to a nature vs. nurture discussion of life in the modern world. Why do women play Tetris and not Brute Force (because it is a game of intellect and skill rather than physical force)? Why do people always sit next to their same sex on the bus (the subliminal damage of the battle of the sexes)? The fact that there are occasional flame wars on this supposedly calm, rather scholarly hotline just goes to show that gender and communication are very hot indeed. Talking dirty on GENDER recently led to a fascinating discussion on gender and swearing online—is it worse to call someone a "prick" or a "cunt?" Why? Postings often arrive in a digest form—a thread at a time. ✓**INTERNET**→*email* comserv@vm.its.rpi.edu

✍ *Type in message body:* subscribe gender <your full name> WEEKLY

GEOGFEM (ml) The GEOGFEM list was designed for discussion of gender and space, and feminism and geography, and as a forum for women in the discipline itself. Country names on maps have been changing at a rapid rate during the last few years, but GEOGFEM has much more on its mind than the boundaries of Serbia. Here one can find serious, spirited discussion of feminist issues like abortion from a unique, often international, perspective. An Indian woman recently entered into a spirited debate with an American male professor about the greater meaning of a new law in India prohibiting parental notification of the sex of a fetus to prevent the abortion of girl children. ✓**INTERNET**→*email* listserv@ ukcc.uky.edu ✍ *Type in message body:* subscribe geogfem <your full name> WEEKLY

SocPol-L (ml) A sociologist from Maryland asks, "Is it possible to create a feminist welfare state?" A social worker from Georgia responds that "bureaucracy is by nature patriarchal." Social Politics: Gender, State and Society complements the journal *Social Politics* but is by no means limited to discussion of the journal's contents. It is a very active forum for those committed to changing the modern state. Personal stories of welfare mothers follow detailed plans for welfare reform. Liberals, libertarians, sociologists, social workers, and scholars are all welcome (real conservatives seem to be absent) and engaged in a number of debates—heated at times. Issues like health care benefit from the list's global perspective. ✓**INTERNET** →*email* listserv@vmd.cso.uiuc.edu ✍ *Type in message body:* subscribe socpol-l <your full name> WEEKLY

Generations

Oldsters, thirtysomethings, Gen Xers, teenagers—it's all about stereotyping. The trick

to navigating the numerous age-oriented venues online is finding what suits your needs—political debate, soul-searching, pick-ups, whining, reminiscing, or goofing. Tapehead teens go to AOL's **TeenChat**, prepubescents to FidoNet's **Kids**; "anything goes" on Prodigy's **Teen BB**. Stereotypically self-involved, apathetic postboomer Gen Xers live up to their image on the WELL's **GenX**, while equal numbers live the image down on the **Gen-X** mailing list. AOL's **Over Forty** probes deeply, while Prodigy's **Seniors BB** is heavy on reminiscence. You get the idea, but always have your favorite seminal TV show, event, or Top 40 tune in mind to prove your eligibility.

On the Net

Teens & kids

The Club BB OOOOHHH. Giggle, gush—I think he likes you! The Club is the hangout for the Prodigy preteen set. These kids aren't talking about sex or drugs; instead, it's "middle-school myths," or they're trading "fave foods and fave hobbies." Here you can form your own club—a seventh-grade boy advocates "a chillin

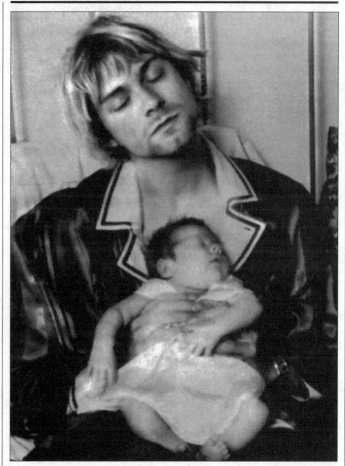

Kurt Cobain and baby—from http://www.ludd.luth.se/misc/nirvana/gifgallery2.html.

club with no bosses," and the eighth-grade girls unite to discuss how to become supermodels in "a cool fashion club (ACFC)." The Club is the launching place for future online singles—boys who say "All cute girls write" grow up into men asking the same of "all hot babes." ✓**PRODIGY** →*jump* club bb→Choose a Topic HOURLY

Kids (echo) "im a single white female and im 12.heres some info about me\ hair color blue/eye color [[/i mean hair color blond/eye color blue. i live in kansas when are you turning 14??????????????????? ??????/" Where are 12-year-olds not single? The preteen lament "I'm bored" rises from keyboards around the world and finds company here. Not yet victims of ennui, these kids name their favorite colors as a mode of introduction. A New Yorker mentions offhand that the crime rate has gone down, an Alberta 12-year-old notes the beauty of the mountains outside her window, a New Zealand teen complains about the snow in July to another trapped in Seattle on a rainy day. They are gearing up for the next phase, young girls practicing putdowns of cocky guys—but at least they're not bored anymore. ✓**FIDONET** DAILY

Teen (echo) Here they are, Rush fans and feminists going at it, just like their parents. Discussions about racism, sexism, and gay rights arouse strong feelings. There is also more traditional teen bonding: A 17-year-old male Wiccan from Arizona chats up a 14-year-old Scottish lass (probably Presbyterian). A wag from England describes how best to embarrass older saleswomen: by asking the price of massage oil. A girl explains her absence from the conference— "My boyfriend's trying to run my life. We've been together for 23 days." Friends or not, teens develops longlasting relationships here. ✓**RELAYNET** DAILY

Teen Chat Teenagers like music. Teenagers like trendy music. Teenagers seem to think of little else. "Primus sucks, and because of that they rule." "Rap takes no talent—that's why it rhymes with crap." "NIN rules!" If your identity is defined by the contents of your tape deck, you've found your niche. While the occasional adult tries, for some inexplicable reason, to masquerade as a snotty 14-year-old Beastie Boys fan, it's hard to cop that energy without seeming studied. ✓**AMERICA ONLINE**→*keyword* people→Rooms→Teen Chat

Teens BB This board is all over

Richard Nixon—downloaded from CompuServe's Graphics Forum.

the place. Kevin asks if "they" can test your system for acid, while a nervous high-school freshman asks how best to attract boys. Pack animals that teens are, this bulletin board is full of trends and pop-culture banter. You can be cool here—or at least get some ideas of how you might be. Lots of pick-up chat, with and without sexual innuendo. Debate, too—with name-calling (men are evil, women "feminazis"). Here you'll read a defense of cheerleaders against charges of airheadedness and a lament on the plight of Native Americans. There is also down-to-earth encouragement to stand up to abusers and to get off drugs. ✓**PRODIGY**→*jump* teens bb→Choose a Topic HOURLY

Youth Rights (ml) "I don't think adolescents could possibly be more ignorant of the issues or do a worse job of it than the adult electorate," says Chris from New Jersey. MTV urges teens to take charge and evidently they are listening. Founded by a young man more interested in weighty issues like kiddie porn, AIDS, murder, and gay marriage than in the "right" to have the car on Saturday night, this international forum welcomes "counselor-types" and the few older activists who show up, but it is really for

teens. ✓**INTERNET**→*email* listserv@ sjuvm. stjohns.edu ✍ *Type in message body:* subscribe y-rights <your full name> WEEKLY

Generation X

alt.society.generation-x (ng) The highly touted generation of underachievers, technogeeks, and criminal misfits—"slackers, hackers, and carjackers," as one posting explains with admirable concision—gets yet another media outlet, and uses it to confirm virtually all of its own stereotypes. Gen Xers like pop music and hate literature. Gen Xers like beer and hate their parents. Gen Xers would

> "The highly touted generation of underachievers, technogeeks, and criminal misfits— 'slackers, hackers, and carjackers,' as one posting explains with admirable concision—gets yet another media outlet, and uses it to confirm virtually all of its own stereotypes."

wear underwear on their head if MTV told them to. Kurt, Kurt, why hast thou forsaken them? How much can you say about a newsgroup that spends much of its energy wondering if its messages should be cross-posted to alt. angst? ✓**USENET** DAILY

Gen-X (ml) If the media casts Generation X as whiny, apathetic post–baby boomers, the denizens of this list don't want to hear it. Refusing all stereotypes, this diverse and prolific group even debates whether the generation can be limited by age. "Gen-X is a state of mind," insists one list member. There are no boundaries to the unmoderated discussions. Fiery political debates over gun control and hiring quotas mix easily with sillier topics such as "Name the most embarrassing album you own." (One Gen Xer: "I have the first Tiffany album. Beat that." The response: "Preferably with a large, blunt object to prevent further human suffering!") Get the digest version if you cannot handle 50–200 posts a day. ✓**INTERNET**→*email* listproc@phan tom.com ✍ *Type in message body:* subscribe gen-x <your full name> HOURLY

Generation X Twentysomethings might not be the most superficial generation ever, but they are certainly members of the most superficial generation ever to have this much media technology at its callow fingertips. Where else are you likely to find more than 200 messages reponding to the question "Where were you when you first heard 'Rock Lobster'?" or extensive discussion of cereal commercials, *Ren & Stimpy*, Wesley Crusher, Mr. Rourke, Buckaroo Banzai, *Beavis & Butthead*, and Taco Bell ("The Official Snack Center of the Slacker Genera-

Moonwalk—downloaded from galaxy.uci.agh.edu.pl.

tion")? If you are in this pipeline, the conference may seem like heaven on earth; otherwise, there may be far too many cultural touchstones to handle.

Serious subjects

And while the conference sometimes tries to tackle serious subjects—how is AIDS affecting modern life? Is the Justice Department to blame for the fate of the Branch Davidians?—the discussion tends to slide into surface-skimming of slacker angst. For a quick fix on things that shouldn't matter but somehow do, it just doesn't get any better than this. ✓**WELL**→*g* genx HOURLY

Under 30 Remember *Square Pegs*? Madness? Do you eat canned ravoili two nights a week so you can afford beer? And are you still living at home? Echo provides a virtual home for you in the Under 30 conference. Compare parents, gripe about the job market, find out how others your age are coping with money, sex, and angst, and attend raucus roof parties (real life) in the New York area. The biggest gripe of Echo's Generation X crowd? Being called Generation X. Get in while you can—when you turn 30 you're booted out. ✓**ECHO**→*j* under WEEKLY

Thirtysomething

#30plus Curious about that station you caught on the radio as you drove through Pittsburgh, the one playing old songs? Well, not too old. Older. On #30plus, they can tell you the call letters (WPGH). Engineers, graphic designers, couch potatoes with chronic fatigue syndrome, and journalists give each other backrubs and confess they wish they'd bought a lottery ticket this morning. The more ambitious wish they'd started a biotech company. There's flirtation, but it's mellow. This laid-back group trades email and GIFs; recent offline get-togethers were held in Washington, D.C., and Kansas City. ✓**INTERNET** →*irc* /channel #30plus

Thirtysomething Of all the rooms in AOL's People Connection, this is perhaps the most aggressively talky—thirtysomethings, you see, not only have substantial angst but seem to have an inexhaustible desire to describe, dissect, and define their lives. For a quick sampling, we logged on and pretended we were just turn-

> "If you know the name of Howdy Doody's cousin or all the words to the *Brady Bunch* theme you are welcome on AOL's Baby Boomers bulletin board."

ing 30, and asked what we could expect. "I think you'll find that this room is devoted to lots of talk about sex, marriage, and divorce." "Money worries. I have house payments to make, and will be making them for the rest of my life." "We are mature, thinking adults, and behave as such." "I treasure this time, because it reminds me of college. These are the only substantive discussions I have during the day: my husband and I both work, and there's so much to do with the kids." But perhaps the most telling response came from a St. Louis businessman: "M or f? And if f, would you like to go private?" ✓**AMERICA ONLINE**→*keyword* people→Rooms→Thirtysomething

40-plus

#40plus Spence will likely pull up a wingback chair for you when you log on. Everyone will say hello. You might see Cowboy rubbing Barbie's feet and, if you're lucky, Spence will bring out a tray of hamburgers, with all the fixings. Take one—everyone else will except perhaps Layla, who's dieting. Imagine this IRC channel on a veranda somewhere in West Texas, behind mosquito netting. You'll be offered a Pepsi, but you can ask for a Heineken. ✓**INTERNET**→*irc* /channel #40plus

Baby Boomers Club If you know the name of Howdy Doody's cousin or all the words to the *Brady Bunch* theme you are welcome on AOL's Baby Boomers bulletin board. It's hosted by two married boomers with kids, and the chat ranges from serious to silly—dealing with aging parents to the worst songs ever written. Here Melanie, a "conservative" Navy wife from Virginia meets Jenny, a veteran of the California commune movement, to discuss day

Jackie —downloaded from CompuServe's US News & World Report Forum.

care. There's a lot of nostalgia—missing John Lennon, wincing at the memory of a Carpenters song played at your wedding. Boomers provides a place to locate classmates from a previous life and ways of dealing with the hassles of present life in sections like "Boomers on Prozac," "Gender Roles," and "Combining Work and Family." You also get to make fun of Gen Xers to your heart's content. ✓**AMERICA ONLINE**→*keyword* boomers WEEKLY

Over Forty In the youth market of online services, subscribers over 40 are almost senior citizens, logging on with the Centris they bought for their kids and touring Cyberspace with an endearing mix of apprehension and cynicism. On AOL's People Connection, the Over Forty rooms are dominated by lightweight conversation about golf, cars, kids, and (of course) sex—the small talk of men and women saddled with immense emotional and economic responsibilities. But there's more: When one woman confesses, "I never had an orgasm that shook me until I was 42. Up until then I was always watching myself in my mind's eye," and a man responds that, "I feel the same way about my job," it's both hilarious and

tragic. The "mindless drivel," as one man calls it, is rarely only that. ✓**AMERICA ONLINE**→*keyword* people→ Rooms→Over Forty

Seniors

Senior Citizens (echo) "The greatest achievement of our generation was landing and retrieving a man from the moon. Our worst was the creation of the baby boomers." You won't find singles ads or many reminiscences here. The seniors here are involved in the world around them, and while they share a generation, they don't share a single viewpoint—an "in my day" is sure to be countered by a forward-looking regular. These seniors are not content to sit back and criticize instead they encourage each other to set goals and to continue to make their voices heard over the din of the younger generations. ✓**RELAYNET** DAILY

SeniorNet Online One very active section is entitled "How SeniorNet changed my life." Some people met traveling companions; others located long-lost pals. There are subsections for every

> **" 'The greatest achievement of our generation was landing and retrieving a man from the moon. Our worst was the creation of the baby boomers.' "**

> **"SIXTIES-L attempts to make sense of a decade in which a bad trip did not mean your luggage went to Belgrade while you went to Club Med."**

specific senior interest imaginable—Health and Wellness, Investment, Politics, and Keeping an Open Mind—as well as forums for gay and lesbian seniors and World War II war brides. Pat told of her cancer diagnosis on Women Sharing and had 50 concerned responses in one day. The Singles section does seem to be dominated by one gentleman calling himself "The Hunk" (who's not too successful at wooing), but plenty of flirting gets done in other sections. For live chat, visit the friendly community center. Many regulars have formed fast friendships and visit each other offline. ✓**AMERICA ONLINE**→*keyword* seniornet→Senior-Net Forums <or> Community Center DAILY/LIVE

Seniors BB Like most Prodigy bulletin boards, Seniors BB is peppered with singles advertising for mates. Don't expect any calls for shuffleboard partners though—more likely an "adventurous soul over 60." Many of the boards here are organized by birth year—and people get together to reminisce about "the good old days" or find lost friends from the 1930s on the Lower East Side or co-workers at Los Alamos during the war or just to pass on a good joke over "The

Backyard Fence." There's also advice on finance, retirement and just plain living. No one responded to the inquiry about nuclear-powered pacemakers—but many are banding together online to lobby Congress for their interests in health-care reform. ✓**PRODIGY**→*jump* seniors bb→Choose a Topic DAILY

Nostalgia

MEMORIES (echo) Do you lie awake nights trying to remember the name of Top Cat's fat sidekick (Babalooey)? Do you have a yen to chat with others who bought their fruit from pushcarts instead of buying it shrink-wrapped at A&P? This is a multigenerational forum—people with memories of 10-cent movies and TV-generation boomers meet here. Trivia discussions and timeless experiences—the first time you rode a bike or the most painful traffic ticket. ✓**FIDONET** DAILY

Sixties-L (ml) You say you want a revolution. Yeah! You know, we all wanted to change the world. SIXTIES-L attempts to make sense of a decade in which a bad trip did not mean your luggage went to Belgrade while you went to Club Med. Cultural historians, sociologists, and just plain people over 30 meet here to dissect, lament, and reflect—proof positive that Oliver Stone doesn't own the era. Recent threads have included mild (hey, man!) disagreements over the accuracy of film versions of the age (too drug-oriented) and more heated altercations about the Vietnam War's place in the past and present. And SIXTIES-L helps perpetuate the revolution: A dad writes in asking how his daughter can paint her car like Kesey's Magic Bus. ✓**INTERNET** →*email* listproc@jefferson.village.virginia.edu

✍ *Type in message body:* subscribe sixties-l <your full name> DAILY

CYBERNOTES

"During WWII every kid in my hometown (pop. 8,000) would play this really stupid game.

"When walking to and from anywhere, when an empty Camel cigarette package was spotted lying on the ground, a kid would run to the package, stamp on it and shout: 'Hits or cracks.'

"The person or persons accompanying him/her would then choose to reply with either 'Hit' or 'Crack.'

"The person who had originally stamped on the cigarette package would then carefully peel open the bottom of the packgage and look for the letter 'H' (for Hit) or 'C' (for Crack).

"It didn't dawn on me until I was about 50 that the 'C' was simply some sort of packaging code for 'C'amels.

"There never was any 'H.'

"Obviously this was highly regionalized. I've never found anyone in any other town who was dumb enough to play this moronic game."

—FidoNet's **Memories**

New Age consciousness

Eating meat, wearing clothes all the time, never reading the horoscope, having just one

life, treating colds with Vicks, equating witches with that one writing "Surrender Dorothy." These attitudes just aren't '90s! But the Net makes it easy to move into the New Age. You don't have to live in Santa Fe anymore; you can live in Cleveland and be spiritually attuned. CompuServe and FidoNet both offer very active gathering places for "alternative" views—be they Wiccan, spiritualist, Eastern, or Eck. Practitioners of a higher level of astrology than the Sunday paper cast the stars in the moderated **Astrology** mailing list or the less consistently friendly **alt.astrology** (who let the fundamentalists in?). Tarot readers delve deeply into the ancient mysteries in **BOTA-L**. For a second opinion many choose either the **Holistics** mailing list or the WELL's **Holistic** conference. The meat-free meet on **Veg-life**, and the real radicals, the vegans (no cream in your coffee or woolen muffler; just ideals to warm you), find support on **Vegan-L**. And the people who are naked off-line more than not head to AfterDark's **Natural** conference.

Pyramid—downloaded from GEnie's Graphic Images RoundTable.

On the Net

Across the board

alt.consciousness (ng) Any interest in philosophy, spirituality, brain machines, or smart drugs? They're all covered in this New Agey forum with a large number of amateur philosophers and pranksters. To wit: "It's really too bad that people don't recognize cockroaches as conscious entities. It shows how ethnocentric people are." Despite the roach debate, the group also engages in a number of serious discussions: e.g., the nature of reality, the need for language in society, and fractal consciousness and mystical experience. ✓**USENET** DAILY

HU-Talk (ml) "Love in Eck" concludes nearly every posting on HU-TALK, the mailing list for practitioners/devotees of the spiritual teachings of Eckankar. HU-Talk welcomes all searchers for serenity and serves up friendship and instruction. Newcomer Felicia got help in remembering the gifts

of the Dream Master here, and Bob, who moved away from his ECK group, found a spiritual community online. Cyberspace appears to be an important meeting ground for ECKers—one young mother became so addicted to her online spiritual quest she forget to "treasure the world." HU-TALK offers big things to its appreciative audience: "immediate inner communication…soul to soul." ✓**INTERNET**→*email* listserv@ jug.eng.sun.com ✍ *Type in message body:* subscribe hu-talk <your full name> WEEKLY

New_Age_Echo (echo) New Age is a catch-all category for anything neo-pagan, other-dimensional, or found in Santa Fe. People meet here to talk about their past lives and their visions, their gurus and their shamans, astral projection and visitors from other

> "The group is more understanding than your family or people on the street—you can talk about when you were Lolita de Mendoza and no one will raise an eyebrow."

worlds. The group is more understanding than your family or people on the street—you can talk about when you were Lolita de Mendoza and no one will raise an eyebrow. These people are mellow—healing their inner children—except when confronted with lurking fundamentalists. ✓**FIDONET**

New Age Forum Ever wanted to know how to walk on burning coals? Is it okay to hex a rapist? How do you get one of the dearly departed to visit you? Do starfish have souls—and if so what happens when you cut them up and they rejuvenate? Are the phone lines going dead because of Mercury's heavenly position? If these are the kinds of questions you are prone to ask, the New Age Forum may be the place for you. Because New Age means anything William F. Buckley laughs at—vegans here confront back-to-native crossbow hunters and witches chat with channelers over cups of hemlock tea about "the trouble with patriarchy." With the exception of the "meat" debate, the forum is by nature a very friendly place peopled by the likes of Steve—a "letter carrier trying to spread joy," and Neil, a lonely British soul battling his nation's contempt for therapy and spirituality. ✓**COMPUSERVE**→*go new age*→Messages DAILY

talk.religion.newage (ng) Users here don't "post"; they "share." Nearly all are devoted to their spiritual ideology of choice, be it Qi meditation, tantric sex, channeling, or neopagan druids. Nonbelievers do pop up: One user asked, tongue in cheek, why, if the Universe was so abundant, he could not find a girlfriend. Quite a few serious replies followed; one told him that all he had to do was "convince himself that he was ulti-

> "Nonbelievers do pop up: One user asked, tongue in cheek, why, if the Universe was so abundant, he could not find a girlfriend. Quite a few serious replies followed."

mately more worthy than other men" and that his belief would "vibrate out from him in his fields and manifest itself." ✓**USENET** DAILY

Astrology

Astrology (ml) The Astrology mailing list was formed as a low-traffic alternative to alt.astrology, a Usenet group typically cluttered with flame wars, discreditors, and advice-seekers. This list offers seasoned astrologers and students a relaxed, unmoderated environment in which to discuss the nuances of chart interpretation and client consultation. Professionals share thoughts on topics such as counseling ethics, the future of astrology, and determinism vs. free will. Students can ask questions ("How do I calculate a solar progression?") and expect prompt, personal replies. The traffic here is light, but subscribers can expect plenty of substance and very little noise. ✓**INTERNET**→*email* astrology-request@festival.ed.ac.uk ✍ *Write a request* WEEKLY

BOTA-L (ml) The Magician, the

High Priestess, the Lovers, the Fool, The Wheel of Fate (not Fortune)…turn over the card and see. BOTA-L is a very active list devoted to the practitioners of tarot—some call themselves readers, others magicians. These are devoted people, delving into the ancient mysteries and minutiae of the symbolism of stars and cards. Here tarot is not just a telling of the future but a way of guiding one's life, using one's power—ordering the universe. College students encounter real-estate agents to discuss the nature of evil or how best to make magic work when out of town. Interested amateurs are welcome but may be lost in some discussions—and nonbelievers are non-existent!? ✓**INTERNET**→*email* listserv @netcom.com ✍ *Type in message body:* subscribe bota-l <your full name> DAILY

Holistic

Holistic (ml) Does the Senate health-care plan include mind machines sending out binaural beat frequencies, kombucha tea, oak trees, and the light of the full moon? The Holistic list does. Those who frequent this list have in common a basic discontent with the medical profession and a willingness to experiment with alternative forms of treatment. The prescriptions here vary from New Age visualization to folk healing to technology-based methods that treat the whole person. The list members are very familiar with natural science and nutrition, and many informative FAQs are posted. Regulars also keep tabs on one another's medical progress, providing encouragement and sympathy along with the tea. ✓**INTERNET**→ *email* listserv@siucvmb.bitnet ✍ *Type in message body:* subscribe holistic <your full name> DAILY

Holistics Sure, doctors are smart—hey, they've been through all that school—but they don't know everything. Sometimes you have a pain that they can't identify, or a funny feeling that escapes their notice. And they don't always treat the whole patient—the hundreds of psychological, physical, mental, emotional, and spiritual variables that contribute to well-being. Or at least that's the premise behind the WELL's holistic-medicine conference. Whether displaying a healthy skepticism toward vaccines, explaining kinesiology, detailing vitamin therapy, or wondering aloud about the harms of microwaves, the participants in this conference agree that feeling good is more than a pair of aspirin and a morning call. ✓ **WELL**→*g* holistic WEEKLY

Nudism

Natural (echo) Though there's no way to prove that the people who write into After Dark's Natural conference are sitting at their desks in the buff, some of them claim that they are. Anything else, they say, would be hypocritical, especially for a group that advances the philosophy that "the naked body is a beautiful thing, and should not be covered out of shame." Most of the naturists seem to be men and women in their early forties, upstanding citizens who comply with societal norms in so many ways that a little public nudity now and then—washing the Volvo in one's birthday suit—hardly seems rebellious. ✓ **AFTERDARK** DAILY

Vegetarianism

Vegan-L (ml) If you are a serious vegan (no leather shoes, no silk undies, no honey in your tea—no animal products at all) this list is it! Come here for your survival strategies—how to take photos without using gelatin-based film, how to make rayon look as fancy as silk. True vegans are committed to a difficult lifestyle and thus have a very strong bond. But they see the future as theirs. And—holy cow!—they have a sense of humor too, discussing the pros and cons of turning housecats vegetarian, and the aftereffects of the latest *Star Trek* movie, which mentioned pepperoni pizza. ✓ **INTERNET**→*email* listserv@vm.temple.edu ✍ *Type in message body:* subscribe vegan-l <your full name>

VegLife (ml) "If we didn't eat beef what would happen to all the cows?" Cattle retirement communities. This is a warm and friendly list providing vegetarians of all sorts a chance to feel some kinship in the dead-flesh-loving world. A few recipes are exchanged, but the meat of this list is more good-humored fellowship and veggie activism. How to get your kids to like tofu and how to get carnivores to stop offering us hot dogs are prime topics—tall orders both. ✓ **INTERNET**→ *email* listserv@vtvm1. cc.vt.edu ✍ *Type in message body:* subscribe veglife <your full name> DAILY

Castaneda (ml) A mailing list for the devotees of the popular Don Juan series of books by Carlos Castaneda (and his spiritual guide, DJ). The discussion is concerned with exploring classic Castenada issues like "How does a person become aware of something that they currently aren't aware of?" The members are a combination of aging hippies, New Age spiritualists, and college students discovering Don Juan and altered states while away from home. ✓ **INTERNET**→*email* castaneda-request@earth.com ✍ *Write a request* WEEKLY

Religion

Serious astrologers long ago announced that the Age of

Aquarius would bring a frenzy of worldwide communication. How fitting, then, that as we enter this era—in which mankind, it is hoped, will reach a higher level of consciousness—the Net spans the globe, and chatter ascends to the heavens so happy and uninhibited that it makes the Goddess giggle. And not unlike the apostle Boniface, who entered Frysia to evangelize the peasants, many disciples of smaller and larger religions have set foot in Cyberia to discuss their respective versions of Absolute Truth. Except that, while you may get flamed in Cyberspace, you'll never get burned. We're hopping religions like TV channels—from **alt.pagan** to **soc.religion.bahai** to **Quaker-P**. We're discussing theological matters as if they were shopping lists—such as the onomastic issue of how we can call God "God"—and we're sharing tips about our rituals as if there were no Inquisition. And—damn!—we're having a hell of a time at it too! Even on **alt.zen** they're getting a little zany every now and then.

Jesus—downloaded from America Online's Mac Graphics Forum.

On the Net

Across the board

Ethics & Religion Forum Maintains separate message folders for all major faiths—atheism, Buddhism, Christianity, Islam, Judaism, and paganism, among others—and also embraces related disciplines such as history and ethics. The Ethics board draws the largest discussion, with abortion, abortion, and abortion the main topics. The large Christian Fellowship category encompasses the Christian spectrum—from Mormons to Catholics to Jews for Jesus. Christian and single? There's a topic devoted specifically to personals for Christians. As on GEnie, forum members share an interest in the less popular religions, like Rosicrucianism. Occasionally, members head to The Front Porch Room for real-time religious talk.

✓**AMERICA ONLINE**→*keyword* religion→Ethics & Religion Message Center *or* The Front Porch Room WEEKLY/LIVE

Religion & Philosophy Round-Table The godhead of all online religion chat sites is GEnie's Religion bulletin board, which boasts an awe-inspiring breadth of categories—not only separate categories for most Protestant sects but also spiritual fasts, religion and science fiction, tithing, and Mormon humor. Hard-core hermeneuts flock to GEnie's Bible Discussion categories, and many members have serious interests in Rosicrucianism, Zoroastrianism, Taoism, Satanism, Mithraism, Baha'i, and even Freemasonry.
✓**GENIE**→ *keyword* religion→Religion & Philosophy Bulletin Board WEEKLY

Religion BB Everything going to hell? The Religion boards on Prodigy offer a variety of solutions for you. If you have your bags already packed you might want to check out the millennialist fest in topics like "1994 End Signs— READ OR PERISH," where everything from Disney cartoon characters to gun control foretells the coming of the horned beast. But this bulletin board also offers fellowship, solace, advice, and debate. There are sections for every religion and denomination from Baha'i to Pentecostal, as well as open forums for discussion of volatile issues like woman priests, abortion, and homosexuality.

Prayer for a daughter

People come here seeking understanding—like the woman whose prayer for a daughter had gone unanswered. Some come for religious guidance—like the children of Holocaust survivors wanting to know Orthodox positions on artificial insemination. Some need help with worldly problems—like the Mormon woman's questions about incest. If they do not find an answer here they do find comfort—or so it seems from the high volume. Make no mistake, there are many willing to condemn others here, but there are more willing to listen. ✓**PRODIGY**→*jump* religion bb→Choose a Topic HOURLY

Religion Forum If the number of posts reflects popular support, religion on CompuServe is embattled. The two groups with the heaviest traffic on the Religion Forum are "Free Thought," home of atheists and agnostics, and "Limbo," which is short for "Location for Informing the Masses of Bunny Organizations" (aka the Church of the Bunny, with its estimable Vice-Pope Doug). Thanks to strict rules and sysop monitors, however, serious religion does survive. In fact, CompuServe's religion forum has hundreds of messages posted hourly on such message boards as Christianity, Judaism, Eastern Religion, Islam, Interfaith, Pagan, and Religion and Science. A pastor posts encouraging words to a young man starting seminary. Reports sift in of a revival church near the Toronto airport. Jews debate whether the great rabbis had anything to say about credit cards, and Catholics argue over ordination of women, natural family planning, and poor old Onan. Online groups also study the Talmud, the Bible, and a book called *A Course in Miracles*. Although the sysops forbid it and are watchful, some here are proselytizing for what seem to be cults; just say no to unwanted file transfers. ✓**COMPUSERVE**→*go* religion→ Messages DAILY/LIVE

Spirituality Some of the best soul food you're likely to taste. Interested in learning the 9 billion

> ## "Everything from Disney cartoon characters to gun control foretells the coming of the horned beast."

names of God? Want to find out more about women and spirituality? How about chanting, or Werner Erhard, or the role of drugs in religion? An electronic gateway to the houses of the holy may feel strange at first, but the strangeness soon fades, and at least one respondent to a speculative theology topic—"The new ten commandments: here's your chance to play supreme being for a day"—has proposed a fitting imperative for the electronic age: Thou shalt log in. ✓**WELL**→*g* spi DAILY

Atheism

alt.atheism (ng) Hard to say who is more abrasive, the Christians or the atheists. Insults such as "bigot" and "demagogue" are traded faster than bullets in a De Palma film. A Christian proposes that because of a genetic deficiency, atheists live in a virtual reality where they cannot perceive God. An atheist suggests that religious people should be thought of as having a "conditioned rational dysfunctionality." Choose your poison: Do you like them loopy and pushy, or haughty and condescending? Occasional posts from almighty@omnipotent.omnipresent.com. ✓**USENET** *FAQ:* ✓**INTERNET**→*ftp* rtfm.mit.edu→ anonymous→<your email address> →/pub/usenet-by-hierarchy/alt/ answers/atheism→faq DAILY

Christianity

Bible-L (ml) Like it or hate it, it's indisputable that the Bible lies at the center of Western society and has great impact on world culture (without it, for instance, there would be no *Paradise Lost*, and Charlton Heston certainly would never have donned his beard for Mosaic ends). Even if you're not very religious, you have probably had some experience with the Good Book, as it's sometimes called. The Bible-L mailing list treats all aspects of the Bible as text, from the vexed matter of its origins (while one man calls it "God's inspired Word, given by inspiration to His faithful servants who wrote it down in Hebrew, Aramaic, and Greek," others may disagree) to more specific hermeneutic questions.

Symbolism of the flood

Want to suggest a new interpretation for Revelations? Interested in working out the symbolism of the flood? There's plenty of chance to do so here. While the level of expertise varies—seminarians are well represented, as are people whose main connection with the Bible is the occasional hotel visit—the mix makes for an interesting community. And in the end, that's the beauty of the Bible—it is accessible to anyone. As one man says, "I have taught Old Testament and related courses for 27 years. I have read the Bible through many times, which does not make me more knowledgeable, merely older." ✓**INTERNET** →*email* listserv@gitvm1.gatech.edu ✎ *Type in message body:* subscribe bible-l <your full name> DAILY

bit.listserv.catholic (ml/ng) As the subscribers to this group recognize, the Catholic Church is not only a religious denomination but the world's most powerful corporation, and much of bit.listserv. catholic concerns itself with internal business. Who gets hired? Who gets fired? What should be done with disobedient and problematic employees? And, finally, is the pope fallible? This last question provokes intense debate, including a vituperative response from a man who suggests that those who dare conceive of a fallible pope "reflect on the pride and disobedience to Christ that [their] words entail." The group isn't all housekeeping, though, and there's a decent amount of reflection on other Catholic issues—C.S. Lewis's *Screwtape Letters*, birth control, Mary-cult, and even the Kennedys. ✓**USENET** ✓**INTERNET**→ *email* listserv@american.edu ✍ *Type in message body:* subscribe catholic <your full name> DAILY

Christian Fellowship Not the most popular online chat area in People Connection, Christian Fellowship is frequently fascinating, with large numbers of young Christians exploring the boundaries of their faith. Like other teens, they love to talk about bands—"Isn't Christian contemporary music cool? And I mean the stuff that rocks!"—and occasionally confess sexual or emotional crises. The adults in the group aren't as interesting, primarily because they aren't in flux in quite the same way. ✓**AMERICA ONLINE** →*keyword* people→Rooms→ Christian Fellowship

---

Orthodox (ml) Orthodox Christianity refers to a variety of Eastern churches—not only Greek Orthodox but also Russian Orthodox and several affiliated traditions. In short, Eastern beliefs afford primacy of honor to the patriarch of Constantinople, and maintain seven ecumenical councils. The top-

ics on this mailing list ranges from Eastern Orthodox news to general discussions that you might find in the *American Review of Eastern Orthodoxy* to hard-core theology. On the topic of theological onomastics (how can we call God "God"?), a man writes that "in reply to my previous message, you suggested that a theology 'that distinguishes the energies of God from the Essence of God usually has no need to fear being charged with pantheism.' My point is that I think the human ability to understand is so limited that it (I) cannot understand either energies or Essence. I can read words that define the terms, but my understanding is still human, not divine." ✓**INTERNET**→*email* listserv@iubvm.ucs.indiana.edu ✍ *Type in message body:* subscribe orthodox <your full name> DAILY

Quaker-P (ml) The Quakers, of course, aren't responsible only for oats—also known as the Society of Friends, this religous sect has existed since the 17th century, and their belief in pacifism and a gentle, almost colloquial approach to religion has persisted with very little change. This mailing list treats a wide variety of Quaker peace and social-justice issues, and while some of the postings offer brief bi-

> **"A Christian proposes that because of a genetic deficiency, atheists live in a virtual reality where they cannot perceive God."**

ographies of pacifist activists (there's an oxymoron in training), others clarify the role of Quaker thought in the travesty-a-minute world of the nineties. As one woman writes of C.S. Lewis's *Chronicles of Narnia*: "This is a typical tale of 'justifiable violence,' setting the world out in terms of good vs. evil, and I was not surprised that Lewis had written it. As a metaphor for might and Empire, it works fine but I am still mystified as to why a pacifist would think that this was good or instructive reading for children." ✓**INTERNET**→*email* listserv@uiucvmd. bitnet ✍ *Type in message body:* subscribe quaker-p <your full name> DAILY

---

soc.religion.christian (ng) If your parents asked you to kill someone, which commandment (No. 4 or No. 5) would take precedence? A Jew explains the rule of "*pikkuach nefesh*," whereby one is not only permitted, but required, to break a commandment to save a life. A Muslim quotes Muhammad: "There shall be no obedience to a creature, in what is a disobedience to the Creator." A Christian prioritizes Jesus' new commandment to "love thy neighbor." When soc.religion.christian is debating doctrine, it's an informed, speculative community. Unfortunately, undergraduate atheists bait readers with old chestnuts like premarital sex, the rock too big for God to lift, and bad things that happen to good people, and instead of turning the other cheek (where is it written that thou shalt not killfile?), Christians here flame back. ✓**USENET** DAILY

Eastern Religions

alt.zen (ng) A few Zen fans can be overheard comparing translations of the *Lotus Sutra*, but a

More religion chat...

Across the board

Belief-L (ml) Discussion open to all belief systems. ✓**INTERNET**→ *email* listserv@brownvm.bitnet ✍ *Type in message body:* subscribe belief-l <your full name>

Religion (echo) Catch-all religious discussion. ✓**ILINK**

Religion (ml) Discuss religion. ✓**INTERNET**→*email* listserv@harvarda.harvard.edu ✍ *Type in message body:* subscribe religion <your full name>

Religion (echo) General religious discussion. ✓**RELAYNET**

talk.religion.misc (ng) Religious debate. ✓**USENET**

Atheism

alt.atheism.moderated (ng) A moderated discussion about atheism. ✓**USENET**

#atheism Chat channel for atheists. ✓**INTERNET**→*irc* /channel #atheism

Buddhism

alt.buddha.short-fat-guy (ng) Zen Buddhism is the topic, but the discussion is as often silly and sarcastic as serious. ✓**USENET** *FAQ:* ✓**INTERNET**→*ftp* rtfm.mit.edu→ anonymous→<your email address> →pub/usenet-by-group/alt.answers→alt-buddha-short-fat-guy-faq

Buddhist (ml) Chat about Buddhism. ✓**INTERNET**→*email* listerv@ jpntuvm0.bitnet ✍ *Type in message body:* subscribe buddhist <your full name>

#buddhist Live talk in a channel reserved for Buddhists and Buddhist topics. ✓**INTERNET**→*irc* /channel #buddhist

Zenbuddhism-L (ml) Discussion about Zen Buddhism. ✓**INTERNET**→*email* majordomo@ coombs.anu.edu.au ✍ *Type in message body:* subscribe zenbuddhism-l

Christianity

alt.religion.christian (ng) Debate and discussion about Christianity and biblical interpretation. ✓**USENET**

alt.religion.quaker (ng) Discussion for Quakers. Group has been superseded at some sites by soc.culture.quaker. ✓**USENET**

Anglican (ml) A discussion forum for Anglicans. ✓**INTERNET**→*email* listserv@auvm.bitnet ✍ *Type in message body:* subscribe anglican <your full name>

Baptist (ml) A discussion forum for Baptists. ✓**INTERNET**→*email* listserv@ukcc.bitnet ✍ *Type in message body:* subscribe baptist <your full name>

Bible Studies (echo) Scripture analysis and discussion. ✓**RELAYNET**

bit.listserv.christia (ml/ng) Discussion of practical Christian living. ✓**USENET** ✓**INTERNET**→*email* listserv@asuvm.inre.asu.edu ✍ *Type in message body:* subscribe christia-l <your full name>

#christian A fellowship channel for Christians. ✓**INTERNET**→*irc* /channel #christian

Elenchus (ml) Academic discussion about Christianity in Late Antiquity. ✓**INTERNET**→*email* listserv@ acadvm1.ottawa.ca ✍ *Type in message body:* subscribe elenchus <your full name>

GLOBLX-L (ml) Discuss Christianity from a global perspective. ✓**INTERNET**→*email* listserv@qucdn. bitnet ✍ *Type in message body:* subscribe globlx-l <your full name>

Holy_Bible (echo) For serious Bible study. All points must be supported by Scripture. ✓**FIDONET**

#jesus Live chat for Christians— rarely serious. ✓**INTERNET**→*irc* /channel #jesus

Liturgy (ml) Discuss the Christian Liturgy. ✓**INTERNET**→*email* mailbase @mailbase.ac.uk ✍ *Type in message body:* subscribe liturgy <your full name>

Quaker-L (ml) Intimate list for Quaker discussions. ✓**INTERNET**→ *email* listserv@uvmd.cso.uiuc.edu ✍ *Type in message body:* subscribe quaker-l <your full name>

soc.religion.christian.bible-study (ng) Biblical debate and interpretation discussions. ✓**USENET**

soc.religion.quaker (ng) Discuss the Religious Society of Friends. ✓**USENET** *FAQ:* ✓**INTERNET** →*ftp* rtfm.mit.edu→anonymous→ <your email address>→/pub/ usenet-by-group/soc.religion.quaker→soc.religion.quaker_Answers_ to_Frequently_Asked_Questions

UUS-L (ml) Discussion group for Unitarian Universalists. ✓**INTERNET**→*email* listserv@ubvm.bitnet ✍ *Type in message body:* subscribe uus-l <your full name>

More religion chat (continued)

Visions (ml) Discuss visions and apparitions within a Christian context. ✓**INTERNET**→*email* listserv @ubvm.bitnet ✍ *Type in message body:* subscribe visions <your full name>

Eastern religions

alt.meditation (ng) Discuss meditation techniques and experiences. ✓**USENET** *FAQ:* ✓**INTERNET**→ *ftp* rtfm.mit.edu→anonymous→ <your email address>→/pub/ usenet-by-group/alt.meditation →Meditation_FAQ

alt.philosophy.zen (ng) Discuss Zen Buddhism. ✓**USENET**

Taoism-studies (ml) Forum for discussing Taoism. ✓**INTERNET**→ *email* majordomo@coombs.anu. edu.au ✍ *Type in message body:* subscribe taoism-studies

Universal Zendo (ml) A Zen Buddhist discussion list. ✓**INTER-NET**→*email* zendo-request@lysator. lui.se ✍ *Write a request*

Hinduism

alt.hindu (ng) Moderately active discussion about Hinduism. ✓**USENET**

Islam

alt.religion.islam (ng) Islamic discussion. ✓**USENET**

#islam Live chat channel frequented mainly by Muslims. ✓**IN-TERNET**→*irc* /channel #islam

MSA-L (ml) Discussion list for members of the Moslem Student Association. ✓**INTERNET**→*email* listserv@psuvm.psu.bitnet ✍ *Type*

in message body: subscribe msa-l <your full name>

soc.religion.islam (ng) Active forum for Islamic discussion. ✓**USENET**

Sufism (ml) Discuss Sufism. ✓**IN-TERNET**→*email* majodomo@world. sdt.com ✍ *Type in message body:* subscribe sufism

Judaism

israel.bridges (ml/ng) Feminist Jews discuss religion. ✓**USENET** ✓**INTERNET**→*email* listserv@nysernet. org ✍ *Type in message body:* subscribe bridges <your full name>

Kesher_Halacha (echo) Discuss Jewish law from an Orthodox perspective. ✓check local bulletin board systems ✓**FIDONET**

Liberal-Judaism (ml) Judaic discussion from a liberal perspective. ✓**INTERNET**→*email* faigen@ aero.org ✍ *Write a request*

Torah-Talk (ml) Discussion of the Torah. Moderated by a Rabbi. ✓**INTERNET**→*email* listserv@jeru salem1.datadrv.co.il ✍ *Type in message body:* subscribe torah-talk <your full name>

Paganism

alt.religion.all-worlds (ng) Discuss the Church of All Worlds. ✓**USENET**

alt.religion.gnostic (ng) Forum for discussing issues related to gnosticism. ✓**USENET**

#pagan Live chat for pagans. ✓**INTERNET**→*irc* /channel #pagan

Pagan (echo) Discussion of all things pagan. ✓**RELAYNET**

Satanism

alt.satanism (ng) Say the outrageous—the more foul the better. ✓**USENET**

Shamanism

alt.religion.shamanism (ng) Discuss shamanism. At some sites, the group has been superseded by soc.religion.shamanism. ✓**USENET**

soc.religion.shamanism (ng) Discussion about shamanism. ✓**USENET**

Other

SSREL-L For the discussion of the social and scientific study of religion. ✓**INTERNET**→*email* listserv@ utkvm1.bitnet ✍ *Type in message body:* subscribe ssrel-l <your full name>

Buddhist monk—downloaded from America Online's Mac Graphics Forum.

more typical alt.zen debate was sparked by the question "Do our dogs perceive us as dogs or as people?" Zen here is often a pretext for silliness—"The Bodhisattva holds on to nothing but Prajnaparamita (Sanskrit for 'peanut butter sandwich')"—and can sometimes descend to the level of bad Generation X ad copy: e.g., "the unconditional acceptance of what is." One budding zippie thought it should "be mandatory to use acid a few times before considering Zen," because people who used LSD "made breakthroughs faster." Fortunately, someone else pointed out that people who used sledgehammers were just as speedy. Not limited to Zen, the newsgroup is sort of a San Francisco–style burrito of non-Western philosophies. ✓**USENET** DAILY

Buddhist These days, more and more celebrities are turning to Buddhism—Richard Gere, Courtney Love, Bernardo Bertolucci. That, along with the hundreds of millions of noncelebrity Buddhists, makes the religion a hot topic, and the WELL's wonderland conference attempts to explain this Eastern spiritual system by training its gaze on all things Buddhist. Topics range from practical matters—a bulletin board to list Buddhist activities in major cities—to more complex discussions on Buddhist dreams, Buddhist poetry, and Buddhism and sex. If you sometimes get your tantra and your sutra mixedup, this conference will help you clarify. ✓**WELL**→*g* wonder DAILY

soc.religion.bahai (ng) If you've ever been to Evanston, Illinois, you may have seen the Baha'i temple, looming like a vision just north of Northwestern University. As the Baha'i newsgroup explains, Baha'i is an oddly benign reli-

Muslim—downloaded from America Online's Graphics Forum.

gion—its theology insists upon the oneness of man, the oneness of religion, independent investigation of truth, religion as a source of unity, the evolutionary nature of religion, and the peaceful coexistence of science and religion. Despite this high level of tolerance, there are still interesting topics to discuss, such as the specifics of the Baha'i marriage ceremony, the aesthetics of Baha'i verse, and even the Baha'i stance on birth control ("The problem for a Baha'i is that the intrauterine device prevents fertilized eggs from implanting, and therefore if you interpret 'conception' to mean 'sperm and egg joining,' then use of the IUD prevents what may in the end be a large number of souls from passing through this world"). ✓**USENET** DAILY

soc.religion.eastern (ng) Since Toshi, the moderator, deters the unenlightened from posting, soc.religion.eastern is as donnish as an Oxford common room. Any scholar imprudent enough to equate Zarathushtra with Parashurama on this newsgroup can expect mild, politely worded aspersions. If you ask for a book on T'ai Chi, those in the know will chuckle and make the koanlike recommendation of a book on a

topic that cannot be understood by those who do not practice T'ai Chi. This is not the place to gush about *The Tao of Pooh*: Here they write poems to the dharmakaya, analyze each other's close readings of sloka 16 of the *Bhagavad-Gita*, and debate the extent of and limits to the authority of Panini, the Sanskrit grammarian. ✓**USENET** WEEKLY

Islam

Islam-L (ml) Islam-L is essentially two lists. About half the postings are very detailed debates over the interpretation of the Koran. To take part in these frequent dialogues one would have to be a well-trained religious scholar. The other half of the postings are of a more general nature, focusing on Islamic history and culture. One might be wary of voicing an opinion on a list with a religious component, but all posters are not Muslims, and those who are do not seem in any way bothered by frank debate about female circumcision, censorship in Arab countries, or how Islam can deal with contemporary issues like transsex-

> "Zen here is often a pretext for silliness—'The Bodhisattva holds on to nothing but Prajnaparamita (Sanskrit for "peanut butter sandwich")'"

ualism. ✓**INTERNET**→*email* listserv @ulkyvm. louisville.edu ✍ *Type in message body:* subscribe islam-l <your full name> WEEKLY

Judaism

CJ-L (ml) Conservative Judaism is the middle of the road on the great Jewish highway, not as rigid as Orthodox Judaism but more closely connected to the Orthodox tradition than the immensely popular Reform movement. Much of the Conservative Judaism mailing list treats specific religious issues— "[While] Jules wrote that poetry should be of relatively low priority in terms of translating prayers," says one woman, "I really do disagree. I simply cannot daven from the Silverman siddur because the language is so stiff. Esthetics must be a central concern." While complaints about the Silverman siddur may seem esoteric, the list also gestures toward larger social issues such as Zionism, kosher laws, immigration policy, and Jewish literature. ✓**INTERNET**→*email* listserv@ uacsc2.albany.edu ✍ *Type in message body:* subscribe cj-l <your full name> DAILY

Paganism

alt.pagan (ng) This newsgroup is the international gathering spot for tens of thousands of pagans, Wiccans, and goddess-worshipers. Participants are free to discuss anything that touches their lives, so the topics vary greatly. Ongoing threads include discussions of Magick, mythology, and the struggle for religious acceptance in a Christian society. Others reveal the problems of wearing a pentacle in public, or keeping a cat seated upon an altar during a ritual. ("Have you tried double-sided tape?") The newsgroup serves as a regional bulletin board, allowing

pagans to network with others in their vicinity. Expect dozens of new posts daily, as this is by far the most popular site on the Net for followers of earth-based religions. ✓**USENET** *FAQ:* ✓**INTERNET**→*ftp* rtfm.mit.edu→anonymous→<your email address>→/pub/usenet-by-hierarchy/alt/pagan→ALT. PAGAN_Frequently_Asked_Questions_(FAQ) DAILY

Paganism (ml) Amy writes "I am a solitary witch who is very into Tarot and herbalism." In Paganism, Amy encounters a large group dedicated to exercising their freedom of religion—making witches and pagans a welcome part of every community. Pagan mothers meet to discuss school-board issues and non-baptisms; others boycott a video chain because of its prohibition of pentagrams. These techno-age practitioners of ancient craft share ideas for a hypertext *Book of Shadows* and techniques for clearing your crystals. Very supportive—some busy witches post weekly notes addressing each member by name. Remember to keep your sleeves out of the sacrificial flame! ✓**INTERNET**→*email* uther+pagan-request@ drycas.club.cc.cmu.edu ✍ *Write a request* DAILY

#wicca They're a huggy bunch who hang out on the Wicca channel—just don't call them witches! Discussions are generally of a spiritual, Wiccan nature, but off-topic friendly chatter is welcome. ✓**INTERNET**→*irc* /channel #wicca

Scientology

alt.religion.scientology (ng) Scientology is, of course, the fever dream of the late ex–Navy man L. Ron Hubbard, and while opponents deride it as a spiritual farce that borders on being a cult, the

Scientology adherents on alt.religion.scientology insist that it's a legitimate religion, albeit one that exposes its own economic apparatus. While there's a small amount of conversation about the spirtual tenets of the religion, most of the newsgroup is devoted to either condemning or commending Hubbard for his avaricious vision. Did he really say, "The best way to make a million dollars is to start a religion"? ✓**USENET** DAILY

CYBERNOTES

"I just heard Dr. Joseph Stowell, President of Moody Bible Institute, give a message tonight, and he raised what I think is a more interesting question: 'Why did Jesus hang around for as long as He did (40 days) after the resurrection?' In other words, if at the resurrection, it was finished, why didn't He ascend immediately? Any comments?"

"Because the silly apostles finally had a clue about what had actually been going on for the last three years, and He had to give them time to get used to the idea. St. John, in both what he says and what he does not say, makes this abundantly clear."

—from **soc.religion. christian**

Veterans

War is hell...but was it always? Those who faced Hitler don't always see eye to eye with those who battled Ho Chi Minh. But in Cyberspace there are several virtual V.F.W. posts for reminiscing, debating, and support. Prodigy's **Veterans BB** has a very active lost-buddy locator service, putting units back together. RelayNet's **Veteran's Echo** is heavily populated with WWII vets reliving the glorious battles under Patton and Mac-Arthur. Less easygoing is FidoNet's **Vietnam Vets**, still as divisive as the war itself—full of flames and fury. What will happen when girls or gays hit the battlefield? Should we go to war against X,Y, or Z? For general chat check out soc.veterans, where vets from a range of wars add their two cents to policy discussion.

On the Net

Across the board

soc.veterans (ng) Amid the flood of newsletters from anti-imperialists and exposés of military atrocities (remember, this is Usenet), military men debate the pros and cons of service, reminisce, and search for old buddies. The quality of today's soldiers and military policy are ongoing discussions, and political talk is consis-

Norman Schwartzkopf—downloaded from Exec PC.

tently conservative. Not hyperactive by any means, the group blossoms when someone mentions the name of a military vessel, base, or other touchstone that members can relate to. ✓**USENET** WEEKLY

Veterans (echo) Starting a conversation is often as simple as mentioning where you were stationed during the war, whom you served under, or what job you held. "Allen, great to hear from a fellow 'water-cooled machine gunner.'" Everyone's a bit of a military historian, and following careers is a favorite pastime. Who knew General Cota? What was he like? "One who could get down in the dirt with the rest of the guys and slug it out." A VA representative participates in the conference, often helping members figure out what they're entitled to. But anyone who thinks the government owes them more, is critical of U.S. policy (not liking Clinton is fine), or belittles the efforts of soldiers in other wars or branches of service should prepare for some flak. The World War II crowd is here in

force. ✓**RELAYNET** DAILY

Veterans BB A World War II vet looks for the pal he last saw on the beach at Normandy. A Desert Storm pilot reminisces about how "great it felt to do some real damage." A depressed Vietnam vet listens to his online comrades' pleas to hang in there. The board can be lighthearted—sailors comparing "best liberty"—or it can be harrowing. Most of all, it enables people to make strong connections. "If you can't rap to another brother, who can you reach out to?" ✓**PRODIGY**→*jump* veterans bb→ Choose a Topic DAILY

Vets A service for those who have served. Discussions of news events, listings of reunions and tributes, passionate debates about more general topics: How well does the country treat its veterans? What are the best movies about war? What should be done about gays and lesbians in the military? ✓**WELL**→*g* vets DAILY

Vietnam veterans

Vietnam_Vets (echo) Anger and arguments heavily outweigh support. While vets often share painful memories—"Hope you weren't at Hamburger Hill, that one really sucked! Never saw so many dead good guys...still dream about it sometimes"—political debates here are passionate and can erupt into shouting matches that polarize the conference. Hillary's a Marxist. Slick Willie's leading us into another war we won't be able to get out of. The National Vietnam Veterans Association is selling out. There's a lot going on (including several internecine wars), so you may want to set up a twit filter to cut down on the noise. ✓**FIDONET** DAILY

Part 7

Support

Illness and disability

The sick and the dying, and their relatives, friends, and caregivers want to meet people too.

They have the same need (perhaps more of a need) to share thoughts and experiences and to meet other people with concerns like theirs as the well and unburdened. In the **Carcinoma** echo you'll find people cheering each other on through chemo. In the **CFS** echo you'll find a world without skepticism. In the AIDS support groups you can flirt as well as pick up the latest treatment tips. Prodigy's **Health BB** brings together an active group looking for holistic answers. In the real world you might feel alone; online you won't.

On the Net

Across the board

disABILITIES There's a dizzying array of support groups here, covering learning disabilities, blindness, deafness, physical disability, cerebral palsy, multiple sclerosis, mental health, and assistive technology. The popular topic of attention-deficit disorder rages through almost every one of them. AOLers confer on how to find work if you're housebound, how to wean yourself from your ventilator, and where to get legal advice to fight your child's school district. But unless you're combating someone over a hot issue—does pornography cause mental ill-

AIDS ribbon—downloaded from AOL's Mac Graphics & CAD Forum

ness?—you'll have a little trouble feeling connected; AOL is just too massive and diffuse. If you disappear, no one's going to notice. Read the "Online Chats, Self-Help Schedule" for dates and times of live discussions. Real-time sessions like "Endometriosis Self-Help," "Herpes Self-Help Group," and "Living With Cancer Self-Help Group" are regularly scheduled. ✓**AMERICA ONLINE** *keyword* →Disabilities Message Center *or* Equal Access Cafe DAILY

Health BB Take two tablets of blue-green algae and dial Prodigy in the morning. Although there are a doctor, dentist, and nutritionist online here to answer questions, most of the discussion ranges outside the medical establishment. Holistic-medicine practitioners suggest cures for impotence; the angry recipients of silicone breasts band together to fight back. John, a 36-year-old man considering liposuction to get rid of love handles, wonders if his torso will be an odd shape after the procedure. Steve replies yes—

watch out for lumps. There are folk remedies—raisins in rum for arthritis, cod-liver oil for sinus headaches, air-conditioning for sleeplessness. Plus there is sympathy from fellow sufferers—an outpouring of support for a young pregnant woman who experiences panic attacks from others with the same fears. Bodybuilders trade exercise routines and wannabe parents ask whether there is really any way to determine the sex of your baby. No question is too naive ("Can you be pregnant and get your period the first month?") or too off-the-wall ("What do those dreams of being naked in public mean?") to get an answer here. ✓**PRODIGY**→*jump* health bb→ Choose a Topic HOURLY

Medical Support BB Judy wrote on August 15 that she had been diagnosed with breast cancer that day. "I would like to hear from survivors. I am scared. I don't want to die." Many women responded with encouragement and advice about treatment programs. Two days later Judy decided to have a radical mastectomy. "I'm beginning to feel more HUMAN now…Thanks so much for writing." But Judy will likely not disappear from Medical Support— where concerned regulars keep track of each other's progress and psyche. Here you can be as scared, as angry, or as elated as you feel. These people know the side effects of the meds, they've told loved ones they have HIV, they've worried in the night about losing another eight-week pregnancy to miscarriage, they've confronted an abuser. Prodigy warns all who come to the board to seek expert advice—but that is not really what the board offers. It offers the real gift of no longer feeling alone. ✓**PRODIGY**→*jump* medical support bb→Choose a Topic HOURLY

AIDS

AIDS Though the traffic on this conference has diminished considerably in recent months, it remains a rich source of news and opinion on the dominant social issue of our generation. From transcriptions of Usenet AIDS postings to speculations on the origins of the disease, from personal anecdotes of AIDS sufferers in San Francisco to reactions to needle- distribution programs nationwide, almost 70 topics are covered; some, such as one that speculates on the link between HIV and AIDS, comprise more than 200 messages. And while HIV-positive participants are well represented, the population is very diverse—you're just as likely to find coming-to-terms-with-death postings from suburban parents as you are to find hard-core polemics from full-time activists. ✓**WELL**→*g* aids WEEKLY

AIDS_HIV and AIDS/ARC (echo) Members in both of these conferences regularly post news, debate government policies (especially concerning the FDA and White House), and turn to each other for advice about treatments, medication, and sex. Questions rarely go unanswered, and usually lead to personal stories. Someone asks for a book recommendation on living with a lover who has AIDS and soon he's telling the conference about his recent separation, opening up a conversation carried on in both conferences about emotional and sexual relationships with lovers who have AIDS. There are regulars from Eu-

rope and New Zealand, an RN named Linda in New York City who's offered to answer questions, a guy named Bobo Bear who's thinking of writing a play about AIDS, and others like Tall Paul and Mustang who write all the time. Reality checks are constant, with people dropping in to say that they've just tested positive, regulars posting about their T-cell counts or funeral plans, and occasionally even a post about a member who has died. ✓**FIDONET** WEEKLY

HIV/AIDS Share personal experiences with others who are living with HIV/AIDS and discuss new and alternative treatments along with safe-sex practices. There's a raging, often flaming, debate in the Does HIV Cause AIDS? folder. Need an uplift? Browse the Lighter Side of HIV, where members post Erma Bombeck–like anecdotes about the reality of living with HIV. Nothing, apparently, is too serious that it can't be laughed at. ✓**AMERICA ONLINE**→ *keyword* glcf→Message Boards→ HIV/AIDS Issues DAILY

HIV/AIDS Support Group Meeting every Sunday at 9 p.m., this moderated support group is held in a private room in order to provide a safe and confidential space where individuals may express themselves in an atmosphere of mutual respect, encouragement, and support. You must be HIV-positive, or at least say you are, to attend. All aspects of living and coping with the disease are discussed as well as medical information, current trials, disclosure problems, etc. The emphasis is on a positive attitude toward living the best life possible after diagnosis with HIV. Email MARTY HWRD confirming your HIV status and he will forward you a set of guidelines and the name of the

Private Room. ✓**AMERICA ONLINE**→ *keyword* glcf→Lambda Lounge→ Rooms→Private Room→HIV/AIDS Support Group

Living with AIDS In addition to regular CDC bulletins and information on AIDS drugs, treatments, and policy, the forum is home to a knowledgeable community. If you ask, they'll explain the byzantine world of immunology, parsing CD4s and CD8s from CD3s, or point you toward other resources (*Poz* magazine's email address, for instance: pozmag@ aol.com). At least one forum member was logged on from his hospital's intensive-care unit, from where he launched a lively thread opposing crucifix decor. If your doctor wants you to quit your job and go on disability in order to pay for a prophylactic drug regimen, this would be a good place to discuss it, and flirt a little while you're at it. ✓**COMPUSERVE**→*go* aids→Messages *or* Conferences HOURLY

Diabetes

Diabetes (echo) People come

> "At least one forum member was logged on from his hospital's intensive-care unit, from where he launched a lively thread opposing crucifix decor."

here to vent about the chocolate bar they can no longer eat, the depression that sometimes overcomes them, and the related ailments that plague them. Discussion jumps from griping about health insurance to verifying rumors—"Who invented Humulin? Some people at our temple say that it is an Indian man, who sometimes comes here"—to welcoming back a member of the conference who just suffered a stroke. ✓**FIDONET** DAILY

Diabetes Forum At times, the shoptalk about insulin sounds like it's coming from a jazz critic admiring an inspired riff: 70/30 premix "crests and rides unevenly," but Lilly Humulin Nph is "smooth." Come here to commiserate with other people who injected their insulin while it was still cold (ouch) or whose irritable spouses won't stick to their regimen. Compare your regimen with others', and find out if your doctor is skimping on injection frequency at a cost to your health. This tight-knit but welcoming band is also quick to veer off-topic and reminisce about Sperry UNIVACs, earthquakes, and life among the Apache. ✓**COMPUSERVE**→*go* diabetes→Messages *or* Conferences HOURLY

Hearing-impaired

bit.listserv.deaf.l (ml/ng) Pertaining to any and all aspects of deafness and deaf culture, this group is populated by friendly deaf, hearing, and hearing-impaired people. A majority of the posts come from Gallaudet University (the world's only deaf liberal-arts university) and other deaf academic programs. Most of the hearing people have friends, family, or co-workers who are deaf. Topics range from simple requests

> "William posts a message asking whether someone would be willing to write to his mother, who has just finished chemotherapy."

or announcements (specialized software, job information, social events) to lengthy and heated debates on issues that affect the deaf (cochlear implants, ASL vs. oralism, deaf existence in a hearing world). New users are welcomed cordially. ✓**USENET** ✓**INTERNET**→ *email* listserv@siucvmb.bitnet ✍ *Type in message body:* subscribe deaf-l <your full name> DAILY

Silent_Talk (echo) The latest telephone technology for the hearing-impaired, movie captions in the cinemas, deaf musicians (music in general is a big topic with those not completely deaf), sign language, careers, and a host of other topics are discussed here. Members get to know each other through their interests—a deaf-ed student seeks out another deaf-ed student; musicians chat back and forth. A few members are both deaf and blind. ✓**FIDONET** WEEKLY

Other illnesses

ADHD (echo) Attention-deficit disorders have recently received a lot of attention (a *Time* magazine cover story, for instance), but many of the members of this group have been struggling with the disorder or with family mem-

bers and friends who have the disorder for a long time and they've done so without a lot of understanding. Together conference members have passed along information, compared insurance coverages and treatment plans, fumed over the government's failure to classify the disorder as a disability, and chatted as they tried to cope.

Bonnie, a 35-year-old divorced mother of two, had been lurking on and off in the conference for years before she introduced herself. Both of her children have the disorder, as does her "significant other," Scott. In her introduction, she described the long road to diagnosis and treatment of her oldest daughter, Heather ("Last Sunday, we celebrated a year at home with no hospitalizations. Heather and I are both very proud of ourselves"), her shame at not recognizing it in her younger son, and the relationships she now has with her children and Scott. "I am going to leave the discussion of Scott to him. I think that he will also be joining us here shortly." ✓**FIDONET** DAILY

C-Palsy (ml) The people with cerebral palsy on this mailing list are pragmatic and curious about their disease, and proud of how they have adapted to it so far. A man who remembers that he moved more freely after childhood boat rides is now a doctor studying the effect of vestibular stimulation on muscle spasms. A librarian details the exercise regimen she has found helpful. Parents recommend the software and keyboards that have worked for their children. Everyone shares theories and experiences in a spirit that mixes scientific inquiry and well-deserved boasting. ✓**INTERNET**→*email* listserv@sjuvm.stjohns.edu ✍ *Type in message body:* subscribe c-palsy

Illness and disability Support

<your full name> DAILY

Carcinoma (echo) William posts a message asking whether someone would be willing to write to his mother, who has just finished chemotherapy for ovarian cancer. Paula, with the same type of cancer, promises to get a letter out that weekend. People don't hold back in this conference. While details about tumor sizes, pain, and related ailments are common, so are the stories of triumph—"Had a barbecue at the park to celebrate my first year of surviving cancer."

Day in and day out people check in to talk about their treatments: "I want it done and finished. Then I'll only see the doctor every three months...geez, I just won't know how to behave!" writes Lydia. "Still waving my flag for your finish of all those treatments!!!!...I'm standing right here...are you ready for a HUG yet?",responds Mary, who with her son runs the conference. Religion is often part of the discussion here, especially since Mary appears to be a very religious person, but the group is by no means preachy. ✓**FIDONET** WEEKLY

CFS (echo) "I don't think a person

> ## "Questions like 'Why do I have CF?' and 'Why doesn't my sister have it?' tear at my soul. Does anyone out there have a good answer for a 5-year-old?"

without CFIDS or some other chronic, debilitating illness will ever be able to understand just how much pride and enjoyment we take from being able to do simple things that they take for granted." If ever there was an "I know how you feel" conference, it's this one. No skepticism and lots of empathy here for people suffering from chronic fatigue syndrome, a disease that drains people of energy and is not always acknowledged as being a real physiological illness. Always cold—freezing, in fact? "Yes. I know exactly what you mean about the cold." Can't finish what you need to get done, or even what you want to do? "It's time to do the vacuuming the next time I have some energy." Discussion is split among comparing symptoms, voicing resentment against the medical establishment, and sharing advice and encouragement. It's a comfortable environment to vent frustrations and fears—no need to answer "Fine, thank you" when someone here asks how you're feeling. ✓**FIDONET** DAILY

Chronic_Pain (echo) People here understand what it's like to live every day with pain, often without any hope that the pain will pass. New pain medications as well as names of doctors and clinics are always being recommended on this group, but members are here less for referrals than for the company. They've formed a small community where talking about bad days, describing the pain, and letting people know what the doctor said doesn't brand you as a "chronic complainer" or a burden. ✓**FIDONET** DAILY

Cystic-L (ml) Ross writes, "Questions like 'Why do I have CF?' and 'Why doesn't my sister have it?' tear at my soul. Does anyone out

CYBERNOTES

"We actually have six senses!! Smell, Taste, Feel, See, 'Sense of Humor,' AND 'Special-Effect See' (we usually spot things that hearies would have overlooked!!)."

"Yeah, I noticed that Hearies don't have that sense. For example, when I went out to eat lunch with Deaf friends, I found an empty table in a crowded place, and sat down waiting for the other Deafies to come around. I had no problem catching their attention in less than a few seconds by simply waving one hand, even though they were very far away. Once I went out with Hearies, and I practically jumped up and down waving both hands forever like crazy to catch Hearies' attention, even though they were only a few feet away! I even screamed with my Deaf voice. Not working. Oh well... I start to wonder what kind of senses the Hearie has???"

—from **Deaf-L**

there have a good answer for a 5-year-old?" Cystic-L brings together parents, spouses, researchers, and cystic fibrosis sufferers, from South

Africa to France, for support and information exchange. This is a warm and encouraging environment. Here frightened new parents get advice from old pros, who can joke about "beating the snot" out of their kids. A 31-year-old survivor exchanges insurance advice with a 63-year-old, while a Gen Xer is thankful for baggy clothes that hide her back brace. There is detailed exchange of treatment information. ✓**INTERNET** →*email* listserv@yalevm.cis.yale. edu ✍ *Type in message body:* subscribe cystic-l <your full name>

Disabled (echo) Conversations get intensely personal, almost as if people were sharing secrets—the breakups of marriages have been chronicled here. Often messages will call out to a specific reader asking about "your situation." How's your father doing? Have you left the house lately? Unlike some support groups, personal rather than medical issues dominate the discussion. Messages often lead to telephone calls or face-to-face meetings. Kathi, who has multiple sclerosis, is one of the group's most active posters. In one "Dear Kathi" message a 46-year-old grandfather who also has multiple sclerosis and is on active duty in the Navy as a chaplain began by telling her how important it was to him to get one last promotion before retiring. Soon he was sharing his experience in dealing with his diagnosis and encouraging Kathi to contact her local MS Society. ✓**RELAYNET** DAILY

Down-Syn (ml) A father has heard through the grapevine that removing a child's adenoids and tonsils may make it easier for him to chew his food. Does anyone's experience confirm this? One parent says yes; another's experience refutes it. A therapist outlines her

> "I feel like the whole world is caving in around me. I am trying to live day by day but each day, it seems another piece crumbles."

theory that difficulty with food chewing is related to the trouble Down's syndrome children have in processing textures. Two-texture foods like tapioca are harder to manage than one-texture foods like applesauce. Yet another parent writes up a questionnaire on the topic, so they can pool their experiences more systematically, and responses pour in. Down-Syn members are enterprising and well informed. Emotions here are more subdued and even-keeled than on most support groups; the support members give each other is practical and polite. ✓**INTERNET** →*email* listserv@ndsu vm1.bitnet ✍ *Type in message body:* subscribe down-syn <your full name> DAILY

Parkinsn (ml) The Parkinsn list is not just for those suffering from this debilitating disease but for care givers and others concerned with treatment and progress in the field. Members here gather for support and action, including lobbying Congress for increased research funding. This is also a place to make connections with others fighting the same battles. When a firefighter from Canada with Parkinson's staged a 48-hour pole-sit to publicize the disease, the list helped to spread the news and brought international support from members. ✓**INTERNET**→*email*

listserv@vm.utcc.utoronto.ca ✍ *Type in message body:* subscribe parkinsn <your full name> WEEKLY

Stress_Mgmt (echo) While stress-prevention techniques—from meditation to diet—are perhaps the most common topic of discussion, members also turn to each other when they're feeling overwhelmed. "I feel like the whole world is caving in around me. I am trying to live day by day, but each day it seems another piece crumbles," writes Nancy to Joanna. A diverse bunch of people hang out here: the discussion moderator is a 52-year-old who rides motorcycles; there's a 22-year-old worried about gray hair, a 24-year-old worrying about what he's going to do with his life, a Vietnam vet looking for help with post-traumatic stress disorder, and a 50-year-old woman exploring Zen Buddhism for stress prevention. ✓**FIDONET** WEEKLY

Witsendo (ml) A young woman faces an agonizing decision; get pregnant right away, have a hysterectomy, or continue to suffer with a painful disease. She turns for advice here. WITSENDO (Endometriosis Treatment and Support) is an active support and discussion group. Since the causes of endometriosis are not fully known, WITSENDO provides much vital information on possible causes as well as treatments. "Hazardous Waste News" makes a frequent appearance, with advice for avoiding suspect substances like dioxin. There are often recent medical papers placed on line, followed by discussion by both sufferers and the several MDs on the list who provide advice and medical contacts. ✓**INTERNET**→*email* list serv@dartcms1.dartmouth.edu ✍ *Type in message body:* subscribe wit sendo <your full name> DAILY

Electronic therapy

Feeling glum? Having trouble dealing with co-workers? Experiencing flare-ups of sexual

anxiety with your second husband? Chances are, you're not alone. Therapy groups range from bona fide cybercommunities—AOL's RecoveryLink—to quirky newsgroups, such as **alt.support.shyness**. What results is an endearing network of analytic relationships. Jan, who overcame her agoraphobia during graduate school, can pass along the fruits of her wisdom to Edith, and the sexually abused Paul can share his story with the abusive Don. Everything's covered, from drugs to alcohol to gambling, from paranoia to anhedonia. In fact, the only problem that's not discussed with an almost embarrassing candor is Net addiction.

On the Net

Across the board

Homelife BB Imagine *Better Homes and Gardens* meets Dear Abby with a good dose of real trauma thrown in. I guess everyone knows that "home" is not a Norman Rockwell painting all the time, and this board shows it. Homelife is a mixed bag of topics—Home Repair, Domestic Violence, Gardening, and Single Parenting. Here a confused wife wonders if her husband's mid-life crisis

Sigmund Freud—downloaded from CompuServe's Archive Forum.

will go beyond a red Camaro. A former husband cautions against an affair; a former wife advises self-respect. A dad responds with gentle wisdom to a teen's post "I Hate My Dad," thinking his own daughter might have written it.

Sanctuary

Domestic-violence tales routinely receive home addresses to ensure sanctuary. But Homelife can also be funny. Amateur Erma Bombecks, for instance, unite in "Life Abhors a Vacuum." Homelife also fosters new relationships—a message in the Single Parents topic boasts a wedding announcement—an online *Brady Bunch* courtesy this BB. ✓**PRODIGY**→*jump* homelife bb→ Choose a Topic HOURLY

Psychotherapy

I'll tell you the truth: I'm having some trouble in my life. It seems I have this prob-

lem that I can't get past. It's like a weight on my head. I've tried everything—talking to friends, throwing myself into my work, embarking on a series of pointless affairs—but nothing seems to help. Therapy? Well, no. I don't really believe in therapy. Electronic therapy? Now I'm especially suspicious; who wants to get shrunk online? Yes, I know that the WELL's therapy conference covers a wide variety of topics, including couples counseling, cross-cultural therapy, abuse of power by therapists, even the Buddhist stance on psychotherapy. And I know that the only way to get better is to begin by helping myself. Well, we'll see. Thanks for the recommendation. To tell you the truth, I feel much better. Bill me. ✓**WELL**→ *g* therapy DAILY

Anxiety/Depression

alt.support.depression (ng) According to a recent, informal survey, most readers of alt.support.depression dread sunny days. When one group member disagreed and called it "crazy" to prefer rain, she was gently upbraided for her word choice.

There's a strong sense of community here. Flaming is frowned upon and rare. Despite the occasional undergraduate prankster, it feels like a safe place to admit you're sad or at wits' end, and many people do.

Newbies learn that their symptoms aren't unusual (a veteran reassured a man confused by his mood swings that depression and anxiety "go together like cream cheese and a bagel"), while old hands compare the merits and side effects of Zoloft, Prozac, and lithium. ✓**USENET** *FAQ:* ✓**INTERNET**→*ftp* rtfm.mit.edu→anonymous→<your email address>→/pub/usenet-by-group/alt.support.depression HOURLY

Anxiety (echo) With some members skeptical of medication and others desperate for any release that drugs can provide from panic attacks and anxiety, the talk about medication is what bonds people here—talk is along the lines of "currently taking Zoloft"; "recently took me off of Prozac for my depression, and started me on Effexor"; "currently on Klonopin (Rivotril)."

Men and woman of all ages (although you'll find a lot of teens and twentysomethings here) write in with their fears—being dependent on medication, being taken off medication, being on the wrong medication. But, there are also messages about therapy, the shame of being ill, and the moments of anxiety themselves. ✓**FIDONET** WEEKLY

Walkers in Darkness (ml) The Walkers in Darkness, aka the Bearers of Light, are people helping each other cope with depression. They keep tabs on each other and often respond quickly and energetically to calls for help. When, for example, a woman despaired that she had become the "black sheep" of the Walkers, just as she had in other social groups, "electronic hugs" flooded in.

Off the beaten path

As a mailing list rather than a newsgroup, the Walkers are a little off the beaten path; the group therefore has a more intimate feel than alt.support.depression and is safer from pranksters. A good list for people who have not yet come to terms with depression. ✓**INTER-**

> **"Like the member who reported having eaten six Monterey Jack Chicken Soft Taco Supremes, you'll get consoling pats on the back and help figuring out what happened."**

NET→*email* majordomo@world.std. com ✍ *Type in message body:* subscribe walkers DAILY

Dieting

alt.support.diet (ng) Can't remember which is the "good" cholesterol and which is the "bad" one? On alt.support.diet, they'll give you the answer, and throw in a few calorie-reducing tips: Sniffing peppermint oil will fool your brain into thinking you've already eaten. Floss and brush in early evening to avoid nighttime munchies. Newsgroup members enjoy critiquing and comparison-shopping for weight-loss programs. (Women who had paid to eat Jenny Craig's specially prepared food had little good to say about it.) Come here for your Taco Bell postmortems, and like the member who reported having eaten six Monterey Jack Chicken Soft Taco Supremes, you'll get consoling pats on the back and help figuring out what happened. ✓**USENET** *FAQ:* ✓**INTERNET**→*ftp* rtfm.mit.edu→anonymous→<your email address>→/pub/usenet-by-

group/news.answers/dieting-faq→part1 *and* part2 *and* part3 HOURLY

Diet (ml) Oddly, food and weight loss are almost never mentioned on this mailing list; instead, young mothers swap child-rearing tales and videos of Barney. You're more likely to find a recipe for homemade Play-doh here than for low-fat brownies. There's a lot of small-town small talk—when Alice's husband cleaned out her closet without consulting her, everyone sent condolences—but the support seems real. Group members visit each other when they go traveling; if someone is in trouble, friends will ask the group to send supporting email and to remember her in their prayers. ✓**INTERNET**→ *email* listserv@ubvm.cc.buffalo.edu ✍ *Type in message body:* subscribe diet <your full name> DAILY

Shyness

alt.support.shyness (ng) "I asked her out," a young man writes, "—now what?" Many posters on alt.support.shyness are unsure how to approach the opposite sex, and their anguish, though genuine, has a kind of 1950ish charm. It's like Wally all nervous because he wants to ask the homecoming queen to the prom. Although most of the advice is the earnest and practical sort that Wally would get from the Beaver or his parents, Eddie Haskell also has a few things to say. I'd be wary, for instance, of the intentions of the author who posted "Shy Married Ladies Look Here." Spoofers are also common but can easily be spotted by their hostile garrulousness. For the shy person with a level head. ✓**USENET** DAILY

INTP (ml) "This list is for sharing information and experiences between persons who are rated as INTP (Introverted iNtuitive Thinking Perceivers) on the Myers-Briggs Temperament Index."

There are 30–50 messages a day on this list—INTP does not mean shy. The regulars are interested in dissecting how their introversion and intuition affect them in every day life—making them withdraw during crises, for example. Discussing these emotional states seems to make them easier to deal with. These are not unhappy people but sensitive ones, and they're glad to recognize themselves in others. A shared "rating" has led to friendships, and much time is spent just joking or sharing thoughts. ✓**INTERNET**→*email* listserv@satelnet.org ✍ *Type in message body:* subscribe intp <your full name> DAILY

Complaining

alt.bitterness (ng) Miserable is an understatement. Some people, a vast majority of them Generation Xers, drop by the group to complain when things go wrong; others, like Piglet, are always here—finding pain, anguish, and unrealized expectations at every turn. It's a bonding process of sorts. So your life sucks too? Still living at home? Girlfriend deserted you? Probably going to get fired? I totally understand. Still not done complaining? Drop by alt.whine. ✓**USENET** WEEKLY

12 Steps

alt.recovery (ng) There's a Jesuitic tone among the alcoholics, addicts, and overeaters who discuss the process of recovery here. Are you still sober if you eat food cooked in alcohol? The debates are for the most part even-tempered and seldom lead to confrontation and flames. ✓**USENET** DAILY

RecoverNet The network has bursts of activity and painful lulls. The Alcoholics Anonymous and Narcotics Anonymous conferences consistently draw the most traffic. Other conferences include CoDependency, 12step, Over Eaters Anonymous, Sober Sex, Fun, Youth Recovery, Grateful Recovery, Meditation, Alanon, and Survivors. People travel between the groups, making the network seem almost like one extended conference. Members contribute to several conferences at once. While the RecoverNet discussions tend to be more freewheeling and less focused than other recovery discussions, members are still quick to respond to any call for help. LifeLine BBS (310-823-6686) is the main hub. ✓check local bulletin board systems WEEKLY

Recovery (echo) Don't look for philosophical discussions or poetic writing; people are here to write about their temptations and depressions. "It's wonderful to finally talk to people who know exactly what I'm going through, my demon temptations and internal battles with them." Family members of alcoholics and addicts also find relief in the conference. "At times I am not even sure if my problem is serious enough to post but I do have the need to talk myself out," writes a mother with a teenage son addicted to drugs. ✓**FIDONET** DAILY

Recovery (echo) Almost everyone here is participating in a 12-step program. Most are recovering alcoholics sharing the success of their sobriety ("5 years old today") or the fear of falling off the wagon ("I am in need to write and write and write, so that I don't drink"). Diverse participants in the group include a prep-school-educated writer and a self-proclaimed "dude" from the 'hood. ✓**RELAYNET** WEEKLY

Recovery Link Devoted to "people in 12-step and other programs who are recovering from various addictions," AOL's Recovery Link encourages its addicts and ex-addicts (mainly alcoholics, although there are a few drug users and the occasional rageaholic) to gain control over their experiences, to make meaning by making narrative.

This tactic results in good talk—long stories about that first needle in the vein, or the Lost Weekend, how "I used to go on benders, and I didn't know that the Friday-afternoon drinks I was sneaking at the office at five of 5 weren't just ways of guaranteeing that I would have a good time that night." Like most behaviors that are both seductive and self-destructive, addiction is equivocal—while tales from the front have a morbid magnetism, it's not always productive to have the Voice of Experience regale you with an anecdote about the last time he fell off the wagon. ✓**AMERICA ONLINE**→*keyword* people→Rooms→Recovery Link

#12step Promptly at 8 p.m. on Sunday evenings, people start fil-

> "'Hi, I'm new,' types Dick. 'I came to this meeting last Sunday and fought over whether to pick up the beer at my feet...'"

ing in, greeting each other, and settling down. John checks in from his vacation at the Cape; Jesse sends greetings from Atlanta; members from across the country welcome each other. The chair (chosen at the end of last week's meeting) sends private greetings to newbies, announces the rules (don't "crosstalk"—i.e., interrupt someone who's speaking), and calls for someone to begin.

"I'm an alcoholic"

Immediately, the hands go up (people type an "!") and someone is called upon. "Hi, my name is Jesse and I'm an alcoholic." This is a real AA meeting. "Hi, I'm new," types Dick. "I came to this meeting last Sunday and fought over whether to pick up the beer at my feet..." For an hour or so, alcoholics and other addicts tell their stories, talk about their progress and weaknesses, and get instant feedback and support. Meetings are announced on the newsgroup alt.recovery. ✓**INTERNET** →*irc* /channel #12step

12_Steps (echo) Most members are in the early stages of recovery programs—their problems and questions lead the discussion. Don, for instance, asks the group about his attraction to women in his program. Steve confesses that he only became involved in a recovery program because of a court order. Members flood the conference with messages to Steve, sending encouragement and personal stories of triumph. "Hi Steve! Ya need to talk? Talk to me!...I have been sober 16 years," wrote one member to Steve. "Perhaps up till now you haven't been able to be sober for long," another member counsels Steve, "but for me today, thanks to God and you folks, words like *can't* are disappearing from my

vocabulary." ✓**FIDONET** DAILY

Codependency

alt.recovery.codependency (ng) Whether it's a son declaring he no longer wants or needs to be friends with his unloving father or a girlfriend fearing that she's projecting the problems of past relationships onto her present involvement, members eloquently share their codependency struggles. A core group of members talk each other through their insecurities, fears and needs on a daily basis. Newcomers should introduce themselves before jumping into the discussion. Support, not criticism, is the rule of the group. ✓**USENET** DAILY

Smoking

alt.support.stop-smoking (ng) You smoked a pack a day for 20 years, you quit on Monday, and this morning you chewed your 2-year-old daughter's head off for dropping her breakfast cereal on the floor. Is quitting worth it? Will you stick to your resolve? The other quitters here will understand your nicotine-deprived rage, congratulate you on each smoke-free day, and see through your rationalizations. Yes, taking a drag of your friend's cigarette does count. You'll also get a sustaining fix of tobacco-company paranoia and advice on how to avoid situations where you might relapse (recommended: moving to California). There's not too much continuity here; people quit or they don't, and in either case, they move on. But the conversion narratives are inspiring—one man lost his craving for cigarettes when a vision of his future came to him in an incense-filled church in Chiapas, among the highland Maya. ✓**USENET** DAILY

Appendices

Netted!

A selection of the smartest, steamiest, funniest, and most obnoxious chat in Cyberspace

Absolutely Do Not Miss

alt.fan.oj-simpson (ng) ✓**USE-NET** HOURLY

#bdsm ✓**INTERNET**→*irc* /channel #bdsm *or* /channel #bondage

FurryMUCK ✓**INTERNET**→*telnet* sncils.snc.edu 8888→connect guest guest

The Gay Member Rooms on AOL ✓**AMERICA ONLINE**→*keyword* people→Rooms→Available Rooms →Member Rooms

MediaMOO ✓**INTERNET**→*telnet* purple-crayon.media.mit.edu 8888 →connect Guest

rec.arts.tv.soaps (ng) ✓**USENET** *FAQ:* ✓**INTERNET**→*ftp* rtfm.mit. edu→anonymous→<your email address>→/pub/usenet-by-group/ rec.arts.tv.soaps DAILY

Most Loquacious

Allmusic (ml) ✓**INTERNET**→*email* listserv@american.edu ✍ *Type in message body:* subscribe allmusic <your full name> HOURLY

rec.arts.movies (ng) ✓**USENET** *FAQ:* ✓**INTERNET**→*ftp* rtfm.mit.edu

→anonymous→<your email address>→/pub/usenet-by-group/ rec.arts.movies HOURLY

Sappho (ml) ✓**INTERNET**→*email* sappho-request@mc.lcs.mit.edu ✍ *Write a request* HOURLY

SF-Lovers (ml) ✓**INTERNET**→*email* sf-lovers-request@rutgers.edu ✍ *Write a request Archives:* ✓**INTERNET**→*ftp* elbereth.rutgers.edu→ anonymous→<your email address> →/pub/sfl DAILY

Best Sense of Humor

alt.fan.pratchett (ng) ✓**USENET** DAILY

alt.alien.visitors (ng) ✓**USENET** HOURLY

Start Your Morning With...

alt.fan.howard-stern (ng) ✓**USENET** *FAQ:* ✓**INTERNET**→*ftp* rtfm.mit.edu→anonymous→<your email address>→/pub/usenet-by-group/alt.answers/howard-stern→faq DAILY

Finish Your Day With...

alt.fan.letterman (ng) ✓**USENET** *FAQ:* ✓**INTERNET**→*ftp* rtfm.mit.

edu→anonymous→<your email address>→/pub/usenet-by-hierar chy/alt/fan/letterman→alt.fan.let terman_Frequently_Asked_Ques tions_(read_before_posting) DAILY

Best Places to Meet Someone

Gen-X (ml) ✓**INTERNET**→*email* list proc@phantom.com ✍ *Type in message body:* subscribe gen-x <your full name> HOURLY

Human Sexuality Forums ✓**COMPUSERVE**→*go* human→Mes-sages *or* Conferences DAILY/LIVE

People Connection ✓**AMERICA ONLINE**→*keyword* people

Best Places to Flirt

alt.romance/alt.romance. chat (ng) ✓**USENET** *FAQ:* ✓**INTER-NET**→ *ftp* rtfm.mit.edu→anonymous →<your email address>→/pub/ usenet-by-group/news.answers/ romance-faq→part* DAILY

Foothills ✓**INTERNET**→*telnet* mar-ble.bu.edu 2010→<your handle>→ <y or n>→<your gender>→continue

#sex ✓**INTERNET**→*irc* /channel #sex

Netted

Raunchiest

Cunt ✓**ADULTLINKS** DAILY

OrgyRoom ✓**ADULTLINKS** DAILY

Sex-L (ml) ✓**INTERNET**→*email* list serv@tamvm1.tamu.edu ✍ *Type in message body:* subscribe sex-l <your full name> DAILY

Ben's Favorite Sex Group

alt.sex.voyeurism (ng) ✓**USE-NET** DAILY

°Most Gender-bending

AnimeMUCK ✓**INTERNET**→*telnet* tcp.com 2035→connect guest guest

FurryMUCK ✓**INTERNET**→*telnet* sncils.snc.edu 8888→connect guest guest

Human Sexuality Forums ✓**COMPUSERVE**→*go* human→Messages *or* Conferences DAILY/LIVE

Smartest Talk

Mozart (echo) ✓**ILINK** DAILY

soc.culture.african.american (ng) ✓**USENET** DAILY

soc.culture.asian.american (ng) ✓**USENET** *FAQ:* ✓**INTERNET**→*ftp* rtfm.mit.edu→anonymous→<your email address>→/pub/usenet-by-group/soc.culture.asian.american→FAQ_for_soc.culture.asian.american DAILY

soc.culture.indian* (ng) ✓**USE-NET** *FAQ:* ✓**INTERNET**→*ftp* rtfm.mit.edu→anonymous→<your email address>→/pub/usenet-by-group/soc.culture.indian→[soc.culture.indian]_FREQUENTLY_ASKED_QUESTIONS HOURLY

Victoria (ml) ✓**INTERNET**→*email* listserv@ubvm.usc.indiana.edu ✍ *Type in message body:* subscribe victoria <your full name> HOURLY

Dumbest Talk

alt.revisionism (ng) ✓**USENET** DAILY

#bored ✓**INTERNET**→*irc* /channel #bored

soc.men (ng) ✓**USENET** HOURLY

Hottest Flame Wars

alt.abortion.inequity (ng) ✓**USENET** DAILY

talk.politics.guns (ng) ✓**USENET** HOURLY

Hippest Fans

alt.music.alternative.female (ng) ✓**USENET** DAILY

alt.tv.real-world (ng) ✓**USENET** DAILY

Weirdest

alt.devilbunnies (ng) ✓**USENET** *FAQ:* ✓**INTERNET**→*ftp* rtfm.mit.edu→anonymous→<your email address>→/pub/usenet-by-group/alt.answers/devilbunnies-faq→part1 *and* part2 DAILY

alt.fan.oj-simpson (ng) ✓**USE-NET** HOURLY

Most Obsessive

Encounters Forum ✓**COM-PUSERVE**→*go* encounters→Messages DAILY

rec.arts.anime* (ng) ✓**USENET** *FAQ:* ✓**INTERNET**→*ftp* rtfm.mit.edu→anonymous→<your email address>→/pub/usenet-by-group/ rec.arts.

anime HOURLY

Most Sensitive Members

Mail-Men (ml) ✓**INTERNET**→*email* mail-men-request@summit.novell.com ✍ *Write a request* HOURLY

Are These People Serious?

tlhIn gan-Hol (ml) Klingon Language List. ✓**INTERNET**→*email* tlhIn-gan-Hol-request@klingon.east.sun.com) ✍ *Type in subject line:* subscribe DAILY

Be Careful Of...

#teensex ✓**INTERNET**→*irc* /channel #teensex

In the Worst Taste

alt.sex.cthulhu (ng) ✓**USENET** WEEKLY

alt.sex.fetish.orientals (ng) ✓**USENET** DAILY

Most Exclusive

AAGPSO (ml) ✓**INTERNET**→*email* (by invitation only) DAILY

Human Sexuality Forums ✓**COMPUSERVE**→*go* human→Messages *or* Conferences DAILY/LIVE

Most Pretentious

MediaMOO ✓**INTERNET**→*telnet* purple-crayon.media.mit.edu 8888→connect Guest

DeepSeas ✓**INTERNET**→*telnet* muds.okstate.edu 6250→connect guest guest

Most In-Your-Face

alt.aol-sucks (ng) ✓**USENET** DAILY

Most Like *Cheers*

alt.callahans and #callahans (ng) √**USENET** √**INTERNET**→*irc* /channel #callahans *FAQ:* √**INTERNET**→*ftp* physics.su.oz.au→anonymous→<your email address>→ /mar/callahans HOURLY/LIVE

#cheers √**INTERNET**→*irc* /channel #cheers

Kelly's Favorite

alt.usenet.kooks (ng) √**USENET** DAILY

Most Like Real Life

Homelife BB √**PRODIGY**→*jump* homelife bb→Choose a Topic HOURLY

Most Women

PernMUSH √**INTERNET**→*telnet* cesium.clock.org 4201→create <your character's name> <your password> *FAQ:* √**INTERNET**→*ftp* rtfm.mit.edu→anonymous→<your email address>→/pub/usenet-by-group/alt.fan.pern/→Welcome*

RRA-L (Romance Readers Anonymous) (ml/ng) √**INTERNET** →*email* listserv@ kentvm.kent.edu ✍ *Type in message body:* subscribe rra-l <your full name> √**USENET**→ bit.listserv.rra-l DAILY

Neatest Spin on Chat

#12step √**INTERNET**→*irc* /channel #12step

Top TV Talk

alt.tv.nypd-blue (ng) √**USENET** DAILY

Court TV √**AMERICA ONLINE**→*keyword* court tv→Message Board WEEKLY

Nathaniel's Favorite Music Site

Beastie List (ml) √**INTERNET**→ *email* majordomo@ world.std.com ✍ *Type in message body:* subscribe beastielist DAILY

Adult boards

by area code

201

Bytes 'n Bits
437-4355
Evergreen
398-2373

203

Adults 'R' Us
583-0715
Chronicles BBS
445-0607
Jump Start BBS
735-5357

205

The Corral BBS
852-8127
Shadoevision Cbis
306-0486
Southern Stallion
322-3816

206

Bangkok Express
838-7908
Merlins Castle
377-5950
Raptor Zoo
522-4873
Scheherazade BBS
371-7219

207

Swamplands BBS
457-2273

209

The Outhouse BBS
634-5395

210

Necronomicon
675-4787
X-Factor
648-3874

212

Fpx2
627-0531
Molecular Beam
873-3559

213

Mr Wonderful's Lair
261-8055
A_p_a_p BBS
296-1151
Blues Cafe
638-1186
Night Lights BBS
480-8170
Technoid's Toybox
226-6017

215

Anterra Network
675-3851
DSC/Voicenet
443-7390
The Hotline BBS
393-8594
The Keep BBS
855-0401
The Motherboard
295-2625
Newton Express
860-9724
Night Wind
497-3912
Prince Of Porn
272-5799
Quantum Leap
536-8823

The Storm Front BBS
788-4339
Swingers Connection
727-8409
Twelfth Step
657-4870

216

Bottom's Up Spanking
961-1921
The Dragon's Lair
671-0850
Paradox Online BBS
686-7900
Swingles
749-1020

217

2/3 Board
877-1138
The Backdoor BBS
762-8349

219

Michiana Online
873-0994
The Rock Pile BBS
288-8950

301

The Alternative BBS
864-5292
The Jellicle Cat
779-5946
Network East
738-0000
Taesar's Palace
417-6952
The Yellow Pages
737-5344

302

The Nut House
674-5496
Theorem Beach BBS
284-3570

303

Cat's Dog House
341-5933
Nix Pix
375-1263

305

Adults Only Mansion
594-4526
Alpha 2000
752-9439
The Bad Boys Club
271-2000
Big Bobber's BBS
572-3357
Daybreak Mail System
771-0041
Misty Moonlight
473-2314
Pair O' Dice
753-9259
Playhouse BBS!
968-8139
The Rockcreek BBS
432-8698
South Beach BBS
572-4287
Starware BBS
428-0012
Turbo Soft
247-1305

306

Technology Transfer
372-4903

310

Hedonism
631-7697
Lifeline BBS
823-6686

312

The Billboard BBS
284-5508
Fourth Dimension
284-7133

313

Lan Solutions
542-9615

314

Hartz Foundation
281-4362
Ourplace BBS
745-2082

315

Excalibur System
736-3792
The Meeting Place
433-0916
Walt's Pleasure
797-5415

317

The Users Choice
894-1378

319

Rich's Disk Cafe
372-3673

402

Atomic Dustbin
291-2896
Mirrored Dragon's
734-2073

404

Club Erotica
333-0008
Eagles Landing
944-3717
Intimate Visions
244-7059

406

Pc-Montana BBS
284-3120

407

Adonis BBS
881-8641
Adult Expectations
852-2007
Dirty Deeds BBS
290-5189
The Door BBS
682-3132
Hy-It Express
295-0594
Infinite Space 3
240-1790

412

Jbj Systems Pcboard
341-9323
The Nuthouse BBS
229-9560
Ooohhh-Zone BBS
635-0814
Voyager Ii Pcboard
746-1447

413

Shangrila
527-7360

414

The Back Doors BBS
744-6003

415

Graveyard Shift
397-1038
Hints BBS
572-8219

417

Laura's Lair
683-5584

Adult Boards

Laura's Lair
683-5534

501

After Five
835-5830
Ferrett Face
791-0124
Moonman BBS
562-7399

503

Lost In The Ozone
461-4634
The Machine BBS
236-3266
Nightfire BBS
296-9834
Nwcs Online
620-5910
Rose City On-Line
257-7264
Sadie's Swingshift
245-2006
T&E Verbal Abuse Network
368-2903

508

Auto Exec
833-0508

509

Zulu Alert Facility
244-2460

510

Bust Out BBS
888-1443
Clawmarks
452-0350
The Gift Shop
689-4686
Team H BBS
236-5114

513

Basic Concept
573-9201
Ccc
752-8248
Modem Zone
424-7529

514

Linq
522-3866

516

The -=Bunny Hutch=-
328-1844
Substation BBS
364-4450

519

Images At Twilight
649-2672

601

Magnolia Cadlelight
939-5622

602

Boardwalk Hotel
955-9338
Fire! And Ice Hotel
246-9132
The High Mountain
527-8404
The Petting Zoo
493-1937
Rusty's Wild Kat BBS
936-3892

609

The Beckett BBS
467-3898
Bill's BBS
853-0384
Compu-Data
232-1245

The —Detour—>BBS
896-3673
Electron Symentry
768-5689
Galaxy BBS
678-5360
La Dolce Vita BBS
722-0415
Online In D'hood
645-7080
Polymath One
392-5953
The Union Lake BBS
327-5553

613

Tron BBS System
537-8344
The Viking's Cove
394-0685
Wayne's World BBS
831-0632

614

Gbl BBS
445-8180
Masterlink
384-4072

615

Cheyenne Social Club
361-5956
Distant Mirror BBS
648-1782
Goat Shack BBS
842-8758
Third Eye
227-6155

616

Northern Data BBS
347-0942

617

Channel One
354-5776

619

Bare Bones BBS
384-2824
Stephanie'splayhouse
462-8788
Wee Cabin
278-5959
West Coast Connectio
449-8333

702

Nighthawk
644-1537

703

The Advocate
498-4007
Springfield Connect
451-0624

704

The Big Byte
279-2295
Mot's Place
598-1025
The Rabbit Hole
563-8474

706

Fubar BBS
860-7209

707

Rapture BBS
573-0927

708

Aquila BBS
820-8344
Intimate Mansion
934-3045

713

A-Mega BBS
488-6077

After Hours
937-0504
The Macaw's Roost
495-3730

714

Big Blue Mac
493-4779
Black Pines
539-9374
Calypso BBS
492-1045
Fantasia Services
579-7022
Fantasia Services
579-7022
Mistress's Digs
836-0131
Software Exchange
552-3515
The Solar System BBS
837-9677

717

Terminal Paradise
292-0497

718

Mega-Source
545-3881
Moondog BBS
692-2498
Paradise Network
241-9007
Systematic BBS
716-6198
The Treasure Chest
525-5610

804

Coma BBS
293-2400
Phantom's Lair BBS
723-1227
Pleasure Dome
490-5878
Pleasure Dome BBS
490-Lust

Sinbad's Shack
482-6578
Splitsville BBS
467-9640
The Video Zone!
474-9635
The Zoo BBS
431-9363

805

The Computer Factory
995-1299
Tom Cat Pictures
482-8030

810

Black River Computer
679-2408
Legend Onlineamerica
776-1975

812

Digicom BBS
479-1310
Elmer T's
282-3837
Elmer T's BBS
282-3837
Kentuckiana Mag
948-9670

813

Bandit BBS
977-5600
Godfather
289-3314
Mercury Opus
321-0734

814

Compuphile Ii
398-2950

815

The Mchenry BBS
385-5031

Adult Boards

816
Night Moves BBS
322-5494
Pizazz
468-6900

818
The Continuum BBS
441-2625
Crystal Palace
765-2171
Mog-Ur's Ems
366-1238
Odyssey
358-6968
Panasia BBS
569-3740
The Sports Club
792-4752

819
Synapse
561-5268

901
Second Wind BBS
388-8358

904
Dream Land BBS
837-9105

Electric Blue
479-2855
Exotica's Pet/Stuff
563-0066
Queen Of Hearts
789-6843
Shuttle Pad BBS
766-8938
The Vandal's Castle
456-9972

908
Arrakis
638-5766
The Backroom Ii
758-1122
Dream Homes BBS
888-3959
The Pleasure Den
549-5996

909
Bits And Bytes BBS
356-4636
Nightvision
369-6556
Nothin' But
338-6716

913
Colossus]Ii[System
897-6667

Night Prowler BBS
784-6177

914
Dirty Hacker
794-5306
The Dirty Hacker BBS
796-4566
Intimate Inn
961-0398
The Machine
883-6612
The Voice
664-1844

916
Bigtime's Exchange
668-9453
For Adults Only
962-3964

918
Cat-Tastrophe
663-1249

Chat Boards

by area code

201

Arc Xchange BBS
429-1317
Beacon Studios BBS
863-5253
The Cave of Wonders
387-0640
Cobra's Triangle BBS
335-1652
Compucon
887-7463
Computer Connections
798-0065
Frankly Speaking STS #3 Synergy System
633-0569
Harry's Place
934-0861
Headquarters Information Service
672-8969
In The Wind BBS
646-0227
Jezebel's Parlour
927-2932
The Rainbow Connection
967-1061
The Silver Bullet BBS
812-9352
The Starship Enterprise
283-1806
Tower of Silence
963-8007
UNitek Research BBS
678-1367
The Vortex BBS
751-5608

203

C-C-Chat
438-5577
The Candle Light Base
777-0168
Computer Caddie
444-0731

The Download America BBS
676-1708
The Libertarian BBS
257-1960
New Horizons BBS
373-1448
Our House BBS
599-3970
Sea of Noise
886-1441
Urban Express
966-5662
The Wolf's Revenge
261-4963

205

The Anchor Inn
675-8406
The Byte Swap BBS
355-2983
The Computrion BBS
595-0183
The Crenshaw County BBS
335-3968
DFG Financial BBS
745-0579
The Fulda Sector
653-5986
Genesis Online
620-4150
Inferno BBS
837-7715
Intoxicated State University
456-3052
KickAxis BBS
733-0253
Montgomery PC Users' Group
277-3889
ShadoeVision BBS
306-0486
Shoot the Bull BBS
556-3067

206

The Board For The Bored
789-0085
Cameron's Railroad
659-2132
Capital City OnLine!
956-1123
GameLand Plus!
260-0957
Guns & Hoses
653-9581
More Then Meets the Eye
787-5339
The Party Line
857-8701
Pony Express BBS
367-9131
Starlight BBS
782-3221

207

The 64th Dimension BBS
883-1904
Circular Logic BBS
873-4981
The Great Northern BBS
325-4103

208

After Hours BBS
345-6121
Idaho Central Interchange
677-2028
Idaho Interactive BBS
345-4987
Indigo BBS
734-6592
Night Flight
529-4248
V&K After Hours
237-5707

Chat Boards

209

Fresno Public Access
277-3008
MicroLink BBS
591-8753
The Wrong Number BBS
943-1880

210

G.C.E.M.S. BBS
997-6028
Newberry Bulletin Board System
233-4877
Olde Guard BBS
684-4470

212

FPX2
627-0531
The Invention Factory
274-8110
NYPC BBS
679-6972
Real Exposure
691-2679

213

PhotoPro BBS
223-9285
US Pompeii
878-2801
The Westside
933-4050
Westwood S.B.
295-2084

214

The BucketBored!
414-6913
THe GaRBaGe DuMP BBS!
644-6060
Midnight Angel Express
243-0378
Texas Talk
497-9100

215

C.B.B.S.
433-3370
ClockWork BBS
546-7088
The Computer Shop BBS
395-9823
DSC BBS
443-7430
Entertainment Technologies
335-9850
The Hotline BBS
393-8594
LOGON: Philadelphia
572-8240
The National Cheese Emporium BBS
673-0261
The Shelter
945-1152

216

The Ace of Spades
339-4592
BBS-Ohio
951-8938
Christian Network #1
741-6244
City Senders
734-1477
The Dragon's Lair BBS
671-0850
Flip Flop
951-9150
The Menagerie BBS
651-1095
The Musician's BBS
639-9508
PC Ohio
381-3320
The Scientist's BBS
639-9508
The Silicon Dreame
641-0311

217

LTM Computer Systems BBS
539-6545
PDC BBS
347-0280

Suburbia BBS
337-6312
The Temples of Syrinx
787-9101
The Ultimate BBS
792-3663

218

Computer Enterprises BBS
326-4205
The Esko BBS
879-9466
Northern Light BBS
828-9302

219

Magicland BBS
879-7184
NetConnect
420-1326
River Bottom BBS
273-0936
Tech BBS
654-3210

301

Altered Reality BBS
431-0239
The File Factory
599-8382
InterConnect
208-2547
Maryland Catholic (Washington Node)
596-3230
Network East
738-0000
Sandy's Castle
753-8230
Tan_d-Link BBS
946-6056
Tim's House of Fun BBS
705-7115

302

The Krystal Palace
762-9245
The Small Blunder
234-2792

303

The Chicken Coop
328-5642
Colorado Connection
423-9775
Denver Matchmaker
232-5523
DLS Infonet
347-2921
The Forum
226-4218
The Garbage Dump
457-1111
The Horizon
766-3104
The Hot Line
245-1147
Nix*Pix
375-1263
North Street BBS
884-1391
The OS/2 Source
744-0373
Star One
429-0597
Wizards Mansion
980-8486

304

Bandit Boy BBS
664-9421
The Bit Bank
728-0884
Boot Camp BBS
872-6029
Canaan Valley Report
478-3524
The Clubhouse BBS
485-9232
Interfaith Experience BBS
845-1108
The Red-Eye
846-6229
Seneca Station
636-9592
The Spencer BBS
927-3532
Stand Fast BBS
926-8304
Telephone Technologies
697-5769

The White Knight
346-3419
WildCat! West Virginia
636-9097

305

A Midnight Rave
270-6780
Astro Cafe
245-6393
Bullitt-80 Opus BBS
751-7903
Comport I BBS
971-1677
The Data Center BBS
436-5070
The Info Exchange
534-5770
The Library BBS
581-5162
Silver Bullet BBS
238-2106
The TechLands BBS
971-0130
Ups and Downs
434-8403
Wild Palms BBS
472-4431

306

The Sage's Desk
545-2943
Saskatoon Online Entertainment
933-0538

307

Rocky Mountain Rendezvous BBS
638-8506

308

The Panhandle Connection
487-5505

309

Buzzard's Roost
691-5416

The Data Stream
688-7713
EPE On-Line
694-7725
Hacker's World
672-4405
NightWatch BBS
963-6060
The Phoenix
792-2543
Rod's Place BBS
836-1432

310

After Hours/18+
842-7995
Independent Filmmakers Forum
425-0012
Miller's Party Board
815-0117
ModemBoy BBS
659-7000
Surfboard II BBS
631-1434

312

The Billboard BBS
284-5508
CEBBS
902-3599
Home Again
665-7319
The Power Palace
594-0643

313

The Bloom County BBS
582-0888
Bruce's Place BBS
562-0051
The Danger Zone
782-4524
Data Land BBS
572-7980
The Death Star BBS
429-0567
Detroit Data Exchange
885-4222

Chat Boards

Gateway Online
291-5571
MSS Support Line
761-8256
Toledo's TBBS
854-6001
The UnStoppable Dragons BBS
697-0609

314

The Bone Yard BBS!
447-7999
The Data Express BBS
431-3777
The Insider/NGN Netmail Server #01
731-3871

315

Dreamscape
458-3482
Ham-Net BBS (StormNet Int'l HQ)
682-1824
Solid Foundation Information Exchange
458-7662
The Way, The Truth, The Life
392-2368

316

BJ's Brass Monkey BBS
945-7860
The Hole
529-8880
The MicroChip Dungeon BBS
241-7803
The MotherLode
441-0047
Popcorn BBS
552-4577

317

Absolute Connection
861-9333
Bill and Ted's Excellent BBS
883-4510

CCS-BBS
781-5799
Graffiti on the BBS Wall
448-2842
Luck of the Irish BBS
887-5665
Pandaemonium BBS
580-1531
Trader's Connection
359-5199
Workplace Connection
742-2680

318

Bible Bulletin Board
949-1456
The Dataexchange BBS
239-2122
Techie Tavern
387-8264

319

The Electric Nightline BBS
337-0674
Reality Check BBS
373-5355
Rush Hour
568-6370
The Short's BBS
381-1591
Visionary
927-4474

401

Information Resource System
783-7559
The Springboard
232-0088

402

The Badger's Byte
376-3120
HAWG! WILD! BBS
493-2737
The Mages Inn
734-4748
Outnet
496-9987

403

Terminal Frost
437-6820

404

Chaos Inc.
498-9646
Club Torgy BBS
974-0460
Michael's Lair
735-6454
The Night Shift BBS
478-9700
Rubber
433-8213
Skid Row BBS
319-0307
Windows Online America
477-8942

405

Crazy Horse BBS
232-4030
The Funny Farm
233-7474
Sword's Point BBS
682-1628

406

The Cultural Wasteland BBS
782-7941
The Homeport BBS
228-2902
Midnight BBS
587-8163
Montana MediaNet
549-6325

407

The Black Hole
639-1822
The Eagle's Hideout
547-4233
The Ice Cave
793-8598
JumpStart BBS
337-2559

My Cozy Kitchen BBS
687-9355
Narcoossee BBS
892-8483
Osceola Express
348-5295
Politically Incorrect BBS
632-7549
The Shire Scribe BBS
633-1026

408

Comp-U-Ease
286-8332
The Lazer Board
268-4863
Monterey Gaming System
655-5555

409

Bay City Beginnings
244-9530
Little Flock BBS
769-6880

410

AACyberNet
674-5427
The Abingdon Info Exchange
569-8336
The Core
840-9356
Falling Star BBS
778-9688
Forces Unknown
644-5100
Greg's Corner
781-6735
Hotline BBS
799-8102
HouseNet BBS
745-2037
Hunter's Cabin
257-7249
Maryland Catholic (Baltimore Node)
997-5262
Maryland State Firemen's Association
536-1935

The Sin Bin BBS
796-0819
Tilt
521-4808
Waterfront East
687-6890
The Weatherstation
882-8887
Wishbringer BBS
269-6607

412

The Annex BBS
635-9165
The Hufftown BBS
836-7326
Moment Online
439-6163
Mtn. View Electronic Micro Mall
821-8431
The ooohhh-Zone BBS
635-0814

413

The Archives BBS
525-2804
Shangri-La
527-7360
The VideoTex BBS
445-6812

414

Computer Plus
677-4499
The Crystal Barrier
457-8399
Digital Data Exchange
423-0441
Exec PC
789-4360
Link Tek
384-1055
Network Cabling
764-6706
The Shadow BBS
235-4006
Zforce Solar Systems
657-5566

415

California Online
331-4081
Eye Contact
703-8200
Fun University Network
327-4591

416

Baudeville BBS
283-0114
BlackBoard International
449-0799
CRS Online
213-6002

419

The BackDoor BBS [CIN]
675-0823
Fox On-Line Information Systems
352-7544
The Message Base
866-0554
The Oak Grove BBS
535-6116

501

Castle of Dreams BBS
771-0126
The Chicken Coop
273-2442
The Cutting Edge
663-3343

502

The Barbarian's Hut
352-2169
The FlightLine BBS
886-7146
The Scrapyard
942-0864
StarLink Information Services Inc.
964-7827
The V.I.N.E. BBS
636-5595

Chat Boards

503

The Advanced System BBS
657-3359
CF BBS
523-2513
Magnetic Inx the Machine
476-0729

504

Baud Horizons
436-9590
The Chatter Box
775-7825
DataCom BBS
275-2605
Heavy Metal BBS
872-3043
The Laboratory
837-0155
Night Moves BBS
927-6492

505

Construction Net #6
662-0659
Coyote Run
351-4693
THe GaRBaGe DuMP BBS
294-5675
The Hermit's Outlook
454-8364

506

Fundy Isle BBS
662-8342

508

The Adult Hangout BBS
746-6010
Dark Realms
695-3420
Dreamer's BBS
991-6058
Pure Coincidence BBS
677-2472
Stealth BBS of New Bedford
997-4982

Twilight Zone
643-3253
White Pine RBBS
378-3847

509

CEO & Chairman of the Board
758-6022
The Moonflower
927-1184
Pro-Greens BBS
588-3519

510

Aardwolf Express
797-8700
Bay Area Mega Board
247-8300
Bust Out BBS
888-1443
Caxius BBS
895-6961

512

Austin Matchmaker
458-1172
Bermuda Triangle
416-7826
DatSource BBS
219-6629
The Graveyard
445-0301
RagBBS
719-3542

513

Authors' Area Writers' Forum
848-4288
The Cottage by the Stream
235-2605
Enginet
858-2688
Epsilon Computing
563-6475
Mind Expansion
864-5964
Type Too Basement
451-8990

514

Ephesus Online
426-0110
Media Spectrum
366-0670

515

Advanced Cryptographic Services BBS
869-3662
The Other Side BBS
232-0969
RBBS of Newton
791-9288

516

Ace's Place
599-1209
Around Town-Islip Terrace
859-0703
Artificial Intelligence
822-8909
Defcon BBS
437-1659
The Game Peddler BBS
493-0785
Long Island BBS
326-9809
Long Island File Exchange
249-0275
The Midnight Star BBS
371-0539
Mistral BBS
921-6806
Monitor-1 BBS
395-4507
The Nut House
862-2274
PC BBS
795-5874
Point Blank
755-3000
Sherlock's Haven BBS
433-1843
Spock's World
349-0178
Stages
823-0732
Tele-Net Online!
579-0050

Tower of Power
981-8372
Utopia Tech BBS
579-7507

517

C4 Yourself BBS
423-3667
PJ Systems
451-2072

518

The Access Network
283-5716
The Active Access BBS
371-4932
The Assassin's Lair
432-6771
Cow Land
861-8718
The Florida Keys
587-0317
Tidal Wave BBS
861-6770

519

The Edge BBS
974-4603
New Edge Data Systems
371-8383
New Gold Dream BBS
725-1744
River Spills BBS
862-2396

601

After Hours BBS
371-0423
Fireball BBS
627-9376
Hacker's Heaven
388-3745
Mississippi Online
627-4811
Neon Blue
329-3247
Psychobabble
332-9453

602

The Arizona Speed Trap
768-6584
Chairman Paul's Journal
831-0464
Circle of Fellowship
942-8921
The Danish Tower BBS
459-6514
Demodulator
290-2807
Empty Pockets BBS
831-7979
THe GaRBaGe DuMP BBS
331-1112
GraF/X
282-9035
Quantum Leap
937-1356
Scott's Spot BBS
982-6156
Sunwise
584-7395

603

American Amiga
679-1762
Botnay Bay, EIS
431-7090
Computer Castle BBS
382-0993
Icehouse BBS
863-3537
Whiz Data Network
647-3068

604

Double Exposure BBS
939-9540
Earthshine BBS
361-9053
Mary and Thyme
646-2243

606

Cincidel
282-9803
Kentucky Explorer BBS
271-1451

Magic$oft BBS
371-6337
The Niche BBS
885-4757
Playland BBS
268-0776

607

The Forum BBS
272-1371
The Messed BBS
844-9216
Sugar Mountain
732-4565

608

The Connecting Line
365-2302
The Doghouse
788-9657
Mac Line
233-9487
The RF Deck
356-4777

609

Compu-Data
232-1245
The Dark Side BBS
391-0987
Planet-X
730-1656

610

The Cosmic Forge
926-1213
The Docksider BBS
678-0350
The Other Reading
370-9470
POP's BBS
272-5799
Rick's Cafe Americain
740-9886
Sports and More BBS
995-2155
Time-Out BBS
857-2648

Chat Boards

612

Fort Weyr BBS
654-8516
SpareCom
445-5655

613

Programmer's Source BBS
837-0413
Proton Palace Professional BBS
829-0909

614

Computer Connection
922-5042
Deafened Psychosis
382-6886
Megabyte City BBS
682-7594
Metrodata BBS
777-2030
SOCS BBS
432-2899
The Wizard's Gate BBS
224-1635

615

Bigfoot's Lair
792-1888
The Byte Board BBS
878-2286
Coles Kingdom
657-5708
Out of Bounds
336-1620
The Software Club BBS
745-8516

616

The Derby BBS
429-2935
The Eau Claire Connection
461-6801
EifenVille Multiline
323-1016
Files Galore
365-0659

The Jungle BBS
392-3477
Macatawa Multiline
399-1141
Shoestring BBS
969-4216
The Taz's BBS
373-4231

617

Dalliance/Vortex BBs
899-7534
Donna Dee's Dungeon
894-3090
The Outpost BBS
871-2683

618

Genesis Station
876-8806
Smurph Land BBS
345-5243
Uniq Computer Consultant BBS
996-3102
World Horizon Network
482-5239

619

Gray's Anatomy
778-1866
Public Access BBS
665-8028
Rendezvous BBS
689-8550

710

Dakota Central Tele-Net
674-8115

702

AmigaBoard BBS
423-8352
Heavy Metal BBS
825-5951
Superboard
423-4739

Vega$ Online BBS
222-0409

703

The Advocate
498-4007
Another Dimension
667-3530
The Arts Place
528-8467
Back Woods II
663-0840
The Contraxx
573-5255
The Cracker Barrel
899-2285
Elite Few BBS
765-4539
Images BBS
629-8727
The Pedaler's Palace
532-3051
Red Dwarf BBBS/2
631-0041
SkyNet BBS
552-8767
UFOria
803-6420

704

Digital Dreams/2
254-0345
The Eclectic Board
865-7126
The GTS BBS
866-7353
Private Investigators Exchange BBS
563-5480
The Transporter Room
567-9594

706

Furbar BBS
860-7209
Populus
569-0773
The Potter's House
637-9276

707

Anathema Downs
792-1555
Color Galaxy Milky Way (RCISNET.ORG)
585-8246
The Party Line BBS
588-8055
Sonoma Online
545-0746

708

American Archive Electro Mail BBS
426-8903
Cair Tuatha
393-7750
The City of Illusions
361-2436
Com One
717-9370
The File Sponge BBS
548-6103
The House of Games
918-8421
Obsidian Systems
386-2825
RadioComm
518-8336
Scintillation BBS
953-4922

712

Midwest Connection BBS
276-6534
The Virtual Reality BS
737-3960

713

Data Warp Computers
335-6107
HAL-PC BBS
963-4100
Photo-Play
467-0032
The Recovery Room BBS
242-9674

714

4Next GT BBS
956-4698
American Survival network BBS
441-0789
The Desktop BBS
898-7269
Happy Trails BBS
547-0719
Real Estate Online
969-9624
Vertrauen
529-5313
The Viewlink BBS
650-4612

715

CompuLine/PIDS
732-1036
The Infinite Realm
682-8573
The Magic Of Krynn
344-4142
The Neighborhood BBS
341-4016
Nothern Lights!
426-9886

716

Blue Moon Online System
874-8941
The Flaming Chalice
271-6323
Mac's Last Stand BBS
247-9056
Media Online
798-5549
The Neon Rainbow
735-9493

717

Bitt's Place
387-1725
Cyberia - The Final Stop in Cyberspace
840-1444
Cybernetics BBS
738-1976

Dark Corners
343-4865
The Eclipse
637-3939
The Lycoming Link BBS
321-6440
The Northeast File Bank
876-0152
The Tower of High Sorcery
696-2236
The Tusk BBS
560-1750

718

ABC On-Line
446-2157
Bay Cafe
636-3081
City-Net BBS
373-5529
The Electric Line BBS!
822-6997
Expressways BBS
636-1844
The Icebox BBS
793-8548
Impax Online
932-7710
Innovations BBS
575-2914
InterCom Online
252-6720
The Midnight Connection
357-0429
Mind Matters BBS
951-6652
More BBS
251-9346
Overnight BBS
967-3789
The Paradise BBS
497-5665
Paradise Network BBS
241-9007
Pic & Flics BBS
885-0555
Ray's World BBS
234-4113
Shadowdale BBS
934-1843
Spark*Net Online Systems!
447-5544

Chat Boards

The Sports Pages BBS
761-9513
Tree Branch Online!
739-5845

719

P*PCompAS
591-1453

801

The Darkside
465-1367
The Lower Lights BBS
272-5451
The Nightmare Enterprise
394-5956
Random Lunacy
221-0928
The Sandbox II [ASV]
774-5574
This Old BBS
489-0638
The Unbelievers
466-4261
The Zion Curtain BBS
723-6117

803

Blackbeard's Tavern
294-9657
Chaos
469-9267
Charleston Computer Connection
767-4190
The Cosmic Connection BBS
862-7789
The Synapse BBS
695-1917

804

Central Station BBS
545-0447
The Digital Empire
739-6747
The Hegelian Solution, Inc. [PIN]
358-3286

Joe's Place
520-0536
Joe's Room
887-2569
The Midnight Foundation BBS
296-2066
The Music BBS!
739-7289
Servant of the Lord BBS
590-2161
Talisman BBS
467-5507
Valhalla BS
560-0701

805

The Computer Factory
995-1299
EnigmaScape
541-4012
The FunZone
988-0549
Quality of LifeMentor BBS
393-5332
Searchlight of San Luis Obispo, CA, BBS
549-0961
The Seaside
964-4766
Tehachapi Mountain
822-6587
Ventura County's Information Network
485-8982

806

Byte the Bullet
796-3464
Excelsior BBS
745-8220
The Hub
745-9144
Sherwood Forest
763-4975

808

The Aloha Network
621-8845
The Country Cupboard
488-0617

Hawaii OnLine
246-8887
The "In-Touch" BBS
521-2359
One Step Beyond BBS
695-8352
Paradise BBS
625-5120
TBird's BBS
423-3152

810

Bad to the Bone BBS
749-3581
Battle Zone
949-8839
The Carnival BBS
235-0158
Electronic Lucidity
680-8861
The g Force BBS
852-4444
Legend On-Line America
776-1975
The Totem Pole BBS
238-1178

812

The Hotseat
279-2143
SpellSinger II
232-1821
The Top of the Hill
824-8682
The Tradin' Place
334-0442

813

The Alternative
882-3887
Budville BBS
593-0061
Close Encounters
528-2582
The Eagle's Nest Trading Post
528-8256
The Inner Sanctum
848-6055
Longbow BBS
961-3653

The Nuthouse
625-8233
Southern City Central BBS
749-0664
Supersonic BBS
467-9794
Tampa Connection
961-8665
Wizard's World 2
694-4882

814

Cheers
539-6648
Erie's Westside BBS
459-8901

815

Digital Dreams
227-9455
Electric Estates BBS
886-0109
Rockford College BBS
394-5153

816

The Cave BBS
665-7157
Night Watch and Night Moves BBS
322-5494
The Wolf's Den
361-7670

817

Electric Knights
922-8900
The ShadowCat BBS
246-8657

818

The Annex
786-5600
Barter Exchange
999-1829
BlockBuster Bulletin Board
831-9942

The Castle
985-6075
Ghost Town
996-9913
Hawks Haven
348-0278
Hottips BBS
248-3088
KBBS Los Angeles
886-0872
Merchants of Wonder BBS
508-0214
Millers Party Board
769-2302
Spectrum
757-3532
The Sports Club BBS
792-4752

819

Barbarian's BBS
762-0632
Info Tech
375-8452
The Klingait BBS
897-8255

901

The Fridge
427-0132
Metroplex BBS
327-1895
The Shoreline BBS
775-3190

903

Botany Bay
509-8518
The Gate
872-0903
Tupelo Pflash
872-8088

904

Beach BBS
426-8726
The Beachside
492-2305

The Black Lodge
794-5263
The City Lights
786-9914
Digital Underground
373-0237
Esoteric Oracle
332-9547
The Hard Drive Cafe
721-8831
The Jungle BBS
666-8470
Late Night
735-0531
Nightmare Cafe
874-2296
The Ship's Log BBS
441-1941
Southern Accent
777-0694
Terrapin Station BBS
939-8027
The Toy ShopPC BBS
688-9124
Victory Station
693-3147
The Wall BBS
730-8659

905

After Shock BBS
578-5048
Alpha City BBS
579-6302

906

InfoBase
632-4478

907

The Comet's Tail
488-4387
The Play Room
338-7049

908

The County Jail BBS
787-7459

Chat Boards

The English Palace
739-1755
Gneric BBS
389-8473
High Voltage BBS
234-0249
Hudson's Info BBS
525-8478
Isle-Net
495-6996
The Manor BBS!
493-3936
The POW/MIA BBS
787-8383
Toys in the Attic BBS
475-4138

909

Castle of the Dark Sun
468-0621
Empire BBS
980-2306
The Enchanted Forest BBS
883-2552
GMS Support Online
688-3104
Hacker's Den BBS
678-3412
NewAge Connection
276-3248
Nothin' But
338-6716
Sat's BBS
338-3971

910

Ansi-Mation Alley
346-6543
The Fine Ride
799-8412
The Generic BBS
567-5819
PC-Motorsports BBS
595-8073
The Tarheel Connection
643-9570
Terminal Entry BBS
895-0368
UNA-USA BBS
722-5164

Victory BBS
222-6014
WhiTech BBS
944-1165

912

Baudville Station BBS
741-8722
Code Plus BBS
953-1053
DOS Connexion BBS
431-0836
The Hot South BBS
245-1865
Microlink
786-5888

913

Adcon Network
271-7107
Country BBS
478-0334
Databank
842-7744
Lawrence OnLine/TBBS
865-1440

914

The Apple-Wize BBS
961-0663
The Brewster BBS
279-2514
The Bridge
856-5309
Executive Network
667-4567
MHS:BBS
794-8904
New York Metro Chat BBS
242-8227
New York Telephone I
368-2819
The Space Station BBS
292-0670
Stromi's Place [LCC]
234-1284
Ultra Tech BBS
227-7889

915

The Black Gate
585-3701
Kilroy's Zer0 BBS
530-0227
The Lost Isle Of Melnibone
520-5453
Telegraph Road BBS
561-5115

916

Artisan Crafts BBS
331-7865
The Compass Rose-Sacramento
447-0292
The Compass RoseDavis
758-0292
The Dixon Sub-Station BBS
678-8383
FAO Bulletin Board System
962-3973

The Miata BBS
224-9890

918

AGRI-Specialists BBS
255-6542
The Billboard BBS
831-5278
Black Gold BBS
272-7779
Broken Arrow
252-2236
The Ham Radio Emporium
272-4327

919

The BC BBS
217-9540
The Black Forest BBS
787-6198
Downtown BBS
383-4905
The Island BBS
354-4753
Legend of Sleepy Hollow
492-5353

Internet providers

National

CR Laboratories ☎→*dial* 415-837-5300 (vox)/212-695-7988/713-236-9200/617-577-9300/415-389-8649 ✓**INTERNET** ...→*telnet* crl.com→guest ...→*ftp* crl.com→anonymous→<your email address> ...→*email* info@crl.com ✉ *Email for automated info*

Delphi ☎→*dial* 800-544-4005 (vox)/800-365-4636→JOINDEL-PHI→INTERNETSIG ✓**INTERNET** ...→*telnet* delphi.com→joindelphi→free ...→*email* info@delphi.com ✉ *Email for automated info*

Millennium Online ☎→*dial* 800-736-0122 (vox) ✓**INTERNET**→*email* info@mill.com ✉ *Email for automated info*

Netcom Online Communication Services Dozens of area codes for many parts of the U.S. ☎→*dial* 800-501-8649 (vox) ✓**INTERNET** ...→*telnet* netcom.com→guest→guest ...→*ftp* ftp.netcom.com→anonymous→<your email address>→/pub/netcom ...→*email* info@netcom.com ✉ *Email for automated info*

PSILink ☎→*dial* 703-709-0300 (vox) ✓**INTERNET** ...→*ftp* ftp.psi.com→anonymous→<your email address>→/info ...→*email* all-info@psi.com ✉ *Email for automated info*

Your Personal Network (YPN) ☎→*dial* 800-NET-1133 (vox) Run by the editors of this book. ✓**INTERNET** ...→*telnet* ypn.com→guest ...→*ftp* ypn.com→anonymous→<your email address>→/pub ...→*www* http://www.ypn.com ...→*email* info@ypn.com ✉ *Email for automated info*

Alabama

Nuance Network Services ☎→*dial* 205-533-4296 (vox) ✓**INTERNET** ...→*ftp* ftp.nuance.com→anonymous→<your email address>→/pub/NNS-INFO ...→*email* jkl@nuance.com ✉ *Email for info*

Arizona

Data Basix ☎→*dial* 602-721-1988 (vox)/602-721-5887→guest ✓**INTERNET** ...→*telnet* Data.Basix.com→guest ...→*ftp* Data.Basix.COM→anonymous→<your email address>→/services/dial-up.txt ...→*email* info@Data.Basix.com ✉ *Email for automated info*

Evergreen Communications ☎→*dial* 602-230-9330 (vox) ✓**INTERNET**→*email* evergreen@libre.com ✉ *Email for info*

The Illuminati Online ☎→*dial* 512-447-7866 (vox)/512-448-8950→new ✓**INTERNET** ...→*email* info@io.com ✉ *Email for automated info* ...→*telnet* io.com→new ...→*ftp* io.com→anonymous→<your email address>

Internet Direct, Inc. ☎→*dial* 602-274-0100 (vox)/602-274-9600/602-321-9600→guest ✓**INTERNET** ...→*telnet* indirect.com→guest→guest ...→*email* info@direct.com ✉ *Email for automated info*

California

a2i communications ☎→*dial* 408-293-8078 (vox)/415-364-5652/408-293-9010 ✓**INTERNET** ...→*telnet* a2i.rahul.net→guest ...→*ftp* ftp.rahul.net→anonymous→<your email address>→/pub/BLURB ...→*email* info@rahul.net ✉ *Email for automated info*

Dial n' Cerf USA ☎→*dial* 800-876-2373 (vox) ✓**INTERNET** ...→*ftp* ftp.cerf.net→anonymous→<your email address>→/cerfnet_info/cerfnet-general info.txt ...→*email* info@cerf.net ✉ *Email for automated info*

E & S Systems Public Access ☎→*dial* 619-278-8124/619-278-9127/619-278-8267/619-278-9837 ✓**INTERNET**→*email* steve@cg57.esnet.com ✉ *Email for info*

Express Access 714-377-9784 908-937-9481 ☎→*dial* 800-969-9090 (vox)/714-377-9784→new ✓**INTERNET** ...→*telnet* access.digex.net→new→new ...→*ftp* ftp.digex.net→anonymous→<your email address>→/pub ...→*email* info@digex.net ✉ *Email for automated info*

HoloNet ☎→*dial* 510-704-0160 (vox)/510-704-1058→guest ✓**INTERNET** ...→*telnet* holonet.net→ guest ...→*ftp* holonet.net→anonymous→<your email address>→/info ...→*email* info@holonet.net ✉ *Email for automated info*

Institute for Global Communications (IGC) ☎→*dial* 415-442-0220 (vox)/415-322-0284 ✓**INTERNET** ...→*ftp* igc.apc.org→anonymous→<your email address>→/pub ...→*email* info@igc.apc.org ✉ *Email for automated info*

KAIWAN Public Access Inter-

net Online Services ☎→*dial* 714-638-2139 (vox)/714-452-9166/818-579-6701/818-756-0180/310-527-4279/714-539-5726/714-741-2920 ✓**INTERNET** ...→*ftp* kaiwan.com→anonymous→ <your email address>→/pub/kai wan ...→*email* info@kaiwan.com ✍ *Email for automated info*

The Portal System ☎→*dial* 408-973-9111 (vox)/408-973-8091/408-725-0561→info ✓**INTERNET** ...→*telnet* portal.com→online→ info ...→*ftp* ftp.shell.portal.com→ anonymous→<your email address> →/portal.info ...→*email* info@por tal. com ✍ *Email for automated info*

The Well ☎→*dial* 415-332-4335 (vox)/415-332-6106→guest ✓**INTERNET** ...→ *telnet* well.com→guest ...→*email* info@well.com ✍ *Email for automated info*

Colorado

Colorado SuperNet, Inc. ☎→*dial* 303-273-3471 (vox) ✓**INTERNET** ...→*ftp* csn.org→ anony-mous→<your email address>→ /CSN/reports/DialinInfo.txt ...→ *email* info@csn.org ✍ *Email for automated info*

Community News Service ☎→*dial* 800-748-1200 (vox)/719-520-1700/303-758-2656→ new→newuser ✓**INTERNET** ...→*tel-net* cscns.com→new→newuser ... →*ftp* cscns.com→anonymous→ <your email address> ...→*email* info@cscns.com ✍ *Email for auto-mated info*

Old Colorado City Communi-cations ☎→*dial* 719-632-4848 (vox)/719-632-4111→newuser ✓**INTERNET** ...→*telnet* oldcolo.com→ newuser ...→*email* thefox@oldcolo. com ✍ *Email for info*

Connecticut

The John von Newmann Computer Network ☎→*dial* 609-897-7300 (vox) ✓**INTERNET**→ *email* info@jvnc.net ✍ *Email for automated info*

DC & Maryland

CAPCON Library Network ☎→*dial* 202-331-5771 (vox) ✓**IN-TERNET**→*email* capcon@capcon.net ✍ *Email for info*

Express Access 714-377-9784 908-937-9481 ☎→*dial* 800-969-9090 (vox)/301-220-0462→new ✓**INTERNET** ...→*telnet* access.digex. net→new→new ...→*ftp* ftp.digex. net→anonymous→<your email ad-dress>→/pub ...→*email* info@ digex.net ✍ *Email for automated info*

Merit Network, Inc ☎→*dial* 313-764-9430 (vox) ✓**INTERNET** ...→*telnet* hermes.merit.edu→help ...→*ftp* nic.merit.edu→anonymous→ <your email address> ...→*email* info@merit.edu ✍ *Email for auto-mated info*

Delaware

Systems Solutions ☎→*dial* 302-378-1386 (vox) ✓**INTERNET** ...→*ftp* ssnet.com→anonymous→ <your email address> ...→*email* info@ssnet.com ✍ *Email for auto-mated info*

Florida

CyberGate, Inc. ☎→*dial* 305-428-4283 (vox) ✓**INTERNET**→*email* info@gate.net ✍ *Email for auto-mated info*

The IDS World Network ☎→*dial* 401-884-7856 (vox)/305-534-0321→ids→guest ✓**INTERNET** ...→*telnet* ids.net→guest ...→*email*

info@ids.net ✍ *Email for automat-ed info*

Illinois

InterAccess ☎→*dial* 800-967-1580 (vox)/708-671-0237→guest ✓**INTERNET** ...→*ftp* interaccess. com→anonymous→<your email ad-dress>→/pub/interaccess.info ...→*email* info@interaccess.com ✍ *Email for automated info*

MCSNet ☎→*dial* 312-248-8649 (vox)/708-637-0900/312-248-0900→bbs→new ✓**INTERNET** ...→ *ftp* ftp.mcs.com→anonymous→ <your email address>→/mcsnet. info ...→*email* info@mcs.net ✍ *Email for automated info*

Prairienet Freenet ☎→*dial* 217-244-1962 (vox)/217-255-9000→visitor ✓**INTERNET** ...→*telnet* prairienet. org→visitor ...→*email* info@prairienet.org ✍ *Email for automated info*

XNet Information Systems ☎→*dial* 708-983-6064 (vox)/ 708-983-6435→guest→new ✓**IN-TERNET** ...→*telnet* net.xnet.com→ guest ...→*email* info@xnet.com ✍ *Email for automated info*

Louisiana

NeoSoft's Sugar Land Unix ☎→*dial* 713-438-4964 (vox) ✓**IN-TERNET**→*email* info@neosoft.com ✍ *Email for automated info*

Massachusetts

Merit Network, Inc ☎→*dial* 313-764-9430 (vox) ✓**INTERNET** ...→*telnet* hermes.merit.edu→help ...→*ftp* nic.merit.edu→anonymous→ <your email address> ...→*email* info@merit.edu ✍ *Email for auto-mated info*

NEARnet ☎→*dial* 617-873-8730

(vox) ✓**INTERNET** ...→*ftp* ftp.near.
net→anonymous→<your email address> ...→*email* nearnet-join@
near.net ✍ *Email for info*

North Shore Access ☎→*dial*
617-593-3110 (vox)/617-593-
4557→new ✓**INTERNET** ...→*telnet*
shore.net→new ...→*ftp* shore.net→
anonymous→<your email address>
→/pub/flyer ...→*email* info@shore.
net ✍ *Email for automated info*

NovaLink ☎→*dial* 800-274-2814
(vox)/508-754-4009/800-937-
7644→new ✓**INTERNET** ...→*ftp*
ftp.novalink.com→anonymous→
<your email address>→/info ...→
email info@novalink.com ✍ *Email
for automated info*

The World ☎→*dial* 617-739-
0202 (vox)/617-739-9753→new
✓**INTERNET** ...→*telnet* world.std.
com→new ...→*ftp* std.com→anony-
mous→<your email address>→
/world-info/description ...→*email*
world.std.com ✍ *Email for info*

Michigan

Merit Network, Inc ☎→*dial*
313-764-9430 (vox) ✓**INTERNET**
...→*telnet* hermes.merit.edu→help
...→*ftp* nic.merit.edu→anonymous→
<your email address> ...→*email*
info@merit.edu ✍ *Email for automated info*

MSen ☎→*dial* 313-998-4562
(vox) ✓**INTERNET** ...→*telnet* msen.
com→newuser ...→*ftp* ftp.msen.
com→anonymous→<your email ad-
dress>→/pub/vendor/msen
...→*email* info@Msen.com ✍
Email for automated info

Minnesota

MRNet ☎→*dial* 612-342-2570
(vox) ✓**INTERNET**→*email* info@mr.
net

New Hampshire

MV Communications, Inc.
☎→*dial* 603-429-2223 (vox)/603-
424-7428→info→info ✓**INTERNET**
...→*ftp* ftp.mv.com→anonymous→
<your email address>→/pub/mv
...→*email* info@mv.com ✍ *Email
for automated info*

NEARnet ☎→*dial* 617-873-8730
(vox) ✓**INTERNET** ...→*ftp* ftp.near.
net→anonymous→<your email ad-
dress> ...→*email* nearnet-join@
near.net ✍ *Email for info*

New Jersey

Express Access ☎→*dial* 800-
969-9090 (vox)/908-937-9481/
609-348-6203/714-377-9784/
908-937-9481→new ✓**INTERNET**
...→ *telnet* access.digex.net→
new→new ...→*ftp* ftp.digex.net→
anonymous→<your email address>
→/pub ...→*email* info@digex.net
✍ *Email for automated info*

**The John von Newmann
Computer Network** ☎→*dial*
609-897-7300 (vox) ✓**INTERNET**→
email info@jvnc.net ✍ *Email for
automated info*

New Mexico

New Mexico Technet ☎→*dial*
505-345-6555 (vox)

New York

Echo Communications ☎→*dial*
212-255-3839 (vox)/212-989-
8411→newuser ✓**INTERNET** ...→*telnet* echonyc.com→newuser ...→
email info@echonyc.com ✍ *Email
for info*

MindVox ☎→*dial* 212-989-2418
(vox)/212-989-1550→guest ✓**INTER-
NET** ...→*telnet* phantom.com→guest
...→*email* info@phantom.com ✍
Email for automated info

PANIX Public Access ☎→*dial*
212-787-3100 (vox)/212-787-
6160→newuser ✓**INTERNET** ...→*telnet* panix.com→help ...→*email*
info@panix.com ✍ *Email for automated info*

The Pipeline ☎→*dial* 212-267-
3636 (vox)/212-267-8606/212-
267-7341→guest ✓**INTERNET** ...→
telnet pipeline.com→guest ...→*ftp*
pipeline.com→anonymous→<your
email address> ...→*email* info@
pipeline.com ✍ *Email for automated info*

North Carolina

CONCERT-CONNECT ☎→*dial*
919-248-1999 (vox) ✓**INTERNET**
...→*ftp* ftp.concert.net→anonymous
→<your email address> ...→*email*
info@concert.net ✍ *Email for automated info*

Vnet Internet Access, Inc.
☎→*dial* 704-334-3282 (vox)/919-
406-1544/919-851-1526/704-347-
8839→new ✓**INTERNET** ...→*telnet*
vnet.net→new ...→*ftp* vnet.net→
anonymous→<your email address>
→/vnet-info ...→*email* info@vnet.
net ✍ *Email for info*

Ohio

APK Public Access ☎→*dial* 216-
481-9428 (vox) ✓**INTERNET** ...→*telnet* wariat.org→bbs ...→*ftp* ftp.
wariat.org→anonymous→<your
email address> ...→*email* info@
wariat.org ✍ *Email for automated
info*

Oregon

Rain Drop Laboratories
☎→*dial* 503-452-0960 (vox)/503-
293-1772/503-293-2059→apply
✓**INTERNET** ...→*telnet* agora.rdrop.
com→apply→<your name> ...→*ftp*
agora.rdrop.com→anonymous→
<your email address>→/pub ...→

email info@agora.rdrop.com ✍ *Email for automated info*

Teleport ☎→*dial* 503-223-4245 (vox)/503-220-1016→new ✓**INTERNET** ...→*telnet* teleport.com→new ...→*ftp* teleport.com→anonymous→<your email address> ...→*email* info@teleport.com

Pennsylvania

The John von Newmann Computer Network ☎→*dial* 609-897-7300 (vox) ✓**INTERNET**→ *email* info@jvnc.net ✍ *Email for automated info*

Telerama Public Access Internet ☎→*dial* 412-481-3505 (vox)/ 412-481-5302/412-481-4644→new ✓**INTERNET** ...→*telnet* telerama.lm. com→new ...→*ftp* telerama.lm. com→anonymous→<your email address>→/info ...→*email* info@lm. com ✍ *Email for automated info*

Rhode Island

The IDS World Network ☎→*dial* 401-884-7856 (vox)/401-884-9002→ids→guest ✓**INTERNET** ...→*telnet* ids.net→guest ...→*email* info@ids.net ✍ *Email for automated info*

The John von Newmann Computer Network ☎→*dial* 609-897-7300 (vox) ✓**INTERNET**→ *email* info@jvnc.net ✍ *Email for automated info*

Texas

The Black Box ☎→*dial* 713-480-2685 (vox)/713-480-2686→ guest ✓**INTERNET**→*email* info@blk box.com ✍ *Email for automated info*

DFW Net ☎→*dial* 817-332-6642/817-429-3520→info ✓**INTERNET** ...→*telnet* dfw.net→info ...→

email info@dfw.net ✍ *Email for automated info*

The Illuminati Online ☎→*dial* 512-447-7866 (vox)/512-448-8950→new ✓**INTERNET** ...→*email* info@io.com ✍ *Email for automated info* ...→*telnet* io.com→new ... →*ftp* io.com→anonymous→<your email address>

NeoSoft's Sugar Land Unix ☎→*dial* 713-438-4964 (vox) ✓**INTERNET**→*email* info@neosoft.com ✍ *Email for automated info*

RealTime Communications ☎→*dial* 512-451-0046 (vox)/512-459-4391→new ✓**INTERNET** ...→*telnet* vern.bga.com→new ...→*ftp* ftp.bga.com→anonymous→<your email address> ...→*email* hosts@ bga.com ✍ *Email for info*

South Coast Computing Services, Inc. ☎→*dial* 713-917-5000 (vox)/713-917-5050→newuser ✓**INTERNET** ...→*ftp* sccsi.com→anonymous→<your email address>→ /pub/communications ...→*email* support@nuchat.sccsi.com ✍ *Email for info*

Texas Metronet ☎→*dial* 214-705-2900 (vox)/817-261-1127/214-705-2901→info→info ✓**INTERNET** ...→*telnet* metronet.com→info→info ...→*ftp* ftp.metronet.com→anonymous→<your email address>→ /pub/info ...→*email* info@metro net.com ✍ *Email for automated info*

Virginia

CAPCON Library Network ☎→*dial* 202-331-5771 (vox) ✓**INTERNET**→*email* capcon@capcon.net ✍ *Email for info*

Express Access ☎→*dial* 800-969-9090 (vox)/703-281-7997/ 714-377-9784/908-937-9481

→new ✓**INTERNET** ...→*telnet* access. digex.net→new→new ...→*ftp* ftp. digex.net→anonymous→<your email address>→/pub ...→*email* info@ digex.net ✍ *Email for automated info*

Wyvern Technologies, Inc. ☎→*dial* 804-622-4289 (vox)/804-627-1828/804-873-0748→guest ✓**INTERNET** ...→*ftp* infi.net→anonymous→<your email address> ...→ *email* system@wyvern.com ✍ *Email for info*

Washington

Eskimo North ☎→*dial* 206-367-7457 (vox)/206-742-1150/206-367-3837/206-362-6731 ✓**INTERNET** ...→*telnet* eskimo.com→new→ <your name> ...→*email* nanook@ eskimo.com ✍ *Email for info*

Halcyon ☎→*dial* 206-455-3505 (vox)/206-382-6245→new ✓**INTERNET** ...→*ftp* ftp.halcyon.com→ anonymous→<your email address> →/pub/info ...→*email* info@halcy on.com ✍ *Email for automated info*

Olympus ☎→*dial* 206-385-0464 (vox) ✓**INTERNET**→*email* info@pt.olympus.net ✍ *Email for automated info*

Canada

UUNET Canada, Inc. ☎→*dial* 416-368-6621 (vox) ✓**INTERNET** ...→*ftp* ftp.uunet.ca→anonymous→ <your email address> ...→*email* info@uunet.ca ✍ *Email for automated info*

Communications Accessibles Montreal ☎→*dial* 514-931-0749 (vox)/514-596-2255/514-596-2250 ✓**INTERNET** ...→*ftp* ftp.CAM. ORG→anonymous→<your email address> ...→*email* info@CAM. ORG ✍ *Email for automated info*

Glossary

@ | Separates the **userid** and **domain name** of an Internet address. Pronounced "at."

AberMUD | An adventure-based MUD program named after the University of Aberstywyth, where it was written.

anonymous FTP | Method of logging in to public file archives over the **Internet**. Enter "anonymous" when prompted for a **userid**. See **FTP**.

anonymous remailer | Service that encodes the return address in **email** and then forwards it. Good remailers allow replies to be sent back without revealing the original identity. Anon.penet.fi is the most popular remailer on the **Internet** (see pages 18-20).

Archie | A program that lets you search **Internet FTP** archives worldwide by file name. One variant is called **Veronica**.

ASCII | A basic text format readable by most computers. The acronym stands for American Standard Code for Information Interchange.

backbones | The high-speed networks at the core of the **Internet**. The most prominent is the NSFNet, funded by the National Science Foundation.

bandwidth | The maximum transmission speed that a computer connection can handle.

baud | The speed at which signals are sent by a **modem**, measured by the number of changes per second in the signals during transmission. A baud rate of 1,200, for example, would indicate 1,200 signal changes in one second. Baud rate is often confused with **bits per second (bps)**.

BBS | "Bulletin-board system." Once referred to stand-alone desktop computers with a single modem that answered the phone, but can now be as complicated and interconnected as a commercial service.

binary | A file format in which data is represented by binary numbers (based on 1s and 0s); generally used to store software and pictures. One binary integer is called a bit (see **bits per second**).

binary transfer | A file transfer between two computers that preserves **binary** data.

bits per second (bps) | The data-transfer rate between two **modems**. The higher the bps, the higher the speed of the transfer.

bot | A computer program with humanlike behavior (short for "robot"). In live-chat areas like **IRC** channels or **MUDs**, bots are often programmed to represent their creators, to moderate games, or to perform such tasks as

Glossary

delivering local **email** messages.

bounced message	An **email** message "returned to sender," usually because of an address error.
bye	A log-off command, like "quit" and "exit."
carrier signal	The squeaking noise that modems use to maintain a connection. See also **handshake**.
cd	"Change directory." A command used, for example, at an **FTP** site to move from a directory to a subdirectory.
cdup	"Change directory up." Can be used at an **FTP** site to move from a sub-directory to its parent directory. Also **chdirup**.
channel operator	User with special powers in an **IRC** channel, most notably the ability to kick other users off the channel.
character	A term used in adventure or **role-playing** games to refer to the persona a player assumes in the game. Choosing a character name is usually one of the first things a player does.
chdirup	See **cdup**.
client	A computer that connects to a more powerful computer (see **server**) for complex tasks.
collaborative fiction	The literary version of **role-playing**, where players/authors write up their **characters**' adventures as part of a group effort to create an ongoing story.
commercial service	General term for large online services (e.g., America Online, CompuServe, Prodigy, GEnie).
compression	Shrinkage of computer files to conserve storage space and reduce transfer times. Special utility programs, available for most platforms (including DOS, Mac, and Amiga), perform the compression and decompression.
cracker	A person who maliciously breaks into a computer system in order to steal files or disrupt system activities.
dial-up access	Computer connection made over standard telephone lines.
dino	A long time **MUD**der.
dir	"Directory." A command used to display the contents of the current directory.
domain name	The worded address of an **IP number** on the **Internet**, in the form of domain subsets separated by periods. For example, cunix.columbia.edu would be the address of a **server** named cunix located at Columbia University, which is in the .edu hierarchy (refers to educational institutions). Other domain hierarchies include ".com" (for companies, such as

ypn.com), ".org" for organizations (such as eff.org), ".net" for network provider (such as sura.net), ".gov" for government addresses (such as whitehouse.gov), and ".mil" for military facilities (such as nic.dnn.mil). Sites in foreign countries have a two-letter country abbreviation as the last subset of their domain name. The full address of an **Internet** user is **userid@domain name**.

email	"Electronic mail."
emoticon	See **smiley**.
Ethernet	A fast and widely used type of **LAN**.
FAQ	"Frequently asked questions." A file of questions and answers compiled for **Usenet newsgroups**, **mailing lists**, and games to reduce repeated posts about commonplace subjects.
file transfer	Transfer of a file from one computer to another over a network.
finger	A program that provides information about a user who is logged into your local system or on a remote computer on the Internet. Generally invoked by typing "finger" and the person's **userid**.
flame	A violent and usually ad hominem attack against another person in a **newsgroup** or message area.
flame war	A back-and-forth series of **flames**.
fluxer	As in "influx." Alternate for **newbie**.
Free-Net	A community-based network that provides free access to the **Internet**, usually to local residents, and often includes its own forums and news.
freeware	Free software. Not to be confused with **shareware**.
front end	A program used in conjunction with another program to alter the appearance—for visual appeal and ease of use—of the screen. The front end is often run locally on a user's machine.
FTP	"File transfer protocol." The standard used to transfer files between computers.
furry	An anthropomorphic animal; a popular type of character for **Net** role-players embarking on sexual adventures.
get	An **FTP** command that transfers single files from the **FTP** site to your local directory. The command is followed by a file name; typing "get file.name" would transfer only that file. Also see **mget**.
GIF	Common file format for pictures first popularized by CompuServe, standing for "graphics interchange format." Pronounced with a hard *g*.
gopher	A menu-based guide to directories on the **Internet**, usually organized by

subject.

GUI
"Graphical user interface" with windows and point-and-click capability, as opposed to a command-line interface with typed-out instructions.

hacker
A computer enthusiast who enjoys exploring computer systems and programs, sometimes to the point of obsession. Not to be confused with **cracker**.

handle
The name a user wishes to be known by, often in some sort of gaming system (e.g., a **MUD**). A user's handle may differ significantly from his or her real name or **userid**.

handshake
The squawking noise at the beginning of a computer connection when two modems settle on a protocol for exchanging information.

Home Page
The main **World Wide Web** site for a particular group or organization.

hqx
File suffix for a BinHex file, a common format for transmitting Macintosh binary files over the **Internet**.

hypertext
An easy method of retrieving information by choosing highlighted words in a text on the screen. The words link to documents with related subject matter.

IC
"In character." A game player who is IC is acting as his or her **character**'s persona.

Internet
The largest network of computer networks in the world, easily recognizable by the format of Internet **email** addresses: **userid**@host.

Internet Adapter, The (TIA)
A new commercial UNIX program that emulates a **SLIP** connection over a standard **dial-up** connection.

Internet provider
Wholesale or retail reseller of access to the **Internet**. YPN is one example.

IP connection
Full-fledged link to the **Internet**. See **SLIP**, **PPP**, and **TCP/IP**.

IP number
The unique number that determines the ultimate **Internet** identity of an **IP connection**.

IRC
"**Internet** relay chat." A service that allows **real-time** conversations between multiple users on a variety of subject-oriented channels.

jpeg
Common compressed format for picture files. Pronounced "jay-peg."

knowbot
An experimental computer program designed to retrieve information anywhere on the **Net** in response to a user's request.

LAN
"Local area network." A network of computers limited to a particular physical site, as opposed to the massive cyber-sprawl of the **Internet**, which encompasses networks all around the world.

LPMUD	A combat-oriented **MUD** program. Named after the original creator, Lars Penji.
ls	"List." A command that provides simplified directory information at **FTP** sites and other directories. It lists only file names for the directory, not file sizes or dates.
lurkers	Regular readers of messages online who never post.
lynx	A popular text-based **Web browser**.
mailing list	Group discussion distributed through **email**. Many mailing lists are administered through listserv.
mget	An **FTP** command that transfers multiple files from the **FTP** site to your local directory. The command is followed by a list of file names separated by spaces, sometimes in combination with an asterisk used as a wild card. Typing "mget b*" would transfer all files in the directory beginning with the letter *b*. Also see **get**.
modem	Device for establishing a connection between two computers, usually over standard phone lines. Most modem **bandwidths** range between 2,400 and 28,800 **baud**. From the technical name "MOdulator-DEModulator."
MOO	An object-oriented **MUD**. Many MOOs have an education or research orientation. The LambdaMOO **server** is the most popular type of MOO.
MUCK	A social **MUD** and a variation of **TinyMUD**. Also called a TinyMUCK.
MUD	"Multi-user dimension" or "multi-user dungeon." A computer program designed to create the illusion of rooms, worlds, and time periods through text descriptions. Players use commands to "walk" through the MUD, chat with other **characters**, solve quests, and fight monsters. Used generically to refer to any of the MUD variants like **MOO**, **MUSE**, **MUCK**, **MUSH**, etc. The first MUD was written in 1979.
MUD God	The system administrator of a **MUD**.
multi-tasking	The capability of a computer to perform more than one job simultaneously.
MUSE	A social **MUD** and a variation on a TinyMUSH that includes a class system and combat. Also called a TinyMUSE.
MUSH	"Multi-user shared hallucination." A social **MUD** and a variation of a **TinyMUD** that allows building. Also called a TinyMUSH.
Net, the	A colloquial term that is often used to refer to the entirety of Cyberspace: the **Internet**, the **commercial services**, **BBSs**, etc.
Net guru	A person with unimpeachable **Net** expertise who can answer any question.

Glossary

netiquette The rules of Cyberspace civility. Usually applied to the **Internet**, where manners are enforced exclusively by fellow users.

newbie A newcomer to the **Net**, to a game, or to a discussion. Also called **fluxer**.

newsgroups The **Usenet** message areas, organized by subject.

newsreader Software program for reading **Usenet newsgroups** on the **Internet**. (See page 17.)

NIC, the Short for the InterNIC ("Network Information Center"), the Virginia-based authority that, among other things, registers **Internet domain names** on a famous first-come, first-serve basis. Pronounced "nik."

nick Short for the nickname you set for yourself in **IRC**.

OOC "Out of character." Someone who is OOC is acting as himself rather than as his **character**.

port number A number that follows a **telnet** address. The number connects a user to a particular application on the telnet site. LambdaMOO, for example, is at port 8888 of lambda.parc.xerox.com (lambda.parc.xerox.com 8888).

post See **posting**.

posting The sending of a message to a **newsgroup**, bulletin board, or other public message area. The message itself is called a **post**.

pwd A command used at an **FTP** site to display the name of the current directory on your screen.

real-time The **Net** term for "live," as in "live broadcast." Real-time connections include **IRC** and **MUDs**.

remote machine Any computer on the **Internet** reached with a program such as **FTP** or **telnet**. The machine making the connection is called the home, or local, machine.

RL "Real life."

role-playing A type of gaming where players act and respond in the nature of the **character** they play. Role-play can be heavily moderated and tied to specific themes and rules (for example, PernMUSH or FurryMUCK), or the play may be "free-form," with few rules.

RPG "**Role-playing** game."

server A software program, or the computer running the program, that allows other computers, called **clients**, to share its resources.

shareware Free software, distributed over the **Net** with a request from the programmer for voluntary payment.

sig	Short for **signature**.
signature	A file added to the end of **email** messages or **Usenet** posts that contains personal information—usually your name, email address, postal address, and telephone number. **Netiquette** dictates that signatures, or **sigs**, should be no longer than four or five lines.
SLIP and PPP	"Serial line **Internet** protocol" and "point-to-point protocol." Connecting by SLIP or PPP actually puts a computer on the Internet, which offers a number of advantages over regular **dial-up**. A SLIP or PPP connection can support a graphical **Web browser** (such as Mosaic), and allows for multiple connections at the same time. Requires special software and a SLIP or PPP service provider.
smiley	Text used to indicate emotion, humor, or irony in electronic messages—best understood if viewed sideways. Also called an **emoticon**. The most common smileys are :-) and :-(
snail mail	The paper mail the U.S. Postal Service delivers. The forerunner of **email**.
spam	The posting of the same article to multiple **newsgroups** (usually every possible one) regardless of the appropriateness of the topic (e.g., "Make Money Fast"). Virtual hangings of spammers take place in the newsgroup news.admin.misc. Thought to come from the mind-numbing repetition of Monty Python's "Spam Song."
sysop	"System operator." The person who owns and/or manages a **BBS** or other **Net** site.
TCP/IP	The "transmission control protocol" and the "**Internet** protocol." The basis of a full-fledged Internet connection. See **IP Connection**, **PPP**, and **SLIP**. Pronounced "T-C-P-I-P."
telnet	An **Internet** program that allows you to log into other Internet-connected computers.
terminal emulator	A program or utility that allows a computer to communicate in a foreign or nonstandard **terminal mode**.
terminal mode	The software standard a computer uses for text communication—for example, ANSI for PCs and **VT-100** for UNIX.
thread	Posted **newsgroup** message with a series of replies. Threaded **newsreaders** organize replies under the original subject.
timeout	The break in communication that occurs when two computers are talking and one takes so long to respond that the other gives up.
TinyMUD	A social **MUD** where players explore and build. **TinyMUD** is the program used in the original **MUD**.

tinysex   The use of **MUD** commands and "descriptive prowess" to imitate sex acts.

tty   A plain-vanilla terminal protocol for transmitting text over computer connections. Comes from "teletypewriter," the original electromechanic typewriter that could transmit and receive messages by electrical signals carried over telephone wires.

URL   "Uniform resource locator." The **World Wide Web** address of a resource on the **Internet**.

Usenet   A collection of networks and computer systems that exchange messages, organized by subject in **newsgroups**.

userid   The unique name (often eight characters or less) given to a user on a system for his or her account. The complete address, which can be used for **email** or **finger**ing, is a userid followed by the @ sign and the **domain name** (e.g., Bill Clinton's address is president@whitehouse.gov).

Veronica   See **Archie**.

VT-100 emulation   Widely used terminal protocol for formatting full screens of text over computer connections.

WAIS   "Wide area information server." A system that searches through database indexes around the **Internet**, using keywords.

Web browser A **client** program designed to interact with **World Wide Web servers** on the **Internet** for the purpose of viewing **Web pages**.

Web page   A **hypertext** document that is part of the **World Wide Web** and that can incorporate graphics, sounds, and links to other **Web pages**, **FTP** sites, **gophers**, and a variety of other **Internet** resources.

wizard   A player in a **MUD** who has won the game or been appointed to help run the MUD by **MUD Gods**.

World Wide Web   A **hypertext**-based navigation system that lets you browse through a variety of linked **Net** resources, including **Usenet newsgroups** and **FTP**, **telnet**, and **gopher** sites, without typing commands. Also known as WWW and the Web.

zip   File-compression standard in the DOS and Windows worlds.

Index

Index

Index

Really Deep Thoughts, 64
amputee fetish, 51
Amwest-H, 164
anal sex, 53
anarchism, 139
Anderson, Laurie, 89
Andy Griffith Show
    Mayberry, 82
Anglican, 214
Animal_Rights, 132
Animaniacs, 98
animation, 98-99
    AnimeMUCK, 102-103
    See also cartoons, comics
anime, 98-99, 102-103
#anime!, 98 150
AnimeMUCK, 102-103
Anne Rice, 95
anon.penet.fi, 19-20
anonymity, 19-20
anonymous remailer, 19-20
anxiety, 226-227
AOL Neighborhood Singles
    Groups, 31
AOL Romance Connection, 26
#appleIIgs, 150
Arabic, 183
    #egypt, 151
archeology
    Dinosaur, 166
Argic, Sedar, 90
ArizonaM4M, 47
art, visual, 161-162
Artcrit, 162
Artifact, 164
Arts, 162
ASA-L, 178
Asia, 179-181
Asia
    movies, 75
    See also Asian-Americans,
        Hong Kong, Taiwan
#asian, 150
Asian-Americans, 181
Asimov, Isaac, 85
Astr-L, 161
astrology, 209
#astronomy, 150
atheism, 212, 214
#atheism, 214
Atlanta Braves, 105
Atlanta Falcons, 107
Atlanta Hawks, 106

attention deficit disorders (ADD),
    223
Australia, 182
    #aussies, 150
    #melbourne, 152
#australia, 150
Avant Garde, 161
avant garde
    alt.fan.laurie-anderson, 89
    See also alternative music
#aynrand, 150

B

ba.motss, 193
ba-sappho, 193
Babble List, 64
baby boomers, 206
    #40plus, 151
    See also 30 somethings
Baby Boomer Club, 206
Babylon5, 86
BackRoom, 53
Backstreets, 66
Bahai, 216
Balkans
    Mideur-L, 182
Baltimore Orioles, 105
bands
    See music, musicians/bands
Baptist, 214
Barney, 114, 51
baseball, 105-106
basketball, 106-107
    #nba, 153
#bawel, 150
BayMOO, 156
BBS off-line reader, 19
BBSs, 7-8, 236-252
#bdsm, 57, 150
Beakmans World, 82
#bearcave, 49, 150
bears, 49,150,191
Beastie Boys, 63
Beastie List, 63
Beatles, 66, 70
Beavis and Butthead, 79
Belief-L, 214
#beijing, 150

bestiality, 51
Beverly Hills 90210, 79, 82
Beyond, 117
Bi-Sexual, 48
BiAct-L, 190
Bible-L, 212
Bible Studies, 214
#biblestud, 150
BiCuriousMen4Men, 47
BiMen4BiMen, 47
#bisex, 49, 150
Bisexu-L, 190
Bisexual, 33
bisexuality, 33, 48-49, 150, 190
bit.listserv.catholic, 212
bit.listserv.christia, 214
bit.listserv.deaf-l, 223
bit.listserv.gaynet, 187
Bithry-L, 190
bitterness, 228
bizarre humor, 113-114
Black Sabbath, 66
BlackExperience, 179
Blake7, 82
Blue, 39
Blue Oyster Cult/Hawkwind, 66
Blues-L, 68
Blues Traveler, 68
bOING bOING, 124
bondage, 56-58,150,
#bondage, 57, 150
Bong (Depeche Mode), 70
Books, 168
Books, 93
books
    See fiction, literature
Books and Writing BB, 93
#bored, 150
Bosox Mailing List, 105
#boston, 151
Boston Bruins Mailing List, 108
Boston Celtics Mailing List, 106
Boston Red Sox, 105
BOTA-L, 209
Brady Bunch, The, 82
#brasil, 151
breasts, 51
Brontë Family, 169
Bronte-L, 169
Buddhism, 213-216
Buddhist-L, 214
Buddhist, 216
#buddhist, 214, 151

Index

Index

Index

Index

Q

QMS, 71
Quaker-L, 214
Quaker-P, 213
Quakerism, 213-214
Quantum Leap, 82, 85
Quayle, Dan, 88
Quebec Nordiques Mailing List, 109
Queen, 65, 71
QWK message format, 19

R

R.E.M., 63
Rand, Ayn, 140, 150
rap music, 72
rape, 201-202
rave, 69-70,153
#rave, 69, 153
Real World, The, 80
Really Deep Thoughts, 64
rec.arts.anime, 99
rec.arts.books, 169
rec.arts.comics.misc, 101
rec.arts.movies, 74, 91
rec.arts.sf.fandom, 83
rec.arts.sf.movies, 83
rec.arts.sf.science, 83
rec.arts.sf.tv.quantum-leap, 82
rec.arts.sf.written, 83-84
rec.arts.soaps, 81
rec.arts.startrek.current, 86
rec.arts.theatre.misc, 162
rec.arts.tv, 77
rec.arts.tv.mst3k, 82
rec.arts.tv.uk, 82
rec.food.historic, 165
rec.music.beatles, 66
rec.music.bluenote, 65
rec.music.christian, 66
rec.music.country-western, 66
rec.music.dylan, 66
rec.music.funky, 66
rec.music.gdead, 67

rec.music.indian, 180
rec.music.industrial, 66
rec.music.misc, 64
rec.music.phish, 64
rec.music.reggae, 73
rec.music.rem, 63
rec.sport.baseball, 105
rec.sport.basketball.misc, 106
rec.sport.basketball.pro, 106
rec.sport.football.misc, 107
rec.sport.hockey, 108
RecoverNet, 228
Recovery, 228
Recovery, 229
Recovery Link, 228
Red Dwarf, 82
reggae, 73
relationships, 34-35
    See also support, singles,
religion, 211-217
    atheism, 212
    Bahai, 216
    Buddhism, 213-216
    Catholicism, 212-214
    Christianity, 211-214
    eastern, 213-216
    history, 167, 216
    Islam, 215-216
    Judaism, 215, 217
    Paganism, 208-209, 215, 217
    politics, 129
    Quakerism, 213-214
    satanism, 215
    science and religion, 215
    Scientology, 217
    shamanism, 215
    Wicca, 201, 208-209, 217
    women, 201
Religion BB, 211
Religion Forum, 212
Religion & Philosophy Round-
    Table, 212
#report, 153
Republican Forum, 140
Republican Party, 140
Review, 39
Rice, Anne, 95, 120
    See also gothic horror
rmusic-L, 64
rock, 65-66, 70-72
Rockford Files, 82
Rocknet, 71
Rocky Horror Picture Show, 75

role-playing, 148
role-playing
    alt.pub.dragons-inn, 148
    AnimeMUCK, 102-103
    BayMOO, 156
    #camelot, 151
    DeepSeas MUSH, 157-158
    FurryMuck, 44
    MediaMOO, 160
    PernMUSH, 97
    Theater des Vampires, 120
Rolling Stones, 66, 70
romance and relationships, 34-35
#romance, 42, 153
romance fiction, 96
#root, 153
Roseanne, 82
RRA-L, 96
RTKBA, 135
Rush, 65
RUSH
    National Midnight Star, 71
Rush Limbaugh, 141
Russia
    H-Russia (history), 167
    #moscow, 153
#russian, 153

S

S_King, 95
sadomasochism
    bondage, 47, 56-58
    gay, 57
    spanking, 58
    women, 58
San Diego Chargers Mailing List, 108
San Francisco, 156, 149
San Francisco, 149
San Francisco 49ers, 108
San Francisco Giants, 106
San Jose Sharks Mailing List, 109
Sappho, 191
satanism, 215
SATB-L, 64
Saturday Night Live
    alt.tv.snl, 82
Saved By the Bell, 82

Index

Index

Michael Wolff & Company, Inc.

Michael Wolff & Company, Inc., digital publisher and packager, specializing in information presentation and graphic design, is one of the leading providers of information about the Net. The company's book *Net Guide*, published with Random House, has spent almost a year on bestseller lists, and is now a monthly magazine published by CMP Publications.

MW& Co., and its team of Net surfers, is embarked upon a project to map all corners of the Net. This means that the growing community of Net adventurers can expect a steady flow of new Net baedekers. *Net Guide* has now been joined by *Net Games* and *Net Chat*, and will shortly be followed by *Net Money, Net Trek, Net Sports,* and *Net Tech.* MW&Co.'s Internet service, YPN—Your Personal Network, features a hypertext version of the entire series. It is the most comprehensive Net source available anywhere.

Among the company's other recent projects are *Where We Stand—Can America Make It in the Global Race for Wealth, Health, and Happiness?* (Bantam Books), one of the most graphically complex information books ever to be wholly created and produced by means of desktop-publishing technology, and *Made in America?*, a four-part PBS series on global competitiveness, hosted by Labor Secretary Robert B. Reich.

Kelly Maloni, who directed the *Net Chat* project, is the managing editor of MW&Co. and, at 25, one of the most experienced travelers in Cyberspace. Senior editor Nathaniel Wice, formerly an editor at *Spin* magazine, has written for *New York* magazine, *Esquire*, and *The New Republic*, among other publications. Senior editor Ben Greenman has written pop-culture criticism for many publications, including *Miami New Times*, the *Chicago Reader*, and *Rolling Stone*.

Net Notes

EXPLORE the INTERNET
——————— FREE!* ———————

Delphi Internet™ offers you full access to the Internet and now you can explore this incredible resource with no risk. You get 5 hours of evening and weekend access to try it out for free!*

Use electronic mail to exchange messages with over 20 million people throughout the world. Download programs and files using "**FTP**" and connect in real-time to other networks using "**Telnet**." Meet people from around the world with "**Internet Relay Chat**" and check out "**Usenet News**," the world's largest bulletin board with over 10,000 topics.

now supporting **9,600 and 14,400 bps** at no extra charge!

If you're not familiar with these terms, don't worry; DELPHI has expert **online assistants** and a large collection of help files, books, and other resources to help you get started. After the free trial you can choose from two low-cost membership plans. With rates as low as $1 per hour, no other online service offers so much for so little.

5-Hour Free Trial!*
Dial by modem, **1-800-365-4636**
Press return a few times
At *Password*, enter NETGCT

GEnie®
The most fun you can have with your computer on.

No other online service has more cool stuff to do, or more cool people to do it with than GEnie. Join dozens of awesome special interest RoundTables on everything from scuba diving to Microsoft to food and wine, download over 200,000 files, access daily stock quotes, talk to all those smart guys on the Internet, play the most incredible multi-player games, and so much more you won't believe your eyeballs.

And GEnie has it all at a standard connect rate of just $3.00 an hour.[1] That's one of the lowest rates of all the major online services! Plus -- since your a reader of *Net Chat* - you get an even cooler deal.[2] If you sign up before December 31, 1995, you'll receive up to $50 worth of free services your first month[3]

You can take advantage of this incredible offer immediately -- just follow these simple steps:

1. Set your communications software for half-duplex (local echo) at 300, 1200, or 2400 baud. Recommended communications parameters: 8 data bits, no parity and 1 stop bit.
2. Dial toll-free in the U.S. at 1-800-638-8369 (or in Canada at 1-800-387-8330). Upon connection, type **HHH** (Please note: every time you use GEnie, you need to enter the HHH upon connection.)
3. At the U#= prompt, type **JOINGENIE** and press <Return>
4. At the offer code prompt enter **GDG225** to get this special offer.
5. Have a major credit card ready. In the U.S., you may also use your checking account number. (There is a $2.00 monthly fee for all checking accounts.) In Canada, VISA and MasterCard only.

Or, if you need more information, contact GEnie Client Services at 1-800-638-9636,TDD 1-800-238-9172 from 9am to midnight, Monday through Friday, and from noon to 8pm Saturday and Sunday (all times are Eastern).

1 U.S. prices. Standard connect time is non-prime time: 6pm to 8am local time, Mon. - Fri., all day Sat. and Sun. and selected holidays.
2 Offer available in the United States and Canada only.
3 The $50 offer is a usage credit and must be used by the end of the billing period for your first month. Please call 1-800-638-9636 for more information on pricing and billing policies.

K.G.B

MAGAZINE
• ON - STAND
• ONLINE

(media culture ideas style)

David Cronenberg · Dennis ... Bros Hernandez · Nick Cave · Atom Egoyan · Philipe ... Mark Leyner · The Future Is Now · Bill Laswell · Prince Pa... Metropolis: Tokyo · Surveillance Fashion · Nintendo Kids ... Dress · Breakfast Drugs · VideoPhone Interviews · SexDriv... TV · Bulletproof Life · Multimedia Technologies · De... ... Los Bros Hernandez ·

• *The Transom*™
transom@reach.com
1.800.475.9689

• *SonicNet*™
info@sonic.com
212.941.5912

• *New York Online*™
info@nyo.com
718.596.6000

subscribe @

**WOW!
10 HOURS
FREE?**

Try PRODIGY Chat FREE!
Call 1-800-PRODIGY ext. 143 today and you'll get 10 Free Hours the first month to try Chat and enjoy all the other features on the PRODIGY Service. Join us, Chat, and explore PRODIGY News & Weather, Business & Finance, Sports, Communications, Entertainment, Reference, Shopping, Computers, Travel, Home & Family & Kids and much, much more.

PRODIGY Chat is Quality Chat
With America's largest online community on the PRODIGY Service you can chat with rooms full of experts, celebrities and people just like you, talking in real time about virtually any and every topic imaginable.

**There's a Chat Room
for You**
See what others have to say in Arts & Writing, Comedy, Computing, Internet, Money and Finance, Parenting, Pets, Sci-Fi, Sports, Seniors and Teen Chat rooms.

Check out what's going on in Chat rooms like Baby Boomers, Blue Note Cafe, Generation X, Great Debate, Hard Drive Cafe, Melrose Space, Paradise Place, Truth or Dare and Vampire Pub. There's bound to be chat rooms you'll want to visit over and over again.

**Instant Messages
Let You Chat Privately**
Instant Messages allow you to send a private message to other members who are using

PRODIGY at the same time. Instant Messages can be sent to members who are in Chat, or anywhere on the PRODIGY Service. And, it's possible to engage in several Instant Message conversations simultaneously. Create your Nickname and you're ready to get started!

PRODIGY®
CHAT